University of Liverpool

Withdrawn from stock

For

The UK Economy
A Manual of Applied Economics

The UK Economy
A Manual of
Applied Economics

Seventh Edition

Edited by

A. R. Prest M.A. Ph.D
Professor of Economics, London School of Economics

and

D. J. Coppock B.A. (Econ.)
Professor of Economics, University of Manchester

Weidenfeld and Nicolson

London

First published 1966
Second impression 1967
Third impression 1968
Second edition 1968
Second impression 1969
Third edition 1970
Second impression 1971
Fourth edition 1972
Fifth edition 1974
Sixth edition 1976
Seventh edition 1978

Weidenfeld and Nicolson
91 Clapham High St London SW4

ISBN 0 297 77532 4 cased
ISBN 0 297 77533 2 paperback

Text set in 10/11 pt. IBM Press Roman, printed by photolithography
and bound in Great Britain at The Pitman Press, Bath

CONTRIBUTORS

Chapter 1
M. C. Kennedy *B.Sc. (Econ.) (London)*
Lecturer in Economics, University of Manchester

Chapter 2
N. J. Gibson *B.Sc. (Econ.), Ph.D. (Belfast)*
Professor of Economics, The New University of Ulster

Chapter 3
J. S. Metcalfe *B.A. (Econ.), M.Sc. (Manchester)*
Lecturer in Economics, University of Liverpool

Chapter 4
J. R. Cable *B.A. (Nottingham), M.A. (Econ.) (Manchester)*
Senior Lecturer in Economics, University of Warwick

Chapter 5
David Metcalf *M.A. (Econ.) (Manchester), Ph.D. (London)*
Professor of Economics, University of Kent
and
Ray Richardson *B.Sc. (Econ.) (London), Ph.D. (Columbia)*
Lecturer in Economics, London School of Economics

Contents

Contents

TABLES

Chapter 1

Chapter 2

Chapter 3

Chapter 4

Chapter 5

FIGURES

Chapter 1

Chapter 5

STATISTICAL APPENDIX

ABBREVIATIONS

(1) Economic Terms

CAP	Common Agricultural Policy
c.i.f.	Cost including Insurance and Freight
FIS	Family Income Supplement
f.o.b.	Free on Board
GDP	Gross Domestic Product
GNP	Gross National Product
MLH	Minimum List Headings
PAYE	Pay as you Earn
PDI	Personal Disposable Income
R and D	Research and Development
REP	Regional Employment Premium
RPM	Resale Price Maintenance
SDRs	Special Drawing Rights
SIC	Standard Industrial Classification
SITC	Standard Industrial Trade Classification
TCF	Total Currency Flow
TFE	Total Final Expenditure at Market Prices

(2) Organizations, etc.

CBI	Confederation of British Industry
CSO	Central Statistical Office (UK)
DE	Department of Employment
DI	Department of Industry
ECE	Economic Commission for Europe
ECSC	European Coal and Steel Community
EEA	Exchange Equalization Account
EEC	European Economic Community
EFTA	European Free Trade Area
FAO	Food and Agriculture Organization
GATT	General Agreement on Tariffs and Trade
IBRD	International Bank for Reconstruction and Development
IFC	International Finance Corporation
IMF	International Monetary Fund
IRC	Industrial Reorganization Corporation
MC	Monopolies Commission
NBPI	National Board for Prices and Incomes
NEB	National Enterprise Board
NEDC(O)	National Economic Development Council (Office)
NIESR	National Institute of Economic and Social Research

NRDC	National Research Development Corporation
OECD	Organization for Economic Cooperation and Development
OPCS	Office of Population Census and Surveys
PB	Pay Board
PC	Price Commission
TUC	Trades Union Congress
UN	United Nations
UNCTAD	United Nations Commission for Trade and Development

(3) Journals, etc.

AAS	*Annual Abstract of Statistics* (HMSO)
AER	*American Economic Review*
BEQB	*Bank of England Quarterly Bulletin*
BJIR	*British Journal of Industrial Relations*
BLS	*British Labour Statistics, Historical Abstract* (HMSO)
BTJ	*Board of Trade Journal* (HMSO)
DEG	*Department of Employment Gazette* (HMSO)
EC	*Economica*
EJ	*Economic Journal*
ET(AS)	*Economic Trends (Annual Supplement)* (HMSO)
FES	*Family Expenditure Survey* (HMSO)
FS	*Financial Statistics* (HMSO)
IFS	*International Financial Statistics*
JIE	*Journal of Industrial Economics*
JPE	*Journal of Political Economy*
JRSS	*Journal of Royal Statistical Society*
LBR	*Lloyds Bank Review*
LCES	*London and Cambridge Economic Service*
MBR	*Midland Bank Review*
MDS	*Monthly Digest of Statistics* (HMSO)
MS	*The Manchester School of Economic and Social Studies*
NIBB	*National Income Blue Book* (HMSO)
NIER	*National Institute Economic Review*
NWBR	*National Westminster Bank Review*
OEP	*Oxford Economic Papers*
PE	*Preliminary Estimates of National Income* (HMSO)
QJE	*Quarterly Journal of Economics*
RES	*Review of Economic Studies*
REST	*Review of Economics and Statistics*
ROT	*Report on Overseas Trade* (HMSO)
SIPEP	*Statistics of Income, Prices, Employment and Production* (HMSO)
SJPE	*Scottish Journal of Political Economy*
ST	*Social Trends* (HMSO)
TBR	*Three Banks Review*
TER	*Treasury Economic Report* (HMSO)
TI	*Trade and Industry* (HMSO)

Foreword to the Seventh Edition

In 1966, when the first edition of this book was published, the foreword began as follows:

> The central idea behind this book is to give an account of the main features and problems of the UK economy today. The hope is that it will fulfil two functions simultaneously, in that it will be as up to date as possible and yet will not be simply a bare catalogue of facts and figures. There are many sources of information, official and otherwise, about the structure and progress of the UK economy. There are also many authors to whom one can turn for subtle analyses of the problems before us. Our effort here is based on the belief that there is both room and need for an attempt to combine the functions of chronicler and analyst in the confines of a single book.
>
> The contributors to these pages subscribe rather firmly to the belief that economists should practise, as well as preach, the principle of the division of labour. The complexity of a modern economy is such that, whether one likes it or not, it is no longer possible for any individual to be authoritative on all its aspects; so it is inevitable that the burden of producing work of this kind should be spread among a number of people, each specialist in his or her particular field. Such a division carries with it obvious dangers of overlap and inconsistency. It is hoped that some of the worst pitfalls of this kind have been avoided and there is reasonable unity of purpose, treatment and layout. At the same time, it is wholly undesirable to impose a monolithic structure and it is just as apparent to the authors that there are differences in outlook and emphasis among them as it will be to the readers.
>
> The general intention was to base exposition on the assumption that the reader would have some elementary knowledge of economics — say a student in the latter part of a typical first year course in economics in a British university. At the same time, it is hoped that most of the text will be intelligible to those without this degree of expertise. We may not have succeeded in this; if not, we shall try to do better in the future.

Despite the usual extensive re-writing, we should still regard this as an accurate description of our intentions.

Chapter 1, 'The Economy as a Whole', is concerned with questions of applied macroeconomics: fluctuations in demand and employment, the management of demand, inflation and economic growth. The chapter ends with a section on the economic prospects in the near future. Chapter 2, 'Monetary, Credit and Fiscal Policies', starts with a brief discussion of the general theoretical background and then analyses in detail the theory and practices of monetary, credit and fiscal policies in the UK in recent years. The final section discusses the policy record and some policy implications of membership of the EEC. Chapter 3, 'Foreign Trade and the Balance of Payments', deals with the importance of foreign trade and payments to the UK economy and assesses UK balance of payments performance over the last two decades. It then looks at current problems and policies in this field and ends with a discussion of the reform of the international monetary system. Chapter 4, 'Industry and Commerce', starts with a brief summary of various theories of the behaviour of firms and the structural characteristics of UK industry. Various aspects of public policy towards nationalized industries, competition policy and consumer protection, regional problems and so on are then discussed, all with due regard to the implications of EEC membership. A final section deals with industrial efficiency. including such issues as planning agreements and price control. The last chapter, 'Labour', sets out the main characteristics of the UK labour force, and then discusses problems of wealth, income distribution, pay and incomes policy. The final section is concerned with trade unions and industrial relations.

Whilst we try to minimize unnecessary overlapping between chapters, we quite deliberately aim at complementary treatment of some topics. Thus different aspects of EEC membership are discussed in the relevant chapters; similarly, wages-inflation relationships appear in both Chapter 1 and Chapter 5. To minimize the use of space, factual material or definitions appearing in one chapter but relevant to another are not always duplicated and so it must be understood that to this extent any one chapter may not be self-contained.

Each chapter is accompanied by a list of references and further reading. The Statistical Appendix has eleven tables dealing with different aspects of the UK economy. There is an index as well as the detailed list of headings and sub-headings given in the Contents pages.

We acknowledge the great help given to us by Mr. P. Temple in preparing the Statistical Appendix and by all those who have rendered secretarial or computing assistance.

London School of Economics   A. R. PREST
University of Manchester   D. J. COPPOCK

April 1978

1

The economy as a whole

M. C. Kennedy

I   INTRODUCTION
I.1   Methodological Approach

This chapter is an introduction to applied macroeconomics. It begins with a brief description of the national income accounts and goes on to discuss the multiplier, the determination of national expenditure and output in the short run, the policy problems of maintaining full employment, the causes of inflation and of economic growth. It cannot claim to give all the answers to the questions raised, but aims, in the space available, to provide the reader with a basis for further and deeper study.

In principle there is no essential difference between applied economics and economic theory. The object of applied economics is to explain the way in which economic units work. It is just as much concerned with questions of causation (such as what determines total consumption or the level of prices) as the theory which is found in most elementary textbooks. The difference between theoretical and applied economics is largely one of emphasis, with theory tending to stress logical connections between assumptions and conclusions and applied economics the connections between theories and evidence. Applied economics does not seek description for its own sake, but it needs facts for the light they shed on the applicability of economic theory.

At one time it used to be thought that scientific theories were derived from factual information by a method of inference known as *induction*.[1] Thus it was supposed that general laws about nature could be deduced from knowledge of a limited number of facts. From the logical point of view, however, induction is an invalid procedure. For example, the fact that ten men have been observed to save one-tenth of their income does not entail the conclusion that all men do so. The conclusion may be true or false, but it does not rest validly on the assumptions. Such conclusions have the status of conjectures and require further empirical investigation.

More recently it has come to be understood that scientific method is not inductive but *hypothetico-deductive*. This means that a hypothesis is proposed to explain certain events, and from the hypothesis it is possible to deduce various other factual consequences or predictions. If these predictions coincide with observations of the factual evidence the hypothesis is said to be confirmed; but if they are contradicted by the facts the hypothesis is said to be refuted or falsified.

It will be clear that this concept of scientific method places the role of factual

---

1 For a highly readable introduction to the problems of scientific method the reader is referred to P. B. Medawar, *Induction and Intuition in Scientific Thought*, Methuen, 1969, and the more serious student to K. R. Popper, *The Poverty of Historicism*, Routledge and Kegan Paul, 1961, and *Conjectures and Refutations*, Routledge and Kegan Paul, 1963.

information in a rather different light from the inductive approach. Facts, instead of being the basis on which to build economic or scientific theories, become the basis for testing theories once they have been propounded. If a theory is able to survive a determined but unsuccessful attempt to refute it by factual evidence, it is regarded as well tested. But the discovery of evidence which is inconsistent with the theory will stimulate its modification or the development of a new theory altogether. One of the purposes of studying applied economics is to acquaint the theoretically equipped economist with the limitations of the theory he has studied. Applied economics is not an attempt to bolster up existing theory or, as its name might seem to imply, to demonstrate dogmatically that all the factual evidence is a neat application of textbook theory. Its aim is to understand the workings of the economy, and this means that it will sometimes expose the shortcomings of existing theory and go on to suggest improvements.

The discovery that a theory is falsified by some factual observation need not mean that it must be rejected out of hand or relegated to total oblivion. Economists, as well as natural scientists, frequently have to work with theories that are inadequate in one way or another. Theories that explain part but not all of the evidence are often retained until some new theory is found which fits a wider range of evidence. Frequently the theory will turn out to have been incomplete rather than just wrong, and when modified by the addition of some new variable (or a more careful specification of the *ceteris paribus* clause), the theory may regain its status. The reader who notices inconsistencies between theory and facts need not take the line that the theory is total nonsense, for it may still hold enough grains of truth to become the basis for something better.

It is often argued that our ability to test economic theories by reference to factual observations is sufficient to liberate economics from value judgements, i.e. to turn into a *positive* subject. This position probably has more than an element of truth in it: when there is clear evidence against a theory it stands a fair chance of being dropped even by its most bigoted adherents. Nevertheless, it would be wrong to forget that a great deal of what passes for factual evidence in economics is somewhat infirm in character (e.g. the statistics of gross domestic product or personal saving), so that it is often possible for evidence to be viewed more sceptically by some than by others.

The discussion of economic policy which also figures in this chapter is partly normative in scope, and partly positive. The normative content of policy discussion consists in the evaluation of goals and priorities. But the means for attaining such goals derive from the positive hypotheses of economics. They involve questions of cause and effect, the hypothetical answers to which are appraisable by reference to evidence. In making recommendations for the achievement of policy goals, however, the economist treads on thin ice. This is partly because his positive knowledge is not inevitably correct, but also because it is seldom possible for him to foresee and properly appraise all the side-effects of his recommendations, some of which have implications for other policy goals. When economists differ in their advice on policy questions it is not always clear how much the difference is due on the one hand to diagnostic disagreements, and, on the other, to differences in value judgements. Indeed it is seldom possible for an economic adviser to reveal all the normative preferences which lie behind a policy recommendation. Thus policy judgements have to be scrutinized rather carefully for hidden normative assumptions. The reader of this chapter must be on his guard against the author's personal value judgements and he must remain critical of the hypotheses adopted.

Economics is a young subject with uncertain answers even to some of the most pressing problems of our time.[1]

I.2   Gross Domestic Product

Most of the topics discussed in this chapter make some use of the national accounts statistics. A full explanation of what these are and of how they are put together would occupy more space than can be afforded and is, in any case, available elsewhere.[2] It will be useful, however, in the next few pages to remind the reader of the main national accounting categories in so far as they affect this chapter.

The most important concept of all is gross domestic product (GDP). This is the value of the total output of the whole economy. Its significance can be most readily appreciated by imagining that the economy is like some simple productive enterprise, such as a farm. Suppose that a farm produces only wheat, the total production during a single year being 100 bushels and the price £1. The value of total production is therefore £100. This is the sum which is divided as income between the various factors of production. It is distributed in the form of rent to the landowners, wages to the labour force and profit to the farmer. Thus total output is equal to total income. Furthermore, total output is equated to total expenditure on the output under the accounting convention that any output which is not sold is recorded as an addition to stocks, and as such regarded as investment expenditure by the farmer. Thus the income and output of the farm and the expenditure on its output are evaluated so as to make them identically equal to each other.

The GDP of the UK, by analogy with the simple production unit, can also be added up in three different ways: from the sides of income, output and expenditure. The first of these, total *income,* measures the sum of all incomes of the residents of the UK earned in the production of goods and services in the UK during a stated period. It divides into income from employment, income from self-employment and profit, and income from rent. These are factor incomes earned in the process of production and are to be distinguished from *transfer incomes,* such as pensions and sickness benefits, which are not earned from production and which, therefore, are excluded from the total. The breakdown of factor incomes for 1976 is illustrated in table 1.1 on page 4.

As with the simple production unit the value of output accruing in the form of unsold stocks is included in total factor output. But a problem arises when the prices at which stocks are valued in the national accounts vary during the course of the accounting period. When this happens the value of stocks held at the beginning and end of the period will have been reported at two different prices, and it is then necessary to make a special valuation adjustment known as the adjustment for *stock appreciation.* A firm holding stocks of wood, for example, may increase its holding

---

1 See E. H. Phelps Brown, 'The Underdevelopment of Economics', and G. D. N. Worswick, 'Is Progress in Economic Science Possible?', both published in *EJ,* March 1972.

2 See, for example, S. Hays, *National Income and Expenditure in Britain and the OECD Countries,* Heinemann, 1971; R. and G. Stone, *National Income and Expenditure,* 9th edition, Bowes and Bowes, 1972: H. C. Edey and others, *National Income and Social Accounting,* 3rd edition, Hutchinson, 1967; or the official handbook, *National Accounts Statistics, Sources and Methods,* HMSO, 1968.

TABLE 1.1
GDP and GNP at Current Prices, UK, 1976

FROM INCOME

	£m	% of domestic income[1]
Income from employment	78,639	68.6
Income from self-employment	10,208	8.9
Income from rent	7,771	6.8
Gross trading profits of companies	12,445	10.9
Gross trading surplus of public corporations and other public enterprises	4,580	4.0
Imputed charge for consumption of non-traded capital	1,012	0.9
Total domestic income (before providing for stock appreciation)	114,655	100.0
less Stock appreciation	−6,557	
Residual error	982	
Gross domestic product at factor cost	109,080	

FROM OUTPUT

	£m	% of domestic output[1]
Agriculture, forestry and fishing	3,116	2.8
Mining and quarrying	2,458	2.2
Manufacturing	30,464	27.0
Construction	7,793	6.9
Services and distribution	68,969	61.1
Total domestic income (after providing for stock appreciation)	112,800	100.0
Adjustment for financial services[2]	−4,702	
Residual error	982	
Gross domestic product at factor cost	109,080	

FROM EXPENDITURE

	£m	% of TFE[1]
Consumers' expenditure	73,656	46.4
General government final consumption	26,562	16.7
Gross domestic fixed investment	23,427	14.7
Investment in stocks	359	0.2
Export of goods and services	34,837	21.9
Total final expenditure at market prices	158,841	100.0
less Imports of goods and services	−36,564	
less Adjustment to factor cost	−13,197	
Gross domestic product at factor cost	109,080	
Net property income from abroad	1,179	
Gross national product at factor cost	110,259	

Source: NIBB 1966-76, tables 1.1, 1.11. *ET*, October 1977.
1 Percentage figures may not add up to 100.0 because of rounding.
2 Deduction of net receipts of interest by financial companies.

from 100 tons on 1 January to 200 tons on 31 December. If the price of wood was £1.00 per ton at the beginning of the year and £1.10 at the end of the year the increase in the monetary value of stocks will show up as (£1.10 x 200) – (£1.00 x 100), which equals £120. This figure is inflated by the amount of the price increase and fails, therefore, to give an adequate record of what the Central Statistical Office (CSO) calls 'the value of the physical increase in stocks'. In order to rectify this the CSO attempts to value the physical change in stocks at the average price level prevailing during the period. If, in the example, the price averaged £1.05 over the period then the value of the physical increase in stocks would be shown as £1.05 (200–100) which equals £105. The difference of £15 between this and the increase in monetary value is the adjustment for stock appreciation. It must be deducted from the reported value of factor incomes in order to reach an estimate of gross domestic income.

GDP is measured from the *production* side by adding up the value of production of the various firms and public enterprises in the country. This procedure presents two types of problem. First, the goods and services produced by one firm may also form part of the output of some other firm. Wheat produced on a farm, for example, is entered as farm output. But it may also be used by a bakery as an input in the production of bread. If so its value will enter into the value of bread output as well as farm output. To eliminate double-counting of this kind a distinction must be drawn in the production accounts between, on the one hand, total final output, which is sold to final buyers and, on the other hand, intermediate output sold to other productive units. Intermediate output must be excluded before arriving at a firm's contribution to gross domestic product.

A second problem arises in the case of imports which often form part of a firm's production (e.g. imported wheat in bread output), but which are produced by enterprises outside the UK. To arrive at UK domestic output, the value of imports must be deducted from the value of total final output. In table 1.1 the various categories in the output column are all evaluated net of intermediate output.

GDP can also be measured from the side of *expenditure.* Conceptually this total is identical to the income and output totals; but in practice the expenditure statistics are collected from independent sources and do not lead to exactly the same figure. The difference between the two estimates is known as the residual error and is sometimes quite large. In 1976 it was £982m, or 0.9% of GDP.

The breakdown of the expenditure total is especially important in the analysis of aggregate demand. Expenditures are undertaken by four types of spending unit: persons, public authorities, firms and foreign residents.[1] Purchases by persons are described as consumers' expenditure, or, more loosely, as consumption. The latter description, however, may be slightly misleading when applied to expenditure on durable goods such as motor cars and refrigerators, the services of which are consumed over several years and not solely in the year in which they are purchased. One form of personal expenditure which is not classed as such is the purchase of new houses. These are deemed to have been sold initially to 'firms' and included under the broad heading of domestic capital formation or gross investment. Fixed investment, other than housing, represents the purchases by firms of physical assets that are not completely used up in current production, but which accrue as

---

1 The distinctions between types of spending units are not always clearcut, e.g. expenditure by self-employed persons is partly consumers' expenditure and partly investment.

additions or replacements to the nation's capital stock. The preface 'gross' warns us
that a year's gross investment does not measure the change in the size of the capital
stock during the year because it does not allow for withdrawals from the capital
stock due to scrapping, or for wear and tear. The concept of gross capital formation
is also carried through into the definition of domestic product itself. Net domestic
product is not easily measured but attempts to include only that investment which
adds to the total stock of capital. It is less relevant to the level of employment than
gross output.

The sum of exports, consumers' expenditure, government current consumption
and gross investment is known as total final expenditure at market prices, or TFE
for short. Each of the four components contains two elements which must be
deducted before arriving at GDP at factor cost. The first is the import content of the
expenditure which must, of course, be classified as foreign rather than domestically
produced output. The simplest way of removing imports is to take the global
import total as given by the balance of payment accounts and subtract it from TFE,
and this is the usual method. Estimates do exist, however, for the import content of
the separate components of final expenditure in the input-output tables, but they
are drawn up much less frequently than the national accounts. The second element
of total final expenditure which must be deducted to obtain the factor cost value of
GDP is the indirect tax content (net of subsidies) of the various expenditures. This
is present for the simple reason that the most readily available valuation of any
commodity is the price at which it sells in the market. This price, however, will
overstate the factor incomes earned from producing the commodity if it contains
an element of indirect tax; and it will understate factor income if the price is
subsidized. The deduction of indirect taxes (less subsidies) is known as the *factor
cost adjustment,* and is most conveniently made globally since it can be found from
the government's records of tax proceeds and subsidy payments. Estimates of its
incidence on the individual components of TFE are available annually in the
National Income *Blue Book.*[1]

Gross domestic product from the expenditure side is thus reached by adding up
the components of TFE at market prices, and by subtracting imports of goods and
services together with the factor cost adjustment. It relates to expenditure on the
total production in the UK of the residents of the United Kingdom. It differs from
the other aggregate concept, gross national product (GNP), in that it does not
include receipts of interest, profits and dividends by UK residents from productive
activity carried out overseas; nor does it exclude the profits of foreign-owned
enterprises producing in the UK. The balance of these two amounts is known as net
property income from abroad and must be added to GDP in order to obtain GNP.
It is a small total representing about 1% of GDP in 1976.

I.3   Gross Domestic Product at Constant Prices

Table 1.1 summarizes the national accounts for 1976 at the prices obtaining in
1976. As such it is a useful source of information as to the way in which domestic
income, output and expenditure were divided in a particular year. If, however, we
wish to compare the *volume* of goods produced in different periods we must use a

1 *NIBB,* 1966-76, table 1.8.

different set of figures. These are the estimates of GDP at constant prices, the expenditure side of which is presented in the Statistical Appendix, table A-1. They show the value of GDP for each year in terms of prices ruling in 1970. Similar estimates are available in index number form for the income total of GDP and for the output total together with its main industrial components. These totals are derived almost entirely from movements in quantities, the various quantities for each year being added together by means of the value weights obtaining for 1970. The result is three conceptually equal but independently derived estimates of real domestic output, and, as with the current price series, there are often large differences between them.[1] The existence of these differences means that there is normally some element of ambiguity as regards both the level of GDP in a particular year and changes between years. Thus the increase in real GDP between 1975 and 1976 was put at 2.7% by the expenditure estimate and at 2.3% by the output and income estimates. Since most macroeconomic discussion is concerned with expenditure relationships it is usual to put the main emphasis on this aspect of GDP.

Gross domestic product is an important entity in its own right and changes in its real amount are the best estimates available of changes in UK production. Even so, it must be remembered that it leaves a good deal out of the picture by excluding practically all productive work which is not sold for money. The national income statistics neglect, for example, the activities of the housewife and amateur gardener even though they must add millions of hours to UK production of goods and services. It is also important to recognize that GDP stands for the production of UK residents, not their expenditure. As an expenditure total it measures the spending of all persons, resident or foreign, on the goods and services produced by the residents of the UK. Thus if national welfare is equated to the expenditure of UK residents it is incorrect to represent it by GDP. The total appropriate for this purpose is GDP *plus* imports *minus* exports. This total is sometimes referred to as 'domestic absorption', and is equal to the UK's total use of resources, which is the sum of consumption, government expenditure and gross investment. It is an amount which can diminish quite substantially when there is a sharp correction to the balance of payments, such as might be expected from a devaluation of the currency.

I.4   Personal Income and Personal Disposable Income

Two further concepts, personal income and disposable income, are of importance in the analysis of consumption and the multiplier. Personal income is not directly obtainable from the income breakdown shown in table 1.1, although two of the categories there, employment income and the income of the self-employed, form part of it. The remainder consists of that part of total rent, dividends and profits which is actually paid to persons (a part of the total shown in table 1.1) and also transfer incomes received by persons from the central government and from charitable institutions. A full breakdown of personal income and personal disposable income is shown in tables 1.2 and A-3 (in the Statistical Appendix). It should be noted that the difference between personal disposable income (derived from the income side of the national accounts) and consumers' expenditure

---

1   These differences are usually referred to as 'the statistical discrepancies' so as to distinguish them from the residual error in the estimates at current prices.

TABLE 1.2
Personal Income, UK, 1976

	£m
Income from employment	78,639
Income from self-employment	10,208
Rent, dividends and interest	10,451
Current transfers to charities from companies	42
National Insurance benefits and other current grants from public authorities	12,822
Imputed charge for capital consumption of private non-profit-making bodies	192
Personal income before tax	112,354
less	
National Insurance, etc., contributions	8,426
UK taxes on income	17,610
Transfers abroad	65
equals	
Total personal disposable income	86,253
of which	
Consumers' expenditure	73,656
Personal saving (before provision for depreciation, stock appreciation and addition to tax reserves)	12,597

Source: NIBB, 1966-76, table 1.2 and *ET,* October 1977, table 4.

(derived from the expenditure side) is the most frequently quoted estimate of personal saving.

II   FLUCTUATIONS IN TOTAL OUTPUT AND EXPENDITURE
II.1   Fluctuations in Output and Employment

The British economy has experienced cyclical fluctuations since the time of the industrial revolution. During the nineteenth century these appear to have followed a fairly uniform pattern with a peak-to-peak duration of seven to ten years and a tendency for 'full employment' (roughly defined) to reappear at each cyclical peak. After the First World War this pattern ceased, and for nearly twenty years there were well over one million unemployed. Unemployment reached 12½% of the work force in the recession of 1926 and 22% in 1932.

Since the Second World War the business cycle has been much milder than before and unemployment has been relatively low. Nevertheless the cycle has not been without interest. Involuntary unemployment is wasteful and demoralizing even when it comes in small doses. And, whilst the national rate of unemployment has been low, rates in some of the regions (notably Northern Ireland, Scotland and the north of England) have been more disturbing. Again, the assumption by the state of responsibility for the level of employment, along with an improved understanding of how it may be regulated, has focused political attention on each phase of the business cycle. Finally, there has probably been some connection between political popularity and the state of the economy.

Cyclical movements are often associated with increases and decreases in national output. In the postwar period, however, the cycle has been very mild with the consequence that there have been rather few actual downturns in the level of GDP. There have been sharp increases in GDP in the upturn of the cycle, but in the recession GDP has simply increased at less than its average rate. Any decline in employment has tended to be more than offset by a rise in output per man. Thus GDP rose in 1963, 1967 and 1971 despite increases in unemployment in those years and an evident easing of the demand for labour. The most recent recession, however, has been deeper than before with the result that GDP fell by 2.4% between 1973 and 1975, and even by 1977 had barely not recovered to its 1973 peak.

The best indicators of cyclical activity are the figures for unemployment and unfilled vacancies as percentages of the labour force (figure 1.1). These indicate peak levels of economic activity in 1960-1, 1965 and 1973-4 whilst the main periods of recession are shown as 1963, 1971-2 and 1975-7. The vacancy series suggest that the pressure of demand for labour was much the same in 1975-7 as in the earlier recessions of 1963 and 1971, whereas the unemployment figures suggest that the most recent recession has been much more serious than earlier. Thus the two sets of figures are in agreement about the *phases* of the cycle but in conflict as to its *intensity* (see p. 11).

The annual movements in employment shown in figure 1.1 tend to follow the same pattern as those of unemployment and vacancies. But they also reflect demographic factors such as movements in the total population of working age and its composition by age and sex, as well as social or institutional changes in the propensity to seek work. During the early 1960s there was still some upward trend in employment due to the demographic factors, with the result, in particular, that there was no decline in its level in the recession of 1963. In the later 1960s, however, the employment figures were affected by a levelling off in the population of working age, by a large increase in student numbers, and by the raising of the school-leaving age in 1973. The level of employment was almost exactly the same in 1977 as it had been fourteen years earlier.

Whilst employment and unemployment move together over the business cycle they seldom display the same relative variations from year to year. In most cycles the proportionate variation in employment exceeds the change in the unemployment percentage. This is probably explained by the presence of 'hidden employment', i.e. various groups of workers, such as married women, who do not register as unemployed when they are dismissed. A second common characteristic of cyclical movements in the economy is for the change in total output to be proportionately greater than the change in employment. This implies that productivity will tend to rise faster on the upturn of the cycle than on the downturn. It is explained partly by the presence of 'overhead labour', such as managerial and supervisory staff who remain on the payroll despite changes in turnover, and partly by a tendency for firms to 'hoard' labour, particularly those with scarce skills, during the recession so as to be sure of having it to hand when demand recovers.

Some of these characteristics are illustrated by the upturn of 1972-3 (see table 1.3), although in the recession that followed the rise in unemployment was substantially larger than the percentage drop in employment.

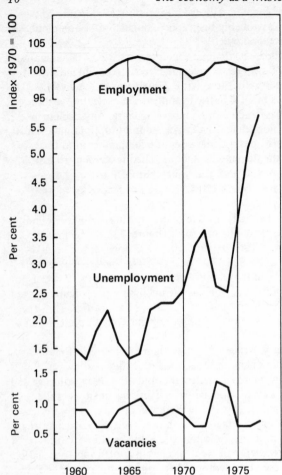

Figure 1.1   Employment, unemployment and vacancies, UK, 1960-77.

TABLE 1.3

Changes in Output, Employment and Unemployment, UK, 1972-7

Percentage change in:	1972-3	1973-5	1975-7
GDP	+5.3	−3.2	+3.2
Employment	+2.0	−0.4	−0.2
Unemployment	−1.0	+1.3	+1.8

Sources: ET, May 1978 (average estimate of GDP and employed labour force); *DEG* (wholly unemployed, excluding school-leavers and adult students as percentage of total employees).

The intensity of peaks and troughs: An accurate measure of the intensity of peaks and recessions is needed for policy purposes. It is important to have complete, sensitive and consistent indicators of inflationary pressure and of the degree of underutilization of resources. There are some grounds for regarding the unemployment series as superior. It can be argued, for example, that unemployment tends to be more completely recorded than vacancies because most of those who register are entitled to unemployment benefit. Unfilled vacancies, however, are recorded only in so far as employers believe it to be worth their while to report them to the employment offices. An employer who has already notified the employment office of vacancies for a particular kind of worker will not always register new vacancies when they arise since the original notice will be sufficient to attract applicants. Thus the vacancy figures are bound to be incomplete, and it is officially estimated that only about one-half of all new vacancies are notified to the Department of Employment.[1]

In the last fifteen years, however, both sets of statistics have been called in question by a sharp change in the relationship between them. A given level of vacancies is now accompanied by a much higher level of unemployment than it used to be. The extent of the change can be seen from the following comparisons:

	Unfilled vacancies		Unemployment	
	(000s, percentages in brackets)			
1962-3 (average)	145	(0.6)	461	(2.0)
1965-6 (average)	262	(1.1)	315	(1.4)
1971-2 (average)	137	(0.6)	777	(3.5)
1973-4 (average)	297	(1.3)	576	(2.6)
1975-6 (average)	145	(0.6)	1055	(4.6)

The figures illustrate a continuing tendency for unemployment to rise relative to vacancies. The comparison between 1962-3 and 1971-2 clearly suggests a rise of 1.5 per cent in unemployment for a constant vacancy rate, whilst that between 1965-6 and 1973-4 (two peak years) may be taken to imply an adjustment to the unemployment percentage of 1.4 per cent (i.e. an actual increase of 1.2 per cent plus 0.2 per cent to allow for a higher vacancy rate). The comparison between 1971-2 and 1975-6, moreover, implies a further shift in the relationship, so that by the time of these last two years a vacancy rate of 0.6 per cent coincided with an unemployment rate some 2.6 per cent higher than would have been observed in the early 1960s. It will be clear that a change of this magnitude makes it very difficult to compare the intensity of the cycle or the pressure of demand for labour over a period of more than a few years.

It is possible to isolate about four different sets of factors which may have been responsible for this dramatic change in the relationship of unemployment to vacancies:

(i)   One explanation is that there has been an increase in the ratio of registered to actual unemployment. Registered male unemployment in 1971 was 71% of the amount recorded by the Census sample of the same date, as against

1 See *BLS*, p. 18.

only 56% at the time of the 1966 Census and 44% at the 1961 Census. The increased reporting rate could have added about 100,000 to the register, or about one-third of the increase noted above. What is not so clear, however, is the underlying reason for the increased reporting rate. It can be argued that it was due to improved monetary incentives to register, such as the earnings-related unemployment benefits introduced in September 1966, and the gradual rise in the ratio of basic benefit to average industrial earnings. But a possible qualification here is that regional figures indicate a higher reporting rate in areas of high unemployment, and this could mean that the rise between the peak of 1966 and the trough of 1971 may have been partly due to the phase of the cycle.

(ii)   A second hypothesis is that better compensation for unemployment could have encouraged workers to spend longer on the unemployment register whilst looking for new jobs, thus raising the unemployment level for any given pressure of demand for labour. It may be significant that the shift in the U-V relationship has been almost totally confined to male workers, a high proportion of whom are entitled to unemployment benefit, whereas there has been practically no shift for female workers, large numbers of whom do not qualify for benefit when they lose their jobs.

(iii)   A third hypothesis is the 'shake-out' theory, which rests on the supposition that since about 1968 employers have become much more economical in their use of labour, and, in particular, that the practice of hoarding labour between cyclical peaks was greatly diminished at about this time. The stimulus to greater economy may have been given by the jolt to expect-ations of recovery after devaluation and by the promise in the Budget speech of 1968 of 'two years' hard slog'. Thus hoarded labour was shaken out, with the result that recorded unemployment increased relative to vacancies. The fact that output per man rose dramatically in 1968 (by 4.8%) is a point in favour of this hypothesis. But a weakness of the hypothesis is that it seems to imply a change in the relationship of vacancies to unemployment only in the recession phase of the cycle. One might expect a recovery of demand to be accompanied by a 'shake-in' – a decline in unemployment faster than a rise in vacancies. This, however, did not happen when the recovery came in 1973. Vacancies rose to their previous peak level whereas unemployment did not fall correspondingly.

(iv)   Two further factors were the raising of the school-leaving age in 1973, which probably produced some additional increase in unemployment relative to vacancies, and the various improvements in the efficiency of the employment service since about the same date. These if anything would tend to have increased the reporting rate for vacancies.

It seems probable that all the factors mentioned have played some part in the shift in the U-V relationship. But their relative importance is difficult to ascertain with much confidence. A tentative conclusion is that the vacancy figures probably functioned as a more reliable indication of the pressure of demand on resources over a period running from about 1961 to 1971, but that from then onwards they may have behaved less consistently than the unemployment figures. This would suggest that the recession of 1971-2 was about equally severe as that of 1962-3 whereas that of 1975-6 was more severe than 1971-2.[1]

II.2   Expenditure in the Cycle

Fluctuations in domestic output have their origins in movements in total spending and its components. Theoretical accounts of the business cycle tend to stress investment fluctuations as the principal source of movements in the total, and this emphasis is largely confirmed by the figures in table 1.4.

TABLE 1.4

Growth Rates of Expenditure (at constant prices) during the Main Cyclical Phases, UK, 1955-77 (*Percentage increases per annum*)

	1955-9	1959-61	1961-3	1963-5	1965-72	1972-3	1973-7
Fixed investment	4.6	9.4	0.8	10.6	3.1	4.7	−2.8
Investment in stocks (expressed as % of TFE)	0.0	0.0	−0.1	0.4	−0.2	1.9	−0.3
Exports	2.0	4.4	2.9	4.7	5.8	11.7	4.2
Government consumption	−0.9	2.7	2.3	2.1	2.2	3.7	2.5
Consumers' expenditure on goods and services	2.5	3.2	3.2	2.4	2.7	4.4	−0.7
Imports	2.6	5.2	2.9	5.5	5.8	12.1	0.6
GDP (average estimate)	1.7	4.0	2.5	4.4	2.3	6.0	0.0

Sources: NIBB, 1966-76; *ET*, October 1977; figures for 1977 from *ET*, May 1978.

Fixed investment has tended to grow at a much faster rate of increase per annum in the upswings of the cycle than in the ensuing downswings. The same is true of investment in stocks which, despite their small size relative to TFE, can swing so violently as to have quite substantial effects upon the level of total demand. The increase in stockbuilding between 1972 and 1973, for example, added nearly 2% to TFE.

Whilst the investment items tend to move in phase with the cycle, they are by no means the only source of fluctuations. The UK is an open economy in which exports of goods and services account for nearly one-fifth of TFE. When there is a recession in overseas markets, whether in the industrial or primary producing regions, the effect is either to reduce UK exports (as happened in 1951-2) or, more usually, to slow down their rate of increase. Table 1.4 suggests that most of the main downswings in the UK economy were associated with a slackening of demand

---

1   There is a large volume of literature on the relationship between unemployment and vacancies. It includes A. Evans, 'Notes on the Changing Relationship between Registered Unemployment and Notified Vacancies: 1961-1966 and 1966-1971', *Economica,* May 1977; J. K. Bowers, P. C. Cheshire, E. A. Webb and R. Weeden, 'Some Aspects of Unemployment and the Labour Market, 1966-71', *NIER*, November 1972, pp. 83-5; J. Taylor, 'The Behaviour of Unemployment and Unfilled Vacancies: Great Britain, 1958-71, An Alternative View', *EJ,* December 1972; D. I. Mackay and G. L. Reid, 'Redundancy, Unemployment and Manpower Policy', *EJ,* 1972; D. Gujarati, 'The Behaviour of Unemployment and Unfilled Vacancies: Great Britain 1958-71', *EJ,* March 1972. For an official view, see 'The Unemployment Statistics and their Interpretation', *DEG,* March 1975.

overseas. Since 1967, exports have also been affected by devaluation and by the floating of the exchange rate.

There is no reason to expect government expenditure to move closely with the cycle or against it. In 1972-3, its increase contributed to the upturn and was part of the government's recovery programme. In the recession of 1955-9, however, the decline in government spending reflected a cutback in defence expenditure, and was not introduced with the express intention of reducing the pressure of demand. Government expenditure can be used for stabilization purposes, but its main movements have originated with changes in social policy or defence.

Whereas government expenditure, investment and exports can be regarded as the principal *autonomous* causes of demand fluctuations, consumption and imports (and also indirect taxes) are often thought to be *dependent* directly upon total income and indirectly upon the autonomous expenditures. This distinction between the autonomous and dependent items cannot be completely watertight since all of the latter are capable of moving autonomously for other reasons. But it is a useful first approximation.

The dependence of consumers' expenditure upon GDP is not as well supported by table 1.4 as might have been expected. The rate of increase has not been noticeably faster in the upturn of the cycle than in the downturns. This is partly because of variations in tax rates. Rates of increase in imports, however, have moved in phase with those of GDP, but their fluctuations have shown a somewhat larger amplitude. This reflects the fact that imports are taken first into stock, and tend to fluctuate with stockbuilding as well as with GDP.[1]

In the next section we describe some of the main hypotheses which have been advanced to explain movements in the components of total demand.

III   THE DETERMINANTS OF DEMAND

The level of national output is determined in the short run by the level of total expenditure. This is the sum of all demands for domestic output, and thus comprises all the elements of TFE net of their import and indirect tax components. A large area of macroeconomics is devoted to the attempt to explain how these expenditures are determined. Such explanations are essential if we are to understand economic fluctuations and to be able to forecast and control them.

III.1   Consumers' Expenditure

Consumers' expenditure is the largest single element in aggregate demand. It accounts for half of TFE (see table 1.1) and, after the removal of its import and indirect tax content, for about the same proportion of GDP at factor cost. Consumption is one of the more stable elements of demand in the sense that its fluctuations are small when measured as percentages of its total. But its total amount is so large in relation to GDP that even quite small percentage variations in it can have important repercussions for output and employment. An understanding of consumption behaviour, therefore, as well as an ability to predict it, are

1 For a further discussion of cyclical fluctuations see J. C. R. Dow, *The Management of the British Economy, 1945-60,* Cambridge University Press, 1964, chapter 4, and R. C. O. Matthews, 'Post-war Business Cycles in the United Kingdom', in M. Bronfenbrenner (ed.), *Is the Business Cycle Obsolete?,* Wiley, 1969.

important objectives for economic analysis. A great deal of attention has been given to consumption, both in theory and statistically, although this work has been more heavily concentrated upon consumption in the US where the relevant statistical data are available for a longer period than for the UK.

The starting point for the early studies of consumer behaviour was the well-known statement by Keynes:[1] 'The fundamental psychological law upon which we are entitled to depend with great confidence both *a priori* from our knowledge of human nature and from the detailed facts of experience, is that men are disposed, as a rule and on the average, to increase their consumption as their income increases, but not by as much as the increase in their income.' Keynes was suggesting that current income was the principal, although not the only, determinant of consumers' expenditure in the short run, and that the marginal propensity to consume (MPC), i.e. the ratio of additional consumption to additional income, was positive, fractional and reasonably stable. In point of fact the MPC, when measured crudely as the ratio of changes in the annual value of consumers' expenditure at current prices to changes in personal disposable income, has not been particularly stable, nor always fractional, nor even always positive. Between 1952 and 1974 the value of MPC varied between 0.7 and 1.2 with an average annual value of 0.9. It was not fractional (i.e. it exceeded unity) in six years.[2]

If we focus attention upon savings rather than consumption it can be seen (figure 1.2) that the ratio of personal savings to personal disposable income has shown a strong upward trend over the postwar period with deviations from trend which are associated with cyclical fluctuations. The savings ratio was above trend in the peak years of 1956, 1961 and 1965 and below trend in the intervening recessions. These movements will have meant increases in the marginal propensity to save (MPS) on the upturn of the cycle and decreases on the downturn. The MPC, inevitably, has tended to rise in the downturn and increase in the upturn.

Cyclical movements in the savings ratio can be accounted for in various ways. One possible explanation is that consumer behaviour is driven partly by habit and convention so that when income declines the individual attempts to maintain his expenditure at its previous level with the consequence that the APC rises and the savings ratio declines. A related explanation can be found in the ideas of the normal income theorists.[3] Their main proposition is that consumption does not depend upon current income but on normal income, a concept which can be defined either precisely as the expected lifetime income of the consumer or much more vaguely as his notion of average income over some ill-defined future period. Thus it is changes in the level of expected income which are likely to change consumption. If current income increases then it will raise consumption only in so far as it raises normal income, and the amount by which it does so will depend upon the expected persistence of the income change. Cyclical changes in income are (by definition) not persistent, and the likelihood is that some consumers, perhaps a majority, will

1 J. M. Keynes, *General Theory*, p. 96.
2 Measured at constant prices over the same period the MPC varied between −0.5 and 2.6. It was not fractional in six years and negative twice.
3 For an examination of these theories, see M. J. Farrell, 'The New Theories of the Consumption Function,' *EJ*, December 1959 (reprinted in Klein and Gordon (eds), *Readings in Business Cycles*, Allen and Unwin, 1966). The classic reference is F. Modigliani and R. Brumberg, 'Utility Analysis and the Consumption Function' in K. Kurihara, *Post-Keynesian Economics*, Allen and Unwin, 1955.

recognize them as such. Thus the APC will tend to be high in depressions and low at the peaks, whilst the savings ratio (see figure 1.2) will do the reverse.

It is quite possible that the normal income hypothesis can also explain the pronounced and steady rise in the savings ratio since 1971 if, as seems plausible, the higher average level of unemployment, the slowing down of real income growth and, more recently, the threat of anti-inflationary policies, have led consumers to revise their long-term income expectations downwards. But a further factor after 1975 was the additional uncertainty of real income expectations due to the rapid inflation. The problem with these explanations, however, is the difficulty of finding objective evidence of income expectations or of the degree of certainty with which they are held.[1]

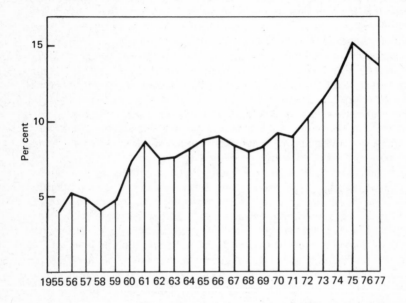

Figure 1.2   Personal saving as a percentage of personal disposable income, UK, 1955-77.

Whilst a change in the climate of expectations may have been partly responsible for the climb in the savings ratio between the 1960s and 1970s, it is not clear why there should have been an uptrend in the 1950s when income expectations were improving. Postponed consumption after the Second World War would explain a very low savings rate in the late 1940s, but it is difficult to believe that it could have been responsible for the savings rate continuing to rise in the 1950s. Thus there may be something in the hypothesis that consumer wants tend, as Keynes once suggested, to become saturated as income increases, or at least that the income-elasticity of consumption in general is less than unity. If so, then consumers would

---

1   In periods when the APS is increasing there is generally an increase in the liquid assets of the personal sector. This is sometimes taken to be the *cause* of the higher savings ratio (see, for example, *BEQB*, March 1976) but in our view is more correctly considered as the *effect* of higher savings.

appear to have behaved differently in the UK from those in the US, where the savings ratio has been roughly stable for a century despite enormous increases in personal income.

An important influence upon consumers' expenditure is the availability of credit, and particularly of credit for financing purchases of durable goods.[1] These goods, which constitute 7-9% of total consumption, are more of the nature of capital equipment than of consumption in that they yield a flow of utility over time. It is natural where income is generally rising that such goods should be bought extensively on credit, and something like one half of their total is financed by hire-purchase. The availability of this form of finance has been subject to government regulation in two main ways: by the stipulation of a minimum HP deposit and by the specification of a maximum period of repayment. The regulations have been varied extensively and have been associated with sharp but short-lived fluctuations in durable goods expenditure. The raising of the minimum down-payment, for example, means that an individual must wait a month or so longer in order to save the additional sum. Thus the effect of such restrictions is to postpone purchases rather than to alter their level in the longer run.

The explanation of aggregate consumption is usually regarded as one of the more satisfactory aspects of aggregate demand economics. In recent years, however, estimated consumption functions have furnished poor predictions of actual consumption,[2] and this has disturbed confidence in the economic theory of consumption. The uptrend in the savings ratio, moreover, and its contrast with US experience, also leave room for further investigation.

III.2 Gross Fixed Investment

Fixed investment or gross domestic fixed capital formation is a heterogeneous total, comprising housing and business investment in both the public and the private sectors. Its breakdown by industry and sector in 1976 is shown in table 1.5. Of the three main components, it is manufacturing investment which is the most volatile. Investment in dwellings is the least volatile of three types of fixed investment. Nevertheless all three sectors vary enough from year to year to have important effects upon output and employment.

TABLE 1.5

Gross Domestic Fixed Capital Formation, UK, 1976 (£m)

	Private sector	Public sector	Total
Dwellings	2,320	2,312	4,632
Manufacturing	3,381	576	3,957
Other fixed investment	7,614	7,224	14,838
Total	13,315	10,112	23,427

Source: NIBB, 1966-76, p. 130; current prices.

---

1 It should be noted that the *Blue Book* definition of durable goods includes cars, motor cycles, furniture, carpets and electrical goods, but, perhaps arbitrarily, does not include clothing, curtains, pots and pans or books.
2 See *NIER,,* February 1976, p. 82.

A hypothesis which goes some way towards explaining the behaviour of manufacturing investment is the capital-stock-adjustment principle. This states that the level of investment is related positively to the level of output and negatively to the existing capital stock (of land, buildings and machinery in productive use). The principle may be expressed as:

$$I_t = aY_{t-1} - bK_{t-1}$$

or, in ratio form, as

$$\frac{I_t}{Y_{t-1}} = a - b\frac{K_{t-1}}{Y_{t-1}}$$

Here I_t stands for gross investment in the current year, Y_{t-1} for last year's level of output, K_{t-1} for the capital stock at the end of the preceding year; and a and b are constant coefficients. The principle may be interpreted in various ways, one of which is to assume (not too implausibly) that technology dictates a fixed proportional relationship between the stock of capital equipment and the level of output. It follows, since net investment is an increase in the capital stock, that its amount will be planned in relation both to the expected volume of production and to the current size of the capital stock. If it is assumed as an approximation that the expected volume of output is equal to the level most recently experienced, then the expressions above may be seen to hold.[1]

Figure 1.3 illustrates the inverse relationship between the investment ratio and the capital-output ratio implied by the stock-adjustment principle. It shows a fairly close correspondence between peaks in one ratio and troughs in the other. An estimate of the relationship by least-squares regression is as follows:

$$\frac{I_t}{Y_{t-1}} = .381 - .091\frac{K_t}{Y_{t-1}}$$

where I_t, K_t and Y_{t-1} all refer to manufacturing industry. The equation fits the data moderately well. The residual errors between the estimated and actual data

---

1   The equations are derived by denoting K_t^* as the desired capital stock, Y_t^* as expected output, R_t^* as desired replacement investment, I_t^* as desired gross investment and I_t as actual gross investment. Then, by definition,

$$I_t^* = K_t^* - K_{t-1} + R_t^*$$

and, by assumption:

$$I_t = bI_t^* = b(K_t^* - K_{t-1} + R_t^*)$$
$$K_t^* = a_1 Y_t^*$$
$$R_t^* = a_2 Y_t^*$$
$$Y_t^* = Y_{t-1}$$

$$\therefore \quad I_t = b(a_1 Y_{t-1} - K_{t-1} + a_2 Y_{t-1})$$
$$= b(a_1 + a_2) Y_{t-1} - bK_{t-1}$$
$$= aY_{t-1} - bK_{t-1} \text{ where } a = b(a_1 + a_2)$$

which is the first of the equations in the text.

averaged out at the equivalent of 3½% of total manufacturing investment, and they exceeded 10% in four years out of the eighteen. The size of the residuals, however, must be judged in relation to an expenditure total which is highly volatile, and in which year-to-year changes exceed 10% in nine years out of eighteen.[1] It seems

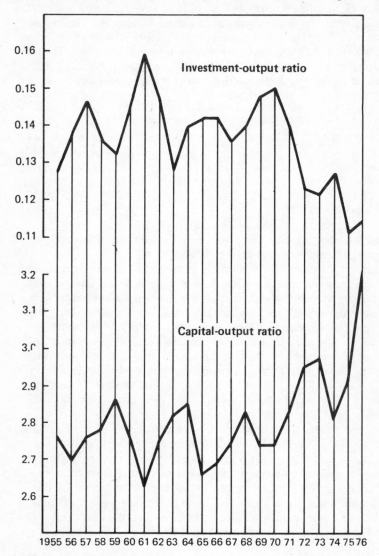

Figure 1.3   Manufacturing investment and capital stock as ratios of manufacturing output, UK, 1955-76

1   The equation was estimated at 1970 prices for 1953-72. Its other statistical characteristics were r^2 = 0.57, t-statistics 7.50 and 4.84 respectively, Durbin-Watson statistic 1.42, standard error of the investment ratio 0.007. The mean prediction error for 1963-72 from a similar equation fitted to 1953-62 data was equivalent to 3.9% of the level of investment. The capital-stock data for 1955-63 were taken from *LCES* and converted into 1970 prices; otherwise *NIBB* 1966-76.

possible to conclude that there is at least an element of truth in the stock-adjustment principle, even though, it is difficult to regard its expectational and technological assumptions as more than approximately true.

Economic theory suggests that there are a number of relevant considerations
ignored by the stock-adjustment principle. One of these is the expected profitability
of the investment, which although related to the volume of expected sales and output is dependent on other factors too. Expected profitability is likely to be guided
by actual profitability which, in recent years, has been exceptionally low. The rate
of return on capital employed fell from 9.6% in 1964-9 to only 4.0% in 1972[1] and
there has been a corresponding decline in the ratio of profits to income:

	Gross trading profits net of stock appreciation as % of total domestic income
1966-9	12.9
1970-2	11.7
1972-5	7.9
1976	6.6

(*Source: ET*, October 1977, p. 121)

There is not much doubt that these trends go a long way to explaining why
investment in the 1970s fell so low relative to GDP.

A further factor is the rate of interest which, as the cost of borrowing, can never
be completely ignored as an influence upon the level of investment. Interest must
be paid on all funds that are borrowed from outside the firm and it must be foregone
on internal funds which could have been lent at interest but which, instead, are used
to finance the firm's own investment projects. If interest rates had fluctuated
violently it would have been necessary to include them as an additional variable in
the determination of investment in the UK. But for many years they showed only
rather modest movements, never rising, for example, by more than 2% in a year over
the period 1958-73.[2] In 1973-4, however, the debenture rate rose from 11.4% to
16.4% and this almost certainly affected investment. The debenture rate fell back
to 13.4% in 1977.

Another factor which must surely be taken into account in any general explanation of investment behaviour is the availability of funds for investment and the
constraints that from time to time have been imposed by credit policy. Investment
is financed predominantly from internal sources and only partly from outside credit
institutions.[3] As far as internal sources are concerned it must be accepted that
company profits, besides acting as a guide to future profitability, will also act as a
financial constraint upon investment. As for external sources of credit, there seems
little doubt that their availability or otherwise must be an influence of some
importance, especially on the investment of small firms.

---

1 *NIER*, February 1976, pp. 83-84.

2 This probably explains why so few econometric studies have found interest rates to be an
   important influence on investment in Britain. See D. Savage, 'The Channels of Monetary
   Influence', *NIER*, February 1978.

3 During 1954-63 some 70–90% of company investment was financed from internal sources.
   See 'Internal and external sources of company finance' reprinted from *ET*, February 1966,
   in CSO, *New Contributions to Economic Statistics*, Fourth Series, HMSO, 1967.

Other business fixed investment does not appear to conform with the capital stock-adjustment principle anything like as readily as manufacturing investment. This may be because the assumption of a fixed relationship between capital and output does not hold well in non-manufacturing industries. It is less easy, therefore, to explain investment in these industries, although it must still be the case that expected sales, profits, interest rates and credit availability are relevant influences. Econometric studies have claimed a role for lagged changes in domestic output,[1] whilst short-term forecasts can be made on the basis of investment intentions surveys such as those carried out by the Department of Trade and Industry, the CBI and the *Financial Times.*

Housing investment needs to be divided between the public and private sectors and examined in relation to demand and supply influences in both sectors. The demand for public-sector building comes indirectly from population trends and directly from the policies of the public authorities. The demand for private-sector building depends upon both population characteristics (family formation and size) and also upon expected lifetime income, the cost of mortgage credit, the prices of new houses and of substitute accommodation. It is subject to the important and highly variable constraints set by the availability of mortgage credit which in turn are determined partly by general credit policy and partly by the policies of the building societies. Among the main influences on the side of supply are the size of the building industry and the number of building workers, the price and availability of building land, and stocks of bricks and other building materials. With such a variety of factors at work it is not easy to construct or present a satisfactory model of the determination of housing investment, and we do not attempt the task in this chapter. The problem of predicting housing investment is eased, however, by the statistics of new houses started, which, with an assumption about completion times, makes it possible to forecast housing for at least a short period ahead.

III.3   Stocks and Stockbuilding

Stockbuilding or investment in stocks is the change in a level — the level of all stocks held at the beginning of the period. In any one year stock investment can be positive or negative, whilst the change in stock investment between successive years can exert an important influence upon GDP. The increase in stock investment in 1972-4, for example, was equivalent to 4.6% of GDP whilst the decline in 1974-5 was equivalent to 1.9% of GDP.

At the end of 1976 the total value of stocks held in all industries was approximately £43,000m, or 39% of the value of GDP in a year. Stocks held by manufacturing industry amounted to £26,000m, or about 75% of the annual value of manufacturing output. Manufacturers' stocks divide into materials and fuel (£9,800m), work in progress (£9,500m) and stocks of finished products (£7,000m).[2]

Stocks of work in progress are held because they are a technical necessity of production, whilst stocks of materials and finished goods are held mainly out of a precautionary motive. They are required as a 'buffer' between deliveries and production; or, more precisely, because manufacturers are wise enough to know that

---

1 For example M. J. C. Surrey, *The Analysis and Forecasting of the British Economy*, NIESR and Cambridge University Press, 1971, p. 32, and HM Treasury, *Macroeconomic Model, Technical Manual*, 1977.

2 *NIBB*, 1966-76, table 12.1. The other main holders of stocks are wholesale and retail businesses.

they cannot expect an exact correspondence between the amount of materials delivered each day and the amount taken into production, or between completed production and deliveries to customers.

For these reasons it seems plausible to assume that manufacturers carry in their minds the notion of a certain optimum ratio between stocks on the one hand and output on the other. If stocks fall below the optimum ratio they will need to be replenished; if they rise above it they will be run down. The reasoning here is the same as that of the stock-adjustment principle which we have already considered in connection with fixed investment. The principle holds moderately well for manu- facturers' stockbuilding, which is by far the most volatile part of stock investment in the UK. Its application is illustrated in figure 1.4, where it can be seen, for

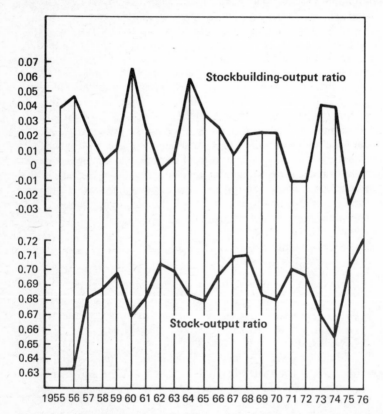

Figure 1.4   Manufacturers' stockbuilding and stock levels as ratios of manufacturing output, UK, 1955-76

example, that the stock investment peaks of 1956, 1960, 1964, 1969 and 1973-4 all coincided with low values of the stock-output ratio.

A regression estimate of manufacturers' stockbuilding using annual data is:

$$\frac{I_t}{Y_{t-1}} = 0.299 - 0.41 \frac{S_t}{Y_{t-1}}$$

where the terms all refer to manufacturing industry and S_t stands for the level of stocks held at the beginning of the year. The quality of this regression equation is less good than that for fixed investment. Its mean residual error (regardless of sign) is about 0.007 in units of the stockbuilding-output ratio, and is equivalent to an average annual error of £80m at 1970 prices. This figure may be put in the perspective of a mean annual change in investment in stocks over the period of £150m.[1] It is probable that this equation would have performed better if we had estimated it for quarterly or semi-annual periods. This is because manufacturers are hardly likely to plan their stock changes for as long as a year ahead.

The stock-adjustment principle is only the beginning of a complete explanation of planned investment in stocks. Other factors are likely to be the level of interest rates, the availability of credit, expected future prices and the degree of uncertainty. *Unplanned* movements in stocks, moreover, will occur whenever sales expectations are falsified. Thus there will be an involuntary accumulation of stocks if sales fall below expectation, and an involuntary run-down of stocks if sales exceed their expected volume.

III.4   Other Expenditures

It remains to discuss two further components of TFE — exports and public authorities' expenditure on goods and services — and two items which have to be deducted from TFE to obtain GDP — indirect taxes (net of subsidies) and imports of goods and services.

There is little to be said about public current expenditure since its amount is determined by the political aims and priorities of the central government and the local authorities. Exports of goods and services depend upon overseas demand which in turn is mainly influenced by the volume of overseas income (both in the industrial and primary producing areas), the sterling price of UK exports and the exchange rate.[2] These matters, however, are discussed more fully in chapter 3.

The components of TFE are normally evaluated at their market prices. If we are interested in UK production and factor incomes we must make the factor-cost adjustment, i.e. deduct from these values the sum of indirect taxes net of subsidies. This is usually done for TFE as a whole, but estimates for the factor-cost adjustment for its main components are given in table 1.6.

Most indirect taxes are levied on consumption goods so that the adjustment tends to be higher here than it is for government expenditure, investment or exports.

The factor-cost adjustment is one of two deductions which must be made in order to progress from TFE to GDP. The other is imports which, since they are produced by foreign factors of production, cannot constitute UK factor income. In 1972, as the table shows, imports came to 18% of TFE; they were a smaller proportion of government spending than of other types of expenditure.

The main determinants of imports are the level of income, stocks of materials

---

1   The estimation period was 1952-70, but excluded 1960 and 1964 which are both well above estimate: $r^2 = 0.40$, the t-ratios were 3.4 and 3.2 respectively, Durbin-Watson statistic 1.94, and the standard error of the equation was 0.009 in units of the stockbuilding-output ratio. A similar equation fitted for 1952-61 predicted the ratios for 1962-70 with a mean error (regardless of sign) of 0.013; the errors for 1971 and 1972 were large.

2   It can be shown that fluctuations in UK exports correlate fairly closely with the index of world industrial production, and that exports to particular countries are statistically linked to output in those areas.

TABLE 1.6

Domestic Output Content of Total Final Expenditure at Market Prices, 1972

Percentages of market price totals

	Consumers' expenditure	*Government current expenditure*	*Gross domestic fixed investment*	*Exports of goods and services*	*Total final expenditure*
Indirect taxes (less subsidies)	16	5	6	4	11
Imports of goods and services	18	9	23	20	18
Domestic output content	66	86	71	76	71

Source: 'Summary Input-Output Tables for 1972', *ET,* April 1976.

and competitive factors. It is probably the latter which are responsible for the sustained upward trend (see chapter 3) in the ratio of imports of goods and services (at constant 1970 prices) to TFE:

1950-4	14.2%
1955-9	14.9%
1960-4	15.8%
1965-9	16.6%
1970-4	19.3%
1975-6	19.8%

It is possible that this trend can be broken down and explained in terms of price competitiveness, trade policy and other variables, but many forecasting equations for imports have simply extrapolated the trend at its average recent rate of increase.

The influence of stocks upon the volume of imports has been recognized for many years and at one time it was thought that every £100m of stockbuilding would add about £50m to the import bill.[1] More recently, however, the influence of stocks appears to have weakened. A recent estimate suggests an import content of stockbuilding of 0.3 rather than 0.5.[2] The reason for the decline in the co-efficients is probably the increased weight of finished manufactures in the import total (see chapter 3).

The underlying explanation of the import content of stockbuilding is to be sought in terms of the stock-adjustment principle which, as suggested above, has a useful part to play in determining stockbuilding and fixed investment. If imports are found to vary directly with stockbuilding, and if stockbuilding follows the stock-adjustment principle, then imports will vary with the level of income and the initial level of stocks. Thus equations in terms of income and stockbuilding can be recast in terms of income and initial stock levels.[3] The more general point is that

---

1   See 'Forecasting Imports' by W. A. H. Godley and J. R. Shepherd, *NIER,* August 1965.

2   M. J. C. Surrey, *Analysis and Forecasting of the British Economy,* op. cit.

3   If $M = mY + nI$ (where M, Y and I are imports, income and stockbuilding respectively, m, the marginal propensity to import and n, the import content of stockbuilding), and if $I = aY - bK$ then $M = (m + na)Y - nbK$. The import ratio is now expressible in terms of the stock-output ratio.

approximately one third of total imports of goods and services consists of items which are used as inputs in the process of production. These are classified in chapter 3 as imports of basic materials, mineral fuels and lubricants and semi-manufactures. They enter into stocks in the same way as domestically produced iron ore or coal, and they are subject to similar laws of behaviour.

IV   THE MANAGEMENT OF DEMAND
IV.1   Objectives and Instruments

Since the end of the Second World War most governments have striven to influence the level of demand in the economy with the intention of maintaining or restoring acceptable levels of employment. This policy was originally advocated in the White Paper on *Employment Policy* (Cmd. 6527) issued in 1944 by the wartime coalition government. The White Paper stated that:

> The Government believe that, once the war has been won, we can make a fresh approach, with better chances of success than ever before, to the task of maintaining a high and stable level of employment without sacrificing the essential liberties of a free society.

The White Paper recommended that there should be a permanent staff of statisticians and economists in the Civil Service with responsibility for interpreting economic trends and advising on policy. It suggested that the execution of employment policy should be examined annually by Parliament in the Debate on the Budget. The White Paper also foresaw that high levels of employment were likely to endanger price stability, and it pointed out the need for 'moderation in wage matters by employers and employees' as the essential condition for the success of the policy.

The task of maintaining a high level of employment proved to be less difficult than had been expected. The White Paper had not laid down any precise target for the level of employment. But the levels attained in nearly every postwar year (with exceptions in 1947, 1971 and 1975-7) were higher than the authors of the White Paper had hoped. It became apparent, moreover, that high levels of employment were compatible with a fairly moderate rate of inflation. The average rate of retail price inflation in the 1950s, for example, was about 4% per year whilst unemployment averaged as little as 1½% of the labour force.

As we observed in section II (above), however, the postwar economy passed through a series of fluctuations with the annual unemployment rate varying between the limits of 1.0% and 5.7%. Part of the reason for these fluctuations could be found in the different views taken by successive governments (or sometimes by the same government at different times) as to the most desirable pressure of demand. The aim of high employment has been in some measure of conflict with the objectives of both balance of payments equilibrium and price stability. A conflict with the balance of payments has been present in so far as governments have been unwilling to make use of instruments of policy, such as exchange rate devaluation or import controls, for dealing with the external balance. Thus fiscal measures, which act upon the level of employment, have at times been directed towards the required balance of payments, with the consequence that the employment objective has taken second place. This conflict of objectives was particularly noticeable in two periods: from 1956 to early 1959 when the government was aiming at a long-term balance of payments surplus and preferred to deflate employment rather than depreciate sterling to achieve it; and also in the period of eighteen months preceding the devaluation of sterling in November 1967. It may be argued, however, that there is no conflict in principle between the balance of payments and employment objectives so long as exchange rate adjustments, or other instruments for dealing with the balance of payments, are effective and permissible.

The employment objective has also been in conflict with that of price stability. Here there is no independent instrument of control to parallel the variability of the exchange rate. Incomes policy, in the sense of voluntary or compulsory guidelines for the rate of increase in wages and prices, has not until recently been found to be particularly successful, and certainly not successful enough to permit nice percentage variations in the permitted rate of inflation. Thus the absence of an independent instrument for controlling inflation has implied a really genuine conflict of aims. It has necessitated a compromise between the two objectives, and the compromise has been struck at different target rates of employment by different governments. This, together with the balance of payments, helps to explain why the target level of employment has not been stable in the postwar period, but has tended to fluctuate according to the priorities of the government of the day.

Once the employment target is settled, the problem of how to attain it becomes an essentially technical issue. It is a matter of how complete and precise is our knowledge of the workings of the economy.

One elementary point concerns the existence of time-lags between the detection of a policy problem and its remedy. This means that it is not sound strategy to wait until unemployment has reached some intolerably high figure before acting or thinking about action to correct it. The unemployment statistics are about a month behindhand; civil servants may take up to six months to advise the appropriate action; Parliament may take three months to enact it; and even after the policy is put into force the full economic effects may not appear for some months afterwards. Thus a strategy based solely upon the observation of past statistics can involve a significantly long time-lag (of twelve months or longer) between the observed need for a change in policy and the effects of that change upon the level of employment.

It is partly for this reason that economic management in the UK is based upon a strategy of looking ahead rather than on response to observed behaviour. This means that the policy-maker relies very heavily upon the use of economic forecasts. If he can *correctly* foresee the emergence of a policy problem then the problem of the delay between the need for intervention and its effects is solved.

There is another reason, too, for relying upon forecasts. This is the need to tailor the amount of intervention to the future size of the problem rather than to what is currently observed. The mere observation of high unemployment or excessive inflation in no way guarantees that it will continue in the same degree of seriousness. The problem may get worse or it may get better. Quite clearly it is essential to form some view of what will happen in the future before deciding the degree and the direction of policy intervention required. Failure to produce a correct forecast of the course of employment over the next twelve to eighteen months could result in an *inadequate* degree of corrective policy action. Or it could actually be *destabilizing*,[1] in the sense that the effect of intervention is to remove the level of

---

1 A more accurate term would be 'perverse' since policy does not necessarily aim to stabilize anything.

output still further from target than it would have been without it.

The last three decades have seen a very considerable advance in the various branches of knowledge which bear upon the problems of forecasting and managing the economy. The chief of these have comprised: (i) an enormous improvement, attributable to the CSO, in economic statistics, and particularly the development of quarterly, seasonally adjusted, constant price, national expenditure figures; (ii) the development of a conceptual framework and quantitative model for forecasting the levels of GDP and employment over a period of about eighteen months; (iii) the development of a conceptual framework and quantitative model for estimating the effects on GDP tax changes and other instruments of demand management.

IV.2   The Effects of Policy Instruments: Government Expenditure

If fiscal intervention is to be tailored to precise targets for employment and output it is necessary for the policy-makers to make a fairly precise quantitative assessment of the effects of their policy instruments upon the level of domestic output. In this section we shall concentrate upon the effects of three such instruments: changes in government expenditure on goods and services, changes in indirect taxation and changes in personal income tax.

The effects of these changes divide into direct effects upon GDP and indirect effects such as the multiplier and accelerator consequences. In the case of an increase in government expenditure on goods and services measured at market prices the direct effects on GDP (at factor cost) will be smaller in volume than the expenditure change itself. This is because there are 'leakages' into imports and indirect taxes which do not influence domestic output. For government spending as a whole the indirect tax content averages 5% and the import content 9%,[1] so that £100m added to government expenditure will raise domestic output by £86m if the goods and services purchased are typical of government spending in general.[2] This also means that government expenditure must be raised on average by £116m to add £100m to GDP.

The indirect effects of the additional expenditure cannot be evaluated without an estimate of the size and timing of the *multiplier*; they are common to all three types of policy change. If GDP is raised by £100m by some initial increase in government expenditure, the question to be asked is how much of this will be re-spent on new domestic output. The problem may be tackled by estimating how much of the additional GDP will find its way into personal income, and by asking how this income is distributed between income tax, saving and consumers' expend-iture. The addition to consumers' expenditure must be broken down into its indirect tax, imported and domestically produced components, and of these it is of course the latter which constitutes the second addition to GDP.

The main quantities involved in this calculation are indicated in table 1.7. It can be assumed that none of the additional GDP is distributed as rent, and if the remainder is divided between profits and income from employment in the same ratio as total incomes from profit and employment (see *NIBB*) then the addition to personal income is likely to be about 82%. The increase in disposable income is

---

1   See table 1.6.

2   If, however, the extra spending is all on the running of a new department in Whitehall the import content could be well below 9%; if it is all on military spending overseas it could be much higher.

found by estimating the marginal tax rate for an average income recipient and the increases in consumption by taking the marginal savings ratio. Next, the indirect tax component of consumption is removed in order to obtain consumption at factor cost. Finally, the import component must be subtracted so as to arrive at the domestically produced increase in consumption. On the basis of the assumptions made, this turns out to be quite a small increase — only 31% of the first addition to GDP.

TABLE 1.7.

Stages in the Multiplier Process

	£m	Assumed marginal relationships
1st round increase in GDP	100	
Increase in personal income	82	$b_1 = .820$
Increase in personal disposable income	56	$b_2 = .683$
Increase (after a time-lag) in consumers' expenditure at market prices	50	$b_3 = .893$
Increase in consumers' expenditure at factor cost	41	$b_4 = .820$
Increase in domestically produced consumption at factor cost (equals 2nd round increase in GDP)	31	$b_5 = .756$

If the initial increase in GDP of £100m is not sustained, but is confined for example to a single quarter's duration, then the indirect effects on GDP will be £31m in the second quarter, 31% of £31m in the following quarter, and so on. Under these circumstances the effects will tend to die out over time. The sequence of quarterly deviations in GDP from the course it would otherwise have followed would be:
£100, 31, 9.6, 3.0, 0.9, 0.3, 0.1 . . . million.
If, however, the increment in GDP is a sustained increase (a continuous injection of demand) then the same sequence is generated in each successive quarter so that the series of quarterly deviations in GDP would be as follows:
£100, 131, 140.6, 143.6, 144.5, 144.8, 144.9 . . . million.
Here the full multiplier effect on GDP is almost wholly realized in four quarters after the initial injection, and even by the third quarter the bulk of the multiplier effect has come through.[1]
The key to the timing of the multiplier process lies in the lag of one quarter which is taken to exist between the receipt of GDP in the form of income and the expenditure of this income on additional consumption goods. The analysis above also assumes that increased expenditure is matched instantaneously by additional

---

1 The full multiplier value is 1.449 and is calculated from the marginal relationships set out in table 1.7 as follows:

$$\frac{1}{1 - b_1 b_2 b_3 b_4 b_5} = \frac{1}{1 - \frac{82}{100} \cdot \frac{56}{82} \cdot \frac{50}{56} \cdot \frac{41}{50} \cdot \frac{31}{41}} = \frac{1}{1 - 0.31} = 1.449$$

This is completely analogous with the simple textbook multiplier save that the marginal propensity to consume is replaced by a composite marginal propensity to re-spend domestic output.

production. This is rather an implausible assumption, and it is almost inevitable that the first impact of any increase in consumers' spending will be met out of stocks. So long as stocks behave passively and production responds to expenditure after a short time-lag, the multiplier time path will be delayed but not altered in any fundamental sense. If, however, stocks are not passive but behave according to the stock-adjustment principle, then it is possible that the replenishment of stocks will cause the time path to wobble on its way to equilibrium.[1] The extent of these wobbles is not well established although our consideration of stock-building behaviour in section III.3 suggests that they must be present in some degree. Hopkin and Godley,[2] in their important discussion of the multiplier effects of policy changes, made small notional allowances for the accelerator both in stocks and in fixed investment. It is probably true to say, however, that these effects are not as well known as they ought to be.[3]

IV.3   The Effects of Tax Changes and Other Instruments

The effects of changes in government expenditure have been discussed above mainly because their evaluation affords an easy introduction to the concept of the multiplier (which is common to all policy changes). In fact government expenditure has not been used extensively as part of short-term employment policy (1972 was an exception). This is chiefly because it is not easy to accomplish changes in this form of spending very quickly or with great precision. Clearly, however, changes in government spending are a potentially useful instrument at times when the economy is severely depressed and when the recovery is likely to take several years to accomplish. The more usual instruments of demand management, however, have been changes in direct and indirect taxes.

The estimation of the effect upon GDP of a change in income tax may be illustrated by reference to the additional 3p on the basic and higher rates (and 8p on the top rate) introduced in the Budget of March 1974. The effect on the income tax revenue of these changes was estimated by the Inland Revenue to be £942m, which implied a reduction in personal disposable income of the same amount.[4] The direct effect of this upon the level of GDP may be found by reference to the coefficients in table 1.7. Thus the change in consumers' expenditure at market prices is obtained by multiplying £942m by b_3 (b_3 being the marginal propensity to consume) and the additional consumption of domestic output is this amount multiplied by b_4 and b_5. Thus the initial effect upon GDP, measured at current prices, is £942m times $b_3 b_4 b_5 = £521$m. This is approximately 0.75% of GDP. The final effect may be found by multiplying this amount by the multiplier value of 1.449, and is almost exactly 1.0% of 1974 GDP.[5]

---

1   In extreme cases there may be severe oscillations or even an explosive time path. On this the classic reference is L. A. Metzler, 'The Nature and Stability of Inventory Cycles' in R. A. Gordon and L. R. Klein (eds), *Reading in Business Cycles.*

2   W. A. B. Hopkin and W. A. H. Godley, 'An Analysis of Tax Changes', *NIER,* May 1965. This article is the basis of the discussion above.

3   For estimates of the effects of policy changes based on econometric models, see J. S. E. Laury, G. R. Lewis and P. A. Ormerod, 'Properties of Macroeconomic Models of the UK Economy: A Comparative Study', *NIER* February 1978.

4   *Financial Statement and Budget Report, 1974-75,* p. 28.

5   Strictly speaking the multiplier is different after the tax change because the coefficient b_2 is changed. But the effect of this is too small to be worth allowing for.

In estimating the effect of a change in indirect taxation it might be thought that the initial effect upon GDP could be found quite simply by taking the additional revenue (as estimated by the Board of Customs and Excise) and applying the coefficients b_4 and b_5.[1] But the problem is complicated by the fact that changes in indirect taxation invariably lead to differential changes in prices. The taxed goods go up in price whereas other prices are unchanged. Elementary economics suggests that there will then be substitution effects as well as income effects so that it is really quite a complicated task to work out the effects of the tax change upon consumers' spending on different articles and the revenue from the tax.[2] An indication of the magnitude involved may be taken from the estimate that a 10% increase in the rates of purchase tax (supplanted in 1973 by value added tax) and the excise taxes on betting, tobacco and petrol would have a direct effect upon GDP of 0.5% and a final effect (including the multiplier) of 0.7%. It can be assumed that the effect of raising VAT from 8% to say 9% would produce effects of the same order of magnitude.

One interesting and important feature of these estimates is that what are regarded as severe changes in taxation appear to have quite small effects upon the economy. If the Chancellor of the Exchequer decided, for example, to raise VAT by 1% in combination with a rise of 3p on the income tax rate, his action would reduce GDP by something less than 2%. There are circumstances, however, when the economic situation calls for a stronger package (in retrospect, 1962, 1971 and 1972 appear to be examples), and when it would be advisable to supplement tax changes by additional instruments of control.

One of the alternatives to tax measures is the control of hire purchase transactions. Alterations in the statutory minimum HP deposit and in the maximum repayment period are used frequently as policy instruments. The effect of raising the down-payment is to choke off purchases until consumers have managed to save the increase in the deposit, whilst a shortening of the repayment period will deter purchasers from buying until they are satisfied that their current income will cover the extra monthly payments. These restrictions cannot be expected to be effective if consumers have access to alternative sources of finance, but the presumption is that a good many of them have no such alternative. The chief objection to the use of HP controls is not that they are not effective but rather that their effects are disturbing to the industries affected and temporary in character. When the restrictions are tightened, they tend to postpone rather than to reduce personal spending, and the period of postponement may be fairly short-lived.

Monetary instruments of demand management are discussed more fully in chapter 2. Increases in interest rates may be expected (if they are sufficiently large) to affect fixed investment, stockbuilding and the purchase of consumer durable goods. These effects, however, are likely to be delayed for many months and their main impact will fall outside the normal policy (and forecasting) horizon of twelve to eighteen months. In this respect they are not as satisfactory as fiscal instruments of control.[3] More rapid effects from monetary policy can, however, occur as a result of cutbacks in the money supply and in the availability of credit. But in this case, although the direction of effect is clear enough, the magnitude in

---

1   We are assuming no initial change in disposable income or the savings ratio.
2   For details see Hopkin and Godley, op. cit.
3   Indeed, in an open economy with a high degree of capital mobility it may be difficult for a single country to dictate its own level of interest rates.

terms of GDP is difficult to estimate. Thus monetary instruments are likely to take second place to fiscal instruments because their effects are either uncertain in magnitude or too long delayed. This need not mean that monetary policy has no role to play, but only that it is reserved for longer time horizons than those of fiscal policy.

IV.4 Economic Forecasts

It has been suggested above that it is not satisfactory to manage the economy simply by reacting to observations of the current situation. If the government is to reduce the risk of unduly delayed, possibly destabilizing, actions it must attempt to forecast the course of domestic output and employment. The difference between the forecast path of GDP and the path required by the employment target determines the direction and extent of budgetary action.

National income forecasts are prepared in the Treasury three times a year. The timing of the three main forecasts is geared to the Budget, which is normally in the first half of April. A preliminary assessment of next year's prospects is generally made in late autumn, and this is brought up to date and extended a further six months in February and March. A third forecast is made in early summer.

From a policy point of view the most important forecast is the one made in February. This extends from the last known figures for GDP (which relate to the third quarter of the previous year) as far as the second quarter of the following year. It covers seven quarters altogether of which the last five quarters, from the second of this year to the third of next, are genuinely in the future. The first two quarters, from last October to March of the current year, represent a kind of no-man's land between an imperfectly known past and an unknown future. The problem here is one of piecing together bits of statistical information such as the monthly figures of exports, imports, retail sales and industrial production into a reasonably coherent picture of the base period. This is always difficult because there is very little monthly information about investment or government expenditure, and the difficulties can be made worse by apparent contradictions between the various monthly figures of production, sales and employment.

Once the base period is established, the forecast proper (i.e. the part relating to the future) can be started. The methods by which this is done need not be described in detail.[1] They have evolved steadily over a number of years and have made increasing use of econometric techniques as a result of the accumulation of economic statistics and their improvement. The forecasting model may best be thought of in terms of dependent expenditures, such as consumption, stock-building and imports, which are determined primarily by the current level of GDP, and autonomous expenditures, such as government purchases, fixed investment and exports which in the short run are largely independent of GDP. In forecasting

---

1 The evolution of the Treasury's forecasting methods may be followed in A. D. Roy, 'Short-term Forecasting for Central Economic Management', in K. Hilton and D. F. Heathfield (eds), *The Econometric Study of the United Kingdom,* Macmillan, 1970, and J. R. Shepherd, 'Short-term Forecasting for the UK Economy', in Sir Alec Cairncross (ed.), *The Managed Economy,* Blackwell, 1970. More recent accounts are J. R. Shepherd, H. P. Evans and C. J. Riley, 'The Treasury Short-term Forecasting Model', Government Economic Service Occasional Papers (HMSO) and finally in HM Treasury, *Macroeconomic Model, Technical Manual* (HMSO), 1977. Any *NIER* will give an impression of the methods used by the National Institute of Economic and Social Research.

the latter a good deal of use is made of direct information from business firms and government departments. Government current expenditure and the government component of fixed investment, for example, can be predicted from information provided by government departments and the nationalized industries. The forecast of business fixed investment is arrived at partly by reference to the sample enquiry into investment intentions conducted by the Department of Trade and Industry. The forecast of housing and investment may be derived largely from figures of housing starts and an assumption about the period of housing construction. The export forecast is made on the basis of expected trends in world trade, and will also be affected by sharp changes in the competitive position such as occurred after the devaluation of 1967. In forecasting the dependent expenditures it is possible to employ behavioural relationships of the type we have suggested in section III. There are many different ways, however, of formulating consumption and invest-ment functions and it is not an easy matter to judge which of them is best. Thus although a large econometric model is now used by the Treasury as part of its forecasting work it may be assumed that parts of the model will be disputed by those responsible for getting the forecast right and that the model, therefore, is not likely to dictate the forecast to the exclusion of all argument and discussion. Furthermore, as every forecaster knows, there are always events which the model is not able to handle (strikes and fuel shortages, for example) and which necessitate judgemental estimation of their effects upon economic activity.

The main upshot of the government forecasting work is a table in considerable detail of the course of GDP and its components, quarter by quarter, over a period of two to three years. The published version of the pre-Budget forecast normally extends to the middle of the calendar year after the Budget.

IV.5   Criticisms of Demand Management

It is not wholly surprising that the demand management has come in for heavy criticism from journalists and economists. This is to be expected of any sphere of government policy, and especially one involving frequent changes in tax rates. In assessing these criticisms it is not always easy to distinguish the positive from the normative.

The criticisms divide into four main groups: (i) that the economy has fluctuated considerably despite the advocacy of 'stable' employment in the 1944 White Paper; (ii) that the technical apparatus of demand management has been inadequate to its task; (iii) that economic policy has been in some sense destabilizing; (iv) that errors in demand management have been connected with the rapid inflation of the 1970s.

(i) On the first of these points there is no doubt that the course of the economy has been something less than stable for most of the period since demand management was inaugurated. This phenomenon (which has sometimes been labelled the 'stop-go' cycle) has been described and charted in section II of this chapter. What is not so clear, however, is the extent to which this instability implies a criticism of the aims of policy (which is largely a subjective matter) or of the technical apparatus for achieving those aims. For even an unstable and highly cyclical time path for the economy may represent a series of changes of mind by successive governments about the best level of employment at which to run the economy. The conflicts or presumed conflicts between economic objectives are sufficiently obvious to make it doubtful whether the target pressure of demand has always been the same. Indeed, in so far as the facts can be ascertained, the target appears to have fluctuated quite significantly.

Fluctuations in targets may be detected from the available information on Treasury forecasts. These forecasts, after allowance for the effects of tax changes introduced at the time, represent the increase in GDP which the government finds acceptable at the time they are made. As such they are tantamount to target increases in output. These targets can be related to the level of *potential output* (the level of GDP in a specific period which can be produced if employment is at some standard rate) so as to obtain an estimate of the intended utilization of potential. A series of these targets running from 1955 to 1975 is shown in table 1.8. It shows intended GDP as a percentage of potential, and the movements in these percentages may be taken as indicating parallel movements in the intended rate of unemployment.

The table shows that the government's intended use of productive potential has undergone fairly large fluctuations in the period since 1955. It fell by about 4% in 1955-9, rose in 1960 and again in 1964, and was fairly stable from 1964 to 1970. The target appears to have dropped abruptly in 1971 and to have recovered equally sharply in 1972. There was another sharp decline in 1975. It can be shown that these fluctuations in the government's short-term objectives are very similar in magnitude (although not in timing) to fluctuations in actual GDP.[1] The amplitude of the intended and actual cycles in economic activity have unfortunately been very similar.[2]

Whilst these fluctuations in the target use of productive potential are regrettable from the point of view of the individual observer, it must not be forgotten that the targets belong to a succession of Chancellors of the Exchequer and to widely differing economic circumstances. It would be rather surprising if a succession of Chancellors of the Exchequer, each of them representing different political parties or different shades of opinion within their parties, had somehow managed to arrive at a uniform target for the pressure of demand over a period of twenty years. Thus the fluctuating time path of budgetary targets must probably be accepted as a fact of political and economic life.

(ii)　As regards the technical apparatus of demand management the key question is whether, and by how much, it has failed to achieve the target levels of employment or GDP. Since the target levels of GDP are equivalent to the government forecasts after allowance has been made for the effects of each Budget, this question is essentially a matter of the accuracy of forecasts.[3] If the Treasury forecasts the increase in GDP incorrectly then it will be led into taking the wrong measures. The result will be that the target level of GDP will be missed by the same amount as the forecast is in error.

The question of the accuracy of Treasury forecasts can only be answered satisfactorily for those forecasts which have been published or described with sufficient clarity to permit comparisons with the outcome. For 1968 and after, the forecasts have been published as part of the *Financial Statement and Budget*

1　See M. C. Kennedy, 'Employment Policy – What Went Wrong?', in Joan Robinson (ed.), *After Keynes*, Blackwell, 1973.

2　One measure of the amplitude of fluctuations is the mean deviation (regardless of sign) from the average utilization rate. This is 2.2% for the intended use of potential and 2.4% for the actual use over the periods shown in table 1.8.

3　Forecasting accuracy is not always simple to interpret: there may be strikes or other events of an unforeseeable nature which affect the accuracy of the forecasts without necessarily discrediting the methods by which they are derived.

TABLE 1.8

Short-term Targets and Forecasting Errors, UK, 1955-77

		Target use of potential output[1] %	Forecast and target change in GDP from year earlier[2] (2) %	Actual change in GDP from year earlier[3] (3) %	Error (forecast less actual) %
1955	(year)	99	2.9	3.7	−0.8
1956	"	98	1.1	1.3	−0.2
1957	"	97	1.3	1.6	−0.3
1958	"	95	−0.4	−0.3	−0.1
1959	(4th qtr)	94	2.8	6.9	−4.1
1960	"	98	3.1	3.8	−0.7
1961	"	94	1.8	2.1	−0.3
1962	"	98	3.9	0.9	3.0
1963	"	97	4.6	6.3	−1.7
1964	"	101	5.4	4.2	1.2
1965	"	100	2.7	2.7	.0
1966	"	98	2.0	1.2	.8
1967	"	97	3.1	2.0	1.1
1968	(2nd half)	97	3.6	5.0	−1.4
1969	"	96	1.9	2.5	−0.6
1970	"	97	3.6	1.8	1.8
1971	"	94	1.1	2.1	−1.0
1972	"	98	5.5	2.8	2.7
1973	"	99	6.0	4.2	1.8 .
1974	"	97	2.6	1.0	1.6
1975	"	91	.0	−3.7	3.7
1976	"	90	3.9	2.5	1.4
1977	"	89	1.5	0.8	0.7

Notes and Sources:

1 Potential output is GDP corresponding to 1.0% unemployment: 1955-64 from M. C. Kennedy, 'Employment Policy − What Went Wrong?' in Joan Robinson (ed.), *After Keynes;* 1955-74 levels are derived from the trend of potential output in University of Cambridge, Department of Applied Economics, *Economic Policy Review No. 1,* February 1975, with 1975-7 extrapolated at 2.5% per annum.

2 Kennedy, op. cit. and *Financial Statement and Budget Reports* (HMSO).

3 Average estimate of GDP, *ET(AS)*, 1977.

Report. But before this date the information is not always as good, and it has to be assembled from official documents or even from forecasts made by other bodies at the same time. Nevertheless, the task is worth attempting even though the results (see table 1.8) cannot be sacrosanct.[1]

The main points to emerge from an assessment of Treasury forecasts over the period since 1955 is that, whilst they have not been as highly accurate as might have been hoped, they have led policy seriously astray on only four or five occasions. There is not much doubt that the 1959 forecast, when the error was 4%, was the worst forecast of all. It meant that an unforeseen recovery in total output was

---

1 The same qualifications apply to the series for the Target Use of Potential Output.

coupled with an expansionary Budget, and the result was a much higher level of employment at the end of the year than the government had actually intended. By contrast, the forecasting error in 1962 went the other way with the result that there was a recession despite the policy aim of a roughly 4% rise in output (implying high employment). The error was put right in 1963, although the recovery went further than intended. The worst forecast of recent years appears to have been 1975 when the Treasury was much too optimistic (by 3.7% of GDP) about the economic outlook.

Taking the whole period from 1955-77 the average error in Treasury forecasts (regardless of sign) was about 1.4% of GDP. This implies an average deviation of about 0.5% between the actual and desired unemployment rate, and is equivalent to an error between the appropriate rate of income tax and the actual rate of about 4p in the £. Unfortunately there is no evidence that the forecasts have become any more accurate with the passage of time. The mean error for 1955-65 in Table 1.8, for example, is 1.1% whereas that for 1966-75 is 1.6%. This increase in the inaccuracy of Treasury forecasts has occurred in spite of a much more extensive use of econometric techniques. It may perhaps be attributed to the greater instability in the economy which has been associated, in particular, with flexible exchange rates and faster inflation. But it remains a matter of some concern that Treasury forecasts have deteriorated rather than improved.[1]

(iii)   A number of writers have sought to show or to deny that demand management has been destabilizing.[2] To do this it is necessary to make assumptions as to the target level of output and the level which output would have attained in the absence of discretionary intervention. Most writers in this field have made somewhat questionable assumptions about the targets and the instruments of intervention. Thus one has claimed that policy was destabilizing because it was demonstrable that 'policy-off' changes in GDP (i.e. after deducting the effects of changes in taxation and government spending) were less widely scattered round the average annual increase in GDP than policy-on (i.e. actual) changes in GDP.[3] It is arbitrary, however, to measure failures of policy in terms of dispersion around an average annual increase in GDP. For there is, first, no presumption that governments were aiming each year at a constant rise in GDP, and secondly, there is every reason (in times of depression or boom) to suppose that they would aim at increases above or below the average.

The stabilizing effectiveness of short-term policy has also been investigated in terms of the stability of GDP around its trend. It has been shown by Artis[4] that for the 1958-70 period the dispersion of quarterly levels of observed GDP from their time-trend was larger than the dispersion of estimated 'policy-off' GDP (i.e. after deducting the cumulative effects of all tax changes introduced after a particular base year) from their time-trend. This result indicates that policy was 'destabilizing' in the sense of this particular method of measurement. But as the author made clear

---

1   For an official calculation of the average error in GDP forecasts and its breakdown by expenditure see *ET,* December 1976, pp. 141-3.

2   For reviews of these and other studies of short-term policies see G. D. N. Worswick, 'Fiscal Policy and Stabilization in Britain' in A. K. Cairncross (ed.), *Britain's Economic Prospects Reconsidered* and M. C. Kennedy, op. cit.

3   B. Hansen, *Fiscal Policy in Seven Countries, 1955-65,* OECD, Paris, 1969.

4   M. J. Artis, 'Fiscal Policy for Stabilization', in W. Beckerman (ed.), *The Labour Government's Economic Record, 1964-70,* Duckworth, 1972.

there was never any presumption that the course of target GDP coincided with trend GDP. It is also questionable whether 'policy-off' GDP should be arrived at by subtracting from actual GDP the cumulative effect of measures taken over several years rather than the effect of those measures taken in the particular year.

(iv)   During the period of fast inflation in the 1970s demand management came in for some further criticisms. One popular source of complaint was that the very fast expansion of demand during 1972 and 1973, together with the high pressure of demand in 1974, were responsible for the acceleration in the rate of inflation. This criticism greatly overstates the case since by far the most important factor in the acceleration of inflation over this period was the massive increase in import prices (almost 100% in two years). This is not to deny, however, that the higher pressure of demand in 1973 and 1974 would have added something to the rate of inflation, or that the very fast pace of the expansion did not create its own special pressures. (The annual rate of increase in GDP between the first quarters of 1972 and 1973 was 8.6%.) But the main factor responsible for the inflation in this period was almost certainly the rise in world commodity prices and its inevitable consequence for UK material and food prices (see section V below).

It has also been suggested[1] that 'the whole intellectual basis of postwar "demand management" by government is undermined if the natural unemployment rate hypothesis is true'. The hypothesis in question postulates that there is some level of the unemployment rate, the natural rate, which is compatible with a zero rate of price inflation provided that the expected rate of price inflation is also zero. If the unemployment target is set below the natural rate then inflation will accelerate. Wage increases will generate price increases which lead to expected price increases and hence to further and larger wage increases. Some of the assumptions behind this hypothesis are rather dubious when applied to the UK economy (see section V). But even if the assumptions were true (and variants of them in the shape of the wage—price spiral hypothesis have been accepted for many years) there is no reason why it should undermine the basis of demand management. Governments which sought to avoid accelerating inflation would simply set the target rate at or above the natural rate of employment.[2] They would seek to achieve their target level of unemployment by exactly the same combination of forecasts and instruments which we have described. Far from destroying the basis of demand management, the natural rate hypothesis simply underlines its importance.

A more acceptable line of criticism is that the Treasury's economic forecasting framework fails to take sufficient note of monetary variables.[3] This omission reflects a deep-seated failure of economics, both monetarist and Keynesian, to provide acceptable estimates of the quantitative effects of changes in the supply of money. The omission is probably most serious in connection with the manner in which Budget deficits are financed. The multiplier effects of tax and government expenditure changes are normally calculated on the assumption that the money

---

1   M. Friedman and D. Laidler, 'Unemployment *versus* Inflation', IEA, Occasional Paper 44, p. 45.

2   According to Professor Laidler (op. cit.) the natural rate is provisionally estimated at 'a little less than 2 per cent'. If this is correct it is difficult to see how recent inflation could have been due to running the economy below the natural rate given that the actual unemployment rate has been in excess of 2% since 1966.

3   See for example D. Laidler, Minutes of Evidence, *Ninth Report from the Expenditure Committee* (1974) HC 328.

supply is adjusted so as to maintain interest rates. But a tight control of the money supply, or an insistence upon the financing of deficits by borrowing from the public, could have effects on expenditure which are not taken into account.

V   INFLATION
V.1   Inflation and its Causes

Inflation is defined variously as *any* increase in the general level of prices or as any *sustained* increase. In this chapter we shall use the wider definition since it enables us to include short-lived increases in the general price level, such as those of 1920, 1940 and 1951-2, within the sphere of discussion without raising the further definitional question of whether they were sufficiently 'sustained' to be called inflations.

In measuring the rate of inflation we have a choice of index numbers. The appropriate index of the prices charged for all goods produced in the UK economy is the implied index number for GDP, so called because it is obtained by dividing the value of GDP at current prices by GDP at constant (1970) prices. The GDP index includes export prices. If an index is required to measure the prices of goods purchased by UK residents the best general measure is the implied deflator for total domestic expenditure, since this is an average of the prices paid for consumption and investment goods, both privately and publicly purchased. If we are chiefly interested in the prices paid for consumer goods and services we have a choice between the implied price index for consumers' expenditure and the index of retail prices. The former, like all implicit indices, is not compiled directly from price data but is found by dividing the current value of consumers' expenditure by the volume estimate as measured at constant prices. By contrast the index of retail prices (the cost of living index) is compiled directly from price data. It registers the prices of a collection of goods and services entering a typical shopping basket. The composition of the basket has been altered from time to time (most recently in January 1975) so as to keep up with changes in the pattern of expenditure. Being a base-weighted index it gradually becomes outdated in coverage. In periods of inflation it is likely to exaggerate the increase in the cost of living because consumers will tend to switch their expenditure patterns towards those goods which are rising less rapidly in price. Nevertheless, it is accurate enough for most purposes.

The 1970s are now well established as the most inflationary decade of the twentieth century. The index of retail prices rose by 137% between 1970 and 1977 and consumer prices by 138%. The average rise in retail prices was 13.1% a year compared with 3.3% in 1953-69, 2.1% in 1934-9 and declining prices in 1925-33.

A theory to explain inflation in an open economy like the UK needs to take account of at least three independent types of inflationary impulse:

(i)   increases in import prices
(ii)   excess demand in the home economy
(iii) wage push.

Any economy which is engaged in overseas trade is exposed to inflationary impulses from the world outside. In the UK, where such a large part of our food and raw materials are imported from overseas, the effects of world inflation are felt primarily through higher prices paid for imported primary commodities and consequential increases in production costs and food prices. Many of our most violent changes in prices, both up and down, can be traced to changes in the world prices of primary commodities.

The second main ingredient in our theory of inflation is the pressure of demand upon productive potential and productive resources. Excess demand is a manifestation of market forces. We should expect wages and/or prices to increase whenever excess demand (i.e. demand less supply at going prices) is positive and to fall when it is negative. In the economy as a whole we can expect positive and negative excess demands to exist simultaneously in different markets so that there is bound to be a mixture of conflicting tendencies with some prices tending to decline as others are tending to rise. From a macro-economic point of view we are interested in the balance of excess demands and excess supplies, and this for most periods can be measured by either the unemployment percentage or the vacancy rate, although neither measure is perfectly satisfactory (see section II). Both these measures relate to the labour market, and there are unfortunately no general statistical indicators of excess demand in the market for goods.

The third main ingredient in our model of inflation is more controversial, and is the potentially independent force of wage-pushfulness. It is necessary to include this as a separate factor because wages are widely fixed by bargaining between the representatives of powerful groups, the union and the firm or employers' federation, each of which has the ability to influence the bargain by threatening to interrupt production and employment. Whilst there are reasons to expect that the pressure of demand for labour will normally be an influence in the bargaining process we cannot exclude the possibility that alterations in the strength of the union, in the loyalty of its members, and in its preparedness to strike, may act as an independent force (i.e. independent of market forces) in determining wage increases.

We can combine these three main initiating causes of inflation into a more complete model by relating them to wage increases, price increases and expected price increases in the manner illustrated in figure 1.5. The model assumes that the *process* by which excess demand leads to price inflation is through the rate of increase in wages. Higher wages mean higher average costs of production and these lead after a time-lag to higher prices. This will happen either because business firms tend to set prices by a constant markup over variable costs or because they seek to maximize profits. Higher prices lead, again after a time-lag, to higher wages since trade unions will tend to claim compensation for increases in the cost of living, or in other words to restore the real wages of their members. Thus the central ingredient of our model is a wage—price spiral which is superimposed upon the excess demand for labour. But besides excess demand the spiral may also be set in motion by exogenous increases in wages coming from wage-push or by increases in import prices as a consequence of movements in world commodity prices.

A possible objection to this manner of presenting the inflationary process is that it does not appear to allow for a direct influence of excess demand upon the rate of price increase. This omission is forced upon us mainly by the dearth of statistical indicators of excess demand in the goods market and partly, too, by the fact that a number of studies have attempted to find evidence of this relationship and have not been successful.[1] However, we do not wish to pretend that

1 For example L. A. Dicks-Mireaux, 'The Inter-Relationship between Cost and Price Changes, 1945-1959', *OEP* (NS) Vol. 13(3). Reprinted in R. J. Ball and P. Doyle, *Inflation*, Penguin, 1969. The model of figure 1.5 is an extension of the relationships estimated by Dicks-Mireaux.

there is no direct effect of excess demand upon prices — only that the main identified connection is through the medium of wages.

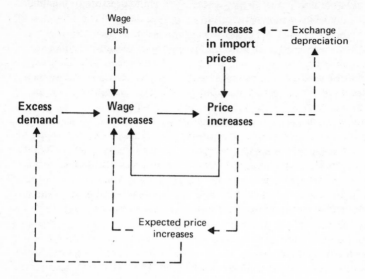

Figure 1.5 Inflationary Processes

A second objection to the model might be that there is no reference to the quantity of money. This lack of an explicit reference, however, does not rule out monetary causation of inflation since additions to the quantity of money will raise prices through the medium of excess demand, and excess demand has a prominent place in the model. This amounts to saying that monetary inflation is a branch of demand-pull inflation. An increase in the money supply will act through interest rate reductions or more directly through credit availability to increase the demand for goods and services, and hence create excess demand. There is no place in our model, or in economic theory in general, for an influence of money upon prices which is not transmitted through the medium of excess demand.

Besides excess demand and the wage-price spiral, figure 1.5 allows for two other possible interactions between wages and prices, both of them operating through the effect of rising prices upon expected future prices. The first of these is the possibility that expectations of future price changes, rather than compensation for past increases, may be a major factor in wage bargaining. It has been suggested by some writers[1] that the expectation of a price increase of, say, 10% in the ensuing twelve months will induce trade unions and employers to settle for increases in nominal wages of as much as 10% more than would have occurred if prices had been expected to be stable. This hypothesis assumes a high degree of sophistication upon the part of bargaining groups and may not be of great relevance to the UK economy during much of its history. Few would deny, however, that really rapid

---

1   For example M. Friedman, 'The Role of Monetary Policy', *AER,* Vol. 58(1), pp. 1-17 and *Unemployment versus Inflation,* Institute of Economic Affairs, 1975.

inflation will force the realization that failure to allow for future price increases can lead to a painful erosion of purchasing power between one wage settlement and the next. Thus expectational wage bargaining is a form of behaviour which is likely to evolve as a consequence of rapid inflation. It is possible that this form of behaviour has emerged in the UK economy over the last few years although it is not clear that it is widespread (or that it would be in the absence of incomes policy).

The second additional link between wages and prices runs from expectations of higher prices to the level of excess demand. As consumers become aware that prices are going to rise rapidly in the future they protect themselves from an erosion of the value of their money by switching out of money into goods. The effects of this form of behaviour will be manifested in a tendency for the savings ratio to decline (which has not happened in the UK) and for the velocity of circulation of money to rise (which has also not happened). We have included it in the figure, along with the link between price expectations and wage bargaining, because it is a mode of behaviour which has been observed in other countries in periods of hyperinflation.[1] It is a form of behaviour which, along with expectational wage bargaining, is likely to develop as inflation gathers pace and as people learn from experience how money can lose its value. The fact that such behaviour can develop adds greatly to the danger of inflation getting out of hand and provides an extremely powerful case for stopping it as early as possible.

A third linkage in the system is that running from domestic prices to import prices. As domestic prices rise the balance of payments deteriorates, the exchange rate depreciates, and this means that the sterling price of imports must rise, thereby adding further to domestic inflation.

One further point which will not be clear from the scheme in figure 1.5 is that increases in the price level always tend to raise the demand for money. If the quantity of money is kept unchanged the effect will be to raise interest rates, thus lowering the levels of real output and employment, and causing a reduction in excess demand which will ultimately check the inflation. This check will be removed, however, if the central bank is aiming to maintain interest rates so as to stabilize the cost of the national debt. It will then have to *increase* the money supply as the demand for money rises. Thus although inflationary processes may be initiated by excess demand, wage push or increased import prices, they may continue only through permissive increases in the supply of money.

V.2　　Imported Inflation

There is a very real sense in which the UK economy takes its price level from the world outside. It can be shown that nearly every annual increase or decrease in UK prices of 9% or more has been associated with a rapid change in world commodity prices and in UK import prices.[2] There were in fact ten such changes between 1920 and 1975 and with one exception they were all initiated by a rapid change in import prices (see table 1.9).

1　See, for example, A. J. Brown, *The Great Inflation*, London, 1955 and P. Cagan, 'The Monetary Dynamics of Hyperinflation' in M. Friedman, *Studies in the Quantity Theory of Money*, Chicago, 1956.

2　We have chosen 9% rather than the round number of 10% because of the rather higher incidence of 9% annual price increases.

TABLE 1.9

Selected Annual Price Changes, UK, 1920-75

	Change in retail prices (%)	Change in import prices (%)	Previous year's change in import prices (%)
1920	15.8	19.0	
1921	−9.2	−33.3	19.0
1922	−19.0	−19.6	−33.3
1940	16.5	38.5	0.0
1951	9.1	33.0	14.9
1952	9.2	−1.8	33.0
1971	9.4	4.7	4.6
1973	9.2	27.3	4.8
1974	16.1	55.5	27.3
1975	24.2	13.5	55.5

Sources: retail prices *BLS, DEG;* import prices 1920-40 *LCES* (average value indices for merchandise imports), 1951-75 *ETAS, AAS* (unit value for merchandise imports).

As the table shows there was only one year in which a dramatic change in retail prices was not accompanied by a large change in import prices. This was 1971 when, as we discuss below, there were exceptionally fast increases in wage rates (apparently not attributable to excess demand) in the same year and the previous year. The price increases that occurred in 1951 and 1952 were associated with the boom in world commodity prices that resulted from the Korean War, whilst the exceptionally fast inflation from 1972 to 1975 was associated with another rapid boom in world commodity prices, especially oil.

Import prices rose by almost 100% between 1972 and 1974, and this led to a protracted spiral of price, wage and further price increases, the effects of which were still being felt several years later. It should be noted that although the rise in import prices in these three years was accentuated by a falling exchange rate, the effect of the exchange rate was small compared with the total change in import prices.[1]

Imported inflation is not readily curable because there is not much prospect of preventing the effect on final prices other than by inducing large reductions in total demand and employment. It is only when the balance of payments is in surplus that a rise in import prices can be offset by an appreciation of the exchange rate.

V.3 Demand-pull Inflation

Whilst external influences seem to have been responsible for the inflation of 1972-5 and for nearly all the more dramatic periods of inflation in UK history, there is no doubt that the internal pressure of excess demand exerts its own influence upon the inflation rate. The evidence for such an influence can be found by examining rates of wage or price inflation at differing demand pressures. Numerous studies have shown a strong negative relationship between the level of unemployment (which is inversely related to excess demand) and the rate of change of money

---

1   See table 1.11 below.

wage rates. One of the earlier studies of this kind, and certainly the most influential, was published in 1958 by Professor A. W. Phillips.[1] This examined the relationship between unemployment rates and the rate of increase in weekly wage rates for nearly a century, and on the basis of data for 1861-1913 suggested that the relationship was negative, as expected, and also nonlinear.[2] The wage increases to be associated with different rates of unemployment were as follows:

Unemployment rate	1.0	2.0	3.0	4.0	5.0
% change in wage rates	8.7	2.8	1.2	0.5	0.1

The relationship became known as the *Phillips Curve* and it implies a changing marginal 'trade-off' between the rate of wage increase and unemployment. Thus the rate of wage increase declines by nearly 6% if the unemployment rate goes up from 1.0% to 2.0%, but by only 1.6% if it goes up from 2.0% to 3.0%. Indeed, the trade-off suggested by the Phillips Curve is a modest one at all but the highest pressures of demand for labour.

One of the more remarkable features of the Phillips Curve, and one which distinguishes it from most similar studies, was that it was found to be highly reliable in predicting increases in wages during much later periods of time than the years 1861-1913 which had been used to derive the equation. Thus Phillips was able to show a very close correspondence for 1948-57 between the wage changes implied by his relationship and those that actually took place (the largest error occurred in 1951 when prices had increased exceptionally fast). It can be seen from the series in table 1.10 that the predictive claims of the Phillips Curve were sustained for a number of years after the publication of Phillips' article. During the period 1958-66, for example, there was not a single error in excess of 2.5% and the mean error (regardless of sign) was only 1.1%; furthermore, the positive and negative errors tended to offset each other so that the mean algebraic error was only 0.1% over this period.

Since 1966, however, the pure Phillips Curve has become increasingly unreliable as a guide to the rate of wage inflation. It under-predicted by about 4-5% per annum in 1967-9, by 10-12% in 1970-73, and by more than 20% in 1974 and 1975 (see table 1.10). These under-predictions can be explained by several factors of which the most important was the omission from the pure Phillips relationship of any allowance for changes in prices. This omission implies that wage adjustment

---

1 A. W. Phillips, 'The Relation between Unemployment and the Rate of Change of Money Wage Rates, 1861-1957', *Economica*, November 1958.

2 The equation for the schedule was:

$$\frac{\Delta W}{W} = -0.900 + 9.638U^{-1.394}$$

It can also be expressed in logarithmic terms as

$$\log \left\{ \frac{\Delta W}{W} + 0.9 \right\} = 0.984 - 1.394 \log U$$

where $\frac{\Delta W}{W}$ is the percentage rate of wage change and U is the unemployment rate.

(Phillips, op. cit.)

TABLE 1.10

Annual Indicators of Inflation, UK, 1953-77

	Change in Retail prices[1] (%)	Change in wage rates[2] (%)	Displacement of Phillips Curve[3] (%)	Unemployment percentage[4]
1953	3.1	3.0	−1.1	1.5
1954	1.8	4.4	−1.6	1.2
1955	4.5	6.9	−0.6	1.0
1956	2.0	7.9	+1.3	1.0
1957	3.7	5.4	+0.3	1.3
1958	3.0	3.6	+1.1	1.9
1959	0.6	1.1	−1.2	2.0
1960	1.0	4.1	0.0	1.5
1961	3.4	3.4	−1.2	1.3
1962	2.6	4.4	+1.6	1.8
1963	2.1	4.3	+2.5	2.2
1964	3.3	3.8	−0.3	1.6
1965	4.8	4.6	−0.6	1.3
1966	3.9	3.3	−1.3	1.4
1967	2.5	5.9	+4.0	2.2
1968	4.7	7.1	+5.2	2.3
1969	5.4	5.7	+3.8	2.3
1970	6.4	13.5	+11.9	2.5
1971	9.4	12.1	+11.4	3.3
1972	7.1	11.0	+10.4	3.6
1973	9.2	12.2	+10.7	2.6
1974	16.1	29.4	+28.9	2.5
1975	24.2	25.4	+25.4	3.9
1976	16.5	11.8	+11.8	5.2
1977	15.8	5.8	+6.0	5.7

Notes: (1) Change from annual level of previous year. (2) 12-monthly change in weekly rates from December of previous year. (3) + underprediction, − overprediction by Phillips equation, op cit., using unlagged unemployment data, GB, including temporarily stopped and school-leavers. (4) Wholly unemployed, GB, excluding school-leavers and adult students.

Sources: DEG, BLS.

concerns money wages rather than real wages, and although this may not have greatly mattered during periods of moderate price rise, it became extremely serious during the fast, and mainly imported, inflation of the 1970s. Another factor was probably the rise in unemployment relative to vacancies (see section II). It was demonstrated by Artis[1] that a modified Phillips Curve, with vacancies rather than unemployment as the indicator of excess demand, and with price changes as a second independent variable, was able to predict wage increases for 1967-9 without serious error. Artis showed that equations of this type failed, however, to predict the wage increase of 1970 by a factor of 6-7%, and it is possible that a wage-push explanation (see below) may have to be admitted for this year. One further factor in the breakdown of the Phillips Curve in the 1970s could have been an increased sensitivity of wage increases to price increases. It seems possible that as inflation became more serious a growing number of trade union negotiators would have

---

1   M. J. Artis, 'Some Aspects of the Present Inflation', *NIER*, February 1971, reprinted in H. G. Johnson and A. R. Nobay (eds), *The Current Inflation*, Macmillan, 1971.

insisted upon full compensation for price increases with the consequence that the causal linkage between price and wage increases became gradually stronger than it had been in the 1960s. Coupled with this factor there was also a tendency to negotiate wage increases at more frequent intervals than previously, and there may also have been attempts to obtain wage increases on the basis of *expected* rather than actual price increases. This last form of behaviour is the type assumed by Friedman and others in the theory of the 'expectations-augmented Phillips Curve'. The theory assumes that the rate of wage increase is determined by both the rate of unemployment and the expected price increase, and in its stronger version it assumes a unitary coefficient for the latter variable. Although this hypothesis has its adherents, and although it seems plausible that expectational considerations must grow in importance if inflation becomes ingrained, it is not certain that the augmented Phillips Curve can claim any general applicability in the UK, although it may apply to some groups of workers. The main factors explaining the break-down of the pure Phillips Curve relationship were probably the omission of the rate of price change and an increased sensitivity of wage increases to price increases.

V.4   Wage-push Inflation[1]

The question of whether wages have increased as a result of unions pushing up wages independently of market forces is controversial chiefly because of the large volume of historical evidence in favour of a demand-pull explanation. This evidence, however, need not preclude the possibility of sporadic outbursts of wage-push inflation. Nor is there any reason in principle why wage bargaining procedures should respond precisely and consistently to the pressure of demand in the labour market.

The main evidence in favour of a wage-push contribution to recent inflation concerns the 'pay explosion' of 1970 when, as table 1.10 shows, the wage increase was about 12% faster than could be predicted by the pure Phillips Curve, and when the relationships estimated by Artis also showed a prediction error of 6.7%. It can be argued that this was a consequence either of the relaxation of incomes policy in late 1969 or of direct wage-push on the part of the trade unions. The two types of explanation are not unconnected because the government was under strong pressure from the unions themselves to bring incomes policy to an end. Evidence in favour of greater union 'militancy', which we may define for our purposes as willingness to strike in order to obtain wage increases, may be seen in the very substantial increase in industrial disputes over this period. The number of days lost in industrial disputes rose very sharply (see table 1.11 below). They more than doubled between 1968 and 1970, whilst between the same two years the propor-tion of stoppages attributed to pay disputes increased from 54% to 64%. The evidence is certainly *suggestive* of a wage-push element in the 1970 pay increase and in the next year or two.

---

1   See Aubrey Jones, *The New Inflation,* Penguin, 1973; D. Jackson, H. A. Turner and
    F. Wilkinson, *Do Trade Unions Cause Inflation?* Cambridge University Press, 1972; P. Wiles,
    'Cost Inflation and the State of Economic Theory', *EJ,* June 1973; E. H. Phelps Brown, 'The
    Analysis of Wage Movements under Full Employment', *SJPE,* November 1971; K. Coutts,
    R. Tarling and F. Wilkinson, 'Wage Bargaining and the inflation process', *Economic Policy
    Review,* No. 2, March 1976, Department of Applied Economics, University of Cambridge;
    M. C. Kennedy, 'Recent Inflation and the Monetarists', *Applied Economics,* June, 1976.

TABLE 1.11

Inflation in the 1970s: possible contributors

	(1) Unfilled vacancies (%)	(2) Change in import prices (%)	(3) Change in exchange rate (%)	(4) Days lost in industrial disputes (m)	(5) Changes in money stock (%)
1964-9 av.	1.0	3.5	*	3.7	6.5
1969	0.9	3.2	−	6.8	4.6
1970	0.8	4.6	−	11.0	6.1
1971	0.6	4.4	−	13.6	12.6
1972	0.6	5.4	−4.8	23.9	23.9
1973	1.4	27.7	−9.3	7.2	26.9
1974	1.3	55.0	−3.1	14.8	18.9
1975	0.6	11.3	−7.7	6.0	9.6
1976	0.6	22.5	−15.3	3.3	10.4
1977	0.7	15.6	−5.0	10.0	8.7

Sources: (1) Adult vacancies, GB, as percentage of labour force: *BLS, DEG.* (2) Unit value index, *ETAS.* (3) Effective exchange rate, *ET.* (4) DEG. (5) M_3, average of 4 end-quarter levels, *NIER.*

*The parity rate was devalued by 14.3% in November 1967.

V.5   Inflation in the 1970s: a summary

In table 1.11 we have grouped together the main factors which have been suggested as causes of or contributors to the particularly rapid inflation of the 1970s. The first column shows unfilled vacancies as a percentage of the labour force, which, to judge from our discussion in section II above, is probably the safest indicator of demand pressure. It suggests that in two years, 1973 and 1974, the pressure of demand was particularly high. The peak vacancy rate of 1.4% of the labour force in 1973 compared with earlier peaks of 1.5% in 1955, 0.9% in 1961 and 1.1% in 1964 and 1965. It must be accepted therefore, that the boom of 1973-4 made a contribution to the inflation. The scale of this contribution, however, is easy to exaggerate because of the sharp rise in import prices which came at the same time. We can, however, make a tentative calculation of the effect of the excess demand *per se* by reference to the Phillips Curve, and this suggests that wage rates might have increased by 5-7% less than they did in 1973 and 1974 if excess demand had been held at the level of 1972.[1] This would probably have taken about 4% off the rate of price increase in these two years. In making this calculation, however, we must bear in mind that 1972 was a year of high unemployment, so that to take it as the norm for the pressure of demand is not entirely satisfactory. More generally, the 1970s were characterized by a rather low pressure of demand, with vacancy rates below the 1964-9 average. Thus apart from the boom of 1973-4 there is not much scope for an excess demand explanation of the inflation.

In the second column of table 1.11 is the factor which, in our view, made by far the largest contribution to the 1970s inflation. This was the quite dramatic rise

---

1   The calculation assumes that unemployment in 1972-4 has to be reduced by 1.5% in order to indicate excess demand consistently with its performance in the 1950s. This means the unemployment rates of 3.6% and 2.5% in 1972 and 1974 respectively are adjusted to become 2.1% and 1.0%. Wage rate changes are calculated from these levels on the basis of the original Phillips equation; see footnote 2 on p. 42.

in world commodity prices, due mainly to the oil price increase but also to an imbalance of world supply and demand for food and raw materials. This had the effect of raising UK import prices by nearly 100% between 1972 and 1974. With imports accounting for one-fifth of TFE this was bound to raise final prices by about 20%, which allowing for lags in the marking up of prices on variable costs, would probably have affected the rate of price increase in 1975 as well as the two previous years. These initial effects on prices, moreover, would have carried through into wages and back again to prices, so that the final effect would have been greater than the initial effect.

It can, of course, be argued that some part of the increase in import prices was a consequence of our own inflation rate being faster than that of other countries, so that the exchange rate was forced downwards. Doubtless there is some element of truth in this contention although as column 3 of table 1.11 shows, the decline in the exchange rate in 1972-4 was not comparable in magnitude to the rise in import prices. It was not really until 1976 that our own relative inflation rate became the cause of the falling exchange rate.

As we have argued in section V.4 above, a further factor in the 1970s inflation may have been wage-push inflation. There was more than a suspicion of this in the 'wage explosion' of 1970, and in the figures of days lost in industrial disputes (column 4 of table 1.11), to suggest that trade union members were more prepared to go on strike for higher pay than they had been earlier. This factor seems to have been primarily a feature of the 1970-2 period.

Taking these various factors together it seems possible to conclude that the initial, but least important, factor in the 1970s inflation was some element of wage-pushfulness or resistance to incomes policies. This was followed in 1972-4 by a simultaneous rise in world commodity prices and a raising of the internal pressure of demand. The higher pressure of demand made a contribution to the inflation, but the main factor in 1972-4, was the dramatic increase in world prices, the effects of which were still being felt well into 1975 and after. This was the single most important cause of the 1970s inflation.

V.6   Monetary Explanations of Inflation

The increased rate of inflation in the 1970s was accompanied by markedly faster increases in the stock of money. As column 5 of table 1.11 shows, the money supply had been rising at an average rate of 6.5% a year in 1965-9 whereas in 1971-4 the rate of increase was very much faster. A number of economists, journalists and stockbrokers have interpreted the connection between the rise in the rate of monetary expansion and the faster inflation rate as cause and effect.[1] Some have attributed to money the sole blame for the inflation.

---

1 For example M. Parkin, 'Where is Britain's Inflation Rate Going?', *LBR*, July 1975, W. Rees-Mogg, *The Times*, 13 July 1976, and for an American example, M. Friedman, *Money and Economic Development*, Praeger, 1973. The monetarist case against the Keynesians is put in D. Laidler, 'Inflation in Britain: a Monetarist Perspective', *AER*, September 1976, and the Keynesian case against the monetarists in Sir John Hicks, 'What is Wrong with Monetarism?', *LBR*, October 1975; Lord Kahn, 'Thoughts on the Behaviour of Wages and Monetarism', *LBR*, January 1976; E. H. Phelps Brown, 'A Non-Monetarist View of the Pay Explosion', *TBR*, March 1975; M. C. Kennedy, 'Recent Inflation and the Monetarists', *Applied Economics*, June 1976.

It is generally accepted in economic theory that increases in the supply of money can lead to higher real output or to higher prices. But they do so by raising the aggregate demand for goods and services, thus adding to the pressure of demand. This means that if the inflation of the 1970s had been caused by the rise in the money supply it would have been accompanied by a rise in vacancies and lower unemployment. These changes, moreover, would have to have been substantial to account for such a sharp increase in the rate of inflation. However, as we have already explained above, there was no general or sustained increase in the pressure of demand in the 1970s. Unemployment was higher than earlier, and the vacancy rate, although high in 1973 and 1974, was lower on average in the 1970s (at 0.8%) than it had been earlier (1.0% in 1964-9). This absence of any increase, let alone any marked increase, in the pressure of demand is fairly compelling evidence against the monetarist point of view.

This conclusion, however, does not prevent us from agreeing that *if* the money supply had not been allowed to increase so fast then inflation in the 1970s would have been less severe. For this would have meant a generally lower pressure of demand, and of course still higher unemployment, with the result that some of the inflationary impact of higher import prices would have been offset. This admission, however, does not mean that monetary expansion caused the inflation. It simply affirms that the money supply is one of several variables which are relevant to the price level.

V.7   Inflation and Economic Policy

In the period when inflation was merely creeping it was possible to regard it as a small price to pay for the benefit of high employment. A gently sloping trade-off between inflation and unemployment made the problem of political compromise minimal compared with the situation in the 1970s. The advocacy of an incomes policy in the 1960s was associated either with those who hoped to be able to run the economy at a pressure of demand which now seems unthinkable, or else with those who sought to use it as an instrument of income re-distribution.

The arrival of fast inflation in the 1970s transformed the policy problem. It resulted in a rapid erosion of real incomes during the intervals between wage settlements, with effects that were socially divisive and disruptive. It also transformed economic behaviour. Economic units learned how to live with inflation and sought to define their real wages either by insisting on a full compensation for past increases in the cost of living or possibly, in a few cases, by bargaining on the basis of price forecasts. This meant that by 1975, if not earlier, there were only two ways of bringing inflation under control. One was to deflate domestic demand to such a low pressure that the effect of unemployment upon the rate of wage increase was large enough to offset that of cost-of-living compensation and/or price expectations. Given that prices in 1975 were increasing by 24% a year this would have necessitated either an intolerably high unemployment figure or an impossibly long period of correction. The other alternative was an incomes policy under which the rate of wage increase was subjected to firm, quasi-statutory control. This was the main course adopted, although unemployment was allowed to increase as well. The incomes policy was introduced in three stages, starting in July 1975 with a maximum wage increase of £6 per week. This policy gave way to limits of £2.50-£4.00 per week in July 1976, and in July 1977 to a 10% limitation on pay increases. The winning of union agreement to the first two stages of the incomes policy was a singular act of diplomacy which may well have saved the UK economy from hyperinflation.

It was certainly the first time that an incomes policy can be said to have made a significant impact upon the rate of wage inflation. The increase in average hourly wage rates which had been 34% in the twelve months ending in July 1975, fell to 18% in the next twelve months, to 5% in the twelve months ending July 1977, and to less than 1.0% in the five months ending in December 1977. In the Budget speech of April 1978 the Chancellor of the Exchequer announced his intention of holding talks with both sides of industry on the question of the appropriate policies to be followed after July 1978.

VI   ECONOMIC GROWTH

VI.1   The Growth of Productive Potential

In ordinary language it is usual enough to speak of any increase in GDP, however it comes about, as economic growth. In economic theory and applied economics it is best to reserve the term for increases in a country's productive potential. This means that demand-induced spurts of economic expansion, such as those occurring in cyclical recoveries, do not qualify as economic growth in the sense we have in mind.

The growth rate of productive potential can only be measured satisfactorily over very long intervals of time or between periods when the utilization of resources was closely similar. Thus the periods indicated in table 1.12, which presents estimates of the growth rate in the UK, have been chosen because they begin and end with similar rates of unemployment or vacancies.

TABLE 1.12

Economic Growth, UK, 1900-76

	GDP	*Percentage increase per annum in* GDP per man	Employed labour force	Capital stock excluding dwellings
1900-13	1.0	0.0	1.0	1.9
1922-38	2.3	1.1	1.2	1.1
1950-60	2.6	2.2	0.4	2.8
1960-70	2.8	2.5	0.3	4.3
1970-76	1.6	1.4	0.2	3.8

Sources: ET, October 1977; *NIBB* 1966-76; *ETCAS*); London and Cambridge Economic Service, *The British Economy, Key Statistics, 1900-1970.*

The table shows that both the growth rates of productive potential and the under-lying trend in productivity have increased since the beginning of this century.

The concept of the growth rate of productive potential is not without its limitations. In the first place it says little or nothing about the causes of growth but simply describes a time-trend. An extrapolation of the growth rate for any period into the future could easily turn out wrong if the forces that determine full employment output are going to be present in different amounts or combinations from those of the past.

A second reservation concerns the interpretation of growth *rates* generally and their relation to *levels*. In calculating growth from 1970 to 1976, for example, one takes the compound rate of increase which will transform the level of GDP in 1970 into that of 1976. This does not tell us anything about the intervening years, during which the level of GDP could have been above or below the suggested time path. Thus the average *rate* of growth is, in general, no guide to the average *level* of output over the period. An allied point is that the *level of potential output* is arbitrarily defined by the unemployment (or vacancy) rate at which it is measured. This does not necessarily represent the maximum attainable level.

One of the questions which the economics of growth must try to answer is why some countries have grown so much faster than others and why, in particular, the underlying growth rate of the UK economy has been slower in the postwar period than that of most other industrial countries (see table 1.13). The answer, if it is to be found at all, must be sought under the more general heading of the causes of economic growth.

The causes of economic growth have been debated by economists since the time of Adam Smith. Growth must depend, in the first instance, upon the increase in the quantity and quality of the factors of production and the efficiency with which they are combined. These increases may be influenced, however, by factors on the side of demand such as the pressure of demand on resources and the degree to which it fluctuates.

The supply of labour depends primarily on the evolution of the population of working age, including net migration, the secular decline in hours worked, and the increase in the length of annual and national holidays. Changes in the pressure of demand, however, affect the size of the labour force and the number of hours worked, and, over the longer period, may influence migration.

The quality of labour must in large degree depend upon the facilities available for education and training, the opportunities taken of them, and the degree to which they match the changing demands for skills arising out of changes in technology and the structure of aggregate demand. Measurement of these influences, however, is difficult and there is little evidence to show which way, if at all, they have affected the international comparison in table 1.13. The mobility of labour from job to job and from area to area is probably an important factor in economic growth in so far as it reflects the degree to which the labour force can adjust to economic change. It has been argued, not without evidence, that much of the relatively fast growth of the German, Italian and French economies can be attributed to the movement of labour from the agricultural to the industrial sectors.[1] But it is still not clear how much of this mobility has been a cause and how much a consequence of the disparity in growth rates between the agricultural and industrial sectors.

One obvious influence on the growth of labour productivity is the rate of increase in the nation's stock of capital, both in quantity and in quality. Some indications of the growth of the UK capital stock are given in Table 1.12, where it can be seen that the rate of increase, like that of productivity, has tended to rise during the course of this century. The stock of capital, however, is extremely difficult to measure. This is because the figures of depreciation in the national accounts are based on data collected for tax purposes and cannot serve as very precise indications of the rates of scrapping and deterioration of existing capital. Moreover, the economic value of a piece of capital equipment is an inherently subjective concept, depending on expectations of future returns and modified by

---

1   A. Maddison, *Economic Growth in the West,* Allen and Unwin, 1964.

TABLE 1.13

Rates of Growth, 1964-74

	Annual percentage rates	
	GDP	GDP per capita
Belgium	4.8	4.3
Denmark	3.9	3.1
France	5.3	4.4
Germany	4.1	3.4
Italy	4.7	4.0
Japan	8.4	7.4
Netherlands	5.0	3.8
Sweden	3.5	2.8
United Kingdom	2.5	2.1
Canada	5.2	3.6
United States	3.6	2.6

Source: National Accounts of OECD Countries, 1974.

problems of evaluating risk. Estimates of the capital stock, therefore, must be treated with a good deal of reserve.

The quality of the capital stock is, perhaps, even more important and even more difficult to measure. According to one widely accepted view the quality of capital depends, by and large, upon its age structure. This view looks upon the capital stock as a series of vintages of gross investment, each new vintage containing machines of higher quality than the previous one. Scientific and technical progress are embodied in new machines, not old ones, so that the most recent capital equipment is likely to be the most efficient. This view is the basis of the 'catching-up hypothesis' which has been advanced to explain the faster growth of some countries in the early postwar period. The argument is that those countries in which the capital stock was seriously depleted by the war were in a position to replenish it with brand-new equipment, and were thus enabled to grow faster than those countries where the bombing and destruction had been less severe. The embodied view of technical progress, together with the difficulties of measuring the quantity of capital, has led a number of economists[1] to emphasize gross rather than net capital formation as the better indicator of the extent to which capital resources have been enhanced. A high rate of gross investment, even if it is entirely for replacement purposes, will reduce the age of the capital stock and increase its quality.

Turning to influences on the side of demand, two aspects of the question need to be distinguished: the average pressure of demand and the size of fluctuations around the average. It can certainly be argued that a low average pressure of demand such as obtained (to choose an extreme example) in the 1930s is inimical to innovation and investment. It hinders investment because capital equipment is under-utilized and because its continuation for any length of time is likely to set an unfavourable climate for expectations. High demand, on the other hand, will generally have the opposite effect. It has also been argued that high demand encourages managers and workers to devise new and better ways of working with existing equipment, thereby making technical progress of a variety which is not embodied in new types of machine. This effect has sometimes been described as 'learning by doing', and it

---

1   For example, A. Maddison, ibid.

fits in with the view that the scale of production problems that have to be solved is itself a stimulus to their solution. Evidence has been produced, for example, to show how the time taken to assemble a prototype airframe has progressively diminished as the work force has gained experience of repeating the same jobs over and over again. On the other hand, it has also to be borne in mind that high demand pressure may work the other way. The presence of a sellers' market with easy profits could also diminish the incentive to innovate and even lead to lazy attitudes to production. Again, extreme pressure can promote mental and physical exhaustion. Thus for any single firm there may be some optimum pressure of demand where technical progress is maximized and beyond which the rate of progress tends to fall. For the economy as a whole the optimum pressure of demand is likely to be a rather complex average of the individual production units, and not something about which it is easy to make generalizations.

Another question is whether the amplitude of fluctuations tends to impede economic growth. It seems probable that the expectation of fluctuations will retard capital formation because profitability will be held down in periods of recession. It may also be the case that expectations of cycles lead to the installation of machinery which can be adapted to use in periods of both high and low output, whereas the prospect of steady growth could enable the introduction of machinery which would be specially designed to produce at a steadier level of sales. In this case it is likely that the extra adaptability will be achieved at some cost to the efficiency of capital, and growth will be slowed down. It may be no coincidence, therefore, that three countries with some of the lowest growth rates in the 1950s — the UK, US and Belgium — suffered sharper fluctuations in unemployment than the others.[1] (Japan was the exception to this rule.)

VI.2   Economic Growth and Policy

Governments prefer a fast rate of growth to a slow rate because it results in greater tax revenues from a given structure of tax rates, and thus permits a larger provision of public services (hospitals, schools and so forth) than would otherwise be possible. Fast growth may also render a policy of income redistribution less painful to the better off than would be so if the growth of income was slow or non-existent. Thus it is not surprising that governments have often announced a faster growth rate as a goal of economic policy.

What is not so clear, however, is whether the means of attaining faster growth are sufficiently well known and understood. There is considerable controversy among economists as to the effects on economic growth to be had from, say, a faster growth of the capital stock and from technical progress. Many would argue that neither are quantifiable, and that the attempts which have been made to quantify them are suspect in a number of ways. Thus it does not seem that growth policy is in the same category as, for example, demand management policies, in which moderately fine calculations can be made as to the effects of changing the instruments of policy by known amounts. Probably all that can be hoped for from policy to promote growth is action, or a series of actions, designed to create a climate which is favourable to worthwhile investment and innovation. It seems doubtful,

---

1   On these points see A. Maddison, ibid, pp. 43-56, and R. C. O. Matthews, 'The Role of Demand Management', in Sir Alec Cairncross (ed.), *Britain's Prospects Reconsidered,* Allen and Unwin, 1970.

however, if even the most determined attempt to alter the environment in this way
would show results within the lifetime of a single government. Nor does it seem
likely, to judge from earlier experience, that dramatic effects can be expected
from the mere announcement of a growth target. This was last done in 1965 when
the government published a National Plan in which the rate of growth of GDP was
to have been 4% per annum for 1964-70. In the event the growth rate turned out to
be only 2.4%, and much of the public investment which had been based on the 4%
growth assumption proved to be excessive. It is still debatable whether the growth
rate would have been any higher if the balance of payments had been managed more
adroitly than it was.[1]

VII   ECONOMIC PROSPECTS AND POLICIES 1978-80

In early 1978 the UK economy was still in recession with unemployment at nearly
1.4 million. The balance of payments, however, had improved a lot, with a current
account surplus of £0.8 billion in the second half of 1977 compared with deficits in
1975 and 1976 of well over £1 billion. The rate of inflation had also come a long
way down from its peak of 24% a year in 1974-5. It was just under 8% for the
twelve months to April 1978. Nevertheless, it was inflation which continued to
be the dominant consideration in economic policy.

There were two main reasons why this should be so. The first concerns the long
period of time which must be taken in order to bring inflation down from 10% for the
year to a tolerable rate. This is because of the lags in the wage—price spiral which
means that in the absence of incomes policy a period of anything from three to five
years is needed to lower inflation to 5%.[2] The second reason was the uncertainty
surrounding the future of incomes policy. The Stage III limit of 10% on earnings
increases was due to expire in July, after which there could be no certainty of TUC
or individual union agreement to a Stage IV policy. If Stage IV could not be agreed
upon there was some danger that the return to free collective bargaining, after three
years of wage discipline, would spark off a pay explosion.

One of the interesting questions about the Budget of 1978 concerns the extent
to which it was influenced by monetary hypotheses about inflation. One of these
hypotheses appears to have been an expectational version of the crude doctrine that
money supply increases of x% imply, without qualification, x% increases in the price
level. This doctrine is incorrect, because monetary expansion may raise real output
rather than prices. But the doctrine still seems to have had its influence on policy,
because of the expectations which were based, or believed to be based, upon it. Thus

---

1   See, however, W. Beckerman *et al.*, *The Labour Government's Economic Record 1964-70*,
    Duckworth, 1972.
2   To illustrate the point, suppose that prices rise, with a lag of 12 months, by 0.8 times the
    previous wage increase, whilst wages rise by the same percentage rate as prices, again with a
    twelve-month lag. It will then take, assuming no changes in import costs, five years to
    reduce a 10% inflation rate to 5%.

Years	0	1	2	3	4	5	6	7
Price increase	10	8	8	6.4	6.4	5.12	5.12	4.10
Wage increase	10	10	8	8	6.4	6.4	4.10	4.10

This example assumed no help from productivity increases. If these are 1.5% per year (as in
1969-76) then the rate of price increase would be 1.2% less each year and the 5% inflation
rate would be attained in three years.

it could be argued that by 1978 enough people in the financial markets believed in this rather crude kind of monetarism for increases in the money supply above the rate expected to raise expectations of inflation. These would lead, in turn, to sales of sterling, exchange depreciation, higher import costs, and force UK prices higher. Thus the behaviour of inflation expectations may have been sufficient in itself to instil an element of truth into what, in all other aspects, was a crude piece of analysis.[1]

The Budget speech of April 1978 made concessions to the monetarist way of thought by announcing a 'target' increase in the money supply (sterling M_3) of 8% to 12% in the financial year. But it was also made clear that this limit would be subject to revision in the light of financial developments and the demand for money. This provision seems to have been intended to give some flexibility to the money supply, such as might be needed in the event of employment and the required budget deficit turning out to be different from forecast.

The main proposal in the Budget of April 1978 was a reduction in taxation, mainly on income, by £2.6 billion for a full financial year. This was calculated to add 0.75% to GDP. The Budget forecasts, allowing for the tax cuts, put GDP as rising by 3.0% between the second halves of 1977 and 1978, and by a further 0.9% in the first half of 1979. These forecasts implied a further rise in unemployment from the high levels of early 1978. Thus the high priority given to inflation carried the unfortunate implication that the return to anything like full employment would have to be postponed until the 1980s. Only an agreement on a tough Stage IV of incomes policy, or perhaps a recovery in world trade, seemed likely to alter this rather gloomy outlook.

REFERENCES AND FURTHER READING

An elementary textbook which introduces most of the policy issues discussed in this chapter is A. K. Cairncross, *An Introduction to Economics,* 5th edition, Butterworth, 1973, whilst intermediate books are F. S. Brooman, *Macroeconomics,* 6th edition, Allen and Unwin, 1977, and D. C. Rowan, *Output, Inflation and Growth,* 2nd edition, Macmillan, 1974. A good short guide to the national accounts is S. Hays, *National Income and Expenditure in Britain and the OECD Countries,* Heinemann, 1971. Economic fluctuations in the UK are described by R. C. O. Matthews in 'Postwar Business Cycles in the UK', in M. Bronfenbrenner (ed.), *Is the Business Cycle Obsolete?,* Wiley, 1969. An advanced treatment of aggregate demand theory is given in M. K. Evans, *Macroeconomic Activity,* Harper and Row, 1969, whilst M. J. C. Surrey, *The Analysis and Forecasting of the British Economy,* NIESR and Cambridge University Press, 1971, is helpful on forecasting. On economic policy there is M. J. Stewart, *The Jekyll and Hyde Years,* Dent, 1977, and W. Beckerman (ed.), *The Labour Government's Economic Record 1964-70,* Duckworth, 1972, together with the articles by R. C. O. Matthews, G. D. N. Worswick and E. H. Phelps Brown in Sir Alec Cairncross (ed.), *Britain's Economic*

---

1 'If markets take the view that the policies pursued by a particular country are likely to damage assets held in that country or in that country's currency, they are likely to behave in ways which can actually enforce a policy change. Market behaviour has become a significant input in policy making' (Sir Douglas Wass, Permanent Secretary, HM Treasury, 'The Changing Problems of Economic Management', lecture to the Johnian Society, Cambridge, 15 February 1978).

Prospects Reconsidered, Allen and Unwin, 1970. D. Morris (ed.), *The Economic System in the UK,* Oxford University Press, 1977, gives an excellent coverage of various aspects of demand management and inflation. Two recent books on inflation are J. S. Flemming, *Inflation,* Oxford University Press, 1976, and J. A. Trevithick, *Inflation,* Penguin, 1977. On the current state of the economy the best general guide is given quarterly in the *National Institute Economic Review* and this may be supplemented by the annual *Economic Policy Review,* Department of Applied Economics, University of Cambridge.

2

Monetary, credit and fiscal policies
N. J. Gibson

I INTRODUCTION: THE POLICY DILEMMA

The previous chapter seeks to convey an overall picture of the UK economy, paying particular attention to fluctuations in economic activity, demand management, inflation, and economic growth. This chapter concentrates on a narrower area, the monetary, credit and fiscal policies of the authorities, that is, the UK government and the Bank of England.

The term 'policy' implies the existence of goals and a strategy or instruments to achieve them. For the greater part of the period since the Second World War the most frequently cited policy goals in the UK have been the maintenance of full employment, price stability and fixed exchange rates, the encouragement of economic growth and the achievement of a 'satisfactory' balance of payments.[1] However, since the late 1960s the emphasis on the maintenance of fixed exchange rates has largely disappeared and instead more flexible exchange rates have become the norm, though this does not mean that the balance of payments has become a matter of little concern. Furthermore, in the last few years a reduction in the rate of inflation, rather than the maintenance of price stability, or full employment, has come to dominate the policy goals of the authorities.

The standard policy instruments at the disposal of the authorities are monetary, credit and fiscal. That is, by changing the money supply, interest rates, the availability of credit and by altering tax rates and government expenditure the authorities may hope to realize some or all of their policy goals. But in addition to the instruments mentioned the authorities may vary exchange rates, restrict imports and impose controls on prices and incomes. They may even go beyond this and introduce rationing and other measures.

Once a set of goals is chosen a host of questions arise. Can they be defined precisely? Are they mutually compatible within the particular economic system, given the policy instruments at the disposal of the authorities? If they are not, which goals should be sacrificed or modified? Are there alternative policy instruments that might be used to achieve one or more of the policy goals? Have the authorities, or for that matter has anyone else, the necessary knowledge about the relationships between instruments and goals? Do they know exactly when and by how much to manipulate the policy instruments or even how many instruments they need?

These questions highlight what might be called the policy dilemma. It is, for instance, not at all certain that full employment and price stability can be attained simultaneously with the help of the policy instruments currently at the disposal of the authorities. The reason, at least in part, is that there is apparently no simple,

---

1 See chapters 3 and 5 respectively for an extensive explanation and discussion of the balance of payments and incomes controls.

well-understood relationship between the policy actions of the authorities and such magnitudes as full employment and price stability. The effects of monetary and fiscal policy may be apparent only after some delay and the delay itself may be variable, depending on the initial economic and other circumstances when the policy actions were first taken, as well as the events that subsequently impinge on the system, including expectations about the future behaviour of the system.

This type of uncertainty and lack of knowledge and information about the precise relationships between instruments and goals has encouraged the search for what are called 'target' and 'indicator' variables. Target and indicator variables are, as it were, intermediate between instruments and goals and may be simply explained by an example.

If it is known in a qualitative if not a precise sense that, *cet. par.*, there is an inverse relationship between the rate of interest and real income, then it may be reasonable for the policy-maker to aim at a particular interest rate or set of interest rates as a policy target though his ultimate goal is the level of real income. However, the target may be affected by other influences besides the actual policy being pursued and so it may be important to have another variable or set of variables which indicate the direction of policy or the policy stance. In the field of monetary policy it might be the reserve base of the monetary system, which in principle is under the direct control of the authorities, and where an expansion of the base would be considered as a policy of ease and a contraction the reverse. Thus on this approach a policy designed to expand real income might be one which had as targets a lower set of interest rates than those ruling at present and also used the cash base as an indicator. Now if the interest rates in these circumstances were to decline as a consequence of a fall in investment expenditures, which could not be observed at the time, the authorities might be inclined to feel that they had already achieved their target. But if at the same time the cash base was being used as an indicator it might be found that this is not expanding as contemplated, thus alerting the authorities that other forces are at work and affecting interest rates. But, of course, the reality is more complicated than envisaged here. This is especially true of an open economy like that of the UK which is heavily dependent on external trade and which may, for instance, find that its ability to affect interest rates or the reserve base is severely limited by conditions in money markets in the rest of the world. Optimal policy in a world of uncertainty and incomplete knowledge poses extremely difficult problems.[1]

Implicit in the foregoing discussion of goals, targets, indicators and instruments are questions concerning both value judgements and how an economic system works. Each of these questions is a recurring theme in this chapter. Section II looks briefly at the theoretical and empirical basis of monetary and fiscal policy. Section III discusses the structure of the banking and financial system and examines some money and credit theories. The taxation system is considered in Section IV which also includes a brief discussion of taxation within the EEC. Finally, in Section V policy since the early 1960s is briefly surveyed and a short discussion of the prospects and possible implications of economic and monetary union within the EEC is also included.

---

1 T. R. Saving, 'Monetary-Policy Targets and Indicators', *JPE*, vol. 75, supplement, August 1967, no. 4, part II, pp. 446-65, also in W. E. Gibson and G. G. Kaufman, *Monetary Economics: Readings on Current Issues*, McGraw-Hill, 1971.

II   SOME THEORETICAL AND EMPIRICAL BACKGROUND
II.1   Certain Keynesian and Monetarist Positions

As implied above, the use of monetary and fiscal policy presupposes some knowledge about policy instruments and goals. One view is that monetary policy is by and large ineffective and that, say, increases in the money supply and reductions in interest rates will have little or no effect as an encouragement to expenditure and hence will have little or no impact on economic activity, whereas fiscal policy in the form of changes in taxation and government expenditure will have substantial effects. Another view, but this time applied to fiscal policy, is that an increase in government expenditure will not stimulate an expansion of output and employment but will only substitute government expenditure for private expenditure. And, similarly, that a reduction in taxation will have no net expansionary effect on expenditure and hence output and employment. In contrast, however, changes in the money supply are believed to have marked effects on an economy.

Implicit in these contrasting statements are different models of the economic system. The first, which completely discounts the importance of monetary policy, is generally associated with an extreme Keynesian viewpoint; and the second, which completely discounts the importance of fiscal policy, with an extreme monetarist position.

It has now been argued persuasively that the first viewpoint does far less than justice to Keynes himself and that it is a serious misinterpretation of his work to attribute to him the general view that 'money does not matter'.[1] On the contrary he was greatly impressed by the power of monetary policy for good or ill as regards the functioning of the economic system. In particular, and despite the experience of the great depression, he was not an adherent of what has come to be called the liquidity-trap hypothesis; that is, that the rate of interest might have a floor below which it would not fall and possibly prevent the achievement of full employment. However, he certainly envisaged this as an extreme possibility and wrote 'whilst this limiting case might become practically important in the future, I know of no example of it hitherto'.[2] At the same time, neither theoretical nor empirical work supports an extreme monetarist position, one which has perhaps been unkindly paraphrased as 'money is all that matters'.[3]

However, to contrast the Keynesian and monetarist positions in this stark way may be unnecessary and even misleading. Recent work on the US economy suggests that, 'in the "short run" both monetary and fiscal policies have powerful effects, first on real output and, more gradually, on prices, with the relative size of the two effects dependent on the degree of slack in the economy'.[4] The same study also states that, 'in the longest run the response of the economy to both monetary and fiscal policy is very much consistent with the views advanced by Friedman and the monetarists. In particular, the money supply does *not* affect real output, or real

1 Axel Leijonhufvud, *On Keynesian Economics and the Economics of Keynes: A Study in Monetary Theory*, Oxford University Press, 1968.
2 J. M. Keynes, *The General Theory of Employment, Interest and Money*, Macmillan, 1936, p. 207.
3 James Tobin, 'The Monetary Interpretation of History: A Review Article', *AER*, June 1965.
4 F. Modigliani, 'The Channels of Monetary Policy in the Federal Reserve – MIT – University of Pennsylvania Econometric Model of the United States', in *Modelling the Economy*, edited by G. A. Renton, Heinemann Educational Books Limited, 1975, p. 241.

interest rates (money is neutral) but only the price level; and a change in real government expenditure, money supply (and tax rates) constant, does *not* affect real output but only its composition, as the expansion in government expenditure tends to displace an equal amount of private demand'.[1]

Though there are dangers in applying uncritically to another economy findings which relate to a particular economy the views expressed in the foregoing quotation are, subject to important qualifications, similar to those which underly this chapter. The qualifications concern the openness of the UK economy in the sense of its large dependence on foreign trade, the ease with which funds can move between UK and other monetary and financial markets and the existence of fixed or floating exchange rates vis-à-vis the rest of the world.

In a regime of *fixed* exchange rates — or, indeed, floating rates if held within a narrow range — and highly developed international capital markets, with freedom of movement of funds between them, the ability of a single country such as the UK to maintain interest rates at levels substantially different from those in the rest of the world is limited. This clearly reduces the usefulness of monetary and credit policy as an instrument of domestic economic policy. However, in the case of fiscal policy and fixed exchange rates the conclusion is rather different; changes in fiscal policy may still affect domestic output and employment. For instance, an expansionary fiscal policy will in the short run generally tend to increase output and employment.

With *flexible* exchange rates the conclusions are more or less reversed. An expansionary monetary and credit policy will tend to depress the exchange rate and thereby stimulate exports and discourage imports and so help to increase domestic economic activity.[2] But an expansionary fiscal policy will tend to increase interest rates and encourage a net inflow of capital, which will raise the exchange rate with adverse effects on exports and hence output and employment. This in turn will tend to offset the expansionary impact of the original fiscal policy. However, these conclusions may of course require modification depending on how the rest of the world responds to the particular policy changes.

For monetarists inflation is essentially a monetary phenomenon and in principle can be controlled by restricting the rate of growth of the money stock to a rate equal to the secular rate of growth of output, making if need be some allowance for population and perhaps real income growth. Furthermore, they believe that the authorities have in principle the power to do so. Monetarists go on to argue that once an inflationary process is under way, economic behaviour is strongly affected by expectations about the future levels of prices and that attempts to reduce the pace of inflation by a more restrictive monetary policy will generally bring about conditions in which output and employment may be static or declining, whilst prices continue to rise. In other words monetarists are not surprised by what has come to be called 'stagflation'. Indeed monetarists tend to believe that inflation in market-based economies cannot be cured without the cost of sluggish or even declining rates of growth of output and rising unemployment in the short run—a phenomenon which has been only too familiar in the 1970s.

---

1 Ibid.
2 The term 'exchange rate', in conformity with British practice, refers to the price of one unit of the domestic currency in terms of a foreign currency. It is frequently much more convenient to follow the opposite practice and define an exchange rate—just like any other price—in terms of the number of units of domestic currency per unit of foreign currency.

Keynesians, and indeed others — with varying degrees of emphasis—are inclined to see inflation not primarily as a monetary phenomenon but as a consequence of a dynamic adjustment process whereby groups of workers and business interests struggle to preserve or improve, largely by wage and price fixing, their relative shares of the real national income.[1] This struggle is seen as often bringing both workers and business into conflict with government, upon which each of them may put such pressure that it feels obliged for electoral or other reasons to pursue permissive monetary and fiscal policies. These policies may seem, at least for a time — which may become shorter and shorter as experience accumulates — to be consistent with the short-term wishes of both workers and business. The *apparent* logic of this approach is to institute a wages, prices and income policy. For it is argued that whilst restrictive monetary and fiscal policies may succeed in reducing the growth of output and increasing the level of unemployment they will do little to come to grips with the fundamental causes of inflation.

On the face of it the so-called monetarist and Keynesian approaches to the explanation of inflation are strongly opposed. The monetarist position would seem to require that the market-based economic system is fundamentally stable and that disequilibria will be self-correcting, provided the monetary framework is controlled in a way that avoids unanticipated changes in the general price level. It is not argued that this requires a constant price level though it is generally accepted that this is probably what should be the target. To achieve this, prices and incomes policies are unnecessary and indeed lead to misallocation of resources and inefficiency.

The Keynesian position seems to imply that conflicts over relative shares of the real national income and, in particular, relative real wages can be resolved at least temporarily through permissive monetary policies and inflation, together with a prices and incomes policy. But this is tantamount to postulating the persistence of money illusion and an inability to learn from experience, hardly a strong base on which to build a theory with such profound economic and social significance. Furthermore, it needs to be stressed that the success to date, other than in the short-run, of so-called prices and incomes policies as a means of avoiding inflation and indeed 'stagflation' would seem to have been extremely limited.[2]

II.2   Views of the Bank of England

The Bank is necessarily committed to pursuing the major policy goals mentioned earlier in the introduction, though the relative emphasis placed on the individual goals may and does change through time. But, in addition, the Bank sees itself as having an overriding responsibility for the financing of the government and the management of the national debt and a general responsibility for the efficiency and stability of the whole financial system. These latter responsibilities, as interpreted by the authorities, are fundamental to an understanding of their approach to monetary and credit policy.

The Bank would argue that its approach to policy is pragmatic and necessarily conditioned by the economic and institutional circumstances existing at any point of time, as well as the general climate of professional opinion about the power of

---

1 This is not to deny that the behaviour of import prices, and capital flows and the like, over which a particular country may have little or no control, may be a further important factor influencing domestic prices, especially under a system of fixed exchange rates. See chapter 1, section V.2.

2 For further discussion of inflation and prices and incomes policy see chapters 1 and 5.

monetary and other policies to influence the economic system. Just how important
these considerations are is illustrated by the following excerpt from a lecture
delivered by a Governor and referring to the period immediately following the
Second World War. 'At the end of the war it was widely believed that interest rates
should be kept low to finance reconstruction as well as to ease the servicing of a
greatly increased national debt; and it was some while before it was universally
accepted that a slump was not after all inevitable. A fairly comprehensive system of
physical controls had been maintained to suppress inflation; and the doctrine of
Keynes, at least as interpreted by his followers. . . had led to a totally new emphasis
on fiscal policy. The active drive for cheap money was succeeded by a period in
which monetary policy went into limbo. There was general scepticism about its
relevance.'[1] There can be little doubt that the Bank shared this scepticism.

But towards the end of 1951 the authorities, largely in response to balance of
payments problems, decided to reactivate monetary policy. This, however, did not
in any sense imply that the authorities had become convinced that careful control
of the money supply was the key to effective monetary policy. On the contrary,
and with the possible exception of a period in the mid-1950s, monetary policy throughout the whole period up to the late 1960s placed major emphasis on influencing
the cost and availability of credit to the various sectors of the economy. Much
reliance was placed on hire purchase controls, the control of bank lending through
quantitative and qualitative restraints, including ceilings on advances, liquid asset
ratios and special deposits. Furthermore, through time the credit controls became
more specific and direct with the authorities detailing the priorities that should be
observed.

Since about 1969, however, the authorities have been more prepared to
acknowledge the disadvantages of quantitative and qualitative controls and,
particularly recently, to give more attention to the growth of monetary aggregates,
including the money supply. But it is only since 1976 that the Bank has been
prepared to announce a target growth rate for the money supply. The present
Governor has stated that 'the most immediate benefit from publicly announced
monetary targets derives from the assurance that money will not itself be a source
of instability. Beyond this, monetary targets give a clear indication to those
responsible for economic decisions — including those affecting the course of future
costs and prices — of the limit to which the authorities are, in effect, prepared to
see inflation financed in the months ahead: the implication being that inflation at a
faster rate will inevitably put output and employment increasingly at risk'.[2] This
represents a fascinating development in official thinking and despite qualifications
and certain protestations is a retreat from the Bank's extreme Keynesianism of
earlier years and a movement in the direction of the monetarists. Moreover, as will
be seen below this new emphasis on the importance of the growth of the monetary
aggregates calls in question the approach of the authorities to monetary policy over
the last thirty years and especially in the early 1970s when they permitted massive
and irregular expansion of the money supply. Indeed it is arguable that the depth

1 'Monetary Management in the United Kingdom', *BEQB*, vol. 11, no. 1, March 1971, p. 41.
   See also, 'The Operation of Monetary Policy since the Radcliffe Report', ibid., vol. 9, no. 4,
   December 1969, pp. 448-60.
2 *BEQB*, vol. 17, no. 4, December 1977, p. 461. See also ibid., vol. 18, no. 1, March 1978,
   'Reflections on the Conduct of Monetary Policy', pp. 31-7.

and duration of the 'stagflation' of recent years is primarily, if not exclusively, a direct consequence of these policies of the early 1970s.[1]

II.3   Some Empirical Work

A great deal of the empirical work on the relative merits of monetary and fiscal policy as stabilization instruments has been carried out in relation to the US economy.[2] The evidence, as indicated above, suggests that monetary policy in terms of acceleration or deceleration of the rate of change in the money supply is important for the behaviour of both nominal and real income in the short-run, though the precise effects on output and prices are not well understood. There is also evidence that fiscal policy affects output, employment and prices. Furthermore, some of the evidence also indicates that for stabilization purposes monetary policy is more powerful than fiscal policy. However, it should be stressed that these conclusions are provisional and should be treated as such. Nevertheless, there is no doubt that since the late 1960s there has been a major shift in professional opinion in the US on the importance of monetary policy as a stabilization instrument, which has frequently been coupled with a reduced emphasis on the significance of fiscal policy, which is not to say that the latter is unimportant.

Unfortunately, as far as the UK is concerned there is rather less empirical evidence available about the relative merits of monetary and fiscal policy as stabilization instruments. Moreover, the evidence that is available is to some extent conflicting.

One study, under the auspices of the National Institute of Economic and Social Research, tentatively suggested that fiscal policy might be more powerful and quicker-acting than monetary policy.[3] This conclusion is, of course, contrary to the analogous conclusions of studies for the US. However the authors of the National Institute study have major reservations about the econometric methods employed in these studies, including their own, and place little confidence in the conclusions of any of them.

Putting aside the fundamental questions relating to the methods used it would seem that the tentative conclusions of the National Institute study are extremely sensitive to the data employed, and perhaps to the time period used. For an alternative study, using different measures of economic activity and fiscal policy as well as a slightly different time period, produces conclusions about the relative effectiveness of monetary and fiscal policy that are consistent with studies for the US.[4]

There remains however some indirect evidence about the potential effectiveness of monetary policy which is worth mentioning. From a number of recent impressive studies by research staff of the Bank of England there is growing evidence that the

1   See section V of this chapter.

2   The term 'stabilization' gives rise to problems of meaning and definition, particularly when a number of different policy goals are being pursued simultaneously. In the rest of this section it is assumed that the primary stabilization objectives are the rate of growth of real and nominal gross domestic product.

3   M. J. Artis and A. R. Nobay, 'Two Aspects of the Monetary Debate', *NIER*, no. 49, August 1969.

4   M. W. Keran, 'Monetary and Fiscal Influences on Economic Activity: The Foreign Experience', Federal Reserve Bank of St Louis, *Review*, vol. 52, no. 2, February 1970.

demand for money in the UK, especially as it relates to M_1, or broadly speaking transactions balances, is stable and with income and interest-rate elasticities which are suggestive of the potential effectiveness of monetary policy in terms of its power to influence income and prices through control of the rate of growth of monetary aggregates.[1]

Nevertheless, the absence of objectively convincing evidence about the merits of monetary and fiscal policy in the UK context makes it very difficult as will be seen below to give a confident assessment of the merits of the policies pursued by successive governments. However, it seems fair to say that much professional opinion in the UK, whilst it may not have moved as much as in the US, is less sceptical about the relevance of monetary policy, in terms of control of the money supply, as an instrument for economic management than it was a few years ago. This is not to say that professional opinion has seriously downgraded fiscal policy. Many British economists would still view it as the more important instrument. But there is perhaps one thing on which professional opinion is more generally agreed and that is that neither monetary nor fiscal policy can, in the present state of knowledge, be used with confidence for 'fine tuning' or, alternatively, sensitive, short-run control of the economic system; and some would add that the attempt to do so may increase uncertainty and exacerbate the situation. Others would go further and argue that the theoretical case for macro-economic intervention is seriously weakened if individuals in the system respond to changes in the light of all the information available and in that sense behave rationally. In short the balance of professional opinion in Britain would seem to be shifting slightly and becoming more sympathetic to the monetarist notion that monetary and fiscal policy should be carried on in a way which helps to provide a stable framework for economic decision making, in particular a stable price level, and that the adherence to appropriate target rates of growth of the money supply may be crucially important to this end. A notable exception to this viewpoint, however, is the National Institute of Economic and Social Research.[2]

III THE BANKING AND FINANCIAL STRUCTURE AND MONEY AND CREDIT CONTROL

III.1 The UK Banking Sector

The UK banking sector consists of UK offices of all those banks which observe the uniform reserve ratio introduced in September 1971 and, in addition, the Banking Department of the Bank of England, the discount market and the National Giro. The banks which observe the uniform reserve ratio are known as listed banks classified into three main groups, British, Overseas and Consortium banks. The British banks include the London clearing banks, the Scottish clearing banks, the Northern Ireland banks, Accepting houses and other British banks. The Overseas banks are made up of three main groups, American banks, Japanese banks and other overseas banks. Consortium banks are banks which are owned by other banks but in which no single bank holds more than 50% of the share capital and where at least one of the participating banks is an overseas bank.

---

1 See R. T. Coghlan, 'A Transactions Demand for Money' *BEQB*, vol. 18, no. 1, March 1978, pp. 48-60 and Graham Haache, 'The Demand for Money in the UK: Experience since 1971', *BEQB*, vol. 14, no. 3, September 1974, pp. 284-305.

2 See 'Summary and Appraisal', *NIER*, no. 83, February 1978, pp. 3-6.

Perhaps the most notable feature of the UK banking sector in recent years is its remarkable rate of expansion in terms of the number of banks involved and in the growth of deposits. The growth in numbers has been concentrated amongst other British banks, Overseas banks and Consortium banks. At the end of 1977 some 360 institutions were covered by the official UK banking sector tables published by the authorities. Ten or so years ago the figure was perhaps one-third of this number.

Because of the growing number of banks which get incorporated in the statistics there are difficulties in determining precisely the growth of deposit liabilities in the UK. However, bearing this in mind, at the end of 1970 total deposits of the UK banking sector were about £32,000m, whilst by the end of 1977 they had reached almost £136,000m, a compound rate of growth of some 23% p.a. Of these totals over £16,000m and £43,000m respectively were sterling deposits and the rest were denominated in other currencies. Thus sterling deposits grew at about 15% p.a. These developments have the most profound significance for the operation and control of the monetary and financial system of the UK. This point is returned to below in discussing the major categories of banks included in the UK banking sector.

III.2   The Bank of England

The Bank of England acts as banker to the government and plays a basic role in smoothing government cash transactions and in administering and managing the national debt — broadly speaking, the debt liabilities of the State to its nationals, to its own agencies and to overseas holders. As agent of the government the Bank helps to regulate and control foreign exchange transactions and manages the Exchange Equalization Account, which controls the official gold and foreign exchange reserves of the UK.[1]

The Bank is divided into two parts for accounting purposes; it produces two balance sheets, one for the Issue Department and one for the Banking Department. The origin of the double balance sheet system is to be found in monetary controversies during the first half of the nineteenth century and was introduced under the Bank Charter Act, 1844, separating the note issue function from all other functions of the Bank. But the two balance sheets still retain a certain, if somewhat artificial, significance in that the Issue Department is classified in the national accounts of the UK as belonging to the public or government sector, whilst, as already mentioned, the Banking Department is classified for banking purposes with the banking sector. The position of the Issue Department in December 1977 is shown in table 2.1.

TABLE 2.1

Issue Department (selected items), 14 December 1977 (£m)

Liabilities		Assets	
Notes:			
In circulation	8,019	Government securities	7,095
In Banking Dept.	6	Other securities	930
	8,025		8,025

Source: BEQB.

1   See 'The Exchange Equalisation Account: Its Origins and Development', *BEQB*, vol. 8, no. 4, December 1968.

The notes in circulation are necessarily held by persons, companies and financial institutions. Notes in the Banking Department would, of course, disappear from the accounts if the two balance sheets were amalgamated. The assets of the Issue Department, except for some commercial bills, local authority debt and some holdings of company securities, such as British Petroleum ordinary stock, under the heading of 'other securities', are classified as government securities but also include government-guaranteed securities, Treasury bills and Ways and Means Advances to the National Loans Fund. Any increase in the note issue generally implies an equal addition to holdings of government securities. In other words, when the Issue Department supplies additional notes, which it does via the Banking Department, it obtains interest-earning government securities in exchange. Indeed the note issue may be looked upon as a means by which the government helps to finance its expenditure.

The assets of the Issue Department are a means of helping the government to organize its finances in another way. The government is continuously concerned with the issue and redemption of the national debt; it may need to borrow new funds or pay off maturing obligations. The Issue Department under-writes all new issues of government stock, taking up any that is not bought by the public on the day of issue and subsequently selling it as demand appears. Similarly, the Issue Department purchases stocks nearing redemption, avoiding large cash payments to the public when the actual redemption date arrives. The Issue Department may in fact be in the market as a buyer or seller of government securities or both almost continuously. That is, it engages extensively in open market operations.

The balance sheet of the Banking Department is shown in table 2.2.

TABLE 2.2

Banking Department (selected items), 14 December 1977 (£m)

Liabilities		*Assets*	
Deposits:			
Public	23	Government securities	1,591
Bankers	428	Advances and other accounts	486
Reserves and other accounts	586	Premises, equipment and other securities	154
Special deposits	1,185	Notes and coins	6
	2,222		2,237

Source: BEQB

Note: The balance sheet does not exactly balance because certain subsidiary items have been omitted. This is also true of other balance sheets summarized in this chapter.

Public deposits are all government balances. They include those of the Exchequer, the National Loans Fund, HM Paymaster General, the National Debt Commissioners and Dividend Accounts. The total amount involved is relatively small by comparison with bankers' deposits despite the enormous scale of government transactions. The main reason for this is that government attempts to keep these balances as low as possible consistently with carrying out its operations. Any so-called surplus balances are used to retire government debt in an attempt to keep down costs. Net payments from the government to the community will have an immediate effect on bankers' deposits, increasing the cash holdings of the banking system. The reverse is also true and smoothing out movements of funds between public and bankers' deposits is a major pre-occupation of the Bank day to day.

Bankers' deposits belong to the London and Scottish clearing banks, other British banks, Northern Ireland banks, Overseas and Consortium banks, discount houses and the National Giro. As bankers' deposits necessarily appear as assets in the balance sheets of these financial institutions and will therefore be discussed later, nothing more is said about them at this point.[1]

Reserves and other accounts include balances of overseas central banks, certain dividend accounts, local authorities and public corporation accounts, as well as unallocated profits of the Banking Department. The accounts of the Bank's remaining private customers are also included here. These accounts are not without importance but they are not central to this chapter and so are not discussed further.

Special deposits were a new category of deposit, first introduced in April 1960, that the London clearing banks and Scottish clearing banks were from time to time obliged to transfer to the Bank in support of its monetary and credit policy. This scheme came to an end on 15 September 1971 when all outstanding special deposits were repaid. Since then two new schemes have been introduced, the first on 16 September 1971 for interest-bearing special deposits and the second on 17 December 1973 for non-interest-bearing supplementary special deposits. Both are discussed below.

Government securities introduce the assets of the Banking Department and include Treasury bills and longer-dated government securities and Ways and Means Advances to the Exchequer.[2] These advances occur if the Exchequer finds itself short of funds at the end of the day and wishes to make up its balance; the advances are generally only overnight loans, being repaid the following day.

The Banking Department, through sales and purchases of government securities, affects the volume of bankers' deposits and hence the cash holdings of the banking system. In general, government securities in the Banking Department can be used in much the same way as those in the Issue Department to facilitate debt management and monetary policy. However, the assets at the disposal of the Banking Department are much smaller than those available to the Issue Department.

Advances and other accounts are of two main types: advances to the discount houses and loans to the remaining private customers of the Bank. The first are by far the most important to the operation of the monetary and financial system and attention is concentrated entirely on them. They are discussed in the section dealing with the discount market.

Premises, equipment and other securities and notes and coins can be dealt with briefly. Other securities are non-government securities and include bills purchased by the Bank in order to keep a watch on the quality of the bills circulating in the London market. The Bank will not purchase bills of which they disapprove and this acts as a deterrent to their circulation. Other securities also include some holdings of equity share capital of other companies. Notes are the counterpart of the item in the Issue Department and some coin is held for ordinary business purposes.

---

1 See below, p. 74.

2 A 'bill' in the sense used here is a piece of paper which is evidence of indebtedness on the part of the person or body on whom it is drawn. The bill is said to be 'discounted' when it is purchased at a price below its value on maturity. Hence Treasury bills are evidence of indebtedness of the Treasury. These bills have usually ninety days to run to maturity and might be acquired by the discount houses at, say, £97.50 per £100, which would represent a discount of approximately 10% per annum on the value at maturity.

III.3   Money and Credit Control and the Bank of England

It was indicated above (p. 60) that in the late 1960s the Bank became increasingly concerned that its use of quantitative and qualitative controls for the purposes of monetary and credit policy adversely affected the efficiency and operation of the banking and financial system. After very careful study it issued in May 1971 a consultative document entitled 'Competition and Credit Control', setting out proposals which purported to have 'the objective of combining an effective measure of control over credit conditions with greater scope for competition and innovation'.[1]

The main proposals in the document were:

(i)   to introduce right across the banking system a uniform minimum reserve assets ratio fixed at 12.5% of its sterling deposit liabilities,
(ii)   to extend the special deposits scheme to all banks, enabling the Bank to call for additional deposits to be made with it; and
(iii)   that the London and Scottish clearing banks should abandon their cartel arrangements for the fixing of interest rates.

The foregoing proposals, after detailed discussions with the interested institutions, became effective from 16 September 1971. Separate proposals were put before the discount houses and finance houses; these are considered later.

The detailed definition of sterling deposit liabilities or what are now called eligible liabilities of the banks gives rise in practice to certain difficulties. The Bank has, for instance, excluded from the total, deposits, except certificates of deposit, having an original maturity of over two years, since it considers these to be more akin to loan capital, but it includes sterling arising from switching foreign currencies into sterling. Inter-bank transactions, including transactions with the discount market, and transit items both within individual banks and between banks are dealt with in special ways in order to eliminate double counting.

From the point of view of monetary policy the most important question about the eligible liabilities total is whether or not it is the appropriate aggregate for stabilization purposes. In other words is there a reasonably stable and predictable relationship between the chosen aggregate and some measure of economic activity such as nominal income? A necessary condition for this to be true would seem to be that the components of the chosen aggregate should be 'highly substitutable one with another but largely complementary with other assets excluded from the aggregate'.[2] In the present case this is unlikely as eligible liabilities vary from demand deposits at one end to term deposits at the other, with, as mentioned previously, a maximum life of two years. This has led to the surmise that the Bank chose the eligible liabilities total not primarily for the reason indicated above but because in the implementation of monetary policy it wished to treat all banks more or less equally since, for many years, it has been arguable that the London and Scottish clearing banks bore the brunt of restrictive monetary policies.[3] However, to impose *equal* reserve ratios on banks which would ordinarily operate

---

1   *BEQB*, vol. 11, no. 2, June 1971, p. 189.
2   H. G. Johnson, 'Harking Back to Radcliffe', *The Bankers' Magazine*, September 1971, p. 117.
3   Ibid.

with very different asset and liability distributions is to affect their earnings very differently and in this respect is not equal treatment at all – the uniform reserve ratio may, in fact, be regarded as a form of discriminatory taxation. But it may be presumed that the authorities felt that in the interests of monetary and credit control over a greatly enlarged banking system these considerations had to be put aside.

The assets which are eligible for inclusion as reserve assets are very carefully defined. They 'comprise *balances with the Bank of England* (other than special and supplementary deposits); *money at call* (secured and immediately callable) with the listed discount market institutions . . . and with listed brokers; British government and Northern Ireland government *Treasury bills*; UK *local authority bills* eligible for rediscount at the Bank of England; commercial bills eligible for rediscount at the Bank of England – up to a maximum of 2% of eligible liabilities . . . , and *British government stocks* and stocks of nationalized industries guaranteed by the Government with one year or less to final maturity'.[1] In addition, the London clearing banks have to maintain as part of their minimum reserve ratio the equivalent of 1.5% of their eligible liabilities in balances at the head office of the Bank of England. Till-money is not eligible for inclusion as reserve assets.

The most striking features of the reserve assets are their variety and their concentration directly and indirectly on government securities. As far as the first point is concerned, it is widely agreed that for the purpose of effective control of a monetary aggregate it is essential for the reserve base to be under the control of the authorities and that the demand for it 'from the banks and the rest of the economy (be) both highly stable and highly predictable'.[2] This is generally felt to be true of cash holdings and hence helps to explain the historical attachment to the cash base as a means of controlling the money supply. However, it did not seem likely that this would be true of the assets eligible for inclusion in the reserve assets ratio and the evidence so far would seem to bear this out. The banking sector would appear to have had little difficulty in satisfying its reserve asset requirements since the introduction of the new scheme and indeed has been able to support a massive increase in deposits.[3] In principle, however, the Bank could have prevented or at least slowed down this growth of deposits if it had been prepared to restrict the expansion of the cash base of the system – notwithstanding the existence of the reserve assets ratio – always assuming of course, a reasonably stable and predictable relationship, which is not to say a constant relationship, between the cash base and the volume of deposits. It seems highly plausible to suppose that whatever the authorities may have said from time to time about the growth of deposits they were not – perhaps for good economic, social and political reasons – prepared to take the kind of actions required to curtail their rapid expansion. This statement,

---

1 Additional notes to table 3, *BEQB*, vol. 18, no. 1, March 1978. The listed discount market institutions are the discount houses, discount brokers and the money trading departments of listed banks – there are five of the latter. Listed brokers comprise money brokers and jobbers on the stock exchange. Eligible commercial bills are bills which are payable in the UK and have been accepted by certain approval banks (ibid).

2 M. J. Artis and J. M. Parkin, 'Competition and Credit Control: A General Appraisal', *The Bankers' Magazine*, September 1971, p. 113.

3 See below, p. 105. See also E. V. Morgan and R. L. Harrington, 'Reserve Assets and the Supply of Money', *MS*, March 1973, no. 1. pp. 73-87 and Michael Parkin, 'The Discount House's Role in the Money Supply Control Process under the Competition and Credit Control Regime', ibid., pp. 89-105.

however, needs some qualification as in the last few years the authorities have paid increasing attention to the rate of growth of deposits.

But to place excessive emphasis on the use of the reserve assets ratio as a means of controlling the supply of deposits is to misunderstand the intentions of the Bank. For spokesmen of the Bank made it abundantly clear at the time that they saw the new credit controls as an important means of retaining influence over *interest rates* in the short end of the market and not primarily as a means of controlling the volume of deposits. The then Governor of the Bank stated that 'It is not expected that the mechanism of the minimum asset ratio and special deposits can be used to achieve some precise multiple contraction or expansion of bank assets. Rather the intention is to use our control over liquidity, which these instruments will reinforce, to influence the structure of interest rates.'[1] Nevertheless, it is doubtful if a spokesman of the Bank would be prepared to make this statement today.

At the same time as the authorities announced their minimum reserve assets ratio they amended and extended the coverage of their interest-bearing special deposit scheme.[2] The initial version of the scheme required that each bank should be prepared to deposit with the Bank of England a uniform percentage of its eligible liabilities, that is, its sterling deposits suitably defined. The Bank intimated, however, that in the future it might want to call for special deposits at different percentage rates on domestic and overseas deposits.[3] And subsequently the Bank announced a revised scheme.

Under the revised scheme the Bank may as before decide to operate a uniform rate of call for special deposits applied to *all* eligible liabilities or — and this is new — a variable rate of call. The variability may be achieved in a number of ways. First, eligible overseas liabilities may be subject to a lower rate of call or be exempted from a particular call. Alternatively, the Bank may call for special deposits in relation to the *increase,* if any, in eligible overseas liabilities over a specified time period. The call may be in addition to or separate from a call applied to the *total* of each bank's eligible liabilities. The revised scheme clearly gives the Bank considerable flexibility in differentiating between domestic and overseas deposits in making calls for special deposits.

In December 1973 the Bank announced a non-interest-bearing special deposits scheme as a supplement to the existing scheme. The supplementary special deposits scheme is designed to curtail the growth of the banks' interest-bearing deposits and works as follows.

The Bank specifies a maximum or target rate of growth over a given time period for interest-bearing eligible liabilities and any growth in excess of this is subject to progressively higher rates of call for supplementary deposits. The initial maximum rate of growth specified by the Bank was 8% for the six months from November 1973 to May 1974, the November figure being defined as the average amount of interest-bearing eligible liabilities outstanding on the make-up days for October, November and December and likewise for the May figure. For rates of growth in excess of the 8% maximum the Bank announced calls for supplementary special deposits at the following rates: for an excess of 1% or less the rate of call was 5%;

---

1 'Key Issues in Monetary and Credit Policy', *BEQB*, vol. 11, no. 2, June 1971, p. 197.

2 The rate paid on interest-bearing special deposits is adjusted weekly to the nearest $\frac{1}{16}\%$ per annum to the average rate of discount for Treasury bills issued at the latest weekly tender.

3 'Competition and Credit Control: Further Developments', *BEQB*, vol. 13, no. 1, March 1973, pp. 51-5.

for an excess of over 1% but not more than 3% the rate was 25%; thereafter the rate of call was 50%.

The Bank subsequently announced revised targets and arrangements for the supplementary special deposits scheme. For August 1974 the reference level for calls and releases of supplementary deposits became 9.5% above the October–December 1973 average of interest-bearing eligible liabilities, rising to 17% for January 1975. The rates of call for a growth in eligible liabilities in excess of the permitted targets were changed to 5% for an excess of 3% or less, 25% for an excess over 3% but not more than 5%, and 50% thereafter. The scheme was temporarily suspended in February 1975, re-introduced in November 1976, suspended again in August 1977 and re-activated in June 1978.

Since the supplementary special deposits scheme has been operative for such a short period it is difficult to assess its significance as a restraint on the growth of interest-bearing eligible liabilities. However, there can be little doubt that it was designed, in effect, as a form of incremental tax to make 'excess' growth highly expensive to the banks. But like all such schemes directed at a particular area of a complex and interdependent monetary and financial system it very likely encourages institutions both subject to and outside the scheme (it also applies to finance houses) to provide alternative outlets for interest-seeking deposits. To the extent that that happens the scheme only succeeds in diverting money and credit flows away from the banks (and finance houses). And in so far as one of the proximate causes of the growth of interest-bearing deposits is the expansion or permitted expansion of the cash base of the system by the authorities themselves the scheme may in the longer term turn out to be relatively ineffective, at least as regards the overall problems of monetary and credit growth. In the short term, however, it may be somewhat more effective as it takes time for institutions, borrowers and lenders to find ways to circumvent such controls. However, that the institutions affected find the controls to be uncomfortable can scarcely be doubted since they have come to be called the 'corset'.

The foregoing discussion implies some scepticism about the effectiveness of the minimum reserve assets ratio and the special and supplementary special deposits schemes as instruments of monetary and credit policy and hence as means of influencing the pace of economic activity, inflation and other economic magnitudes. The fundamental reason for this scepticism is the relative unwillingness – at least until recently – of the authorities to curtail the rate of growth of bank deposits. In other words the authorities have been prepared to provide the cash that enables the growth to take place. No doubt the reasons for this are complex and indeed the problems of controlling the cash base of the monetary system in an open economy subject to large capital flows should not be underestimated. Having said this, however, there remains the strong misgiving that the attention given to the minimum reserve assets ratios and the special deposits schemes is in part an evasion of the basic problem of the availability of cash to the system. Why this should be so raises many difficult problems including the scale and role of government financing and debt management and ultimately perhaps the functioning of our whole economic, political and social system.

III.4 The Discount Market

The discount market is officially described as being made up of thirteen discount houses, two discount brokers and the money trading departments of five banks

which all carry on essentially the same type of business. The discount houses are a
special type of financial institution which borrows a substantial proportion of its
funds from the clearing banks and other institutional lenders such as accepting
houses, other British banks and overseas banks. Most of these funds are at call or on
overnight loan and hence lenders may demand their repayment immediately or
subject to very short notice. The discount houses use these borrowed funds to
acquire both sterling and other currency assets. The assets include short-dated
British government securities, Treasury bills, commercial bills, local authority bills
and securities and certificates of deposit. Under the new credit control arrangements the discount houses were first obliged to hold a minimum of 50% of their
eligible borrowed funds in 'British government and Northern Ireland government
Treasury bills, local bills and bonds and British government-guaranteed and local
authority stocks with not more than five years to run to maturity'.[1]

In practice, however, the Bank found that the operation of the compulsory
minimum public sector debt ratio had many disadvantages. In particular, it
produced interest rate distortions in short-term money markets and complicated
'the Bank's task of securing adequate influence over credit extended by the
discount market'.[2] The distortions arose primarily when a house or houses were
operating near to the limit of their public sector debt ratio. In these circumstances
if a house wished to acquire other assets it could only do so by simultaneously
purchasing public sector assets. This had the effect of pushing rates on the latter to
relatively low levels in comparison with rates on other assets. Similar problems
arose when the Bank attempted to give help to the market through the purchase of
public sector assets.

For reasons such as these the Bank abolished the public sector debt ratio
and replaced it from 19 July 1973 with a new form of control. This limits for
each member of the discount market its aggregate holdings of what are clumsily
called 'undefined assets'—largely private sector assets— to a maximum of twenty
times its capital and reserves.[3] The actual ratio these undefined assets bear to capital
and reserves is known as the 'undefined assets multiple'. The new control should
avoid at least some of the major distortions that arose from the use of the former
public sector debt ratio. Nevertheless it still discriminates in favour of the public
sector and could clearly give rise to difficulties for members experiencing a loss
of reserves and thus inhibit their ability to expand. The capital resources base for
the calculation of the multiple was £147m for 1978; it is calculated as a three-year
moving average of the end of December figure of the net worth of each member. If
the clearing banks or other lenders demand repayment of their loans and the
discount market cannot borrow elsewhere or otherwise obtain funds, the members
turn to the Bank of England which makes funds available to them against suitable

---

1 'Competition and Credit Control: the Discount Market', *BEQB,* vol. 11, no. 3, September
   1971, p. 314. Company tax reserve certificates were also eligible for inclusion in the public
   sector lending ratio.
2 'Competition and Credit Control: Modified Arrangements for the Discount Market', *BEQB,*
   vol. 13, no. 3, September 1973, pp. 306-7.
3 Undefined assets are all assets other than the following: balances at the Bank of England;
   UK and NI Treasury bills, British government and local authority stocks with not more than
   five years to final maturity; local authority and other public boards' bills eligible at the
   Bank; local authority negotiable bonds; and bank bills drawn by nationalized industries
   under specific government guarantee. Source: *BEQB,* vol. 18, no. 1, March 1978.

TABLE 2.3

Discount Market (selected items), 14 December 1977 (£m)

Borrowed funds		*Assets*	
Sterling: Bank of England	246	Sterling: UK and NI	
Other UK banking sector	2,963	Treasury bills	1,052
Other UK	325	Other public sector bills	182
Overseas	76	Other bills	1,031
Other currencies:		Certificates of deposit	509
UK banking sector	73	Other funds lent	170
Other UK	15	British government stocks	557
Overseas	54	Other investments	286
		Other currencies:	
		Certificates of deposit	115
		Other assets	32
	3,752		3,934

Source: BEQB
Note: Total undefined assets £1,945m; undefined assets multiple 15.9.

collateral which, except for eligible bank bills, consists of the public sector assets formerly included in the public sector debt ratio. Furthermore, the collateral must include a minimum proportion of Treasury bills. The members of the discount market are the only financial institutions which have automatic access to the Bank in this way. This privilege was extended to the discount houses on the understanding that they apply each week for the full amount of the Treasury bill issue.

The traditional practice was that the Bank acted as lender of last resort to the monetary and financial system, through the intermediation of the discount houses, by lending to them at or above a rate called Bank rate. But with the increased flexibility of short-term rates following the introduction of the new credit control arrangements in September 1971 the significance of Bank rate, which had formerly been a major reference point for other rates, declined. By September 1972 the rate on Treasury bills which historically had always been below Bank rate jumped to almost 1% above it. With the approval of the Chancellor of the Exchequer the Bank published 'new arrangements for determining and announcing their minimum rate for lending to the (discount) market. From 13 October 1972, the lending rate was to be ½% above the average rate of discount for Treasury bills at the most recent tender, rounded to the nearest ¼% above'.[1] The Bank, however, retained the right to depart from these arrangements and if need be announce independently of them a change in the *minimum lending rate* – the title which has superseded Bank rate.[2] And on 11 March 1977 a further modification was made; 'where the operation of the formula would bring about a reduction in the rate, the Bank reserve the right, exceptionally, either to leave the rate unchanged, or to change it by less than would result from the operation of the formula.[3]

---

1 'Commentary', *BEQB*, vol. 12, no. 4, December 1972, p. 443.
2 The Bank did in fact depart from the minimum lending rate formula on 13 November 1973 when it raised the rate from 11¼ to 13%. The operation of the formula was restored when market rates adjusted to the new rate. On 25 May 1978 it was announced that minimum lending rate would be determined by administrative decision and any change would normally be announced at 12.30 pm on a Thursday; the new rate would become effective immediately (*FS*, June 1978).
3 See Additional notes to table 9, *BEQB*, vol. 18, no. 1, March 1978.

Traditionally, Bank rate was described as a penal rate as it was generally at a level in excess of what were called 'market rates' — the rates ruling in the market for Treasury bills and prime bank bills. The theory was that if the discount houses were borrowing at Bank rate they were therefore making losses and would hasten to pay off their debts to the Bank, with a consequential reduction in the cash base of the banking system. However, there were periods when public sector debt of the kind held by the discount houses yielded more than Bank rate. Thus the penal rate argument would not be valid for borrowings from the Bank against these securities and a similar argument holds as regards the minimum lending rate. Moreover, it is conceivable that if the discount houses were expecting a reduction in interest rates they might be prepared to borrow for a time at the so-called penal rates to take advantage of capital appreciation and high running yields on some or all of their asset holdings. The Bank, of course, has the option, which it may or may not use, to charge more than the minimum lending rate or to raise it. However, it is clear that the penal rate argument is not totally convincing, though the Bank is now in such a powerful position in relation to the very existence of the market that it is almost inconceivable that it would flout the wishes of the authorities.

For many years, however, the Bank has helped to relieve cash shortages in the money market by purchasing bills from the members at market rates, as well as providing funds at Bank rate (or, now, minimum lending rate) or above, depending on which the Bank felt was more appropriate in the light of monetary and economic conditions. Furthermore, in June 1966 the Bank introduced an important modification in its method of lending. Previously *loans* to the discount houses had usually been for a minimum period of seven days and charged at Bank rate or occasionally above. But since then the Bank is prepared to lend overnight and generally at market rates.

Thus the Bank now exercises great flexibility in the supply of funds to the discount market. The Bank is also prepared to absorb by sales of bills to the discount houses surplus funds that they cannot otherwise conveniently employ. The Bank is therefore in a commanding position to influence day-to-day rates in this money market.

The discount houses occupy a very special position in the market for Treasury bills. Before the introduction of the new credit control arrangements the discount houses tendered as a syndicate at a single rate for the whole weekly issue of Treasury bills. Under the new arrangements and with the encouragement of the authorities they still tender for the whole issue but no longer at an agreed rate.

Covering the tender has the merit from the point of view of the Treasury that it 'guarantees' them the funds and probably helps the authorities to stabilize Treasury bill and other short-term rates. However, from another point of view the procedure is an odd one. For in the final analysis the discount houses are able to tender for the whole Treasury bill issue because, as already explained, the Bank stands ready to support them. Moreover, they would presumably become concerned if they could only cover the tender over a sustained period by borrowing at minimum lending rate. To avoid this the Bank may, as has been shown, supply the discount houses with funds at market rates. The discount houses then use the funds to acquire the new Treasury bills. But this is tantamount to the Bank lending directly to the Treasury and so increasing the cash base of the banking system, as the Treasury spends the funds, unless the whole process is offset in some other way, such as by the Bank selling securities to the non-bank public.

There may be, in fact, an element of charade about the whole procedure of the discount houses tendering for the full Treasury bill issue. The danger is that the charade hides what is really happening – the financing of the Treasury by borrowing from the Central Bank. This may tend to subordinate monetary policy to the exigencies of government financial needs; and there is a lot of evidence to suggest that the consequences of this may be inflationary. Moreover, the procedure, and indeed the whole treatment of the discount market is inconsistent with the competitive determination of interest rates by market processes, emphasized by the Bank in introducing the new credit control arrangements.

III.5   The London Clearing Banks[1]

The London clearing banks are so named because they are all members of the Committee of London Clearing Bankers. Up to 1968 there were eleven clearing banks, although not all of them were independent. But with the mergers of 1968 and 1970 only six clearing banks remain and these also are not all independent. The banks are dominated by the big four, Barclays, National Westminster, Lloyds and Midland, who between them control over 95% of total deposits and have a network of over 12,000 branches. The clearing banks' primary function is the management of the payments system in England and Wales, although they necessarily carry out all the usual commercial banking functions and, since the introduction of the new credit control arrangements and the greater freedom that has gone with them, have shown themselves increasingly willing to compete for time deposits, including negotiable certificates of deposit.

For many years the clearing banks acted as a cartel in fixing the interest rates they paid on deposits and charged on advances. These practices had come in for increasing criticism because of the encouragement they undoubtedly gave to uneconomic non-price competition, especially in the form of branch extension, and the general lack of dynamism they had imparted to the whole system. It would, however, be false to argue that the banks had totally stood aside from competing in terms of price for deposits and in granting credit. For many of them had done so through subsidiaries and associated companies such as finance houses (described below) and other financial institutions. To be unduly critical of the banks may be unjustified as it is highly likely that the authorities, with their predilection for short-run stability of nominal interest rates, condoned the existence of the cartel arrangements and would not have welcomed interest rate competition by the banks for deposits and advances.

Sight deposits and time deposits are the main liabilities of the London clearing banks. Sight deposits, which may or may not be interest-bearing, are withdrawable on demand and transferable by cheque; they are the most important means of payment in the economy. Until the introduction of the new credit control arrangements in September 1971 time deposits were interest-bearing and subject to notice of withdrawal, generally seven days, and not ordinarily transferable by cheque. However, these conditions could be waived, though usually with some loss of interest. Since September 1971, however, the London clearing banks have in addition been prepared to take what are called fixed term deposits; that is, deposits

---

1   Limitations on space do not permit discussion of the Scottish clearing banks and the Northern Ireland banks which carry on very similar activities in Scotland and Northern Ireland respectively.

for fixed periods which may be far in excess of seven days. Deposits and other items of the balance sheet of the London clearing banks for December 1977 may be seen in table 2.4.

TABLE 2.4

London Clearing Banks, 14 December 1977 (£m)

(i) *Liabilities*	Sterling[1]	Other Currencies[2]	Total
Sight and time deposits:			
UK banking sector	1,664	1,076	2,740
Other UK	22,874	538	23,412
Overseas	1,356	3,609	4,965
Certificates of deposit	1,306	271	1,577
Capital and other liabilities	–	–	6,612
	27,200	5,494	39,306

(ii) *Assets*	Sterling	Other Currencies[2]	Total
Notes and coin	867	–	867
Reserve assets: Balance with			
Bank of England	419	–	419
Money at call	1,095	–	1,095
UK and NI Treasury bills	710	–	710
Other bills	522	–	522
British government stocks up to 1 year	321	–	321
Special and supplementary deposits	668	–	668
Market loans and advances (other than reserve assets):			
Banks in UK and discount market	2,945	1,425	4,370
Certificates of deposit	540	108	648
UK public sector	412	685	1,097
UK private sector	219	821	1,040
Overseas	2,545	2,510	5,055
Other advances	14,360	–	14,360
British government stocks over 1 year and undated	1,532	–	1,532
Other investments	980	169	1,149
Bills	340	22	362
Sterling and other currencies miscellaneous assets	–	–	5,092
	28,475	5,740	39,307

Source: BEQB.

Notes: Eligible liabilities £22,799m. Reserve assets £3,067m. Ratio 13.5%.

1 Of total sterling deposits of £27,200m, sight deposits amounted to £13,133m.

2 The figures are affected by changes in exchange rates.

Closely related to the fixed term deposits, though with at least one fundamental difference because of their negotiability, are negotiable certificates of deposit. These too have only appeared in the balance sheets of the London clearing banks since September 1971. The certificates are generally denominated in either sterling or US dollars. In the words of the Bank of England: 'A sterling certificate of deposit is a document, issued by a UK office of a British or foreign bank, certifying that a sterling deposit has been made with that bank which is repayable to the bearer upon the surrender of the certificate at maturity'.[1] The definition of a dollar certificate of deposit is analogous.

A sterling certificate of deposit is generally for a minimum amount of £50,000 and normally a maximum of £500,000 'with a term to maturity of not less than three months and not longer than five years'.[2] Certificates of deposit have advantages for both the issuers and the holders. Issuing banks have found them to be a useful means of raising large amounts for strictly fixed periods—unlike the so-called fixed term deposit where payment may be requested, and be hard to refuse, before maturity. And holders have found them highly convenient as they can sell them in the secondary market if they need liquid funds. The discount houses are the major operators in the secondary market. Certificates of deposit first made their appearance in the UK in May 1966 with the introduction of certificates denominated in dollars. Sterling certificates did not appear until October 1968.

Turning to the assets part of the balance sheet it may be seen that these consist of notes and coin, the various kinds of reserve assets, special and supplementary special deposits, different types of market loans and advances, British government stocks of more than one year to maturity and certain miscellaneous assets. Some of these items require further discussion.

Notes and coin are used by the banks for their day-to-day business. The reserve assets include balances with the Bank of England which the banks use to settle their inter-bank indebtedness and to make payments to the authorities. If for some reason a bank, or the London clearing banks as a whole, find that their cash holdings are tending to fall below some desired ratio to deposits, they can rectify the position in a number of ways. It may be possible for them to sell or exchange some of their assets for cash, drawing on their balances with other UK banks, by selling stocks or negotiating repayment of advances or by recalling some of their money at call — another reserve asset — from the discount market. If the latter happens the discount market may, as already explained, have to turn for assistance to the Bank of England. This will generally happen if the banking system as a whole is short of cash. If the Bank does not wish to lend at its minimum lending rate, perhaps because it is anxious to keep interest rates from rising, then it will normally enter the open market and purchase securities at market rates, paying for them with cheques drawn on the Bank and so relieving the cash shortage. However, if the Bank wishes to see some upward pressure on interest rates it will wait for the discount houses to come to the Bank and only make cash available at the minimum lending rate or even possibly above.

In so far as the Bank is not prepared to make a permanent net addition to the stock of cash available and ruling out a surplus of cash in the rest of the banking system then, unless there is an inflow of funds from abroad and which the authorities do not neutralize, some reduction in deposits of the London clearing banks or in the deposits of the banking sector as a whole may be expected. One of the consequences of this is likely to be upward pressure on interest rates.

Of the remaining reserve assets shown in table 2.4 money at call includes not only funds lent to the discount houses but also funds lent for periods not exceed-

1 'Sterling Certificates on Deposit', *BEQB*, vol. 12, no. 4. December 1972, p. 487. See also 'Sterling Certificates of Deposit and the Inter-Bank Market', *BEQB*, vol. 13, no. 3, September 1973, pp. 308-14; and the 'London Dollar Certificate of Deposit', *BEQB*, vol. 13, no. 4, December 1973, pp. 446-52.

2 *BEQB*, vol. 12, p. 487.

ing one month to money brokers on the stock exchange, discount brokers, jobbers and stockbrokers and bullion brokers. Treasury bills and other bills have been described previously. The London clearing banks, by an understanding with the discount houses and the Bank of England, do not generally bid for Treasury bills at the weekly tender, at least not for themselves, though they may do so on behalf of clients. Bills bought on their own account by the clearing banks are usually held to maturity, though they are, on occasion, sold to the Bank if the latter is looking for maturities that are no longer held by the discount houses. The purchase of bills by the Bank from the clearing banks is one of the ways by which the Bank may relieve pressure on the discount houses and obviate their need to borrow at Bank rate or above. This is described as 'indirect help' to the discount houses as opposed to 'direct help' by means of purchases from the houses themselves.

Special and supplementary special deposits which have already been discussed need not be considered further. Market loans and advances includes a wide range of assets some of which are indicated in table 2.4. Loans to the discount market refer to funds which are not immediately callable and are unsecured in contrast with the money at call included in reserve assets. Advances, which are quantitatively of major importance, comprise not only other advances but also advances in other currencies under various headings and not individually specified. Advances are of two main types, loans and overdrafts. With the loan the customer's account is credited with the amount whereas the overdraft is literally an overdrawing of a current account which is debited accordingly. Advances are generally assumed to be the most lucrative of the banks' assets. Until the introduction of the new credit control arrangements by the London clearing banks, rates on advances were tied to Bank rate under their cartel agreements on interest rates. Each bank now fixes what it calls a *base* rate for advances. The base rate may and does differ between the banks but is generally close to the minimum lending rate of the Bank of England. The actual rates charged for advances varies with the nature and status of the customer but most rates are between 1% and 5% higher than the base rate. The London clearing banks do, however, have uniform rates for nationalized industries borrowing under Treasury guarantee and for certain other government-supported borrowing.

The London clearing banks have responded to the increased flexibility provided by the new competition and credit control arrangements by competing more strongly amongst themselves and with other financial institutions. This is indicated by the marked change in their balance sheets over the last few years, both in terms of their rate of growth and of the structure of their liabilities and assets. They are now much more actively involved in what has been called the parallel money markets, such as the market for negotiable certificates of deposit, the inter-bank sterling deposits market—both as borrowers and lenders—and similarly in the euro-dollar market; that is, the market or markets for US dollars held outside the US. In each of these ways the London clearing banks have in recent years diversified their activities and in so doing have narrowed some of the differences between themselves and other types of bank. However, the London clearing banks, like their Scottish and Northern Ireland counterparts, have a predominant proportion of their assets and liabilities in sterling and remain largely responsible for the day-to-day payments system; other types of bank, as will be seen in the next section, tend to concentrate their activities in other currencies.

III.6 Accepting Houses, Other British Banks, Overseas Banks and Consortium Banks

The business of this group of banks varies substantially amongst themselves, although they have enough in common to allow them to be discussed together. Since about 1957-8, when exchange control restrictions were substantially relaxed and funds could begin to move more freely between international financial centres, the accepting houses, other British banks, overseas banks and, more recently, consortium banks, have greatly expanded, and at a much more rapid rate then the clearing banks. Moreover, these banks have been active participants in the development of new and important money markets.

The term 'accepting house' arose because of the important role the houses played and that many still play in 'accepting' bills of exchange, the commercial or financial bill already encountered in the discussion of the discount houses and the clearing banks. A bill is accepted by signing it and in so doing the acceptor becomes liable for payment of the bill on maturity. The accepting houses accept bills on behalf of clients and in this way earn commissions.

Accepting houses are also known as merchant banks since the banking side of their activities generally emerged as a consequence of their business as merchants, particularly in overseas trade. The activities of the accepting houses are excitingly diverse. The individual houses engage in one or more of the following activities: in the gold and silver bullion markets, the foreign exchange market, the foreign currency deposit business—including certificates of deposit—the making of new issues of both domestic and overseas securities, advising on mergers and takeovers, managing investments on behalf of clients, and acting as trustees.

Other British banks refers to banks with majority UK ownership, leaving aside consortium banks which have foreign participation. The group also includes the offices in GB of the NI banks and also branches of their subsidiaries. The composition of the group is very diverse; it now consists of over seventy members some of whom were formerly classified as finance houses as well as highly specialized banks in the fields of investment and international finance.

The overseas banks are banks which maintain branches or subsidiaries in London but whose main business is overseas. There are now about 190 of these compared with around 80 in the early 1960s; they play a major part in the movement of funds into and out of London and in the finance of international trade. Of the 190 almost 60 are branches and subsidiaries of American banks and some twenty of Japanese banks.

Consortium banks are a recently introduced classification. There are nearly 30 of them and they are predominantly concerned with international finance and the management of foreign currency deposits.

In terms of total deposits this group of banks far exceeds in size the London clearing banks. In mid-December 1977 the former had deposits totalling some £140,000m whilst the latter had some £33,000m. These are, however, gross figures and include inter-bank transactions as well as some internal accounts. This element of double counting inflates the figures of the other types of bank to a proportionately greater extent than it does those of the London clearing banks. Nevertheless, in the last twenty years there has been a radical restructuring of the banking system in the UK with the growth of these banks. The scale of the change can perhaps be appreciated when it is recalled that their deposits totalled less than £1,000m in the late 1950s.

TABLE 2.5

Accepting Houses, Other UK Banks, Overseas Banks and Consortium Banks, 14 December 1977 (£m)

(i)   *Liabilities*

	Sterling[1]	Other Currencies[2]	Total
Deposits:			
UK banking sector	9,486	22,247	31,733
Other UK	9,503	3,269	12,772
Overseas	3,128	76,842	79,970
Certificates of deposit	3,181	12,116	15,297
Capital and other liabilities	–	–	5,706
	25,298	114,474	145,478

(ii)   *Assets*

	Sterling	Other Currencies[2]	Total
Notes and coin	34	–	34
Reserve assets: balances with Bank of England	6	–	6
Money at call	1,536	–	1,536
UK and NI Treasury bills	692	–	692
Other bills	266	–	266
British government stocks up to 1 year	58	–	58
Special and supplementary deposits	436	–	436
Market loans and advances (other than reserve assets):			
Banks in UK and discount market	8,050	22,985	31,035
Certificates of deposit	2,232	1,753	3,985
UK public sector	2,172	3,082	5,254
UK private sector	963	6,439	7,402
Overseas	372	79,302	79,674
Other advances	10,475	–	10,475
British government stocks over 1 year and undated	636	–	636
Other investments	714	1,074	1,788
Bills	323	421	744
Sterling and other currencies miscellaneous assets	–	–	1,440
	28,965	115,056	145,461

Source: BEQB.
Notes: Eligible liabilities £14,832m. Reserve Assets £2,558m. Ratio 17.2%.
  1 Of total sterling deposits of £25,298m sight deposits amounted to £4,957m.
  2 The figures are affected by changes in exchange rates.

It might, however, be argued that to contrast the total deposits of this group of banks with those of the London clearing banks is to exaggerate the significance of the growth of the former since so much of that growth has taken the form of foreign currency deposits or what is widely called euro-currency business, as may be seen in table 2.5. It should be noticed that the foreign currency deposits are roughly matched by foreign currency assets. To the extent that this is the case they do not directly affect the UK gold and foreign currency reserves. However, there may be indirect effects, both on the foreign currency reserves and on the management of monetary and credit policy generally, through the earnings of the banks and through effects on interest rates, which will necessarily have repercussions on the highly integrated London money markets.

But even in terms of sterling deposits this group of banks has come to rival the London clearing banks in terms of size, with liabilities of some £25,000m and £27,000m respectively in mid-December 1977. However, for the purposes of monetary and credit control the eligible liabilities of this group of banks of almost £15,000m in mid-December 1977 remain somewhat less than the nearly £23,000m of the London clearing banks. But there can be no doubting the dramatic changes that have taken place in the UK banking system and there is good reason to believe that those changes accelerated in the past five years or so, in part under the influence of the new competition and credit control arrangements.

Furthermore, it seems doubtful that the reserve assets ratio introduced under those arrangements, as a means of influencing the activities of the banking sector, has been entirely successful. It would not be surprising if the authorities are at some stage forced to reconsider the introduction of cash ratios for the banking sector. This is not to suggest that cash ratios are necessarily a panacea for an effective monetary and credit policy but they just might make it rather more easy to influence the behaviour of the monetary aggregates. Furthermore, the banking sector of the UK now operates on what would appear to be an extremely narrow cash base, with this group of banks in particular holding practically no coin, notes and balances with the Bank of England.

III.7   Finance Houses and Other Consumer Credit Companies

A finance house is an institution which specializes in the financing of hire purchase, credit sales and other forms of instalment credit.[1] There are many companies involved in this business but the bulk of it is carried on by a small number of large firms. Hire purchase and credit sale, though legally distinct, generally take the form of a down-payment by the purchaser with the rest of the debt being paid off by instalments over a specified period. The period varies with the type of product and may be as little as six months for some household goods or as much as five years for industrial machinery; the period for cars—the most important type of hire purchase debt—may be up to three years.[2] The finance houses and consumer credit companies attempt to organize their contracts so that the debt outstanding at any time on the transaction is less than the value of the product being acquired; this gives them some security and indicates why they concentrate on financing the purchase of durable or semi-durable goods rather than perishable goods. In practice hire purchase debt is frequently paid off well in advance of the terminal period. This is important in assessing the liquidity of their assets.

Deposits are the single most important liability of the finance houses and consumer credit companies and are of two main kinds: fixed term deposits, usually for three or six months, and deposits subject to notice of withdrawal, again normally for three to six months. Deposits may, however, be for as long as twelve months or even longer. The deposits earn interest at rates which are greatly influenced by those ruling in the money markets, especially the inter-bank deposits market and the market for sterling certificates of deposit. The chief depositors are the banking sector, industrial and commercial companies, other financial institutions and other residents, as well as a small amount of funds from overseas residents.

---

1   See R. M. Goode 'Reflections on Credit Law', *The Three Banks Review,* March 1978, pp. 26-42.
2   These periods are subject to controls by the authorities.

Current accounts are not unknown amongst the finance houses but do not appear to be a significant part of their business. The banking sector provides most of the remaining funds to the finance houses by means of discounting bills and by advances. Capital reserves are also important.

Hire purchase and instalment credit generally accounts for the greater part of their assets with most of the remainder made up of other advances and loans, leased assets and as regards the finance houses, reserve assets under the new credit control arrangements. Not all the hire purchase and instalment credit outstanding is owed directly to the finance houses; part of it arises from the purchase by the latter of debt from retailers and is known as 'block discounts'. Retailers do of course retain some hire purchase debt, but the finance houses own the bulk of it. Other advances and loans include loans to garages (to finance stocks of vehicles) and to property companies and short-term loans to industrial and commercial companies. Until the introduction of the new credit control arrangements the finance houses held very few assets in liquid form, relying on their ability to attract additional deposits, on their borrowing powers and on the speedy repayment of their assets to meet any liquidity requirements.

The new credit control arrangements for the finance houses which come under the scheme are very similar to those applied to the banks. (Companies with eligible liabilities of less than £5m are exempt so long as they remain below this limit). The minimum reserve assets ratio for those within the scheme is 10% compared with 12.5% for the banks. The main reason indicated by the Bank for the difference is that the imposition of the reserve assets ratio was more of a burden on the finance houses than on the banks since the former in the ordinary way did not hold any eligible assets.

In December 1977 the eligible liabilities of the finance houses totalled only £329m and their holdings of reserve assets were £34.0m giving them a ratio of 10.3%. Like the banks, the finance houses are subject to calls for both special deposits and supplementary special deposits. As regards calls for special deposits the Bank has stated that they 'will normally be at the same rate as calls on the banks, but the Bank will have the right in certain defined circumstances to call special deposits from the finance houses at a higher rate. In no circumstances, however, will the total of reserve assets and special deposits represent a higher proportion of eligible liabilities for the finance houses than for the banks.'[1] Only five finance houses now come under the new credit control arrangements since a number of former finance houses have found it preferable to acquire the status of banks for purposes of the scheme.

It is clear that the introduction of a minimum reserve assets ratio for the finance houses imposed on them a significant burden, especially as the return on reserve assets tend to be below their cost of borrowing. Furthermore, the banking sector as a whole now offers the finance houses much more competition than before the advent of the new competition and credit control arrangements. In terms of size the finance houses and other consumer credit companies, excluding those which are now classified as banks, with total assets in September 1977 of some £2,000m are very small in relation to the banking sector.

To their cost, the finance houses have for many years — with some intermissions — been subject to the special attention of the authorities. From time to time they

---

1　'Reserve Ratios and Special Deposits', *BEQB*, Supplement, vol. 11, no. 3, September 1971.

have stipulated some of the terms on which the finance houses could do business; in particular the minimum down-payments that must be made on different products by borrowers and the maximum repayment periods. These kinds of restrictions on the activities of the finance houses have come in for much criticism because of their arbitrariness and selectivity and the`– at any rate short-run – disruptive effects they can have on the production and sales of certain consumer durable industries, especially the car industry. The Crowther Committee on consumer credit gave great impetus to criticisms such as these, recommending the abolition of terms control and credit ceilings and the encouragement generally of equal competition amongst credit institutions.[1] The new credit control arrangements as applied to the finance houses went some way in this direction, though they might legitimately claim that, as regards the problem of credit control, the authorities pay them more attention than the scale of their activities warrants.

III.8   Building Societies

Building societies are mutual or non-profit-making bodies which specialize in the provision of finance for the purchase of both new and secondhand houses. There are some 380 building societies, about one-sixth of the number some seventy years ago. The individual societies differ greatly in size from some very large ones with a national network of branches to those with only one office.

About 90% of the liabilities of the building societies are shares and deposits. Both are essentially deposits, so that the term share is something of a misnomer. However, the shareholder is a member of the society whereas the depositor is not, and the latter has a prior right of liquidation over the shareholder. Deposits earn a slightly lower rate of interest than shares. Shares and deposits are subject to notice of withdrawal, though in practice both are paid on demand or on very short notice. The interest rates on shares and deposits are quoted *net* of income tax, which is paid by the societies at an average or composite rate and is less than the basic rate of tax. In early 1978 the interest rates recommended by the Building Societies Association were 5.5% on paid-up shares and 5.25% on deposits. These rates are net of tax and are equivalent approximately to 8.2% and 7.8% respectively before deduction of basic tax and, much to the concern of the London clearing banks, are substantially in excess of the rates they offer on ordinary deposit accounts. Furthermore, the rate of growth of the shares and deposits of the building societies had been so rapid in recent years that with a total of almost £32,000m at the end of 1977 they are now substantially in excess of the total sterling deposits of the London clearing banks at £27,200m.

Mortgages usually account for over 80% of the assets of building societies and are predominantly for private house purchase. Most mortgages are for between twenty and thirty years with continuous repayment by instalments. The average life is generally about ten years, making the assets of building societies much shorter-lived than might appear. The recommended interest rate on new mortgages to owner occupiers was 8.5% in early 1978. But this is the gross rate as interest payments on a housing loan – up to £25,000 for a principal residence – are allowable against income tax assessments: if allowance is made for income tax relief at the basic rate the interest rate is reduced to about 5.7% net. For those who pay

---

1 *Report of the Committee on Consumer Credit,* Cmnd. 4596, HMSO, March 1971.

less than the basic rate of tax, or no tax at all, there is an option mortgage scheme, supported by the government, which reduces the cost.

All the other assets, except such things as office premises, are classified as liquid assets by the societies. Liquid assets must be at least 7.5% of total assets and both the type of asset and the maturity distribution are regulated by the Registrar of Building Societies. At the end of 1977 the actual liquid assets ratio was 21.8 of total assets. Cash holdings and balances with banks are relatively small and vary a lot seasonally.

The building societies dominate the market providing finance for home purchase and they are therefore relevant, directly and indirectly, to the activity of the house-building industry. The societies cannot for long expand the supply of finance to borrowers unless there is a corresponding net inflow of funds from new shares and deposits; otherwise they would deplete their liquid assets and in time risk upsetting public confidence in their management. The interest rates the societies pay and the relationship they bear to the competing rates would appear to be a major determinant of the net inflow of funds to the societies.

III.9   Other Financial Institutions

The United Kingdom is particularly rich in the variety and number of its financial institutions. The term 'rich' is used advisedly for financial institutions that are able to mediate freely between borrowers and lenders help to make the allocation of scarce resources more efficient. 'Improvements in their efficiency and the development of new financial intermediaries are analogous to productivity increases and innovations in industry.'[1] However, limitations on space prevent more than a brief mention of some of the remaining major financial institutions.

National Savings Bank and Trustee Savings Banks: The range of services offered by the National Savings Bank, formerly the Post Office Savings Bank, and Trustee Savings banks has increased considerably over the last ten years. Both sets of institutions, whilst remaining important as a means of channelling national savings to the state, now offer banking facilities, including current or chequing accounts and personal loans and overdrafts to their customers.

Basically the National Savings Bank and the Trustee Savings banks have three types of deposit: current accounts, ordinary deposits and investment-type deposits. In April 1978 ordinary deposits earn interest at 5% per year in the National Savings Bank and 4% per year in the Trustee Savings banks; the first £70 of interest is free of all income tax, giving a grossed-up rate of 7.46% for the former and 5.97% for the latter with a basic tax rate of 33%. The National Savings Bank pays 8½% on investment-type deposits subject to a maximum deposit of £50,000. The Trustee Savings banks pay varying rates of interest on investment-type deposits and have no maximum deposit rule.

It is only since 1976 that the number of Trustee Savings banks has been reduced from 72 to 18 and at the same time the current accounts of the ordinary department were combined with the investment-type accounts to form what is called the New department. The National Savings Bank carries on its current account banking and money transfer services through the National Giro, the latter being

---

1   N. J. Gibson, *Financial Intermediaries and Monetary Policy*, Hobart Paper 39, 2nd edition, Institute of Economic Affairs, 1970, p. 20.

officially part of the banking sector. By mid-December 1977 it had gross deposits of only £286m, though it had been in operation for some nine years. It is clearly a long way from being a serious competitor of the clearing banks.

Insurance Companies: There are some 600 insurance companies engaged in business in the UK, but by far the greater part of British business is carried on by the members of the British Insurance Association, which has less than three hundred members.

Insurance falls into two main categories: life assurance, and a catch-all, general insurance, which includes fire, marine, motor and other accident insurance. The insurance companies also operate the pension schemes of many industrial and commercial companies. Life assurance for the most part gives rise to long-term liabilities which the companies must be in a position to meet. This gives them an interest in long-term investments and in assets that may be expected to increase in capital value over the years. General insurance, on the other hand, is carried on much more on a year-to-year basis, ideally with premiums for the year being sufficient to cover the risks underwritten and to allow for expenses and the accumulation of limited reserves. So the disposition of funds arising from general insurance is largely governed by short-term considerations; assets must be quickly realizable without undue fear of capital loss.

The insurance companies, with total investments at the end of 1976 of around £30,000m, are of great importance in the UK's capital markets. They are large holders of both government and company securities.

Investment Trusts: Investment trusts are limited companies which specialize in the investment of funds provided by their shareholders or borrowed from debenture holders or other lenders. Despite the term 'trust' they do not operate, as do the unit trusts, under trust deeds which specify the terms and conditions governing the management of investment funds, but are, in fact, limited companies whose assets consist mainly of company securities and who are not allowed by their articles of association to distribute capital gains as dividends. In addition to investment trusts there are private investment companies and investment holding companies which often perform similar functions. But these are not considered to be investment trusts in the sense used here and are not discussed in this chapter. Attention is concentrated on the group of about 210 investment trusts that currently make returns to the Bank of England.

Investment trusts expand by raising funds from new capital issues, borrowing in the form of loan capital and by retaining some of the income and capital profits from previous investments. But once again it is the asset side of the balance sheets that is of chief interest. At the end of 1977 the total market value of assets of investment trusts making returns to the Bank of England was almost £6,500m. Most of this was invested in company securities, practically all ordinary shares. Some 35% of the company securities were those of overseas companies.

This extremely heavy concentration of investment in ordinary shares is a postwar phenomenon. Before the war investment trusts had substantial holdings of fixed interest securities. But the fear of inflation eroding the real value of fixed interest investments has encouraged the investment trusts to rearrange drastically the distribution of their assets. The size of the investment trusts makes them important operators in the ordinary share market. They also fulfil a useful function in helping to finance small companies by holding their unquoted securities. Their ability to invest overseas has from time to time been seriously affected by government restrictions and tax measures.

Unit Trusts: Unit trusts perform a similar function to investment trusts. But unlike the latter they do operate under trust deeds and have trustees, often a bank or insurance company. The unit trusts are authorized by the Department of Trade and are run by managers who are quite distinct from the trustees. Three hundred and seventy unit trusts made returns to the Bank of England at the end of 1977 and the number continues to grow; in 1960 the figure was fifty-one.

Unit trusts do not issue share capital and are not limited companies but they issue units which give the owners the right to participate in the beneficial ownership of the trusts' assets. The units are highly marketable as they can always be bought from or sold to the managers at prices which reflect the market value of the under-lying assets. As more units are demanded the managers provide more; for this reason they are sometimes called 'open-end' trusts, as opposed to 'closed-end' trusts such as the investment trusts which do not expand in this way.

Like the investment trusts the assets of the unit trusts are almost entirely company securities, made up of ordinary shares. But in contrast to the investment trusts, almost 88% of the assets are currently domestic and about 12% overseas. At the end of 1977 the total assets of the unit trusts were £3,364m. Their rate of growth has been rapid; in 1960 their total assets were only £190m. Their growth may be an attempt by small investors and others to protect themselves against inflation by participating indirectly in ordinary share investment.

The Stock Exchange: The Stock Exchange is an association of stockjobbers and stockbrokers and provides a market for variable price securities, both government and company securities. Without this market where securities may readily be bought and sold, the whole business of raising funds through outside sources would tend to be more expensive and less efficient. Since March 1973 the Stock Exchange comprises the Stock Exchange of the UK and the Republic of Ireland. Before that date, though with close links, they were distinct organizations.

A feature of the Stock Exchange is the jobbing system. Jobbers are traders in securities; they act as principals, buying and selling on their own account and making their profits on the difference between their buying and selling prices, which they generally stand ready to quote for the securities in which they specialize. This function can be extremely important in giving stability to the market which might otherwise be much more volatile and possibly mislead investors.

Brokers generally act as agents for customers, buying and selling on their behalf, usually but not always through jobbers.

Speculation is a term frequently associated with the Stock Exchange and nearly always carries overtones of abuse and criticism. To some degree this may reflect ignorance of the functions of the Stock Exchange, though this is not to imply that speculation is always economically and socially beneficial. But the speculator at his best, if he is doing his job properly, will be helping to keep the price of shares in touch with economic realities, damping down the effects of irrelevant rumours and false information; he will, in fact, be improving one part of the communications network of the economic system. However, the economic, social and moral implications of speculation are much wider and more far reaching than can be dealt with here.

Traditionally the terms 'bulls' and 'bears' have been applied to particular types of speculation though they are now used more generally to refer respectively to markets tending to rise and fall in price. But traditionally a 'bull' was someone who bought securities on a rising market hoping he would be able to sell them at a profit before he had to pay for his purchase. The 'bear' sold the shares that he had not got, on a falling market, in the hope that he would be able subsequently to buy and deliver them at a lower price.

An idea of the scale of Stock Exchange activities can be obtained from the figures on turnover; that is, sales and purchases. The total turnover during 1977 was about £173,000m, a relatively good year. Turnover of British government securities was some £136,000m. Clearly the Stock Exchange is of major importance to the financial activities of both the public and private sectors of the economy.[1]

IV   THE TAXATION SYSTEM
IV.1   Introduction

Taxation and the role of government in society are necessarily closely linked and discussion of the one involves some consideration of the other. It is often said that taxation in a market economy has three main functions: (1) to provide or encourage the provision of goods and services that are not easily or adequately supplied by the market if left to itself, and also to discourage the provision of those goods and services that are considered to have harmful effects on society – and perhaps the reverse for those goods and services which are considered beneficial to society; (2) to redistribute income and wealth; and (3) to facilitate the exercise of fiscal policy as a means of economic stabilization.

The first may be approached by making a distinction between so-called private and public goods and noting a possible discrepancy between private and public costs and benefits; what has come to be called the externalities problem. A private good refers to those goods where the utility a person gets from their consumption depends on how much of them he has and at the same time the more he has the less anyone else gets. Public goods on the other hand are such that once the goods are produced their consumption by one person does not diminish the amount available to others. Any kind of food is an example of a private good and some forms of national defence are an example of public goods. The market system can by and large handle the problem of producing and pricing private goods but not public goods since the price system cannot operate effectively to determine an appropriate amount to produce, nor determine its distribution. It needs to be stressed immediately that pure private goods and pure public goods are extreme cases and that, in general, elements of both may be combined in the same good.

Externalities are said to arise when the costs and benefits are not internalized to the individual producer or consumer. A typical example is what has been called the 'smoke nuisance', when a producer engages in a productive activity that gives off smoke and spreads grime and dirt in the immediate neighbourhood and possibly causes chemical erosion of buildings in the surrounding area. The costs of these nuisances are generally not voluntarily paid for by the producer and reflected in the quantity produced and price of his product. This kind of example could be greatly extended, as could similar examples on the benefits side. Indeed, in so far

---

1   The effects of taxation on the operation of the capital market are touched on below, pp. 94–5.

as a so-called public good was provided privately it would be an example of external benefits being conferred widely throughout a community. Clearly, externalities pose a fundamental problem for society, and in particular suggest that where they are present in a market-based economy, the market if left to itself will produce too much of a good which imposes external costs on the society and too little of a good which confers external benefits on it. In such circumstances there seems to be no simple answer to the question, on the one hand of the appropriate domain of market processes and, on the other, of the role of government. These are difficult and far-reaching issues in political economy.

The second function of taxation – the redistribution of income and wealth – is closely related to the matters just discussed. For there is no self-evident reason why a competitive market economy should lead to an optimum distribution of income and wealth – however difficult that may be to define – so governments have come to use taxation and the revenue raised thereby to bring about some redistribution. It should perhaps be said that there is also no obvious reason why government re-distribution policies will be optimal since the distribution and exercise of political power in society also begs some fundamental and intractable questions.

The third function of taxation as an aspect of fiscal stabilization policy is already familiar from earlier discussion in this chapter and the preceding one.

IV.2   The Size of Government

It is well known that in this century governments have become, in terms of their own activities, far more important in relation to the economic life of the community. Nevertheless, it is by no means straightforward to measure the size of government economic activity relatively to the rest of the economic system. Perhaps the best that can be done is to take a number of different measures.[1]

One of these is the direct claims the general government makes on the volume of goods and services available to the community in any time period. In this context 'general government' includes central and local government, but excludes such things as the nationalized industries or, more generally, public corporations. Table 2.6 shows that government expenditure claimed about 21% of the gross national product in the second half of the 1960s but since then has gradually increased to around 26%. Thus the direct claims of government on the GNP have risen by over one-fifth since the late 1960s, a matter of considerable importance for economic policy.

TABLE 2.6

General Government: Total Expenditure on Goods and Services as a Percentage of GNP at Market Prices, 1966-76

Year	1966	1967	1968	1969	1970	1971	1972	1973
%	21.4	22.7	20.3	21.9	22.2	22.3	22.6	23.0

Year	1974	1975	1976
%	25.1	26.7	25.9

Source: NIBB, 1966-76.

---

1 See A. R. Prest, *Public Finance in Theory and Practice*, 5th edition, Weidenfeld and Nicolson, 1975, for a discussion of some of the latest issues involved.

It is arguable that the foregoing understates the 'size' of government. For instance, no account was taken of subsidies, grants and debt interest paid by the government and its net lending. The reason for this is that these are mainly classified as transfer payments. That is, the government raises the necessary funds by taxation and borrowing and transfers them back to the community and overseas. Thus the government does not buy goods and services directly as far as this type of expenditure is concerned. But there is no doubt that these transfers are extremely important, both in relation to taxation and government borrowing, and do influence the economic system. When they are included in government expenditure then the previous percentages are greatly increased. Table 2.7 shows that for the second half of the 1960s the percentage is raised to around 40% of gross national product and that a marked jump occurred to 47% in 1974 and that a peak of over 49% was reached in 1975. Clearly, grants, subsidies, debt interest and net lending have been increasingly important in recent years as a component of government expenditure and as will be seen have posed a formidable financing problem for government.

TABLE 2.7

General Government: Total Government Expenditure as a Percentage of GNP at Market Prices, 1966-76.

Year	1966	1967	1968	1969	1970	1971	1972	1973
%	37.7	41.2	41.9	40.5	40.2	40.3	41.3	41.5

Year	1974	1975	1976
%	47.0	49.3	47.4

Source: NIBB, 1966-76.

IV.3 The Budget and Borrowing Requirements

The Budget is traditionally the annual financial statement which the Chancellor of the Exchequer makes in the House of Commons either in late March or early April around the end of each financial year. The statement includes an account of the revenue and expenditure for the previous financial year and forecasts for the year ahead. In the ordinary way there is only one budget, but in times of crisis one or more supplementary budgets may be introduced to give the Chancellor the opportunity to modify his earlier policies by altering taxation and expenditure. Tables 2.8, 2.9 and 2.10 bring together in an aggregated form the main features of the 1978-9 budget accounts.

The receipts of the Consolidated Fund which cover gross tax revenue 'and all other public moneys payable to the Exchequer'[1] are shown in table 2.8 and fall under four main headings: inland revenue, customs and excise (including EEC own resources), vehicle excise duties and miscellaneous receipts. The first two refer to the great revenue-collecting departments of state and the major taxes and duties collected by these are discussed below.[2] Vehicle excise duties are collected by the

---

1 *Financial Statistics: Explanatory Handbook,* HMSO, October 1977, p. 34.
2 EEC own resources include revenue from the Common External Tariff, agricultural levies and sugar levies that under the EEC Treaty and subsidiary legislation are considered as belonging to the European Community and available for its Budgetary purposes. See *Official Journal of the European Communities,* 94 of 28 April 1970.

Department of the Environment. Miscellaneous receipts include interest and dividends, broadcast receiving licences and certain other receipts.

The two main categories of expenditure shown in table 2.9 are supply services and consolidated fund standing services. The first is voted annually by Parliament; the second is a standing charge against revenue.

TABLE 2.8

Central Government Revenue, 1978-9 (Forecast) (£m)

Inland revenue		
Income tax	19,310	
Surtax	15	
Corporation tax	4,170	
Petroleum revenue tax	170	
Capital gains tax	375	
Development land tax	10	
Estate duty	50	
Capital transfer tax	320	
Stamp duties	440	
Total Inland Revenue		24,860
Customs and excise		
Value added tax	4,775	
Oil	2,500	
Tobacco	2,450	
Spirits, beer, wine, cider and perry	2,400	
Betting and gaming	350	
Car tax	325	
Other excise duties	10	
EEC own resources		
Protective duties	765	
Agricultural levies	175	
Total Customs and Excise		13,750
Vehicle excise duties		1,120
National insurance surcharge		1,475
Total Taxation		41,205
Miscellaneous receipts		1,541
Grand Total		42,746

Source: Financial Statement and Budget Report 1978-9.

The National Loans Fund was set up in April 1968. Broadly speaking it is intended to carry further the separation of current and capital items in the accounts. Most of the domestic lending of the government and all transactions relating to the National Debt, including its creation, the repayment of loans from the Fund and interest payments thereon, now appear in the National Loans Fund. Table 2.10 clearly shows just how important the central government is as a source of capital funds for the nationalized industries and local authorities. The government must raise these funds either through taxation or by borrowing. In these accounts there is a substantial deficit forecast for the consolidated fund and a large

TABLE 2.9

Central Government Supply Services and Consolidated Fund Standing Services, 1978-9 (Forecast) (£m)

Supply Services

I	Defence	6,886	
II	Overseas Aid and other Overseas Services	1,062	
III	Agriculture, Fisheries & Forestry	535	
IV	Trade, Industry and Employment	3,039	
VI	Roads and Transport	1,266	
VII	Housing	2,618	
VIII	Other Environmental Services	299	
IX	Law, Order and Protective Services	1,249	
X	Education and Libraries, Science and Arts	1,740	
XI	Health and Personal Social Services	6,163	
XII	Social Security	6,683	
XIII	Other Public Services	1,071	
XIV	Common Services	1,157	
XV	Northern Ireland	592	
XVII	Rate Support Grant, Financial Transactions, etc.	7,968	
	Total Supply[1]		42,328
	Allowance for price changes (rounded)		2,400
	Supplementary provision		1,450
	Total Supply Services		46,178

Consolidated Fund Standing Services

Payment to the National Loans Fund for service of the National Debt.	3,160	
Northern Ireland – share of taxes, etc.	786	
Payments to the European Community, etc.	1,237	
Other Services	17	
Total Consolidated Fund Standing Services		5,200
Total		51,378
Consolidated Fund Deficit		−8,632
Grand Total		42,746

Source: Financial Statement and Budget Report 1978–79.
Note: 1 At 1978-9 Estimate prices.

net borrowing of £9,872m by the National Loans Fund and a central government borrowing requirement of £7,937m.

The net borrowing by the National Loans Fund, the 'central government borrowing requirement' and the 'public sector borrowing requirement' (PSBR) are closely inter-related. To get from the net borrowing by the National Loans Fund to the central government borrowing requirement it is necessary to take into account the central government's net indebtedness to certain official funds, namely the National Insurance Fund, Departmental balances and miscellaneous items, and Northern Ireland central government debt. The position for the financial year 1976-7 (complete data for later years is not available) is shown below.

	£m
Borrowing required	6,534
less Surplus of National Insurance Fund	957
plus Deficit of Departmental balances, etc.	347
plus N.I. central government debt	20
Central government borrowing requirement	5,944

The PSBR is the amount the public sector borrows from the other sectors of the economy and from overseas. It includes the central government borrowing requirement and in addition the borrowing of local authorities and public corporations from outside the public sector. For the financial year 1976-7 the figures were as follows:

	£m
Central government borrowing requirement	5,944
plus Local authorities net borrowing from other sources	1,407
plus Public corporations net borrowing from other sources	1,419
Public sector borrowing requirement	8,770

The authorities were able to finance this PSBR by borrowing £8,242m from the non-bank private sector, £333m from the banking sector and £195m from the overseas sector. The borrowing took a number of forms such as notes and coin, national savings, Treasury bills, government securities and other specialized forms of debt.

As regards the overseas sector it should be noted that a fall in the foreign exchange reserves because of an external deficit brings an inflow of sterling to the public sector; it is in effect a selling of an asset — foreign exchange reserves — for sterling. The opposite is, of course, true for an external surplus.

To the extent that the PSBR is financed from the banking sector it can add directly to the money supply and, in so far as the reserve asset base of the banks is increased, lead to further expansion of the money supply unless offsetting action is taken by the authorities. Clearly the budgetary system and monetary and financial system are highly interdependent and so are fiscal, monetary and credit policy.[1]

The annual budget as an instrument of fiscal policy has frequently been criticized because of its inflexibility. In the ordinary way the major taxes such as income tax and corporation tax cannot be varied between Finance Acts.[2] Thus though it might be thought desirable, because of changed economic conditions, to alter these taxes more frequently, this cannot be done without all the inconvenience of a supplementary budget. However, the authorities have more leeway over some other sources of revenue. From the point of view of flexibility one of the most important has been the power, first granted in the Finance Act 1961, to vary the rates of nearly all customs and excise duties and formerly purchase tax by at most 10% and known as the regulator. This kind of power was retained with the introduction of

---

1 All statistics in the text are from *FS*. For further discussion of the public sector borrowing requirement see section V below.
2 The Finance Act puts into law the budget proposals, subject to the Provisional Collection of Taxes Act which allows certain taxes to be collected in advance of the enactment of the Finance Bill and subject to any amendments made to it by the House of Commons.

value added tax in 1973 though the regulator may be used to vary it by as much as 25%.[1] Thus there are now substantial powers to vary taxes between budgets. This, of course, leaves other crucially important problems, such as the timing and scale of tax changes, but these are taken up later.

Alterations in government expenditure are also, in principle, a possible way of making fiscal policy more flexible. But government expenditure may be planned years in advance of its formal inclusion in the budget estimates and modifications of the plans may give rise to problems, since much of the expenditure is on a

TABLE 2.10

National Loans Fund, 1978-9 (Forecast) (£m)

(i) *Payments*

Interest, management and expenses of national debt		6,400
Consolidated Fund Deficit		8,632
Loans (net)		
To nationalized industries	−273	
Other public corporations	294	
Local and harbour authorities	1,123	
Private sector	−4	
Within central government	100	
Total		1,240
Grand Total		16,272

(ii) *Receipts*

Interest on loans, profits of the Issue Department of the Bank of England, etc.	3,240	
Balance of interest services of the National Debt met from the Consolidated Fund	3,160	
Total		6,400
Net Borrowing by the National Loans Fund		9,872
Grand Total		16,272

Source: *Financial Statement and Budget Report 1978–79.*

continuing basis and cannot be easily altered. Furthermore, it may be extremely costly to slow down or postpone some kinds of expenditure, particularly investment expenditure. Hence frequent variation of government expenditure is not an ideal instrument of fiscal policy.

The budget accounts, as already indicated, are incomplete in a number of ways. They deal, for example, only peripherally with local government finances and the national insurance funds.[2] But if general government is considered, it is found that for 1977-8 estimated taxes on income and expenditure, plus national insurance and similar contributions and taxes on capital totalled over £52,000m or around 40%

---

1 Thus if a current rate of duty were 10% it might be varied between 9% and 11% and as regards VAT between 7½% and 12½%.
2 National insurance is discussed further in chapter 5.

of GNP at factor cost[1]. This is a further indication of the scale of government in the UK economy.

IV.4   Income Taxation and Tax Credits

Up to April 1973 individuals were subject to income tax and surtax with the latter chargeable in addition to income tax on incomes in excess of a certain level. From that date, apart from certain residual matters, the existing income tax and surtax were replaced by a single graduated personal tax, known as unified tax. The main aims of unified tax were to simplify the tax structure, permit a smoother graduation in tax rates as income rises and simplify the administration of the whole system. The unified tax is constructed on the concept of earned income and so manages to dispense with the calculation of earned income relief, which was required under the previous system since it was constructed in terms of investment income. As well as earned income and investment income a further concept requires to be mentioned, that is taxable income. Taxable income is the income which remains from all sources after deduction of personal, family and certain other allowances.

The main allowances for 1978-9 are as follows: for single persons £985 and for married couples £1,535. For children under eleven years of age the allowance is £100, for eleven to sixteen £135 and for over sixteen £165. These age allowances are being reduced and in process of being phased out with the introduction of tax-free child benefit. From April 1978 the child benefit is £2.30 for each qualifying child, rising to £3 in November 1978 and to £4 in April 1979. The age allowances for the elderly are £1,300 for a single person and £2,075 for a married couple.

Once taxable income has been determined the various tax rates come into operation. For 1978-9 the tax bands or ranges of income in relation to each tax rate are 25% on the first £750 of taxable income, 33% on the next £7,250 of taxable income and thereafter the rates gradually increase from 40% in steps of 5% to 75% for taxable income between £18,500 and £24,000 and rise to a maximum of 83% for taxable income over £24,000.

The unified tax retains the former distinction between earned and investment income but has been modified in an important way. The first £1,700 or less of investment income is treated in exactly the same way as earned income but investment income between £1,700 and £2,250 (£2,500-£3,000 for pensioners) is subject to a 10% surcharge, and in excess of £2,250 to a 15% surcharge, on the progressively rising rates, making the maximum rate 98%.

It is evident from the foregoing discussion that one of the main features of income taxation is its progressiveness. This is, of course, by design. It can be traced to notions of ability to pay. It is assumed that those with larger incomes are or should be able to pay proportionately more of them in taxation. In addition, progressive taxation lends itself to income redistribution, to the extent that government expenditure benefits the less well-off in the community; and some would argue that greater equality of income is important to the maintenance of a politically stable society. But progressive taxation also diminishes the direct reward for extra work as income increases and may act as a disincentive to more effort.

It has also been suggested that steeply progressive taxation is a disincentive to movement from one job to another; it may be difficult to get a sufficiently large income after tax to compensate for the costs of upheaval and change. If this is correct then the tax system may misallocate resources and be a drag on economic

---

1   Furthermore, from late 1978 the surcharge on national insurance contributions of employers will be at a rate of $3\frac{1}{2}$%.

efficiency and growth. There is also no doubt that highly progressive taxation stimulates tax avoidance – the search for loopholes in the law permitting a reduced tax bill and indeed tax evasion which is, of course, illegal. If it is possible to spend less than a pound on advice to save a pound in tax then clearly this is a powerful incentive. The energies and resources of lawyers, accountants and tax experts generally may thus be diverted into socially costly tasks.

To the extent that some or all of these problems arise, the community may have to make difficult choices between more redistribution and a smaller total income, or somewhat less redistribution and a larger total income, with each choice associated with varying degrees of social and political conflict. Once more there would seem to be no escape from the difficult problems which arise in sustaining the on-going life of a complex and diverse society.

It has long been a goal of taxation policy that the system of taxation should be easy to understand, equitable and cheap to administer. How far this continues to be true of the system in the UK is open to question. Concern has been expressed about the distortions and inefficiencies generated by the complex interdependencies of the whole system of taxation and the social security system.[1] In particular, there is concern about what has come to be called the 'poverty-trap', that is where people under the current system who are in low-paid jobs or unemployed may find that the effective marginal tax on their additional earnings may be extremely high – it has been in excess of 100% in some circumstances – when both taxation and loss of social security benefits are taken into consideration. The introduction of the new 25% tax rate and tax-free child benefit may give some alleviation.

There are, however, various proposals for dealing more radically with these and related problems. One is known as 'the negative income tax' which ideally is designed to permit a single assessment of income and provide either for calculating the tax due if income is above a certain level or for the transfer to be paid if it is below that level. The particular scheme that has received most official attention in the UK is known as a 'tax credit system'. Under this system those who come within the scheme would receive an entirely new form of tax-credit for themselves and their families, which would take the place of the main income tax personal allowances and family allowances[2] where the latter includes family income supplement now paid as cash benefit as part of the social services. However, other means-tested benefits including rent and rates rebates, free school meals and free welfare milk would remain within the ambit of the social services. But under the scheme most national insurance benefits, such as retirement pensions, widows' pensions and sickness and unemployment benefit, as well as most occupational pensions, would be covered and be taxed as if they were income from employment, since they would give rise to a right to tax credits. A further feature of the scheme was that tax due and credit entitlement would normally be settled week by week or month by month, depending on the employment payment period. This form of tax system is described as non-cumulative in contrast with a cumulative system, such as the present pay-as-you-earn system, where personal allowances are spread over the tax year. This would be a radical change in UK income tax arrangements. The tax-credit scheme was meant to cover almost all those in employment, except those on very low incomes, but at least to begin with was to exclude the self-employed.

---

1 See *The Structure and Reform of Direct Taxation*, Report of a Committee chaired by Professor J. E. Meade, The Institute for Fiscal Studies, Allen and Unwin, 1978.
2 Cmnd. 5116, p. 3.

There seems to be little doubt that a tax-credit scheme such as that proposed could achieve some simplification and economies over present arrangements for taxation and in the administration of at least some social security benefits. However, the post-1974 Labour Government has made it clear that it dislikes the details of the proposals, whilst not necessarily rejecting the principles, and so it may be that little change will occur in the short term.

IV.5   Capital Gains Taxation and Development Land Tax

Until the Finance Act of 1971 there were two capital gains taxes, the short-term and the long-term tax, but under this Act the former was abolished, leaving what is called capital gains tax. Under this tax gains are taxable on the disposal of most assets. Important exemptions are principal private residence, private motor cars, National Savings securities, most life assurance policies and betting winnings, gifts to charities and British government and government-guaranteed securities. In addition, the first £1,000 of net annual gains of individuals are exempt with the next £4,000 taxed at 15% and a marginal relief for gains between £5,000 and £9,500. Beyond this the tax rate is 30%. Since 1971 all gains at death are exempt and there are special provisions for gains on the sale or gift of a family business or family trading company. There are provisions generally allowing the offset of losses against gains on those assets that are subject to tax. Gains realized by companies are ordinarily chargeable to corporation tax, which for the year 1977-8 is at 52%. However, from 1973 the effective rate of tax on company gains has been only 30% – achieved by the expedient of leaving out of account a fraction of the gain. Special provisions apply to the taxing of unit trusts, investment trusts, super-annuation funds and other bodies.

The major justification put forward for the introduction of capital gains taxation is on grounds of equity. The argument is roughly as follows. An individual may purchase £100 worth of securities in 1976 and – if he is lucky – find that in 1977 they were worth £200. If he sold the securities and if there were no capital gains tax he could maintain his capital intact and still have £100 to spend, therefore his £100 is essentially income and should be taxed as such. But is this really equitable with progressive income tax rates? It might be that if the £100 were spread over a number of years a lower tax charge would arise. Does this mean that gains should be averaged over a number of years or would a compromise solution be to charge rates somewhat less than income tax rates? The UK capital gains tax seems to favour the latter.

In discussing the £100 gain above, nothing was said about prices. But if prices have risen by 20% over the period then £120 would be required to maintain real capital intact and the remaining £80 would be worth only some £64 in real terms. Is it legitimate to tax nominal gains as opposed to real gains? The equity argument is by no means as straightforward as it might seem; and a really comprehensive discussion of the matter would have to consider the wider issues of the distribution of income and wealth generally in relation to the operation of the social and political system and the problems of indexation in a period of inflation.

Capital gains taxation is, of course, important for other reasons besides those of equity. It may affect investment and saving and the functioning of the capital markets, and pose difficult problems of administration. To the extent that the return on investment takes the form of capital gains – especially the return on risky investment – taxing them may discourage such investment. This discouragement may, however, be mitigated to some extent, since the tax is postponable and payable only on realized capital gains. The allowance of losses as an offset to taxable capital gains also works in the same direction. Nevertheless, the effect may well be to depress investment.

The effects on saving are perhaps even more problematical but may also be adverse, as may the effects on the operation of the capital markets. Since the tax is on realized gains this encourages the retention of the same securities as, of course, the holder has the income on the tax that would otherwise have to be paid if the securities were realized. There is therefore a discouragement to switching between securities which reduces the flexibility of the market and perhaps makes the raising of capital more costly. A possible offset to these effects is the realization of capital losses since these are allowable for tax purposes against corresponding capital gains.

The administrative problems are particularly great where problems of valuation arise. This is especially true of changes in the value of assets which do not ordinarily have a market value; an example is unquoted securities. The problem of valuation may become less acute as time proceeds and the community gets accustomed to the tax.[1]

The Development Land Tax of 1976 makes realizations of development value from land subject to a special development tax and where the tax applies there is no liability to income tax, corporation tax or capital gains tax. The term development value refers to the difference between the base value of the land and its disposal value for development purposes. The base value 'is the highest of: (1) cost of acquisition plus the cost of 'relevant improvements', plus any increase in current use value since the date of acquisition; or (2) current use value at the date of disposal, plus 10% or (3) acquisition cost of the land, including all improvements, plus 10%'.[2] The first £10,000 of realized development value in any financial year is exempt from tax. 'For a transitional period up to 31 March 1979, the next £150,000 in any financial year will be liable at a rate of 66 $\frac{2}{3}$ per cent.'[3] The standard rate is 80%.

Various people and bodies are exempt from development land tax, including the main residence of owner occupiers for land up to one acre, and certain co-operative housing associations provided that if they dispose of dwellings or land they do so to 'a housing association registered with the Housing Corporation or to the Housing Corporation itself'.[4] Disposals of other purchasers are liable to development land tax.

No doubt the development land tax is an attempt by the state to appropriate what it considers to be inequitable capital gains from certain forms of land development. However, it is difficult to see how it can fail to raise the costs of new housing and in so doing confer actual or potential capital gains to owners of existing houses.

IV.6   Corporation Tax, Depreciation and Other Allowances

Corporation tax draws a strong distinction between the company and the shareholder, taxing each as separate entities. A basic argument used in favour of

---

1   These last few paragraphs and section IV.6 rely heavily on Prest, *Public Finance in Theory and Practice,* op. cit.

2   *The British System of Taxation,* HMSO, 1977, p. 24.

3   Ibid.

4   Ibid.

corporation tax is the opportunity it gives the authorities to distinguish between the personal and company sectors for policy purposes. They may wish, for instance, to curtail consumption expenditure with as little adverse effect as possible on investment expenditure. An increase in income tax, leaving corporation tax unchanged, may tend to have the desired effect and may even encourage smaller dividend distributions, leaving more funds available to companies for investment purposes.

The foregoing analysis begs, however, a number of important questions. Among these are the following. Should future consumption be preferred to present consumption, in so far as larger current investment makes possible a larger future income and so consumption? Are the companies with retained profits the ones which should grow? This is not at all self-evident. It means that companies avoid the discipline of having to raise funds in the market and probably favours the larger established company at the expense of the smaller or newer company. Furthermore, greater encouragement of profit retention tends to reduce the flow of funds through the capital market to the detriment of companies dependent on it. The corporation tax also tends to distort the operation of the capital market by encouraging firms to rely more on loan or debenture capital at the expense of ordinary or other forms of share capital, since the interest on the former is allowed as a cost in the calculation of profits and hence liability for tax, whereas this is not true of the latter. It may, of course, be argued that the gains from introducing corporation tax outweigh the disadvantages.

From April 1973 the government introduced a new form of corporation tax known as the *imputation system*. Under this sytem all profits, whether distributed or not, are subject to the same corporation tax rate, but part of the tax is imputed to shareholders, and collected from the company at the time of payment of dividends. If, for instance the corporation tax rate is 52% and the basic income tax rate is 33% then a company whose activities are entirely within the UK and which had profits of 100 would have a corporation tax liability of 52. If during a year it paid a dividend of 20.1 to its shareholders it would be treated as a gross dividend of 30 from which income tax of 33% had been deducted. The company would pay the 9.9 to the Inland Revenue and this, which is called advance payment of corporation tax (ACT), would be credited against the company's corporation tax liability of 52. Shareholders subject to basic rate income tax would be deemed to have discharged their tax liabilities; only in the case of those exempt or subject to lower or higher rates would a refund or additional charge be necessary. Small companies whose annual profits do not exceed £50,000 are subject to a reduced rate of corporation tax with the scale of reduction tapering off for companies with profits up to £85,000.

The imputation form of corporation tax has certain advantages over the two-rate system when it comes to negotiating double-taxation agreements with other countries; it is favourable to the UK balance of payments and should facilitate the movement towards tax harmonization within the European Community, as it puts Britain broadly in line with French and German company taxation and with recent proposals by the Commission.

In assessing liability to corporation tax allowance is made, broadly speaking, for all the costs incurred by the company, including the wear and tear of physical capital and, as mentioned above, interest on loans and debentures but not dividends paid on shares. However, depreciation is not allowed on all physical assets; there are no allowances on such things as retail shops, showrooms and offices.

In addition to depreciation allowances for wear and tear successive governments have attempted to stimulate investment by various kinds of incentive. Two main kinds are operative in the UK: initial allowances, and investment or cash grants. Initial allowances, introduced in 1945, are permitted in the first year in addition to the ordinary depreciation allowances and the two together are known as first-year allowances. In other words the rate at which depreciation may be written off is accelerated; the total amount of depreciation permitted remains 100%.

Investment or cash grants are now largely confined to what are called the assisted areas and are known generally as regional development grants. There are four main types of assisted areas: special development areas, development areas, intermediate areas and derelict land clearance areas. Altogether the areas comprise all of Scotland and Wales, the whole north of England roughly above the Wash, and south-western England. Special investment grants are also payable to the ship-building and computer industries.

The position since the 1972 Budget is that all capital expenditure throughout the UK on machinery and plant, excluding passenger cars, is subject to a first-year allowance of 100%, often called free depreciation; and the initial allowance on new industrial buildings is 50% plus an annual allowance of 4% on the construction cost. Thus as far as these allowances are concerned no distinction is made between the assisted areas and the rest of the country. However, as already indicated, the assisted areas do receive special treatment. In addition to the allowances mentioned the special development areas and the development areas receive regional development grants of 22% and 20% respectively of qualifying capital expenditure on new plant and machinery and buildings. Grants of 20% for buildings have also been available in the intermediate areas and the derelict land clearance areas.[1]

An important feature of the new system of regional development grants is that unlike previous grants they do not affect the recipient's entitlement to the first-year or initial allowances on the *full* amount of the capital investment. This means that the new grant of 22% is the equivalent, for a company making profits, to one of over 30% on the previous basis when allowances were calculated on the *net* amount of the investment after deducting any grants.

With the rapid rise in prices in the last few years many companies found themselves subject to heavy taxation on the increase in the value of their stocks. In November 1974 the government introduced measures giving special tax relief on such increases and these have subsequently been extended in successive budgets. This is an important innovation as it is tantamount to an acceptance, at least in part, of inflation accounting.

The whole system of allowances and grants thus gives rise to many complicated issues, only a few of which can be touched on here. First, should depreciation allowances be on an original or a replacement-cost basis? This question would be of little or no significance if prices were generally stable. But in periods of rising prices it would seem that if the community is to preserve intact its physical stock of capital, allowances should be made on a replacement-cost basis. However, if the problem is approached in a different way the argument may not be so clear-cut. Suppose a firm purchases a piece of equipment and thereafter prices rise, including the price of the equipment, then the capital value of the old equipment rises, giving a capital gain to the firm. If allowances are permitted on a replacement-cost basis the firm is, in fact, receiving untaxed capital gains. Is this equitable in relation to other sections of the community or is it a useful compromise to allow only

---

1 *Industrial and Regional Development*, Cmnd. 4942, 1972.

original costs in calculating depreciation, so that the apparent capital gains are subject to corporation and income tax as, until the recent modification relating to the increase in the value of stocks, was the practice in the UK? The answer is far from obvious but clearly the issues become more acute in periods of rapid inflation.[1]

Initial allowances and investment grants should act as a stimulus to investment. The first may be regarded as reducing the amount of tax payable on a profitable investment. The second is, of course, a direct subsidy-to investment and the benefits do not depend upon the availability of profits. It is not at all self-evident that the subsidy is to be preferred as it may mean that investment takes place in forms of dubious profitability — there is therefore the likelihood of misallocation of resources, at least as determined in relation to market prices.

A major feature of investment grants and regional development grants is the extent to which they are discriminatory. They make investments in certain places more profitable than in others and some types of investment more profitable than other types. This, of course, is by design and is intended to stimulate investment in the places and in the forms the government desires. The basis for this intervention hinges on the conviction that the market, reflecting the interacting decisions of consumers, savers and investors, if left to itself will lead to misallocation of investment and to underinvestment, and to regional imbalance in the levels of employment and economic activity. However, as far as regional employment is concerned, it is not at all obvious that this form of capital subsidization, which cheapens capital relatively to labour, with the latter generally in excess supply, is the best way to proceed.[2] But the issues that regional development grants and investment incentives generally raise are extremely complex. Some of the issues, such as the distribution of income and wealth in society and stabilization policy, were referred to in the introduction to this section but cannot be explored further here, except to say that the empirical evidence, such as it is, suggests that investment incentives have not been very effective in stimulating capital growth in the country as a whole — though they certainly seem to have stimulated growth in the assisted areas — since the overall growth rate has lagged behind that of the US and most western European countries. Moreover, their use as stabilization instruments depends crucially on the timing and actual variation in the grants and allowances. It may be doubted that government or anyone else has the knowledge to manipulate these successfully.

IV.7   Value Added Tax

Value added tax, as its name implies, taxes value added at each stage of the productive process with the final selling price to the consumer being made up of the cost of production plus the rate of tax. An example may help to make the matter clearer. Suppose the value added tax rate is 10% — the standard rate for 1978-9 is 8%[3] — and that a manufacturer buys all his raw materials at a cost of 110 including tax. The 10 is known as input tax. The manufacturer processes the raw materials and sells the final product to a retailer for 220 including tax. The 20 is known as

---

1 See Prest, *Public Finance in Theory and Practice*, for further discussion.
2 See chapter 4, section VI.3.
3 There is also a higher rate of 12½% on a wide range of consumer durable goods and the like.

output tax and the manufacturer pays the difference between the output tax and the input tax to Customs and Excise, namely 10. The retailer may be supposed to sell the product to the consumer for 330 including tax. Thus the output tax of the retailer is 30 and the input tax is 20, so he also pays 10 to Customs and Excise.

Thus the tax, as it were, comes to rest with the consumer, and this is why value added tax is frequently described as an indirect tax on consumer expenditure.

It should be stressed, however, that the foregoing is intended only as a simple arithmetical explanation of the value added tax method and should not be interpreted as implying that the tax is necessarily wholly passed on to the final consumer. The problems of tax incidence are extremely complex and, in principle, require to be examined within the framework of a dynamically adjusting process. And even then most economists would be far from confident that they understood the intricacies of tax incidence. Notwithstanding the difficulties surrounding tax incidence, the matter is returned to briefly below in relation to the form of value added tax in the UK.

The government has given many reasons for substituting a value added tax for the previous purchase tax and selective employment tax.[1] The latter taxes were felt to be over-discriminatory in their effects on the prices of goods and services and they needed to be replaced by a more broadly based indirect tax, causing less distortion of consumer choice and so allowing a more efficient allocation of resources. It was also argued that value added tax would benefit the balance of payments as it is more easily remitted on exports than purchase tax – imports are liable for value added tax. Finally, value added tax has either been adopted or is in process of being adopted by the actual and prospective members of the European Economic Community – as a step towards harmonization – and so the UK had little or no alternative but to move in the same direction.

There can be little doubt that the way purchase tax and selective employment tax were levied certainly distorted relative prices and that difficulties would arise in trying to levy them in a way that minimized this kind of distortion. Thus value added tax may well be superior on the basis of this criterion. However, in solving one problem another one may be created in that it can be argued persuasively that a general tax on consumer expenditure is regressive and discriminates against those on lower incomes. Successive governments have attempted, and it would seem with some success, at least as far as short-run consequences are concerned, to get round this criticism by what is called zero-rating most food, coal, gas, electricity, the construction of buildings, public transport fares, and drugs and medicines supplied on prescription. Zero-rating means that the trader does not have to charge tax on his sales and, in addition, he can claim a refund of any tax he may have paid to his suppliers because of tax paid on inputs entering into the final product.

The balance of payments argument in favour of value added tax is superficially persuasive in that imports bear the tax whereas exports are zero-rated. However, it is not at all clear that balance of payments considerations should be a criterion of the appropriateness of a particular tax as balance of payments adjustment is primarily a question of exchange rate policy and monetary and fiscal policy. This,

---

1   See Green Paper, *Value Added Tax*, Cmnd. 4621, 1971; and *Value Added Tax*, Cmnd. 4929, 1972.

of course, is not to imply that value added tax will not have at least short-run implications for the balance of payments.

Certain other features of value added tax deserve to be mentioned. As well as a zero-rated category of goods there is also an exempted category. For exempted goods the trader does not have to charge tax on his sales but he cannot claim a refund for any tax included in the price of his purchases. Exempted goods and services include land, insurance, letter and parcel post, betting and gaming (which already carry excise duty), finance, education and health services. Small traders with a business turnover of less than £10,000 a year in taxable goods and services are exempt from the tax.

IV.8   Excise Duties and Protective Duties

Until recently the practice in the UK has been to distinguish between customs duties which were imposed on imports and excise duties which were levied on home produced goods and services. Customs duties had two functions; one, to raise revenue in a similar way to excise duties and two, to give protection to British-produced goods or preference to goods from specified countries. However, the accession of the UK to the European Communities obliged her to bring (by the end of the transition period, namely 1 January 1978) her practices into line with the rest of the Community. Thus duties for revenue purposes are now known as excise duties and are levied on both home-produced goods and similar imported goods. Protective duties refer to what was formerly the protective part of customs duties and these have been generally brought into line with the Common Customs Tariff of the European Community. This means that the UK, like other members of the Community, now operates a common tariff on imports from non-members, whilst trade between the member countries is free of customs duty. As may be seen from table 2.8 the large revenue yielders are tobacco, oil and alcohol with a total estimated yield of £7,350m in 1978-9 or almost 18% of total revenue from taxation. Moreover, this does not take account of VAT on these products.

An outstanding feature of the duties and taxes on tobacco, oil and alcohol is their scale, the large proportion that they represent of the purchase price. Ordinarily it might be expected that something which has the effect of substantially increasing the price of a product would lead to less of it, perhaps much less of it, being bought. By and large this does not seem to have happened with these three products – their demands are said to be inelastic with respect to price. However, some doubts are beginning to be expressed about the buoyancy of the revenue from tobacco, though this may be due to other causes besides the scale of taxation. Then at any rate apparent inelasticity of demand with respect to price implies that these duties and taxes may have little direct effect on the allocation of resources. But there will be an indirect effect because the funds withdrawn by taxes from consumers will scarcely be spent by the state in the same way as if they had been in the hands of the former.

It is often argued that indirect taxes are to be preferred because they are less of a disincentive to the supply of labour than direct taxes. This is an extremely difficult issue and depends on many factors, such as the scale of duties and taxes to be substituted, say, for a reduction in direct taxes or for foregoing an increase, and the type and the extent of the goods involved. For an individual, in choosing between additional work or leisure, may well consider not only the direct tax on extra earnings but also the real value of goods and services that can be bought with additional income either now or in the future and either by himself or those who may inherit from him.[1]

It is also arguable that on equity grounds indirect taxes are regressive in that they fall more heavily on the relatively low income groups. There would seem to be some truth in this as far as tobacco and beer are concerned, but possibly to a lesser extent for petrol, though bus fares are obviously affected by oil duties. On the other hand the relatively less well off seem to obtain benefits from government welfare and other services. But if the community opts for extensive government expenditure on welfare services and education it seems unavoidable that one way or another a large proportion of the tax revenue must be raised from the mass of taxpayers. If at the same time the latter are important beneficiaries from government expenditure then they are indirectly paying for perhaps all of or a major part of these benefits. This is in no way to deny, however, the power of taxation, or at least certain forms of it, to redistribute income and wealth.

IV.9   Capital Transfer Tax and Wealth Tax

Capital transfer tax was introduced under the first Finance Act 1975 at the same time as estate duty was abolished. The tax, often called a gifts tax, applies, subject to certain exemptions, to gifts made during life and to transfers on death. Transfers of what is called settled property or property held in trust are also subject to the tax. The tax is chargeable as the gifts or transfers occur and is cumulative. That is, in calculating the tax due on successive gifts or transfers the previous ones are taken into account and progressively higher rates of tax apply. The rates of tax on what are known as lifetime transfers are lower than for transfers on death. The tax is in general payable by the donor but may be recovered from the beneficiary.

The main exemptions are transfers between husband and wife both in life and on death; transfers in any one year of up to £2,000 plus any unused part of the previous year's exemption; outright gifts to any one person during the tax year up to a value of £100; and transfers made out of income after tax as part of normal expenditure which leave the donor sufficient income to maintain his usual standard of living. Marriage gifts are given special treatment; transfers by a parent up to £5,000 are exempt and up to £2,500 by any other ancestor and £1,000 by anyone else. Business owners and working farmers also get special relief; for purposes of the tax, value transferred is reduced by 30% and 50% respectively. Transfers to charities or political parties are completely exempt if made more than a year before death. There are also special provisions relating to the exemption of gifts of works of art and historic buildings made during the individual's lifetime.

The first £25,000 of transfers, after taking into consideration all exemptions, is tax-free whether made during lifetime or on death. The rates for lifetime transfers then rise from 5% on the next £5,000 by gradual steps to 75% on transfers of over £2.01m. Transfers made within three years of death become subject to the rates applicable on death.

The intention of the capital transfer tax and indeed the wealth tax to be discussed below is to reduce the inequality of wealth distribution. It should clearly be more effective in achieving this than the estate duty which it replaced, since the latter was avoidable if gifts were made during lifetime and outside the *inter-vivos*

---

1   See *The Structure and Reform of Direct Taxation,* op. cit.

period. However, it is arguable that an accessions tax, that is a tax on recipients rather than on donors, would have been more effective as a means of achieving greater wealth equality. For an accessions tax would encourage a spreading of gifts between recipients in a way that would reduce tax liability; this is not true of the capital transfer tax.

The precise form of the capital transfer tax and the exemptions it incorporates make it extremely important for individuals with even quite modest capital assets to plan their affairs carefully if they wish to minimize their tax liability. This too could be a source of inequity, depending on the foresight and luck of donors. Finally, like all such taxes it may encourage increased consumption expenditure and perhaps expenditure on education, travel and the like.

The Chancellor announced in his 1974 Budget that the government intended to introduce an annual wealth tax. Subsequently a Green Paper was published outlining the proposals the government had in mind.[1] In a foreword to the Green Paper the Chancellor states that 'income by itself is not an adequate measure of taxable capacity. The ownership of wealth, whether it produces income or not, adds to the economic resources of a taxpayer so that the person who has wealth as well as income of a given size necessarily has a greater taxable capacity than one who has only income of that size.'[2] It is not clear what precise form the wealth tax may ultimately take as it has run into much criticism both in and outside Parliament. A Select Committee of the House of Commons established to examine a wealth tax has not found it possible to present an agreed report and for the present the matter would seem to be in abeyance.

IV.10　Taxation and the European Community

It is evident from the preceding discussion that some of the recent tax reforms of the UK are designed to bring its taxes, or at any rate some of them, more closely into line with those of the European Community. Members are obliged under the Treaty of Rome and subsequent directives to harmonize their tax legislation as regards turnover taxes, excise duties and other forms of indirect taxation. In particular, the Community has adopted value added taxation as its main general indirect tax and this is binding on all members, though many of the details, including the actual tax rates, or range of rates, remain to be determined. Contributions to the Community budget are to be calculated on the basis of the harmonized value added tax. It was hoped this would commence with the 1978 budget but it now seems it will be at least 1979 before this proposal can be implemented. The Community intends to harmonize the main excise duties on tobacco, oil and alcohol, and is pressing this forward in 1978. As far as the UK is concerned this may eventually mean a reduction in the duties on tobacco and alcohol since these are much higher than in most of the countries of the present Community. Corporation tax harmonization is still under consideration within the Community but it seems likely that the credit or imputation system will be adopted and, as was seen earlier, the UK has anticipated this eventuality. The Community does not require harmonization of direct personal taxation.

The fundamental justification for tax harmonization within the Community stems from the very concept of the Community as, amongst other things,

---

1　Wealth Tax, Cmnd. 5704, 1974.
2　Ibid, p. 111.

a common, unified competitive market. This requires, it is argued, the disappearance of all artificial barriers to trade and capital flows between the member countries, including those that might be created by different tax systems. On the basis of this approach the impetus towards uniformity or harmonization of taxation is immense. This is especially clear in the case of value added tax and excise duties and is becoming more so, as far as corporation tax is concerned, with the increasing importance of international companies and the mobility of capital, which the Community is determined to foster among its members. The need to harmonize personal direct taxation is not felt to arise as it is believed that mobility of labour is not greatly affected by differences between member countries in this type of tax.[1]

The whole process of tax harmonization carries important consequences for both the Community and its member countries. By implication it places great stress on the efficient allocation of resources as indicated by the static competitive model. By the same token it neglects, or at least puts on one side, the fundamental questions of externalities and of income and wealth distribution, except to the extent that these will be dealt with by harmonization of social security arrangements and with the help of the Community budget, and by regional policy measures. Up to the present none of these areas is well developed though some progress has been made in each of them. Finally, harmonization is relevant to the whole issue of stabilization policy. It remains to be seen to what extent it will be possible for individual members to vary indirect taxes such as value added tax as an instrument of fiscal policy. This could obviously pose serious problems for member countries and, not least, the relative fiscal power of the Community vis-à-vis its individual members. These matters have, as yet, had far too little public discussion in the UK.

V   POLICY IN RETROSPECT AND PROSPECT
V.1   The 1960s and 1970s

In the brief review of policy below attention is concentrated on the record of the authorities in the pursuit of their major policy goals. For most of the 1960s the authorities were preoccupied with the achievement of full employment, price stability, economic growth, stability of exchange rates and a 'satisfactory' balance of payments. But in the late 1960s the commitment to fixed exchange rates became less strong and was abandoned in the early 1970s; and in the last couple of years a reduction in the rate of inflation rather than price stability has come to dominate the other policy goals, including full employment and economic growth. Indeed the authorities now see the curtailment of the pace of inflation as a necessary means to achieving more employment and faster economic growth.

During the 1960s unemployment in Great Britain averaged less than 2%, though from 1967 onwards it was in excess of this figure. But for the 1970s to the end of 1977 it has averaged 3.8% with the trend ominously rising and in early 1978 was in excess of 6%. Thus the policy goal of full employment, if some 2% to 3% is taken as the norm, is far from being currently achieved and this has also been true of the last few years.

Retail prices rose over the 1960s at a compound rate of some 3.8% a year, with the rate of increase accelerating in the later years to around 5%. However, even this

---

1 However, the Community intends to harmonize such matters relating to direct taxation as tax deduction of dividends at source.

latter rate seems low in comparison with the rates experienced since then. Over the seven years 1970 to 1977 the rate has been almost 14%, almost four times the rate of the 1960s. But even 14% is relatively mild in comparison with a rate of 24% between 1974 and 1975, though since then there has been a decline and the figure. has fallen to 15.8% between 1976 and 1977 with the trend continuing downwards in early 1978. Thus there has been a complete failure to achieve price stability, as measured by retail prices, and the degree of failure has increased dramatically during the 1970s.

If economic growth is measured in terms of gross domestic product then this has grown at a compound rate of around 2.8% a year during the 1960s, though by no means regularly, and just about 1.4% a year between 1970 and 1977. In 1974 gross domestic product declined slightly and in 1975 fell by almost 2%, and has since grown by only some 1% a year. Thus most of the growth took place in the early 1970s between 1972 and 1973 when it reached some 5.5%. Thus whilst economic growth has indeed taken place it has been far from regular, has been low by international standards for developed countries, and in 1974 and 1975 was actually negative—something which had not happened since 1952.

For the first half or more of the 1960s fixed exchange rates were a major goal of economic policy. But in the year or two leading up to the devaluation of sterling in November 1967 this policy came increasingly under question and by 1972 the Chancellor of the Exchequer was prepared to say in his budget speech that 'the lesson of the international balance of payments upsets of the last few years is that it is neither necessary nor desirable to distort domestic economies to an unacceptable extent in order to maintain unrealistic exchange rates, whether they were too high or too low'. In the light of the exchange rate fluctuations in recent years and their repercussions on international monetary and economic cooperation it seems doubtful that such a cavalier statement would be made now, though this is not to say that fixed exchange rates have once more become a policy goal.

Whatever may be true of the official attitude to exchange rates and whether it is to be regarded as a goal or an instrument of policy, there is no doubt about the authorities' concern over the balance of payments. For most of the 1960s and in the 1970s the balance of payments has been a matter of grave concern to the authorities and time and time again they have felt constrained to take drastic action to improve the position. For example, the period 1964-8 was one of sustained crisis for sterling and the balance of payments. In the five years ending in December 1968 the cumulative current balance deficit was £865m and the total currency flow, which includes the current balance, investment and other capital flows, the EEA loss on forwards and the balancing item, was the enormous sum of £3,676m. This was mainly financed by borrowing on a large scale from the IMF and other overseas monetary authorities.[1]

For the next four years from 1969 to 1972 inclusive the current balance was in surplus and considerable amounts of foreign debt had been repaid. But by early 1972 the current balance was beginning to deteriorate, and during the five years 1973 to 1977 inclusive the cumulative current balance deficit was £7,154m, almost half of which occurred in 1974. Since then there has been a marked improvement in the position, accompanied by massive investment and other capital flows, outwards in 1976 but inwards in 1977 when the official reserves increased by

---

1   See chapter 3 for further discussion.

£9,588m. Over this five years, more precisely since June 1972, the exchange rate of sterling has been allowed to float. During 1973 it averaged about $2.45 to the pound, falling to $1.75 in 1977, though it recovered to over $1.90 in the early months of 1978. These developments have been of fundamental importance to the management of monetary policy.

For most of the 1960s and indeed also the early 1970s the authorities would, as has already been indicated, seem to have been sceptical about the effectiveness of traditional monetary and credit policy as exercised through changes in the monetary aggregates or even Bank rate or minimum lending rate as a means of, or targets to be aimed at, in trying to achieve their policy goals. Their attitude would seem to have been strongly influenced by the work of the Radcliffe Committee.[1] With the introduction of the competition and credit control arrangements in 1971 the emphasis changed, with more reliance being placed on flexible interest rates as a policy target. The monetary aggregates, such as the various money stock aggregates, did not begin to figure prominently as either targets or indicators of monetary policy until 1976, though for some years greater emphasis had been placed upon them.[2]

From 1963 I to 1966 I, M_1, which may roughly be thought of as transactions balances, grew at a relatively stable rate of about 5.4% a year. For the next four years to 1970 I the compound rate of growth was irregular being negative over a number of quarters between 1966 and 1967 and again between 1968 and 1969 but averaged about 2.4% a year over the four years. The contrast with the next three years to 1973 I is striking when the rate of growth was some 12% a year. It then dropped to just over 3% during the year to 1974 I, rose to some 16.7% in the year to 1975 I, and in the four years from 1973 IV to 1977 IV has grown at a compound rate of some 15% a year, including for the year ending 1977 IV an extremely rapid rate of 21.9%.

From 1963 I to 1970 I sterling M_3 and M_3 followed a similar growth pattern to that of M_1 but at a rather faster rate at just over 6% a year in each case. However, from 1970 I to 1973 I the annual compound rate of growth of each was almost 18%, some 50% faster than the growth of M_1 over the same period. For the year to 1974 I sterling M_3 and M_3 grew at approximately 24% and 25% respectively in strong contrast with the 3% for M_1. During the three years ending 1977 IV sterling M_3 and M_3 grew at some 12% and 13.7% a year respectively, rather less than M_1 at 15% a year. Furthermore, for the year ending 1977 IV sterling M_3 grew at 10.1% and M_3 at 9.5% respectively, less than half the rate of growth of M_1.

For any economist — not necessarily an extreme monetarist — who believes, or at least suspects, that a relatively stable and low growth of the monetary aggregates, perhaps of the order of 4% to 5% a year, would be conducive to overall economic stability, then he cannot but be dismayed by the behaviour of the monetary

---

1 *Committee on the Working of the Monetary System,* Cmnd. 827, HMSO, 1959.

2 Three definitions of the money stock are used in the text: M_1, sterling M_3 and M_3. M_1 consists of notes and coin in circulation with the public and UK private sector sterling sight deposits. Sterling M_3 equals M_1 plus private sector sterling time deposits (including certificates of deposit) and public sector sight and time sterling deposits. M_3 equals sterling M_3 plus UK residents' deposits in other currencies (including certificates of deposit). Each definition is corrected for items in transit and each series is available in two forms, one adjusted for seasonal variation and the other unadjusted. In the discussion of the trend of the money stock in the text above, seasonally adjusted data are used. See Statistical Appendix A-5 for an unadjusted series.

aggregates over the past fifteen years or so and especially since the early 1970s. It may have seemed to the authorities at the time that they had good reasons for permitting the extreme variability that has taken place in the rates of growth of the monetary aggregates, but that in so doing they contributed to inflation, economic uncertainty and stagflation—namely low or negative rates of growth of output and high unemployment—seems to be increasingly evident, though this remains a controversial judgment. Moreover, it is in no way to deny the importance of the many forces affecting the UK economy in recent years and the difficulties that arise in trying to counteract them, including the oil crisis in 1974, the impact of rising import prices and the problems of controlling the money stock in an open economy, subject to large foreign movements of funds. Nor is it being implied that it would be advisable to take whatever measures were required to reduce forthwith the growth of the monetary aggregates to low and stable rates. Such a policy would probably be highly disruptive of economic activity and very costly in economic and social terms. A move to lower and more stable rates of growth of the monetary aggregates would seem to be best approached gradually over a period of years.

A credit aggregate which has occurred frequently in recent discussions of monetary policy is 'domestic credit creation' (DCE). In the words of the Bank of England, 'It is a measure of domestically generated credit in a form which leads directly to monetary expansion'.[1] It may be looked upon as consisting of three main items, 'that part of the public sector borrowing requirement which is not offset by purchases of public sector debt by the UK private sector other than banks . . . , the increase in bank lending (in sterling) to the UK private sector . . (and) . . . the net increase in the banks' sterling lending to overseas residents'.[2] The reason for including the latter in *domestic* credit expansion is that 'such lending is largely connected with the finance of UK exports and has, therefore, much the same effect on domestic liquidity as direct bank lending to a UK exporter'.[3] The outcome for DCE for the financial year 1976-7 was as follows:

		£m
	Public sector borrowing requirement	8,770
less	Purchases of public sector debt by private sector	7,463
plus	Sterling lending by banks to the private sector	3,414
plus	Banks' lending in sterling to overseas	213
	Domestic Credit expansion	4,934

DCE came into renewed prominence in December 1976 when the Chancellor of the Exchequer undertook to keep DCE within certain levels in his negotiations with the IMF for support for sterling. A target level of £9 billion for 1976-7, which as the above figure indicates was greatly in excess of that achieved, was confirmed and targets of £7.7 billion and £6 billion for 1977-8 and 1978-9 respectively were announced.

DCE may also be related to changes in sterling M_3 in a way which highlights the importance of the overseas sector. The position for the financial year 1976-7 is shown below.

---

1 'DCE and the Money Supply – a Statistical Note', *BEQB*, vol. 17, no. 1, March 1977, p. 39.
2 Ibid., pp. 39-40 (words in parentheses added).
3 Ibid., p. 40.

		£m
	Domestic credit expansion	4,934
less	External and foreign currency finance of the public sector	1,097
less	the increase in overseas sterling deposits	175
less	the net increase in the Banks' foreign currency deposits	58
less	the increase in the banks' non-deposit liabilities	776
	Change in sterling M_3	+2,828

Very broadly speaking the first three items deducted from DCE are 'the counterpart in the balance of payments accounts, of the current account. . . deficit plus any capital flows . . . from the UK private sector (including the balancing item)'.[1] Alternatively DCE may be looked upon as roughly the change in sterling M_3 plus the external deficit in the sense just defined.

The importance attached to DCE seems to vary with the state of the balance of payments with rather less attention being given to it when the latter is in surplus than when it is in deficit. The reason for this would seem to be that when there is a deficit in the balance of payments, a target for DCE necessarily makes the money stock target correspondingly less and clearly has an appeal to international creditors such as the IMF. However, this does not necessarily make DCE a good target for policy purposes and it does not seem to have any straightforward relationship to the operation of the economic system. A similar comment might be made when DCE is viewed primarily as a credit concept and related to the financing of the PSBR.

As regards fiscal policy, difficulties arise in trying to determine whether it is in some sense expansionary, contractionary or neutral. For instance, it is argued that the actual budget balance for some period of time may be a misleading guide to what is called 'fiscal stance' and that a better one would be to assess what the budget balance would be if there were full employment or some other standardized level of economic activity with unchanged taxation and expenditure policies. In particular, with given tax rates, unemployment and social security benefit rates the budget deficit will be markedly less or the surplus greater at 'high' levels of employment and economic activity than at low levels and so it is this kind of 'standardized budget balance' that is a better indicator of fiscal stance.

But this approach, like others, gives rise to difficulties. What precisely is meant by a standardized level of economic activity? It may be difficult to get other than a more or less arbitrary working definition of this term. Furthermore, it would seem that the budget balance should be indexed to allow for inflation. Again, a deficit or surplus may be more or less inflationary or deflationary respectively depending on how it is financed or managed. The effects of, say, a deficit being financed through a net increase in the rate of growth of the money stock, as opposed to the sale of government debt to the non-bank private sector, will generally be very different. This might suggest that in assessing the effects of a change in the budget balance it is desirable to hold monetary policy constant in some sense, perhaps in terms of a constant rate of growth of the money stock. Similar questions arise in relation to exchange rate policy; a constant policy might be to hold exchange rates fixed or at the other extreme to allow them to float, depending on the current policy. All of these points need to be held in mind as a qualification to the following discussion

---

1 Ibid., p. 41.

which concentrates on the planned budget deficits or surpluses at the time of the actual budgets and broadly contrasts them with the immediately preceding budgetary experience.

The budgets of the late 1960s were designed to be contractionary in that they aimed for growing surpluses and had as a major objective an improvement in the balance of payments position.[1] A marked improvement did take place in 1969 and the budget for 1970 would seem to have maintained a roughly neutral stance aiming at much the same surplus as in the previous year.

The budgets between 1970 and 1978 can usefully be looked at as a group. Like its two predecessors the 1971 Budget planned for a substantial surplus, though somewhat less than that of the 1970 Budget, and a *negative* borrowing requirement, thus envisaging a net repayment of debt. During 1971, as for some years previously, the growth of output was sluggish and unemployment began to rise, whilst the balance of payments on current account was strongly in surplus, as it had been for the past two years.

It was against this background that the Budget of 1972 was designed. It was highly expansionary. It planned for a very small surplus and net borrowing of £2,667m – the equivalent of some 17% of the estimated cost of supply services for that year. It was not until 1973 that the economy showed much evidence of a response to this large fiscal stimulus. During 1972 the overall balance of payments was showing signs of serious weakness. Despite the latter the 1973 Budget carried the expansionary process even further with an anticipated deficit of almost £1,200m, over twice the realized deficit for 1972-3, and net borrowing of some £3,650m.

As has already been seen output grew rapidly during 1973, as did prices, and unemployment fell, whilst the current account deficit on the balance of payments got markedly worse. Inevitably, the 1974 Budget had to try and rectify the position. It planned to turn a provisional deficit for 1973-4 of some £1,700m into a surplus of about £980m and provisional net borrowing of £3,100m into one of around £600m. These were dramatic and large changes in relation to overall budgetary figures, though in the event they were not realized, but taken in conjunction with monetary and other measures probably helped to improve the balance of payments position at the expense of the rate of growth of output and increased unemployment.

The 1975 Budget was prepared against a background of world recession, rapidly rising prices at home with unemployment tending to increase and a massive deficit in the current balance of payments for 1974. The consolidated fund surplus of some £980m expected twelve months earlier had become a deficit of over £3,200m and net borrowing had turned out to be almost £6,000m instead of £3,100m. Despite some increases in taxation the Chancellor planned for a deficit for 1975-6 on the consolidated fund of over £2,700m and net borrowing of some £4,600m. As in the previous year these figures were far from being realized. The 1975-6 deficit on the consolidated fund was actually over £6,600, well over twice what had been planned a year earlier, and net borrowing became £8,750m.

By the time of the 1976 Budget it was evident that during 1975 there had been a useful improvement in the balance of payments though it still had a substantial deficit, and the pace of inflation was slowing down but was still large by the

---

1   The budgets referred to are the annual budgets at the end of each financial year. However, the authorities have often found it necessary to introduce supplementary budgets.

standards of other developed countries. However, unemployment had increased markedly. In these circumstances the Budget was designed to be more or less neutral and the government showed its determination to control public expenditure by putting a strict limit — known as cash limits — on the actual amount of cash that might be spent on a wide range of public services. In the event the deficit for 1976-7 on the consolidated fund turned out to be some £1,100m less than forecast and net borrowing was some £4,100m less than planned.

However, the year 1976-7 was a very difficult one for the UK economy, with sterling under strong downward pressure in the exchange markets, output sluggish, prices continuing to rise rapidly, unemployment increasing and a substantial rise in official borrowing from abroad. Against this background the 1977 Budget planned for a deficit on the consolidated fund of some £5,700m and net borrowing by the National Loans Fund of some £7,600m, each of which figures was around £1,000m in excess of the estimated outturn for 1976-7 and probably implied that in real terms the Budget was essentially neutral, though the authorities saw it as having some expansionary effect.

The forecast for 1978-9 is that the consolidated fund deficit will be about £8,600m and net borrowing by the National Loans Fund almost £9,900m. Once receipts from other departmental funds are taken into account the central government borrowing requirement becomes some £7,900m. Each of these figures is about £3,500m greater than the outturn figures for 1977-8 and on the face of it represent a moderate fiscal stimulus for the economy, though the Chancellor has also announced monetary targets for the same period which, if realized, would constitute somewhat tighter monetary conditions than in the previous year. Unless there is a further fiscal stimulus later in the year, and bearing in mind the expectations for slow growth in world economic activity, there would seem to be little likelihood of a major recovery in the UK economy over the next year and the general stance of monetary and fiscal policy would seem to imply that relatively high inflation in terms of the standards of other industrial countries will persist in the UK for some considerable time.

V.2   Policy and the European Community

Whatever may be the merits or demerits of past monetary and fiscal policy there is no doubt the UK will be affected by steps taken to establish economic and monetary union amongst the members of the European Community. Some eight years ago this was envisaged as involving absolutely fixed exchange rates between members' currencies, free from any exchange rate margins, or, alternatively and preferably, a single Community currency; the establishment of a Community system for the central banks, possibly along the lines of the Federal Reserve System of the United States and with analogous powers; the harmonized management of national budgets under a Community decision-making body which would have authority to influence member countries' levels of revenue and expenditure, as well as the methods of financing the deficits and the disposal of surpluses.[1]

However, these far-reaching proposals received a cool response from member

---

1   *Report* to the Council and the Commission on the Realization by Stages of Economic and Monetary Union in the Community, Werner Report, Supplement to Bulletin 11-1970 of the European Communities.

countries and little progress was made towards implementing them. But more recently the matter was again taken up by the Community and particularly by the President of the Commission of the European Communities.[1]

The Commission has outlined in a paper to the European Council how it now thinks economic and monetary union should be approached. It proposed, in its own words 'a five year programme of action, the details of which would be filled in from year to year, hinging on three key aims — establishment of lasting convergence of the Member States' economies through fuller coordination of short-term economic policies, a return to greater cohesion between European currencies and an increase in the financial resources available to the Community; establishment of a single market through harmonization in the fields of taxation, free movement of goods and services, capital movements and right of establishment; and, lastly, identification of sectoral, structural and social problems which the Community is well placed to help solve by devising an overall strategy'.[2]

Whilst progress has been made in some of the foregoing areas such as harmonization of taxation, free movement of goods and services and the right of establishment, little progress has been made in the co-ordination of economic policies and particularly in the area of exchange rates.

It was against this background that the President of the Commission stressed the need for working towards what he described as monetary union. He put forward seven arguments. One, 'that monetary union favours a more efficient and developed rationalization of industry and commerce than is possible under a Customs Union alone',[3] as it would eliminate exchange rate risks and inflation uncertainties between member states. Two, he believes there is a need for 'a major new international currency' which would provide 'a joint and alternative pillar of the world monetary system', which is now largely dependent on the uncertainties of the US dollar. Three, he argued that monetary union would lead to 'a common rate of price movement' amongst the members and, though be conceded it to be controversial, 'that monetary union could help establish a new era of price stability in Europe and achieve a decisive break with the present chronic inflationary disorder'. He has in mind, very interestingly, a 'European monetary authority' which would 'manage the exchange rate (sic), internal reserves and the main lines of monetary policy' which would adhere to 'a determined and relatively independent policy of controlling note issue and bank money creation [and] would start by adopting target rates of growth of monetary expansion consistent with a new European standard of monetary stability'.

Four, he believes that monetary union and the assumed price and exchange rate stability it would entail would favour investment and expansion and so ameliorate unemployment. Five, he recognizes that monetary union will not necessarily ensure 'a smooth regional distribution of the gains from increased economic integration and union' and so argues, surely rightly, that 'it is indispensable that an associated

---

1   See Roy Jenkins, 'Europe's Present Challenge and Future Opportunity', Jean Monnet Lecture, European Institute, Florence, 27 October 1977, and reprinted in *Lloyds Bank Review*, January 1978, No. 127, pp. 1-14.

2   'Eleventh General Report on the Activities of the European Communities 1977', Brussels, Luxembourg, February 1978, pp. 74-5.

3   This and all subsequent quotations are from the reprint in *Lloyds Bank Review*, op. cit.

system of public finance should also be envisaged', which would give rise to substantial transfers of real resources within the Community.

Six, he examines the implications of monetary union for the relationship between the Community and its members. In doing so he enunciates the important principle that 'we must only give to the Community functions which will, beyond reasonable doubt, deliver significantly better results because they are performed at a Community level'. One of these is, of course, monetary and exchange rate policy. However, this does not require that social and welfare expenditure amounting to around 25% of the GNP of members should become a centralized Community matter. But the amelioration of regional and other disparities within a monetary union would, according to certain estimates, require some 5% to 7% of Community GNP, against present Community expenditure of the order of 1% of GNP. Seven, he sees monetary union as a means of encouraging European political integration.

This new discussion of monetary union seems much more realistic than the Werner proposals of 1970 and granted the upheavals in international monetary arrangements in recent years and the disruptive experience of domestic inflation amongst member countries, it is conceivable that monetary union will be extensively debated in the next few years.

V.3   Conclusions

The policy record of the UK for the period since the 1960s has been extremely disappointing. The simultaneous achievement of the various goals over a sustained period has continuously eluded the authorities. This failure or relative failure raises far-reaching questions about the choice of policy goals, the nature and adequacy of the policy instruments at the disposal of the authorities and the limitations on our knowledge of the detailed and interdependent relationships between goals, instruments and targets. Moreover, these questions ultimately go far beyond the realm of the economic. For if a choice has to be made between the different goals in terms of the degree to which they can be achieved then serious political problems may arise. If, for instance, price inflation can only be reduced at the expense of substantial unemployment and sluggish economic growth then the very political institutions of the society may come under strain. However, the last few years suggest that these strains have been carried more easily than might have been expected.

Furthermore, the discussion in V.1 above suggests that policy errors and mis-judgements have contributed significantly to the economic problems of recent years. In particular, both monetary and fiscal policy have from time to time been used in ways which could only be expected to give rise to future economic problems. In the recent past the monetary and budgetary policies of 1972 and 1973 clearly come to mind and in the present, but to a lesser extent, the policies being pursued in early 1978. However, there seems to be a greater acceptance across a wide range of political opinion that rapid and variable inflation imposes serious costs on the community, putting at risk both employment and living standards; and that both monetary and budgetary policy must be managed in ways that contribute to its curtailment. These developments, if they persist, as must be hoped, augur well for the recovery of the UK economy over the next several years, though this is in no way to imply that sound monetary and budgetary policies are a sufficient condition for that recovery; but the efficiency of industry and the functioning or malfunctioning of labour and other markets is the concern of other chapters.

REFERENCES AND FURTHER READING

Bank of England Quarterly Bulletin

The British System of Taxation, Central Office of Information Reference Pamphlet 112, HMSO, 1977.

Sir Alec Cairncross (ed.), *Britain's Economic Prospects Reconsidered,* Allen and Unwin, 1971.

Andrew Crockett, *Money: Theory, Policy and Institutions,* Nelson, 1973.

Brian Griffiths, *Competition in Banking,* Hobart Paper 51, Institute of Economic Affairs, 1971.

H. G. Johnson *et al., Readings in British Monetary Economics,* Oxford University Press, 1972.

M. A. King and J. A. Kay, *The British Tax System,* Oxford University Press, 1978.

A. T. Peacock and G. K. Shaw, *The Economic Theory of Fiscal Policy,* 2nd edition, Allen and Unwin, 1976.

A. R. Prest, *Public Finance in Theory and Practice,* 5th edition, Weidenfeld and Nicolson, 1975.

Robin Pringle, *Banking in Britain,* Methuen, 1975.

Jack Revell, *The British Financial System,* Macmillan, 1973.

The Structure and Reform of Direct Taxation, Report of a Committee chaired by Professor J. E. Meade, Allen and Unwin, 1978.

D. Swann, *The Common Market,* 3rd edition, Penguin Books, 1975.

3

Foreign trade and the balance of payments

J. S. Metcalfe

I THE UK BALANCE OF PAYMENTS
I.1 Introduction

The importance to the UK of foreign trade, foreign investment and the balance of international payments will be obvious to anyone who has followed the course of events since 1960. The growth of the UK economy, the level of employment, and real wages and the standard of living have been, and will continue to be, greatly influenced by external economic events. It is the purpose of this chapter to outline the main features of the external relationships of the UK and to discuss economic policies adopted to manipulate these external relationships, with the primary focus of attention being on the years since 1960.[1]

To begin with, it is often said that the UK is a highly 'open' economy, and some indication of the meaning of this is given by the fact that, in 1977, exports of goods and services were 30.8% of GNP and imports of goods and services were 30.2% of GNP, both figures being greater than the corresponding figures for the mid-1960s and substantially greater than those for 1938.[2] A high degree of openness implies that the structure of production and employment is greatly influenced by international specialization. For the UK it also means that about half the foodstuffs and the bulk of raw materials necessary to maintain inputs for industry have to be imported. In the sense defined, the UK is a more open economy than some industrial nations, e.g. West Germany and France, but less open than others such as Belgium.

I.2 The concept of the Balance of Payments

The concept of the balance of payments is central to a study of the external monetary relationships of a country but, as with any unifying concept, it is not free from ambiguities of definition and of interpretation. Such ambiguities stem from at least two sources viz., the different uses to which the concept may be put – either as a tool for economic analysis or as a guide to the need for and effectiveness of external policy changes; and the different ways in which we may approach the concept – either as a system of accounts or as a measure of transactions in the foreign exchange market.

From an accounting viewpoint, we may define the balance of payments as a systematic record, over a given period of time, of all transactions between domestic residents and residents of foreign nations. In this context, residents are defined as

---

1 Earlier editions of this volume contain a discussion of external developments between 1945 and 1960. See, e.g., the 5th edition (1974).

2 In 1938 the export: GNP ratio stood at 14% and the import: GNP ratio at 18.9%.

those individuals living in the UK for one year or more, together with corporate bodies located in the UK, and UK government agencies and military forces located abroad. Ideally, the transactions involved should be recorded at the time of the change of ownership of commodities and assets or at the time specific services are performed. In practice, trade flows are recorded on a shipments basis, at the time when the export documents are lodged with the Customs and Excise, and at the time when imports are cleared through Customs. The problem with this method is that the time of shipment need bear no close or stable relationship to the time of payment for the goods concerned and it is this latter which is relevant to the state of the foreign exchange market, although over a year the discrepancies between the two methods are likely to be small. All transactions are recorded as sterling money flows, and when transactions are invoiced in foreign currencies, their values are converted into sterling at the appropriate exchange rate. Because sterling is a 'key' or 'vehicle' currency, and is used as an international medium of exchange, it transpires that 70% of UK exports and roughly 15% of UK imports are invoiced directly in sterling.

Like all systems of income and expenditure accounts, the balance of payments accounts are an ex-post record, constructed on the principle of double entry bookkeeping. Thus each external transaction is effectively entered twice, once to indicate the original transaction, say the import of a given commodity, and again to indicate the manner in which that transaction was financed. The convention is that credit items, which increase net money claims on foreign residents, e.g. exports of goods and services and foreign investment in the UK, are entered with a positive sign, and that debit items, which increase net money liabilities of domestic residents, e.g. imports of goods and services and profits earned by foreign owned firms operating in the UK, are entered with a minus sign. It follows that, in sum, the balance of payments accounts always balance and that the interpretation to be read into the accounts depends on the prior selection of a particular sub-set of transactions. It will be clear, therefore, that there can be no unique picture of a country's external relationships which may be drawn from the accounts.

When analysing the balance of payments it can be useful to make a distinction between autonomous external transactions, transactions undertaken for private gain or international political obligation, and accommodating external transactions, transactions undertaken or induced specifically to finance a gap between autonomous credits and autonomous debits. This distinction is by no means watertight, as we shall see subsequently, but it provides a useful starting point when structuring the accounts and when trying to formulate notions of balance of payments equilibrium.

The Structure of the External Accounts of the UK: It is current practice to divide the external accounts of the UK into three sets of items: (i) current account items, (ii) capital account items, and (iii) official financing items. Current account items and all, or part (depending on taste), of capital account items can as a first approximation be treated as if they correspond to autonomous external transactions, while official financing items may be treated as corresponding to accommodating transactions. The structure of the external accounts and figures for 1973-7 are shown in table 3.1.[1] Current account items consist of exports and imports of commodities (visibles) and services (invisibles, e.g. insurance, shipping, tourist and

---

1   For further details the reader may consult the *UK Balance of Payments 1966-1976*, HMSO, 1977. This annual publication is known as the *Pink Book*.

TABLE 3.1

UK Summary Balance of payments, 1973-7 (£m)

		1973	1974	1975	1976	1977
Current account (credit +/debit)						
Exports (fob) (+)		12,115	16,539	19,462	25,422	32,176
Imports (fob) (−)		14,469	21,734	22,667	28,932	33,788
Visible trade balance		−2,354	−5,195	−3,205	−3,510	−1,612
Government services and transfers (net)		−768	−858	−999	−1,549	−1,901
Other invisibles and transfers (net)		+2,239	+2,538	+2,590	+3,952	+3,478
Invisible trade balance		+1,471	+1,680	+1,591	+2,403	+1,577
Current balance	1	−883	−3,515	−1,614	−1,107	−35
Capital transfers	2	−59	−75	−	−	−
Investment and other capital flows						
Official long-term capital	3	−254	−276	−288	−158	−168
Overseas investment in UK public sector[1]	4	+175	+252	+43	+203	+2,190
Overseas investment in UK private sector	5	+1,652	+2,278	+1,719	+2,062	+2,883
UK private investment overseas	6	−1,848	−1,149	−1,383	−2,154	−1,837
Overseas currency borrowing (net) by UK banks:						
To finance UK investment abroad	7	+595	+270	+320	+165	+620
Other borrowing	8	−70	−564	−85	−271	−28
Exchange reserves in sterling:						
British Government stocks	9	+74	−124	+7	+14	+5
Banking and money market liabilities	10	+87	+1,534	−624	−1,421	−24
Other external banking & money market liabilities in sterling	11	−7	+148	+550	+255	1,471
Import credit	12	+349	+172	+224	+242	+87
Export credit	13	−552	−809	−570	−1,178	−231
Other short-term flows	14	−152	−48	+290	−565	+132
Total investment and other capital flows	15	+49	+1,648	+203	−2,806	+4,802
Balancing item	16	+122	+260	−54	+285	+2,596
Total currency flow	17	−771	−1,646	−1,465	−3,628	+7,363
Allocation of special drawing rights	18	−	−	−	−	−
Gold subscription to IMF	19	−	−	−	−	−
Total lines 17−19	20	−771	−1,646	−1,465	−3,628	+7,363
Official financing						
Net transactions with IMF	21	−	−	−	+1,018	+1,113
Net transactions with overseas monetary authorities plus foreign currency borrowing by H.M. government[2]	22	+999	+1,751	+810	+1,757	+1,112
Drawings on (+)/additions to (−) official reserves	23	−228	−105	+655	+853	−9,588
Total official financing	24	+771	+1,646	+1,465	+3,628	−7,363

Source: BEQB, March 1978.

Notes: 1 Excludes foreign currency borrowing by the public sector under the exchange cover scheme.

2 Including the foreign currency borrowing by the public sector under the exchange cover scheme.

banking transactions), profit and interest payments received from abroad less similar payments made abroad, certain governments transactions, e.g. maintenance of armed forces overseas, and specified transfer payments, e.g. immigrants' remittances and foreign aid granted by the UK government. The rationale for collecting these items together is that the majority of them are directly related to flows of national income and expenditure, whether public or private. In particular, visible and invisible trade flows are closely related to movements in foreign and domestic incomes, the division of these incomes between expenditure and saving, and the division of expenditure between outlays on foreign goods and services and outlays on domestic goods and services. It should be remembered, however, that trade flows may change not because of changes in incomes, but because of spending out of past savings (dishoarding) or because of the need to build up inventories of means of production, changes in which correspond to variations in holdings of assets. Profit and interest flows are classified in the current account because they correspond directly to international flows of income.

Capital account items can be arranged in several ways. One may distinguish official capital flows (line 3) from private capital flows (e.g. lines 4, 5 and 6). Alternatively, one may classify by the maturity date of the assets involved and distinguish long-term capital flows (e.g. lines 3–6 inclusive) from short-term capital flows (e.g. lines 11–14 inclusive). Equally one could, in principle, distinguish capital flows according to the implicit time horizon of the investor undertaking the appropriate decisions. The inevitable limitations of alternative classificatory schemes should not be allowed to hide one basic point, that all capital flows correspond to changes in the stocks of foreign assets and liabilities of the UK, although not necessarily to changes in the net external wealth of the UK. As such these capital flows are generated primarily by the relative rates of return on domestic and foreign assets after due allowance is made for the effects of risk and taxation. Flows of direct and portfolio investment in productive capital assets (lines 5 and 6) thus depend on prospective rates of profit in the UK compared to those abroad, and changes in holdings of financial assets depend on relative domestic and foreign interest-rate structures. A relative increase in UK profit and interest rates will normally stimulate a larger net capital inflow or a smaller net capital outflow, and vice versa for a relative fall in UK profit and interest rates. One important factor which should not be overlooked here, is the influence of anticipated exchange rate changes upon the capital gains and losses accruing to holdings of assets denominated in different currencies. If a sterling depreciation is anticipated, for example, this will provide a powerful incentive for wealth holders to switch any sterling denominated assets they hold into foreign currency denominated assets, in order to avoid the expected capital losses on holdings of sterling assets.[1] The 'capital value' effect is particularly important in creating changes in the flow of short-term capital. It is worth commenting at this stage upon lines 9, 10 and 11 which correspond to changes in sterling balances. Sterling balances arose out of the key currency role of sterling which led to private traders and foreign banks holding working balances in sterling, and which also led governments to hold part of their official exchange reserves in sterling. This latter aspect was particularly important for the overseas sterling area countries (OSA) which traditionally maintained their domestic currencies rigidly tied to sterling, maintained the bulk of their foreign exchange reserves in sterling, and pooled any

---

1 Subject to the possibility that forward exchange cover may have been taken (cf. section III.6 below).

earnings of gold and non-sterling currencies in London in exchange for sterling balances. Furthermore, between 1940 and 1958, OSA countries were linked to the UK through a tightly knit system of exchange controls which discriminated against transactions with non-sterling area (NSA) countries, and especially those in the dollar area. The sterling area was effectively a currency union which allowed members to economize on their total holdings of gold and non-sterling currency reserves. One important consequence of this was that the sterling area system created substantial holdings of UK liabilities by foreigners which had no maturity date and which could be liquidated at a moments' notice, so forming a permanent fund of contingent claims on the UK gold and foreign currency reserves. OSA countries could acquire sterling balances in the following three ways: by having a current account surplus with the UK; as the result of a net inflow of foreign investment from the UK; and from pooling in the UK any gold and foreign currency earned from transactions with NSA countries.[1] At the beginning of World War II, the total of sterling balances stood at approximately £500m; by the end of the war they had risen to £3.7bn, around which figure they fluctuated between 1945 and 1966.[2] In contrast to the stability in the total quantity of sterling balances there were marked changes in the country composition, some countries, e.g. India and Pakistan, ran down their wartime accumulation of balances, while other countries, e.g. some Middle East countries, acquired new holdings of sterling balances.[3] The continued existence of the sterling area financial arrangements depended upon two conditions being satisfied. Firstly, the OSA must have a high proportion of their transactions with each other and with the UK. Secondly, there must be a continued confidence in the ability of the UK, in its role of banker to OSA, to match short-term sterling liabilities with an equivalent volume of official reserves or other short-term assets. From 1958 onwards neither of these conditions were satisfied. The OSA countries began to transact more intensively with NSA countries and the UK moved into a position of seemingly permanent deficit on her basic balance, so increasing short-term liabilities relative to official reserves and other short-term assets and creating the conditions for the sterling crises which became frequent in the 1960s.[4] It was not unexpected, therefore, when the sterling area effectively ceased to exist in June 1972.[5]

---

1 Ignoring reserve diversification activities, the flow increment of sterling balances is equal to the OSA basic balance surplus with the UK, plus the fraction of their basic balance surplus with NSA countries which is pooled in the UK. The changes in UK official reserves, including any change in official foreign borrowing, less the change in sterling balances (the change in the UK's short-term liquidity position, one might say) is equal to the basic balance of the UK. These relations hold only as an approximation; changes in trade credit, for example, would have to be zero for them to hold exactly. The concept of the basic balance is defined below, section I.3.

2 See Statistical Appendix, table A-8, for details of total sterling holdings.

3 Detailed information on this may be found in Susan Strange, *Sterling and British Policy*, Oxford, 1971, chapters 2 and 3.

4 If official short-term and medium-term foreign borrowing by the UK government is subtracted from the official exchange reserves this gives a measure of 'cover' for the sterling liabilities. In 1962 the ratio of 'cover' to total sterling liabilities was 51%. By end 1967, the 'cover' had disappeared entirely; outstanding official borrowing exceeded the official reserves by £3.8bn.

5 Prior to 1972, the OSA consisted of the Commonwealth, except Canada, South Africa, Iceland, Ireland, Kuwait, Jordan and some others. Before June 1972 these countries were known as the scheduled territories but since June 1972 only Ireland and Gibraltar remain in this category.

Recent developments with respect to sterling balances are treated in section III.6 below.

We come next to the balancing item (line 16), which is a statistical item to compensate for the total of measurement errors and omissions in the accounts, arising from, for example, the under-recording of exports and the reliance upon survey data for certain items such as foreign investment and tourist expenditures. A positive balancing item can reflect an unrecorded net export, an unrecorded net capital inflow, or some combination of the two. The major source of changes in the balancing item is likely to be unrecorded changes in net trade credit, reflecting discrepancies between the time goods are shipped and the time when the associated payments are made across the exchanges. As can be seen from table 3.1, the balancing item is very volatile and can on occasions, e.g. 1977, be of a magnitude comparable to or greater than the surplus or deficit on current account. The total of investment and other capital flows together with the balancing item is known as the total currency flow (TCF, line 17), which can, in principle, be treated as the net balance of autonomous transactions.[1] Before we come to accommodating transactions, two adjustments to the TCF have to be made, both of which relate to the UK's membership of the IMF. First, we have the allocation of special drawing rights (line 18) which are treated as a credit item since they effectively add to the official reserves of the UK (line 23). Second, we have the gold subscription to the IMF. When the UK subscribed gold to the IMF, as in 1966 and 1970, the gold element in the official reserves would fall and this reduction in assets has to be entered in line 23 with a positive sign. The entry in line 19 is the requisite double entry to balance the accounts and can be interpreted as the acquisition of assets in the IMF. Note that as from April 1978 the UK is no longer required to subscribe gold to the IMF when making an increase in its quota (see section III.9 below).

The total of lines 17 to 19, the *adjusted currency flow* (line 20), has to be matched by an equal amount of official financing. If, for any year, line 20 has a negative sign then the authorities must reduce the official external assets or increase the official external liabilities of the UK, undertaking the reverse operations if line 20 is positive in sign. There are three ways in which the necessary adjustments can be made. First, the UK may draw upon or add to the official gold and currency reserves (line 23). Throughout the period since 1967 the ratio of UK gross reserves (end year) to UK imports has averaged only 14.5% with a low of 8% in 1976 and peaks of 23% in 1972 and 32% in 1977. Not only must the reserve base be considered inadequate for an economy as open as the UK, its composition has also changed substantially since the mid-1960s with the proportion of reserves consisting of foreign currency increasing from 6% at end 1963 to 93% at end 1977. Unused access to the SDR facility formed only 3% of UK reserves at end 1977. As a second line of defence, the UK can borrow foreign currencies from the IMF. An amount equal to 25% of the UK's quota may be borrowed automatically, the so-called gold-tranche position which is classed as part of the official reserves.[2] The UK has further access to four credit tranches, each of which corresponds to 25% of quota,[3] but access is

---

1 Note that the TCF is now defined as the balance for official financing, the earlier and more useful TCF concept being abandoned in the 1976 Pink Book.

2 Automatic borrowing can exceed the gold tranche position to the extent that the total IMF holding of sterling falls below 75% of the UK quota.

3 Between March 1976 and March 1978 the credit tranches were temporarily raised to 36.5% of quota. See section III.9 below.

dependent upon the UK government adopting economic policies which meet with the approval of the IMF, this being particularly so for drawings beyond the first credit tranche. The maximum amount the UK could borrow at year-end 1977, including the gold-tranche position, stood at £1294m. The points to remember about IMF finance are that it is temporary (borrowings have to be repaid within three to five years), conditional, and cheap (4%–6%), relative to current commercial rates of interest. Finally, the UK has access to a considerable network of borrowing facilities built up with foreign central banks in the 1960s, primarily as a short-term defence against speculative capital flows. These have proved to be of considerable value to the UK, and have been supplemented since 1973 by direct government borrowing, mostly from the Eurodollar market.

It may already be apparent that the distinction between autonomous and accommodating transactions upon which this discussion is based, is not entirely satisfactory. For example, by manipulating UK interest rates the government can create an inflow of short-term capital to accommodate a given current account deficit, even though from the point of view of individuals or banks buying and selling the assets the transactions are autonomous. Similarly, autonomous government items such as foreign aid may be deliberately adjusted to accommodate a deficit elsewhere in the accounts. At a more general level, whenever the government adopts policies to change the balance of payments, the effects of these policies will influence the totals of autonomous transactions so that they cease to be independent of the underlying state of the balance of payments. Despite these difficulties the autonomous-accommodating distinction provides a useful starting point for any arrangement of the external accounts.

So far we have examined the external accounts in isolation but they may equally by examined as an integral part of the national income and expenditure accounts. From this viewpoint, the balance of payments deficit (surplus) on current account is identically equal to the excess (shortfall) of national expenditure over national income and hence to the reduction (increase) in the net external assets owned by UK residents.[1] It follows that the UK can only add to its external net assets to the extent that it has an equivalent current account surplus.

Finally, we should note that, although the accounts separate current account items from capital account items, there are several important links between the two sub-sets of transactions. We have already pointed out that a non-zero current account results in changes in the net external assets of the UK. As these assets and liabilities have profit and interest flows attached to them, any change in the total of external net assets will lead to changes in the interest, profit and dividend flows which appear in the current account. Furthermore, they also result in equivalent changes in national income and so will affect the current account indirectly through any effects on national expenditure and the demand for imports. Similarly, within the context of a given current account position, capital flows which change the composition of external net assets will change the average rate of return on these assets and so react back on the current account. These are perhaps the more straightforward links, but others exist, for example, between trade flows and the balance of export and import credit and between trade and investment flows and changes in total sterling balances. As has often been said, the balance of payments is akin to a seamless web and it can be grossly misleading to treat individual items in isolation from the rest of the accounts.

---

1   Cf. J. Hicks, *Social Framework,* 1971, chapters 8 and 21.

I.3   Equilibrium and Disequilibrium in the Balance of Payments

It is obviously important, both for purposes of economic policy and historical analysis, to have clear notions of balance of payments equilibrium and disequilibrium. However, the formulation of such notions is not easy. As a first approximation, we could define balance of payments equilibrium as a situation in which, at the existing exchange rate, autonomous credits are equal to autonomous debits and no official financing transactions are required. This definition raises three problems. First, that of the time span over which equilibrium is defined. Clearly, a daily or even monthly span of time would be of little value and it is generally accepted that a sufficient span of years should be allowed so that the effects of cyclical fluctuations in income will have no appreciable net impact on external transactions. Second, if the exchange rate is allowed to fluctuate freely to equate the demand with the supply of foreign exchange, then equilibrium is always attained automatically and any notion of payments disequilibrium becomes redundant. Third, and in contrast, if the exchange rate is managed in some way to make it partially or completely independent of market forces, we must then accept that policies can be adopted to manipulate autonomous transactions in such a way as to make them balance. However, the problem which this raises is that the attainment of external equilibrium, at a given exchange rate, may involve unacceptable levels of employment or inflation, an interest-rate structure which is counter to economic growth objectives and a trade policy inconsistent with international obligations. To take account of these issues we can formulate the following definition of equilibrium. The balance of payments is in equilibrium when, at the existing exchange rate, autonomous credits are equal to autonomous debits over a period of good and bad years, without involving: (i) departures from full employment or price stability; (ii) departures from the desired rate of economic growth; and (iii) adoption of tariffs or subsidies inconsistent with accepted international obligations.

The question now arises of the sets of autonomous transactions to be used in this definition of equilibrium. One possibility is to consider current account transactions alone, but equilibrium would then involve a constant level of net external wealth and there is no particular merit in this, particularly for a growing economy. As far as the UK is concerned, two sets of autonomous transactions have been used in discussions of balance of payments performance, the basic balance and the total currency flow.

The basic balance, defined as the sum of the current account and the net flow of long-term capital, attracts attention on several grounds, not least as one indicator of secular trends in external transactions. If the basic balance is in equilibrium, any net outflow (inflow) of long-term capital results in an equivalent increase in the stock of external assets (liabilities) of the UK. Furthermore, all net flows of short-term capital must be matched by equivalent, offsetting changes in official financing. Thus the basic balance puts below the line all capital flows essentially related to the role of the UK as an international banking and financial centre; capital flows which may be particularly sensitive to accommodating monetary manipulation.

Since 1969, however, the UK authorities have preferred to utilize the TCF as the appropriate indicator of external performance. In contrast to the basic balance, this places all short-term capital flows above the line, so that a zero TCF corresponds to a situation of no change in the total and officially held external net assets. There are several arguments in favour of the switch to the TCF, viz., (i) many short-term capital flows are linked to items in the trade balance, e.g. trade credit, or to the financing of long-term investment, and cannot sensibly be separated from items in the basic balance; (ii) short-term capital flows are inherently volatile, therefore they provide poor accommodation and should not be used for that purpose; and (iii) the TCF avoids the problem of separating the balancing item from the basic balance with the attendant danger of a misleading treatment of any errors and omissions. In the short term, of course, the TCF is more volatile than the basic balance, but over the longer run the two measures should coincide, provided that short-term flows net out to zero. A further advantage of the TCF is that it shows the potential increase (decrease) in the UK money supply as a result of a surplus (deficit) in the aggregate of autonomous balance of payments transactions.

I.4   The Balance of Payments 1956—1977

We shall now use our concepts of equilibrium to assess the balance of payments performance of the UK since 1956. To assist in this, table 3.2 contains average annual figures for selected items in the balance of payments in the periods 1956-60, 1961-4, 1965-7, 1968-71 and 1972-7. The first two sub-periods cover complete short cycles ending in a boom year, while the remaining three are somewhat arbitrary and are separated by the 1967 devaluation and the floating of sterling in June 1972. The averages of course hide substantial annual variations but they will suffice for present purposes.

In the *Brookings Report*, R. Cooper suggested that the UK balance of payments position, at least up to 1966, could be summarized in terms of four propositions: (i) the UK is normally a net exporter of long-term capital, with a surplus on the current account; (ii) the visible trade balance is normally in deficit, but the invisible balance shows a surplus more than sufficient to offset this; (iii) the role of the UK as banker to the OSA gives volatile short-term capital flows an important position in the balance of payments; and finally, (iv) the trading, investing and international financial activities of the UK are carried out with a very inadequate underpinning of foreign exchange reserves.[1] Of our five periods, that of 1956-60 comes closest to conforming to this view. The net outflow of long-term capital exceeded the current account surplus by an annual average rate of £53m and this was financed by a short-term capital inflow of £59m. After taking account of the balancing item and other factors the UK was able to add to its official reserves at an annual rate of £79m. Certainly the payments position, on either basic balance or TCF definitions, was nearer to a state of equilibrium than in any of the subsequent periods, coinciding as it did with an average unemployment rate of 1.7%.

The next two sub-periods to 1967 show unmistakable signs of a slide into fundamental disequilibrium. The trade balance continued to deteriorate throughout the two periods, despite a sustained growth of world trade, and so did the current account which moved into deficit. A successful attempt by the government to restrict the growth of overseas public expenditure in 1965-7 only prevented the deficit from being worse than it would otherwise have been. To some extent a reduction in the net outflow of long-term capital helped reduce the deficit on the basic balance, but the improvement here was more than offset by massive short-term outflows induced by the sterling crises of 1961, 1964 and each of the three following years. It was, of course, the weakness in the current account and basic balance, and the perpetual fear of a sterling devaluation which was crucial here. An important consequence of this lack of confidence in sterling was the need to incur

---

1   R. Caves (ed.), *Britain's Economic Prospects,* Allen and Unwin, 1968, Ch. 3.

TABLE 3.2

Trends in the UK Balance of Payments, Annual Averages for Selected Periods (£m) and Average Growth Rates for GDP and World Exports of Manufactures

		1956-60	1961-4	1965-7	1968-71	1972-7
1	Visible balance	−94	−213	−281	−142	−2,763
2	Government services and transfers (net)	−209	−377	−278	−603	−1,532
3	Private invisibles (net)	+439	+559	+484	+1230	+3,123
4	Invisible balance	+230	+182	+206	+627	+1,591
5	Current account balance	+136	−31	−75	+484	−1,171
6	Balancing item	+91	−13	+49	+139	+396
7	Balance of long-term capital	−189	−139	−137	−101	+537
8	Balance of long-term and other capital flows	−130	−181	+498	+367	+541
9	Basic balance (5 + 7)	−53	−170	−212	+383	−634
10	Basic balance plus balancing item (9 + 6)	+38	−183	−163	+522	−216
11	Total currency flow	+97	−225	−524	+927	−235
12	Gold subs., IMF and SDRs	−18	–	−14	+64	+21
13	Total lines 11 and 12	+79	−225	−538	+991	−214
	Official financing					
14	Net foreign currency borrowing by HM government (inc. IMF)	–	+143	+420	−593	+1,501
15	Transfer $ portfolio to reserves	–	–	+173	–	–
16	Drawings on (+) or additions to (−) official reserves	−79	+82	+55	−398	−1,287
17	Total official financing	−79	+225	+538	−991	−214
18	Average annual growth real GDP (1970 prices) (%)	2.36	3.65	2.33	2.63	0.62
19	Average annual growth world exports manufactures (%)	8.77	7.95	6.77	11.50	6.57

Sources: UK Balance of Payments 1971 and 1976 and ET, March 1978. World exports from various issues of NIER.

substantial foreign debts and to liquidate the government's portfolio of dollar securities, in order to maintain the parity of sterling.

The inevitable devaluation, which took place in November 1967, was followed by a substantial turn round in the external payments position, although it is not completely clear to what extent this is attributable to the devaluation, or to the acceleration in the growth of world trade, or to measures to restrict demand growth and DCE after 1968 (between 1969 and 1971 the average rate of growth of real GDP fell to 1.7%). The visible deficit was almost halved and an increase in the invisible surplus resulted in the current account moving back into surplus. When combined with a halving of the net outflow of long-term capital this created a very strong position in the basic balance, especially when account is taken of the balancing item. Apart from this, confidence in sterling returned after 1968, no doubt helped by the Basle arrangements of that year, and short-term capital flowed back into the UK at an annual average rate of £405m. So strong was the improvement in the payments position, that the UK was able to repay a substantial part of the debts raised in defence of sterling in the previous two periods and, at the same time, add to the official reserves. It cannot be claimed that this period saw a return to equilibrium in the external accounts, simply because of the severe restraint on domestic growth which took place. However, it can at least be argued that the foundations were then laid for a return to equilibrium once the foreign debts had been repaid.

That the return to equilibrium has not been achieved is clear from the figures for 1972-7. The most important point about this period is that it was one of substantial disruption to the international trading system. The rise in the relative price of primary commodities and oil, together with the associated slackening in the growth of world trade, created a sharp deterioration in the UK balance of trade during this period which was reinforced, in the short run, by the depreciation of sterling after June 1972. Two factors helped to cushion the effect of this trade deficit on the basic balance; a marked improvement in the net inflow of profits, interest and dividends and a reversal of the traditional UK role of net-exporter of long-term capital, largely the result of foreign investment to exploit NS oil resources. The average basic balance deficit over this period of £634 was financed in two principal ways: (i) a net inflow of short-term capital, as oil-producing countries allocated part of their surplus revenues to sterling assets; and (ii) resort to substantial foreign currency borrowing by the government and public sector bodies supplemented by drawing upon the official reserves. This policy of 'financing' the deficit has not been without its problems. As the events of 1976 and 1977 demonstrated, short-term capital can flow out of the UK as quickly as it may flow in, placing substantial pressures on the exchange rate and the official reserves. Indeed, the official gross reserves fell from $7.02bn at end February 1976 to a low of $4.13bn at end 1976 and were rebuilt even more rapidly to a figure of $20.5bn at end 1977. The policy of official borrowing has added $17.7bn to outstanding public sector debts between end 1972 and April 1977, and raises immediate problems in terms of repayment; $14.6bn is due for repayment by end 1984, and the financing of a current annual interest charge amounting to $1.3bn.[1]

---

1   Cf. *TER*, No. 86, May 1977, and the article 'UK Official Short and Medium Term Borrowing from Abroad', *BEQB*, March 1976, pp. 78-81. Approximately $10.4bn represents borrowing by the public sector, nationalized industries and local authorities, the bulk of which is covered by the exchange cover scheme reintroduced in 1973. A further $4.2bn represents official borrowing from IMF under the oil facility and the standby arrangements negotiated at the beginning of 1977.

There can be no doubt that this last period was also one of fundamental disequilibrium in the UK balance of payments. The basic balance deficits have been incurred at a time of deepening domestic recession, with the unemployment percentage rising from 2.3% at end 1973 to 6.0% at end 1977, and with industrial production falling 10% between end 1973 and end 1975, from which level it had only improved by 2% by end 1977. The improvement in the current account between 1976 and 1977 can hardly, therefore, be taken as an indication of a return towards equilibrium.

To summarize over the period 1956 to 1977, the one crucial factor appears to be the persistent weakness of the visible trade account which more than offset the steady improvement in the invisible trade surplus. The resulting current account deficits combined with the propensity to export long-term capital progressively undermined the ability of the UK to act as an international financial centre by borrowing short and lending long. The principal result of this has been the termination of the UK's role as banker to the overseas sterling area and the persistence of disruptive changes of international confidence in the external value of sterling. The advent of NS oil, of course, raises the possibility of eliminating, at least temporarily, this state of fundamental disequilibrium as the improvement in the current account for 1977 illustrates. However, this still leaves the longer-term question of how the decline in international competitiveness can be reversed before the benefits from NS oil are exhausted.

North Sea Oil: Recent economic policy discussion in the UK has been dominated by the first of these issues, the economic effects of the exploitation of oil and gas resources in the North Sea, the production of oil first becoming substantial in 1976. Although the effect on GDP will be relatively small, effectively offsetting the loss of real income imposed on the UK by the increase in the relative price of oil at end 1973,[1] and the direct effects on employment negligible, the effects on the balance of payments and public sector revenue are substantial. The major effect will therefore be to alter the environment in which economic policy is formulated and to open up prospects of substantial real growth, unimpeded by trade balance constraints, over the next decade. Section III–5 discusses some of the policy options opened up by NS oil; in this section we briefly outline some calculations of the magnitude of NS oil effects on the balance of payments and the difficulties surrounding such calculations.

The major difficulties relate to uncertainties, e.g. with respect to oil yields, trends in exploitation and development costs, the share of extractive equipment provided by UK firms and most importantly the sterling price of oil. This latter element will depend jointly on the ability of the OPEC cartel to determine the future real increase in the dollar price of oil, a decision over which the UK as a minor producer will have no influence, and upon the policies which the UK government adopts with respect to the exchange rate. Other aspects of government policy, as yet uncertain, will be of equal importance. In particular, the production and depletion policy adopted, whether it matches production to domestic demand or allows net exports of crude oil, and the levels of royalty and petroleum revenue tax charged, which will determine the proportion of profits left to the oil producers

---

1   At 1975 prices, NS oil will contribute some 4% extra to GDP in 1977, perhaps rising to 7½% GDP in 1985.

for potential remission overseas. One further obvious difficulty is that the total benefits from NS oil to the balance of payments will not be independent of how the government feels able to exploit these benefits for domestic purposes.[1]

In calculating the overall balance of payments impact, it is important to remember that the exploitation of NS oil has proceeded for several years prior to the build-up of production in 1976. Over the period 1972-6, for example, cumulative net imports of equipment and services associated with the NS programme amounted to £1.84bn which was almost covered by a cumulative net import of capital of £1.34bn.[2]

The Treasury bases its forecast of the potential balance of payments effects on the assumptions that the unemployment rate is constant and that the exchange rate is held at levels which maintain the competitiveness of UK exports. It then calculates a net current account gain in 1978 of £2.7bn rising to £4.3bn in 1980 and £7.6bn by 1985. The overall figures, after taking account of oil-linked capital flows, are £3.4bn, £4.9bn and £7.5bn respectively.[3] Of course, these overall figures reflect the net outcome of several different magnitudes and are subject to all the uncertainties noted above, and, in particular, to those related to the remission of profits and dividends overseas, and to the role of UK firms in supplying the equipment needs of the oil producers.

II THE FOREIGN TRADE OF THE UK
II.1 Structure and Trends 1955-77

In this section we shall examine the major structural features and trends in the foreign trade of the UK between 1955 and 1977.[4] In focusing attention upon certain longer-term trends, we will find evidence of a marked decline in the international competitive position of UK manufacturing industry; a decline which, it may reasonably be claimed, is the proximate source of the unsatisfactory behaviour of the balance of payments noted in the previous section.

Geographical and Commodity Trade Structure: The traditional picture of UK foreign trade is one in which manufactures are exchanged for imports of foodstuffs

---

1   In particular, the exchange rate policy adopted to accommodate to NS oil is an important determinant of the total economic effect on government revenue and the balance of payments. For a useful account of the effect of different exchange rate assumptions see S.A.B. Page, 'The Value and Distribution of the Benefits of NS Oil and Gas, 1980–1985', *NIER*, No. 82, 1977, pp. 41-58.

2   The figures are at current prices. See *TER*, no. 76, July 1976.

3   Derived from *TER*, No. 89, August 1977. The figures are at constant 1976 prices and are not directly comparable with other estimates, e.g. by the National Institute. See Page, op. cit. p. 53, for a comment on this. Similar calculations related to the exploitation of NS gas reserves, often overlooked in discussions of NS wealth, yield potential balances of payments savings of £2.7bn in 1978, rising to £8.0bn in 1985. See *TER*, no. 76, July 1976. The balance of payments savings on gas are clearly of an equivalent order of magnitude to those obtained from oil.

4   Since, over the period, some 65% to 70% of total exports and imports reflected commodity transactions, we here concentrate solely on commodity trade. For a treatment of invisible items in the current account see P. Phillips, 'A Forecasting Model for the United Kingdom Invisible Account', *NIER*, No. 69, 1974. Interest, profit and dividend flows are discussed in section III.7 below. For further details on invisibles, consult the COI pamphlet, *Britain's Invisible Exports*, HMSO, 1970.

Foreign trade and the balance of payments

and raw materials, with the bulk of the trade being carried out with the Common-wealth and overseas sterling-area countries. That this picture is now completely out of date is shown in tables 3.3, 3.4 and 3.5 which illustrate the radical changes in trading structure which have occurred since 1955. To some small extent these changes reflect the relaxation of wartime import restrictions and the general postwar movement toward free-er trade that resulted from the several rounds of GATT tariff reductions. But, in general, they are the outcome of more deep-seated changes in competitive forces.

TABLE 3.3
Area Composition of UK Merchandise Trade, Selected Years 1955-77 (Percentages)

	Imports (c.i.f.)				Exports (f.o.b.)			
	1955a	1972a	1972b	1977b	1955a	1972a	1972b	1977b
Western Europe	25.7	43.9	48.1	53.4	28.9	42.9	48.1	53.2
EEC	12.6	24.5	31.6	38.3	15.0	22.9	30.2	36.4
EFTA	11.4	17.5	14.5	10.8	11.6	16.1	13.8	11.9
Other	1.7	2.0	2.1	4.3	2.3	3.8	4.1	4.9
North America	19.5	16.0	16.0	13.5	12.0	16.4	16.4	11.6
USA	10.7	10.6	10.6	10.1	7.1	12.5	12.5	9.4
Sterling Area: Developed[1]	16.6	11.5	7.4	5.5	23.4	12.9	7.9	5.7
Japan	0.6	2.8	2.8	2.9	0.4	1.8	1.8	1.4
Soviet Union + E. Europe	2.7	3.5	3.5	3.7	1.7	2.8	2.8	2.7
Total developed	65.1	77.7	77.8	79.0	66.4	76.8	77.0	74.6
Sterling Area: Developing[2]	22.8	11.8	11.7	6.3	21.6	11.5	11.2	9.4
Latin America	6.1	3.0	3.0	2.1	3.7	3.5	3.5	2.9
Rest of World	6.0	7.5	7.5	12.6	8.3	8.2	8.5	13.1
Total	100.0	100.0	100.0	100.0	100.0	100.0	100.0	100.0

Sources: *TI* 16 March 1972, 22 March 1973, and 10 March 1978. *MDS* February 1977.
'b' Series differs from series 'a' as follows:
(i) Sterling Area: Developed, includes Ireland in 'a' excludes it in 'b'; (ii) EEC 'b' includes Denmark and Ireland; (iii) EFTA 'b' excludes Denmark.

Notes: 1 Australia, New Zealand, India and South Africa.
2 Sterling Area: Developing list from *TI* 22 March 1973, p. 638.
There are some small discrepancies between the 1977 list of countries and the 1972 list.

The major changes in the geographic composition of UK trade are shown in table 3.3. Several general trends are immediately apparent. In particular, the increase in the proportion of UK trade carried out with the developed nations (the decline in 1977 is likely to prove a temporary reflection of the increase in world primary commodity prices) and the increase in the proportion of trade carried out with Western Europe. Most striking of all is the increase in the proportion of exports and imports exchanged with EEC countries, a development which has largely been at the expense of trade with the more developed countries of the sterling area. It is worthy of note that trade with EFTA, membership of which has often been presented as an alternative to participation in the EEC, has throughout the period accounted for a smaller proportion of the UK trade than has trade with the EEC, even when due allowance is made for changes in the membership of the

TABLE 3.4

Commodity Composition of UK Imports, Selected Years 1955-77 (Percentages)

SITC Group	Description	1955	1960	1965	1970	1977
0.1	Food, Beverages, Tobacco	36.2	33.1	29.7	22.3	16.1
3	Fuel	10.4	10.3	10.6	10.4	14.2
2, 4, 5 & 6	Industrial Materials	47.9	44.8	43.1	42.1	36.5
7 & 8	Finished Manufactures	5.2	11.1	15.3	23.7	31.9
9	Unclassified	0.3	0.7	1.2	1.5	1.3
	Total	100.0	100.0	100.0	100.0	100.0

Source: *TI,* 16 March 1972, p. 437, table 17 and 10 March 1978, p. 561, table 15.
Note: Imports are measured on an overseas trade statistics basis and are valued c.i.f.

two organizations. We may also note the increase in the importance of Japan as a trading partner and the decline in the importance of North America as a market for UK exports. As far as trade with the developing nations is concerned, the most important feature is the decline in the importance of sterling-area countries both as a market for UK exports and as a source of UK imports. One development, not shown in table 3.3, is the increased volume of trade with the oil-exporting nations, which provided 10.3% of UK imports and took 13.1% of UK exports in 1977.

The switch towards a greater trade dependence on the industrialized, urbanized, high per-capita income countries of Western Europe, Japan and North America has

TABLE 3.5

Commodity Composition of UK Exports, Selected Years 1955-77 (Percentages)

	1955	1960	1965	1970	1977
Engineering Products[1]	36.5	42.3	43.5	44.5	40.4
Machinery	21.1	24.9	26.5	27.4	25.0
Road Motor Vehicles	8.7	11.1	11.6	10.7	8.6
Other Transport Equipment	5.7	5.0	3.3	3.7	4.4
Scientific Instruments	1.2	1.4	2.1	2.7	2.4
Semi-Manufactures[2]					
Chemicals	7.8	8.5	9.2	9.5	11.5
Textiles	10.1	6.9	5.8	5.1	3.6
Metals	11.8	12.3	11.8	11.8	8.6
Other Manufactures[3]	12.6	12.0	13.2	13.7	20.3
Non-Manufactures[4]	21.2	18.0	16.4	15.4	15.6
Food, Beverages, Tobacco	6.5	6.0	6.6	6.3	6.7
Basic Materials	5.6	5.1	4.0	3.1	2.7
Fuels	4.6	3.6	2.7	2.6	6.2
Other	4.5	3.3	3.0	3.4	2.8
Total	100.0	100.0	100.0	100.0	100.0

Sources: *TI,* 16 March 1972, p. 430, table 7, and 10 March 1978, p. 561, table 15.
Notes: 1 Sections 7 plus 86.
2 Sections 5, 65 and 67-69.
3 Remainder of sections 6 and 8.
4 Sections 0, 1, 2, 3, 4, and 9.
Exports are measured on an overseas trade statistics basis and are valued f.o.b.

been matched, not unexpectedly, by significant changes in the commodity structure of UK trade, particularly in respect of imports. The changing structure of UK import trade is shown in table 3.4. Most important here is the increase in the proportion of imports of finished manufactures, the share of which increased six-fold between 1955 and 1977, and the decline in the proportion accounted for by foodstuffs, beverages and tobacco. Imports of finished and semi-manufactures now account for some 58% of total UK imports. This same trend has also been experienced by other EEC countries although it remains the case that the UK is more dependent upon imports of non-manufactures than are, for example, France or West Germany.[1] On the export side, table 3.5, changes in structure are less noticeable. While the share of exports of manufactures has increased slightly over the period, this has been matched by a virtually equivalent decline in the importance of semi-manufactures. The decline in the share of engineering products in 1977 is almost certainly a temporary reflection of the world recession. The only major changes seem to be the sustained decline in the share of textiles and the increase in the share of chemicals in total exports. Looking to the future, the possibility of substantial exports of North Sea oil over the next ten years is likely to substantially raise the share of fuels in total exports and to diminish the share of fuels in total imports.

It will be apparent from this that UK trade is increasingly dominated by an exchange of manufactures for manufactures with the advanced industrialized nations. These structural changes would imply that UK manufacturing industry has experienced and will continue to experience greater foreign competition in home and export markets. They also help to explain the disintegration in the sterling-area system which occurred after 1964.

II.2   The Decline in Competitive Performance

The trend towards an increasing trade deficit in the first half of the 1960s, coming as it did after a relaxation of trade and currency restrictions, has been taken as indicative of a widespread lack of competitive edge in UK industry relative to foreign industry. Further evidence in support of the contention is provided by the continuing decline in the share of the UK in world exports of manufactures,[2] by the rising import propensity in the UK and by, for example, the estimates of Houthakker and Magee, who found, for the period 1951-66, an income elasticity of demand for imports in the UK of 1.66, double the corresponding world income elasticity of demand for UK exports of 0.86. Taken at their face value, which would be misleading, these figures suggest that the UK can only grow at half the world rate if balanced trade is to be maintained.[3]

The statistics of the decline in the UK share in world exports of manufactures are dramatic and show that the share dropped from 20.4% in 1954, to 17.7% in 1959, to 11.9% in 1967 and to 8.3% in 1976. Over the whole postwar period, it

1   M. Panic, 'Why the UK's Propensity to Import is High', *LBR,* No. 115, 1975.

2   'World', in this context, means W. Germany, France, Italy, Netherlands, Belgium, Luxemburg, Canada, Japan, Sweden, Switzerland, US and UK. In 1975 they accounted for 88% of manufactured exports from all industrial nations. See *TI,* 3rd December 1976.

3   H. S. Houthakker and S. P. Magee, 'Income and Price Elasticities in World Trade', *Review of Economics and Statistics,* vol. 51, pp. 111-25. This study covered the period 1951-66. For a critique see A. D. Morgan 'Income and Price Elasticities in World Trade: A Comment', *Manchester School,* vol. 38, 1970, pp. 303-14.

seems that an increase in world exports of manufactures of 10% is associated with an increase in UK exports of manufactures of between 5% and 6%.[1]

Of itself, the decline in export share need not give rise to concern, since it may simply reflect a decline in the UK share of world manufacturing production, the natural result, say, of her early industrial start. (In 1899 the UK accounted for 32.5% of world exports of manufactures.) However, this is far too complacent a view. Once it is recognized that between 1959 and 1973 the volume of world trade in manufactures grew at the historically unprecedented rates of 7% to 10% p.a., and that the UK was alone among the major industrial countries in experiencing a substantial drop in export share, there are grounds for disquiet.

On the import side the evidence for loss of competitive edge is equally disturbing. Even though all the major industrialized nations have experienced a rising import share since 1955, the UK seems to be relatively more import-prone than her competitors and to have a relatively high income elasticity of demand for imports.[2] Recent calculations show that over the period 1963-74 the ratio of imports to the value of domestic production grew by 3.6% per annum for the whole of UK manufacturing to reach an average import penetration figure of 19.6% in 1974. This trend is widespread across manufacturing industry and is particularly significant in certain well-publicized sectors, e.g. motor vehicles and miscellaneous metal goods.[3] Some care, however, is required in interpreting these figures since they reflect to some extent the increasing division of labour in the international economy which has occurred particularly since 1958. Similar calculations on the export side indeed show a corresponding increase in the proportion of UK output which is exported, with the average ratio of UK exports to manufacturing sales increasing from 17% in 1968 to 23% in 1976.[4]

To explain these developments in any precise sense is not easy; several interrelated factors are involved and the relative weight to be attached to each is difficult to establish and may vary over time. At the most general level and since it is trade in manufactures which is crucial there would seem to be three potential sources of the poor UK trade performance: a low rate of increase in manufacturing capacity, a relatively slow growth of labour productivity, and a relative inability to market and develop new commodities and production methods in the face of rapidly changing technical and demand conditions.

It is a well-documented fact that over the period since 1950 the growth of output and the growth of labour productivity in the UK has been inferior to that in the

---

1 *NIER*, No. 73, 1975, p. 12. The world recession has been associated with a slight increase in the UK export share to 9.3% for 1977.

2 A. D. Morgan, 'Imports of Manufactures into the UK and other Industrial Countries 1955-69', *NIER*, No. 56, 1971; M. Panic, op. cit.; L. F. Campbell-Boross and A. D. Morgan, 'Net Trade: A Note on Measuring Change in the Competitiveness of British Industry in Foreign Trade', *NIER*, No. 68, 1974, suggest that since 1963, UK manufacturing industry has never been sufficiently competitive to restore the country's trade situation to the position held in 1963.

3 J. J. Hughes and A. P. Thirlwall, 'Trends and Cycles in Import Penetration in the UK', *Oxford Bulletin of Economics and Statistics*, vol. 39, 1977, pp. 301-17.

4 It may be noted that the sectors experiencing the greatest improvement in export performance, e.g. chemicals, electrical engineering, mechanical engineering and scientific instruments, are also the sectors which perform two thirds of the non-aerospace research and development carried out in UK manufacturing industry. For the export figures, see 'The Home and Export Performance of UK Manufacturing Industry', *ET*, No. 286, August 1977.

other major industrial nations.[1] A relatively slow growth of manufacturing capacity will contribute directly to a decline in the UK share of world exports over the long run, while in the short run it makes the degree of import penetration and the volume of exports particularly sensitive to fluctuations in the pressure of aggregate demand in the UK.[2] Boom periods in particular, it is argued, come up against constraints of available production capacity and available labour supply, diverting exports to the home market and raising the volume of imports above trend, with the possibility that a ratchet effect is involved, i.e. markets once lost to foreign goods are not readily recovered when the pressure of domestic demand slackens.

Trade performance is not simply a question of supply but also of demand and thus of the relative price competitiveness of UK production. Here the poor UK productivity record has been a major factor behind the tendency for the relatively faster increase in UK export prices, at least up to 1967. Averaged over the period 1959-67, UK dollar export prices rose at an annual average rate of 2%, compared to 1.3% for the other major industrial nations.[3] It follows that the relative price of UK manufactures rose by some 6% over this period and that, assuming an export share elasticity of −2, this could account for 37% of the decline in UK export share between the two dates.[4] The problem with this line of argument is in applying it to developments since 1967. Between then and 1974, UK relative export prices fell by 9% and yet the UK export share continued to decline. It is true that her export share showed a slight increase in 1977 but only after relative export prices had fallen by a further 2.9% from end 1974 to end 1976. The magnitude of these price changes and the insensitivity of the export share suggests that other factors than relative prices play the dominant role in the UK's export performance.[5]

Of course, the two explanations of a declining export share are not independent and it is not difficult to weave them together. The below average rate of growth of output can be linked with a below average ratio of investment to output in manufacturing and hence to a below-average increase in output per man and investment in innovation. Supply limitations and increasing relative prices each retard the growth of exports and therefore contribute to a below average growth of

---

1 See e.g. E. H. Phelps Brown, 'Labour Policies', in A. Cairncross (ed.), *Britain's Economic Prospects Reconsidered,* Allen and Unwin, 1971, and D. T. Jones, 'Output Employment and Labour Productivity in Europe since 1955', *NIER* No. 77, 1976.

2 Econometric work in this field is fraught with difficulties both of formulation and execution. For evidence on the demand pressure/supply bottleneck hypothesis see e.g. J. Artus, 'The Short-Run Effects of Domestic Demand Pressure on UK Export Performance', *Staff Papers,* IMF, Vol. 17, 1970, pp. 247-267 and J. J. Hughes and A. P. Thirlwall, *op. cit.*

3 Figures calculated from *NIER* Appendix tables, which also provide a valuable summary of international trends in labour productivity, unit costs and industrial output.

4 An elasticity of −3 would account for 66% of the loss in export share. R. Batchelor and C. Bowe, 'Forecasting UK International Trade': A General Equilibrium Approach', *Applied Economics,* Vol. 6, 1974, estimate price elasticities for UK export volume of between −1.13 and −2.80. One difficulty with any elasticity estimates is in evaluating the length of time it takes for the effects of price changes to be fully reflected in volume changes. Some estimates suggest up to five years as being the appropriate time lag. See, e.g., H. Junz, and R. Rhomberg, 'Price Competitiveness in Export Trade Among Industrial Countries', *AER,* May 1973, pp. 413-18.

5 Other econometric research suggests that relative price movements can only account for one half at most of the UK's loss of export share between 1956 and 1976 and one fifth of the loss between 1970 and 1976. See M. Fetherstone, B. Moore and J. Rhodes, 'Manufacturing, Export Shares and Cost Competitiveness of Advanced Industrial Countries', *Economic Policy Review no. 3,* Dept of Applied Economics, Cambridge, 1977.

aggregate effective demand. Profitability is therefore reduced and this, combined with the deflationary effects of policies introduced to correct the associated trade deficit, results in a weakening in the incentive to invest. So we come full circle, back to the causes of low growth of output and labour productivity from which we started.

Since 1967 the relatively poor growth performance of the UK has continued to contribute to the decline in export share. Between 1967 and 1972 the percentage increase in UK manufacturing output was 55%, less than the average for all OECD countries, although between 1972 and 1974, the last year before the onset of general recession, the gap narrowed somewhat to 32%. Against this, however, we must note that since 1967 the UK has exported an increasing share of its total manufacturing output. If this trend continues, it is possible that the UK export share will show a great improvement in the future under the influence of increasing price competitiveness and a narrowing of the gap between UK and other industrial countries' growth rates.

Finally, we must consider the possibility that it is the inability to innovate and market in response to rapidly changing conditions which is the chief source of UK difficulties. The type and quality of manufactures produced, delivery lags and after-sales service, and the general quality of marketing effort have each, it is frequently argued, played a significant role in limiting UK trade performance.[1] This is hardly surprising; the shift in the geographic and commodity composition of UK trade noted above is bound to enhance the importance of non-price competitive factors, e.g. advertising and research and development activity, between firms essentially operating under oligopolistic conditions.[2]

Unfortunately, the precise role of these factors has proved impossible, as yet, to determine, although it is interesting to note that similar explanations of poor British competitive performance were employed at the end of the nineteenth century.[3]

Other Factors: While it is the inadequate industrial growth performance which is chiefly responsible for the poor UK trade performance, several additional factors should not be ignored. On the export side, it is possible that an undue concentration on the supply of relatively slow-growing markets and on the production of commodities for which world demand was growing relatively slowly could explain the decline in export share. Appealing though this hypothesis is, evidence does not support the view that the structure of UK trade is responsible for poor export performance. A recent NEDO study finds no evidence in support of the view that the UK export structure is biased adversely towards the slower-growing commodities in world trade.[4] Furthermore, a study by R. L. Major has shown that only 9% of

1 NEDO, *Imported Manufactures*, HMSO, 1965. A. P. Thirlwall, 'The Panacea of the Floating Pound', *NWBR*, August 1974. NEDO, *International Price Competitiveness, Non-price Factors and Export Performance*, HMSO, 1977.

2 A survey, carried out by DTI in 1973, found that 44% of UK exports were accounted for by 31 enterprises and 74% by 177 enterprises. Foreign-owned companies and subsidiaries accounted for 29% of UK exports. *TI*, 11 April 1975.

3 R. Hoffman, *Great Britain and the German Trade Rivalry, 1875-1914*, Pennsylvania University Press, 1933, pp. 21-80.

4 M. Panic and A. H. Rajan, *Product Changes in Industrial Countries Trade 1955-68*, NEDO Monograph, No. 2, 1971.

the total loss in UK manufacturing exports between 1954 and 1966 can be attributed to exporting to relatively slow-growing markets.[1]

It may also have been the case that preferential trading arrangements have changed to the disadvantage of UK exporters. Isolated examples of this can be found, for example, in the relaxation by certain Commonwealth countries of import quota restrictions, which led to substantial export gains for Japan and the US at the expense of UK producers. To set against this, an EFTA study concluded that UK exports in 1965 were 2% higher than they would otherwise have been, in the absence of EFTA, although there appeared to be no noticeable effects on UK imports.[2] Of much greater importance has been the formation of the EEC, from which UK exports clearly benefited: the positive effects of selling to a large and rapidly expanding market more than offsetting the adverse effects of discrimination against the UK.[3]

One final factor which may be important in explaining the rising share of imports into the UK is the substantial reduction in tariff and other import restrictions which occurred after 1945. Between 1947 and 1959 the wartime restrictions on imports were virtually eliminated,[4] and from 1955 onwards the UK tariff was progressively reduced in line with agreements concluded through GATT. The UK tariff, introduced in 1932, had developed as a two-part structure with many imports from Commonwealth producers entering the UK duty free, and imports from the rest of the world being subject to duties which, in the case of manufactures, ranged from 10% to 33%.[5] Between 1959 and 1975, the average UK tariff on semi-manufactures fell from 16.2% to 10.5% and that on finished manufactures from 21.4% to 12%. Despite the magnitude of these changes a recent study suggests that their overall effect has proved to be relatively small, increasing the import values for semi-manufactures by 13% and that of finished manufactures by 9% relative to the values they would otherwise have had in 1971.[6]

III   ECONOMIC POLICY AND THE BALANCE OF PAYMENTS
III.1   Introduction

The coverage of this section is limited in two ways. First, pressure of space precludes more than a passing reference to events and policies prior to the floating of sterling

---

1 R. L. Major, 'Note on Britain's Share in World Trade in Manufactures 1954-66', *NIER*, No. 44, 1968.

2 EFTA Secretariat, *The Effects of EFTA on the Economies of Member States*, Geneva, 1969, p. 162.

3 UK membership of the EEC is treated in section III.8 below.

4 For details see M. F. W. Hemming, C. M. Miles and G. F. Ray, 'A Statistical Summary of the Extent of Import Control in the UK since the War', *RES*, Vol. 26, pp. 75-109.

5 In 1957 the average margin of preference on dutiable Commonwealth imports was 9%. See PEP, *Commonwealth Preference in the UK*, 1960. The swing in UK trade towards manufactures and the advanced industrialized nations progressively made this degree of preference less important.

6 A. D. Morgan and A. Martin, op cit. It is possible that this study understates the true reduction in protection afforded to UK manufacturing industry because it deals only with nominal tariff rates and not effective tariff rates — the effective rate taking into account the impact of tariff changes on the cost of imported means of production. Recent calculations for the period 1968-72 show that while the nominal rate on manufactures fell by 36%, the effective rate fell by 46%. M. Oulton, 'Tariffs, Taxes and Trade in the UK : The Effective Protection Approach', *Government Economic Service Occasional Papers* No. 6, 1973, p. 9.

in June 1972. Second, the concept of economic policy is limited to government
intervention where the prime concern was to produce alterations in flows
immediately affecting the balance of payments. It may be argued that *all* economic
policy affects the balance of payments since any non-trivial intervention in the
economy is likely to produce at least minor alterations in the balance of forces
affecting trade and payments flows. Some policies may well have major implications
for trade but, for present purposes, are not regarded as balance of payments policies.
Thus, attempts to control inflation or to stimulate efficiency and growth are likely,
if successful, to have substantial impacts on trade flows but these problems are
discussed elsewhere in this book and, in any case, may be judged desirable for
reasons other than those concerned with the balance of payments. Equally, policies
which are directed explicitly at trade flows may involve related adjustments in
'domestic' policy, as we shall see below in the discussion of exchange rate management. Manipulation of tariff and other barriers to trade is a legitimate branch of
balance of payments policy, but, in practice, government action of this nature is
circumscribed by international agreements, and again pressure of space precludes
more than a cursory discussion of what might be done within these constraints.
Entry to the EEC is obviously a policy decision of incalculable magnitude affecting
all aspects of economic behaviour but this section will confine itself to some balance
of payments implications of that decision. The influence of the international
monetary system on UK policy is so important that we conclude the section by
looking at recent developments in that field.

When interpreting the following discussion it is important to remember that the
conduct of balance of payments policy, or for that matter of economic policy in
general, is not a matter of 'fine tuning'. In part this reflects the fact that UK balance
of payments performance is as much determined by the economic policies adopted
in other countries as it is by policies adopted in the UK. On top of this, familiar
problems of forecasting the direction and rate of change of economic variables,
political and other limitations on the values of policy variables, and conflict between
different policy objectives, taken together, mean that practical policy making is
more an art than a science.

III.2   The Exchange Market Framework

It is a familiar proposition that modern industrial economies have evolved by means
of a progressive division of labour and that one important condition for this is the
adoption of a single internal currency, to act as an intermediary in all economic
transactions. The international division of labour has so far, however, proceeded
without this advantage. Since nations continue to maintain separate currencies for
internal use, it follows that international transactions must proceed with the
simultaneous exchange of national currencies, apart, that is, from those transactions
conducted in key currencies. This exchange of currencies takes place in the foreign
exchange market and it is there that the relative prices of different national
currencies, exchange rates, are established.

An important policy issue which faces the government of any country is, therefore,
that of the degree of restraint which it wishes to place on the exchange of its own
currency with the currencies of other nations. Not only will the chosen restraints
limit the type and geographical direction of transactions which domestic residents
may make with foreigners, but they will also have an important bearing upon the
conduct of policy to achieve internal objectives such as full employment and price

stability. Successive UK governments have exercised their options in two ways: by adopting particular forms of exchange rate policy, and by placing restrictions upon the currencies against which sterling may be exchanged for the pursuit of specified transactions, i.e. by exchange control.

Between 1945 and June 1972 the UK operated the foreign exchange market for sterling in accordance with the rules of the par-value system.[1] This required the official adoption of a par or central value for the spot market[2] rate for sterling to be expressed in terms of gold or the US dollar of 1944 fineness, together with the acceptance of a band of fluctuation of the spot rate around the par value.[3]

Provided the spot rate for sterling, as determined by market forces, lay within the permitted band, the UK exchange authorities did not need to take any action. Should the exchange rate be under pressure to stray outside this permitted band then the exchange authorities were obliged to intervene in the foreign exchange market, selling foreign exchange from the reserves when sterling was at its lower limit and purchasing foreign exchange to add to the reserves when sterling was at its upper limit. Thus the par-value system allowed some degree of variability in the foreign exchange rate but required that the UK keep a buffer stock of foreign exchange reserves, which it could use to keep the exchange rate within the specified bounds.

It must be noted that the par value of a currency was not fixed for all time once a country decided to abide by this system. On the contrary, a country could, when its balance of payments was in 'fundamental disequilibrium' and after consultation with the IMF, change its par value. UK governments did this twice, devaluing sterling in 1949 and again in 1967.

In contrast to what is required in the market for spot exchange, IMF rules placed no formal restrictions on the movements of forward exchange rates for a currency. Nor were any necessary. In normal circumstances, the forward exchange rate will stand in a simple relationship[4] to the spot exchange rate, reflecting the role of the forward market in providing cover for the exchange risks inherent in spot-market transactions.

A major change in UK policy occurred in June 1972, when the par-value system was 'temporarily' abandoned and sterling allowed to take whatever values the balance of demand and supply for foreign exchange might dictate. However, a policy of allowing sterling to float has not meant that the exchange market ceases to be an object of policy concern. The government still has to decide to what extent sterling will float freely, without official constraint, and thus to what extent it is

---

1   This is the name given to the exchange rate system adopted by the majority of Western nations after the Second World War. The central body of the system is the International Monetary Fund (IMF).

2   A distinction must be made between the spot market and the forward market exchange rates for a currency. The spot exchange rate is the price of foreign currency for immediate delivery; that is, at the time the rate for the transaction is agreed. A forward exchange rate is the price of foreign currency for delivery at a specified date in the future.

3   Until December 1971 the permitted band of fluctuation was 1% either side of par. Under the Smithsonian reforms of that time the band was widened to 2¼% either side of par.

4   This is the interest parity relationship. Provided interest arbitrage funds are in perfectly elastic supply then the percentage difference between spot and forward exchange rates for any pair of currencies will equal the interest differential on assets of the appropriate maturities denominated in those currencies. However, with arbitrage funds not in infinitely elastic supply, the forward rate will deviate from the interest parity value. In the limit, when the supply of speculative funds to the forward market is infinitely elastic, the forward rate will equal the value of the spot rate expected to hold at the time forward contracts mature.

going to manage the exchange rate. Recent UK experience suggests a considerable degree of exchange management to iron out potentially violent fluctuations in the spot rate without, if possible, influencing its longer-term trend.

The second aspect of UK exchange policy is that of exchange control. This is a complex issue with a detailed history of evolution, so that space precludes more than the most general remarks.[1] The legal basis of exchange control is contained in the Exchange Control Act of 1947, which assigns to the Treasury the authority to formulate exchange control policy. The day-to-day responsibility for implementing the exchange control provisions is delegated to the Bank of England, while, in turn, the daily volume of foreign currency transactions is handled by authorized exchange dealers, e.g. the commercial banks. The Exchange Equalization Account acts only as a residual purchaser or seller of foreign exchange in order to support a given exchange rate. As far as UK residents are concerned, the practice since 1960 has been to allow complete freedom for current transactions[2] but to restrict transactions on capital account in various ways. A brief outline of restrictions on capital transactions is given in section III.7. Exchange control for the UK is greatly complicated by the international reserve and medium of exchange functions of sterling, which result in foreigners holding sterling balances. Since 1958 a distinction has been maintained between two such categories of sterling: external account sterling and resident sterling. External account sterling consists of sterling balances held by non-sterling-area residents. This is freely convertible into any currency for current and capital transactions. Resident sterling consists of sterling balances held by residents of the UK and of the overseas sterling area, the latter being treated in the same fashion as UK residents, i.e. full convertibility on current account but restricted convertibility for capital transactions to non-sterling-area countries.

From 1958 UK exchange control regulations stayed broadly unchanged. However, with the floating of sterling in 1972 several modifications were required, which essentially involved giving the former sterling-area countries external account status. Today the sterling area, for exchange-control purposes, consists only of a handful of countries.[3]

III.3 External Economic Policy with a Floating Exchange Rate

In June 1972 the UK abandoned its commitment to the par-value system and sterling began to float relative to other currencies. By the middle of 1973 sterling had been joined in this respect by all other major currencies so that for the advanced industrial nations as a whole the par-value system had been abandoned. With sterling only one of many currencies engaged in a simultaneous float, there is no simple index of movements in the international value of sterling. Sterling may appreciate in terms of some currencies while, at the same time, it depreciates in terms of others. Current practice is to rely upon the so called 'effective exchange rate'[4], which is a suitably weighted average of the movements of sterling relative to the currencies of those

---

1   A useful historical account of UK exchange control will be found in B. Tew, *International Monetary Co-operation 1945-1970*, Hutchinson, 1971. The interested reader may also consult the IMF *Annual Reports on Exchange Restrictions*.

2   Apart, that is, from certain restrictions on the availability of exchange for foreign travel and for the making of gifts and other transfers to non-sterling-area residents.

3   See section I.2, page 117, footnote 5.

4   For details see *ET*, June 1974, and *BEQB*, March 1977.

countries which are most important in UK trade. The movement in the effective
exchange rate since June 1972 can be described in terms of a steady depreciation,
the effective rate at end February 1978 being 35% below the value in June 1972,
punctuated by two periods of particularly rapid depreciation between April and
June 1975, when the rate fell by 5 percentage points and, more dramatically,
between March and October 1976 when the rate fell by 17 percentage points. Since
October 1976 the effective rate has been on a gradual rising trend. The movement
of sterling relative to the dollar has been much more volatile although the broad
trend has mirrored that of the effective exchange rate. Before we analyse the causes
of this sustained depreciation it will prove useful to outline some of the more
important economic implications of floating exchange rates.

Floating Rates and Economic Policy: The case for floating exchange rates rests, in
large part, upon the alleged simplicity and automaticity of the free-market
mechanism in re-allocating resources in response to changing circumstances. In a
dynamic world in which comparative advantages change rapidly and national
inflation rates differ, changes in exchange rates are necessary if widespread underutilization of productive resources is to be avoided. The advantage of floating rates,
it is argued, is that the necessary changes can occur progressively at a pace dictated
by the costs and profitability of resource allocation, and not, as with the par-value
system, by sudden, discrete jumps dictated by speculative pressure and political
expediency. The resource allocation advantages are only one aspect of the benefits
derivable from the adoption of a floating exchange rate. More important for present
purposes are the implications for the conduct of macroeconomic policy. For it seems
clear that, with a more flexible exchange rate policy the UK could have avoided
most of the policy dilemmas of the period 1960-71 and that the period since 1971
would have generated impossible policy contradictions had the UK adhered to the
par-value system.

There is, first, the minor point that the government no longer has to decide what
constitutes an equilibrium exchange rate; to a large extent, this will be decided
automatically within the foreign exchange market. One cannot go from this,
however, to suggest that the conduct of domestic economic policy can proceed
independently of developments in the foreign exchange market. The correct
management of domestic demand is just as important with a floating exchange rate
as it is with a fixed exchange rate. Balance of payments problems do not disappear
with the adoption of a floating exchange rate, they are simply manifested in
different forms. Developments that would lead to a loss of reserves with a fixed
exchange rate, lead to a depreciation in the foreign exchange value of the currency
if the exchange rate is allowed to float. In the first case, the loss of reserves will
result, unless it is a once-and-for-all loss, in a policy-induced contraction in domestic
income, while with a floating rate, the loss in real domestic purchasing power occurs
automatically as the prices of tradeable commodities rise with the currency
depreciation.

The main advantage of a floating rate is that it allows a greater independence of
domestic economic policy making. In particular, full employment objectives may be
more consistently pursued; there being some value of the exchange rate which will
give exactly a zero currency flow at any, non-inflationary, level of employment.
Furthermore, since a floating rate provides the minimum of linkage between the
national incomes of different trading nations, it follows that a floating exchange rate
will isolate the level of demand for UK goods from changes in foreign incomes and

preferences for UK goods. An increase in foreign demand which, under a fixed rate, would generate a multiple expansion in UK incomes, now generates an appreciation of the sterling rate of exchange, such that the final increase in the value of UK exports is exactly matched by an appreciation-induced increase in the value of UK imports, i.e. in the domestic expenditure on foreign goods. The total demand for UK goods, and, therefore, UK incomes will remain unchanged.[1] The isolation of domestic incomes from external changes in demand has, of course, as counterpart the proposition that the level of domestic income is more sensitive to changes in the level of *domestic* money expenditure. In this respect, an economy with a floating exchange rate will behave in the same manner as a closed economy; the effects of changes in foreign trade upon the circular flow of income are completely negated. The policy consequence of this is that the multiplier repercussions of monetary and fiscal policy will be greater in an economy with a floating exchange rate than in the same economy with a fixed exchange rate.[2] Correspondingly, the cost of mistakes in demand management will be increased with a floating rate and so policy must be conducted with greater attention to underlying economic circumstances.

Other Implications of Floating Rates: The relative merits of fixed and floating exchange rates are matters of considerable controversy among economists. Some of the alleged advantages of flexible exchange rates have already been mentioned. The object of the present section is to deal with two less clear-cut aspects of the controversy. In particular, the view that private speculation will convert floating exchange rates into wildly fluctuating rates, and the view that a floating rate increases the uncertainty faced by international traders and investors to the detriment of the international division of labour.

The case for and against floating rates depends essentially on the view taken of the effects of speculators in the operation of free markets. If these markets are to be cleared continuously, without undue fluctuations in the exchange rate, it is essential that speculators take over the role of the monetary authorities and operate in a stabilizing manner, selling sterling when the rate is temporarily 'too high' and buying sterling when the rate is temporarily 'too low'. Temporary fluctuations in the exchange rate follow, in part, because daily imbalances in the demand and supply for foreign exchange will result from random and seasonal factors, even if the balance of payments is basically in equilibrium over a longer time span, and because, as mentioned above, short-period trading adjustments to relative price changes are likely to be inelastic. The proponents of floating exchange rates argue that speculative activity will be stabilizing and that speculators will be able to predict the trend value of the exchange rate so as to ensure minimal variations in the actual exchange rate around the trend value. Opponents fear that this will not be the case and the exchange market will be dominated by too much uncertainty for speculators to recognize the appropriate trend. Successive waves of optimism

---

1 A more detailed discussion would have to modify this argument, in respect of any change in the aggregate savings ratio which followed the exchange appreciation and the possible effects on demand of any changes in international interest-rate levels.

2 Again this is subject to qualifications, depending upon the sensitivity of international capital movements to policy-induced changes in interest rates and the time span considered for analysis. With floating rates a greater degree of interest sensitivity of capital flows enhances the potency of monetary policy and limits the potency of fiscal policy for the management of aggregate demand.

and pessimism will follow the frequent revision of expectations and generate substantial movements in exchange rates, out of all proportion to the volume of trading.

The difficulty with the above arguments is that we have little or no relevant factual evidence to decide either way. However, should private speculation prove to be less stabilizing than is thought desirable, there is no reason why the authorities should not engage in 'official' speculation, if necessary at the expense of private operators. Indeed this is precisely what the authorities have undertaken when supporting the sterling par value against speculative pressure and when actually managing the exchange rate over various periods since June 1972. The implication is, of course, that even with a floating exchange rate the authorities must maintain a stock of exchange reserves. Widespread adoption of exchange management practices would also require the institution of international co-ordination and surveillance of exchange rate practices; this appears neither impossible nor undesirable within the framework of an existing body such as the IMF (see section III.9 below). Finally, it must not be overlooked that destabilizing speculation can disrupt any exchange rate framework and clearly did so with the par-value system. One of the major drawbacks of the par-value system was that it gave a one-way option to currency speculators. A currency under pressure would be pushed to one of the official intervention limits. This immediately signalled the possibility of a change in par value in a direction in which no one could have any doubt. Naturally, a large and cumulative movement of funds across the exchanges was therefore encouraged. A likely advantage of floating exchange rates is that the problem of a one-way speculative option would be much reduced.

The view taken of the effects of speculation determines the importance of the arguments on uncertainty and the inhibition of trade and investment. Provided that floating rates do not fluctuate wildly there is no reason why the bulk of trade and investment should be seriously affected. After all, exchange risks can always be covered with simultaneous deals in spot and forward markets. For sterling transactions involving the major currencies, the foreign exchange market currently provides active dealings for contracts up to one year in duration. Since some 89% of UK exports are financed on credit terms of less than six months' duration[1] with, no doubt, a similar proportion for imports, there should be no difficulty in traders covering their exchange risks. Longer-term trade contracts and international investment projects will face problems, but then in an uncertain world they always will. In addition it is argued that, should the forward premium on sterling exceed the appropriate interest differential, then traders will have to face extra costs of finance. There are two counter-arguments to this. First, the difference between forward premia and interest differentials will be smaller, the greater is the response of international capital flows to arbitrage possibilities. Provided that capital controls do not limit such flows, there is no reason to expect the costs of forward cover to be prohibitive. Second, suppose it could be demonstrated convincingly that additional exchange rate uncertainty had reduced trade and investment. This could still not constitute an argument against floating rates, until the claimed costs could be shown to be greater than the employment and resource mis-allocation costs imposed under the par-value system.

---

1 See the article 'Direct Exporters and the Credit Terms of Exports', *TI*, vol. 7, no. 2, 13 April 1972, pp. 50-2.

III.4   The Exchange Rate and the Balance of Payments 1972-7

In section I.4 we have outlined the rapid changes in the UK's external position in the 1970s, showing that from an initial surplus the current account moved into substantial deficit during 1973-6 and then recovered in 1977. On the domestic front, as other chapters show, this period saw very rapid and variable inflation rates, high and variable interest rates and the emergence of substantial unemployment. The purpose of this section is to outline some of the major factors leading to the changes in the current account and the exchange rate during the period and their relation to domestic and international events. The first point to be clear upon when interpreting the events of the period is that the exchange rate for sterling has not been allowed to float freely; rather it has been managed quite actively, and this policy has produced economic effects which are a mixture of those occurring under the extremes of fixed and freely floating rates. Since the equilibrium exchange rate at any point in time reflects the balance of demand and supply of foreign exchange it is useful to begin with an outline of the major forces affecting the volume of autonomous transactions in the foreign exchange market.

Purchasing Power Parity: Many economists would argue that over a period of years the values taken by a freely floating exchange rate would be determined by its purchasing power parity. Broadly speaking, this means that the percentage depreciation of the domestic currency relative to some other foreign currency should be equal to the excess of the domestic rate of price inflation over that foreign country's rate of price inflation.[1] The proximate source of the depreciation of sterling since 1972 would then be found in the excess of the domestic inflation rate over a suitably weighted average of the inflation rates of our major trading partners: it being a matter of indifference what the source of this differential inflation is, whether it be due to excessive monetary expansion or the result of excessive wage pushes by trade unions in the UK. Consider now the following evidence. Over the period 1973 to 1977 the consumer price index in the UK increased by 94.5% while the average increase for the whole OECD area was 48.7%, a change in purchasing power parity of 24%. Over the same period the effective exchange rate for sterling, in the calculation of which the OECD countries have the predominant weight, depreciated by only 20.7%, some 83% of that suggested by this, admittedly crude, calculation. One reason for this is that the purchasing power parity theory only holds true if economic structure is held constant during the comparisons; in a full account it is necessary to allow for structural changes and the effect of fluctuations in aggregate demand on the exchange rate. For example, during this period all the OECD countries faced rising unemployment; however, industrial production in the OECD still rose by 5% while industrial production in the UK fell by 4.5% and one would expect this relative recession in the UK, through its effect in reducing imports and raising exports, to hold the value of sterling above the values indicated by purchasing power parity. Furthermore, as section II.1

---

1   Probably the clearest statement of the purchasing power parity theory is still contained in J. M. Keynes, *A Tract on Monetary Reform*, Macmillan, 1971, pp. 70-93. For a recent survey, see L. H. Officer, 'The Purchasing Power Parity Theory of Exchange Rates : A Review Article', *IMF Staff Papers*, vol. 23, 1976.

demonstrated, the UK is currently shifting its trading pattern towards the EEC and this structural change, together with the associated changes in the UK's average tariff, may be another factor creating deviations from purchasing power parity.

More fundamental, however, is the fact that the purchasing power parity doctrine only applies if the exchange rate varies to clear the foreign exchange market, and this has not happened. In each of the years since 1973 the UK has experienced a considerable imbalance in its total currency flow with three years of deficit and one year of surplus, 1977. This imbalance of autonomous transactions has been financed by substantial foreign borrowing by the government and public agencies, see section I, and by alternatively drawing on or adding to the foreign exchange reserves. The years 1975 and 1977 were rather dramatic in this last respect. From a peak of $7.0bn at end February 1976, the UK reserves declined to a low of $4.1bn at end December 1976, then, during 1977, they were rebuilt rapidly, reaching the postwar peak of $20.6bn at end December. Had the exchange rate been allowed to fluctuate freely over this period there would clearly have been far more violent movements in its value than actually occurred. Some reasons why the government may wish to manage the exchange rate are treated below. For the moment we merely note that such management can be a powerful source of temporary deviations from purchasing power parity.

A final element creating temporary deviations from purchasing power parity is that of short-term movements of capital as asset portfolios are adjusted to changes in interest rate and exchange-rate anticipations (see section III.6). Again the years 1976-7 provide a dramatic example of the forces involved. Commencing in April 1976 a capital outflow began which was primarily the result of sales of sterling by the oil-producing countries, afraid that the excessive UK inflation rate made sterling overvalued. Attempts by the authorities to stem this capital outflow, by raising domestic interest rates, and to finance this capital outflow out of reserves proved ineffectual; consequently, sterling dropped from a value of $2.02 at end February 1976 to a low of $1.59 at end October, and the government was forced to negotiate further borrowings from the IMF. During 1977 this process was reversed; the sharp decline in the UK inflation rate as incomes policy continued to hold, the coming on stream of NS oil and the weakness of the US balance of payments all contributed to create a sustained capital inflow into the UK. Until October, the UK government used this inflow to replenish its exchange reserves but later a less active interventionist policy was adopted and sterling rose to end the year at $1.92. The lesson from this is that short-term capital flows can, in the short run, so dominate the exchange rate as to divorce its value from the state of the current account and make its relation with purchasing power parity dependent on the somewhat tenuous state of inflationary expectations relative to the actual rate of inflation.

The Terms of Trade and the Oil Price Increase: We now come to the major factor underlying the balance of payments situation in the UK during this period: that of the sharp adverse movement of the terms of trade which took place in 1973. The primary element here was the increase in the foreign currency prices of imported materials, foodstuffs and oil. The average dollar prices of all primary commodities increased in 1973 by 48% and in 1974 by a further 33% and this increase has been sustained, albeit with fluctuations around the higher level, the end 1977 index of commodity prices being 125% above the end 1972 level. Without question, however, the most significant event of this period was the quadrupling of the posted price of oil by the OPEC nations at the end of 1974 which increased the c.i.f. price of oil to the UK from $3.45 per barrel to $8.70 per barrel.[1] The implications of this development were considerable and worldwide, affecting not only individual economies but also the stability of the international monetary system. Some of the wider issues are treated in section III.9 below. As far as the UK was concerned, the effect in 1974 was to increase the oil import bill by £2.68bn more than the average for the previous three years and thereby contribute substantially to the historically unprecedented current account deficit of £3.67bn. Comparing the terms of trade over the two years to end 1974 we find a total deterioration of 26% which we can decompose, in a purely arithmetic sense, as follows: a 47% increase in export unit values, offset by a 61% increase in the foreign currency prices of UK imports and a 12% depreciation in the effective exchange rate. Since 1974 the terms of trade have shown some improvement but even by the last quarter of 1977 they remained 16% below their 1972 level.

As the short-run elasticity of demand for oil and commodity imports does not differ appreciably from zero, the impact effect of the oil and other price increases was to simultaneously worsen the trade balance and generate deflationary pressure in the UK economy. It is as if the UK government had raised indirect taxes, so cutting the demand for UK output, and had then transferred the tax proceeds to the oil-producing and primary commodity-producing nations. In addition, the similar effects on other industrial economies produced cuts in the demand for UK exports and so provided a further deflationary stimulus, while very little help could be expected in the short run from the spending of OPEC funds on UK-produced goods.

Several options were open to the government to deal with this situation. First, it could have attempted to eliminate the current account deficit either by a severe policy-induced cut in aggregate demand, or by allowing the exchange rate to depreciate sufficiently to improve the non-oil trade balance of the UK at the expense of the other industrialized countries. Neither option has proved to be feasible or otherwise desirable. The only effective policy has proved to be that of substantial foreign borrowing, combined with a broadly neutral stance towards domestic aggregate demand.[2] The net outcome for the UK has therefore been one of rising external indebtedness, combined with falling domestic production as the deflationary effects of the change in the terms of trade worked through to expenditure and demand.

Foreign borrowing has taken place under three separate headings. Prior to 1973, the OPEC oil producers traditionally received about 25% of their oil revenues in sterling and normally deposited them as sterling balances in London. With the increase in oil revenues following the Tehran Agreement, the immediate response was to place much of the surplus in London. In 1974 some 37% of surplus oil funds, a total of $21bn, were placed in London. In the subsequent years the total amount of short-term finance made available in this way declined considerably, in the face

---

1 The posted price should not be confused with the market price of oil. The posted price is the administrative price from which the OPEC countries assess the royalty payments and tax payments due from the oil-extracting companies.

2 Although the March 1975 Budget was intended to produce substantial cuts in the government borrowing requirement, it can be argued that their net effect on the aggregate demand was negligible. See *NIER*, May 1975, p. 11. A more deflationary stance was adopted in 1976 announcing further reductions in future public expenditure. Recent calculations suggest, however, that over the period 1975-7 the net stance of fiscal policy had a small stimulating effect on the economy. See the article 'Why is Britain in Recession?', *BEQB*, March 1978.

of falling surplus oil revenues and an increasing unwillingness to deposit funds in a depreciating currency. In fact, between 1975 and 1977 only $4bn to $4.5bn flowed into the UK on an annual basis, representing 12%-14% of surplus oil funds. The second important source of finance has been nationalized industry and local authority borrowing under the Treasury exchange cover scheme. Much of this has been in the form of OPEC funds taken out of the Eurodollar market in the form of medium-term (three- to seven-year) loans. Some $3.4 billion was raised in this way in the two years to the end of 1975 and a further $3.6bn to the end of 1977. Finally, the UK government has itself engaged in substantial borrowing. Most important here have been the $2.5bn and $1.5bn loans raised from the Eurodollar market in 1974 and 1977, the $2bn borrowed from the IMF at the end of 1975 − 60% of which represented a drawing on the specially created oil facility, and the stand-by agreement with the IMF agreed at the end of 1976 under which the UK may draw $3.9bn from its remaining credit tranches − $1.2bn being taken in January 1977.

While this policy of foreign borrowing has allowed the UK to accommodate its substantial payments deficits it does imply the need for the rapid emergence of a sustained trade surplus to meet the burden of debt servicing and amortization payments. Although drawings on the IMF oil facility carry an interest rate of 7.75%, with interest rates of 4% to 6% on other IMF drawings, the bulk of the foreign borrowing has been raised at higher commercial rates, 10% and upwards. Furthermore, three-quarters of the debts incurred by the government, nationalized industries and local authorities, are due for repayment within seven years; that is by 1983.[1]

It is clear that the coming on stream of North Sea oil will play an important part in creating this current account surplus but it will also require a substantial improvement in the UK's non-oil net exports. Developments on this later front have been mixed. Largely as a result of the world recession, UK export volume declined by 4.5% in 1975 but has subsequently expanded at an average annual rate of 8.4%. Unfortunately, this rapid growth of export volume, compared with the average rates of 3.25% over the period 1960-7 and 5% over the period 1967-72, has been matched by an almost equally rapid growth of import volume, which averaged 6.1% between 1975 and 1977, compared with 6.4% in 1960-7 and 8.6% in 1967-72. It will be clear from the account of section II.2 that the key to the UK's external recovery lies in the driving of a substantial wedge between the growth rates of export and import volume. Unfortunately, this does not for the moment seem likely.

III.5   Management of the Exchange Rate

In the previous section we have seen how the sterling exchange rate has been heavily managed during the period since 1972, the primary weapons in this management being foreign currency borrowing and changes in the stock of UK foreign exchange reserves. As we have also suggested, such management has prevented sterling from depreciating by as much as is indicated by crude purchasing power parity considerations.

There are several important reasons why a government may wish to manage the exchange rate. In the first instance it may view changes in the demand and supply of foreign exchange as temporary and so act as a speculator to prevent such temporary

1 *BEQB*, March 1978, table 24.

changes in the balance of autonomous transactions from influencing the exchange rate. Such a policy of 'leaning into the wind' could be justified as a way to minimize the disruptive effects of temporary exchange rate variations on trade and investment. As a second example, the government may take a view that the balance of autonomous transactions has shifted permanently but at the same time consider that an immediate full adjustment of the exchange rate would be too disruptive to patterns of employment and resource allocation. The exchange rate could then be actively managed toward its new long-run level at a pace which allows the pattern of resource allocation to change smoothly. The effects of the oil price increase could be interpreted in this light, with the government maintaining the exchange rate above its equilibrium value in anticipation of the benefits of NS oil and the possible effect of the energy-saving programme. The problem with this line of argument is, of course, the familiar one: how does the government know the exchange rate appropriate to different sets of internal and external circumstances? Too easily such a policy of 'leaning into the wind' may become a policy of manipulation of the exchange rate to satisfy other objectives.

One such objective, frequently discussed in the UK, would be that of exchange rate management to improve the trade balance. Effectively the government could be acting as if it were maintaining a flexible par value for sterling and devaluing the par value to improve the trade balance, a policy exactly analogous to the devaluation of November 1967. The mechanism of devaluation would be as follows. The impact effect of the devaluation would be to change relative prices, to increase the relative prices of tradeable commodities, exports, imports and their close substitutes, relative to non-tradeable commodities, and in addition, depending on the pricing policies of domestic and foreign firms,[1] the terms of trade would typically deteriorate as sterling import prices rise relative to sterling export prices. The changes in relative prices then induce substitutions in patterns of production and consumption which, though they may at first be negligible, grow in magnitude as contracts are renegotiated and as new plant and equipment is installed to take advantage of changed profit opportunities. Available evidence would suggest that the magnitudes of these quantitative responses do produce a long-run improvement in the trade balance.[2] There may, however, be an initial deterioration as a result of the adverse terms of trade effect, so producing the so-called 'J' curve response to devaluation.

Even if the elasticities of foreign and domestic demand and supply are of the right magnitude the effects do not stop there. To the extent that the trade balance improves in terms of home currency, the aggregate demand for UK goods will have increased and this, via the multiplier effects on income, will create subsequent and partially offsetting increases in the demand for imports. Furthermore, if the economy

---

1 On the pricing policies of UK firms following the 1967 devaluation, see P. B. Rosendale, 'The Short-Run Pricing Policies of some British Engineering Exporters', *NIER*, no. 65, 1973, and the valuable study by D. C. Hague, E. Oakeshott and A. Strain, *Devaluation and Pricing Decisions,* Allen and Unwin, 1974. Professor Cooper has suggested that foreign suppliers cut their foreign currency prices on average by 4%. See A. K. Cairncross (ed.), *Britain's Economic Prospects Reconsidered,* Allen and Unwin, 1971, p. 181.
2 In the special case in which there is initial balanced trade and supply elasticities of traded goods are infinite, then the devaluation improves the trade balance provided that the sum of the foreign and domestic elasticities of demand for imported goods exceeds unity. For a more general statement see Kindleberger, *International Economics,* chapter 19 and Appendix G.

is at or near to full employment, the devaluation-induced expansion of aggregate demand will have inflationary implications which can only be prevented by reducing domestic expenditure to make room for the improvement of the trade balance. Finally, account must be taken of the import content of domestic production, and the effect of the devaluation in raising domestic costs of production and of its effects in creating pressure for higher money wages.[1] The conclusion to be drawn from this is that powerful forces are at work to offset in part the initial effects of a managed devaluation on the balance of trade. Indeed, recent calculations show that the effects of a hypothetical devaluation are largely transitory with respect to the level of output and the current balance of payments but that after six years a devaluation of 5% would produce a 4% increase in the UK's retail price index. These calculations also make clear that the effects of a devaluation depend on the fiscal policies and other policies to control money incomes which accompany the devaluation.[2] Discussion of the inflationary effects of an exchange depreciation raises another reason why a government may wish to actively manage the exchange rate. Some of the arguments here were stimulated by the sharp depreciation of sterling in 1976, which accelerated the rate of inflation after a period in which domestic incomes restraint had reduced the rate of increase of unit labour costs in the UK from 30% in 1974 to 5% in 1975. It has been suggested, therefore, that a managed appreciation of sterling would help to combat domestic inflation. The argument is simply that the rate of inflation is influenced by the pressure of demand in the labour market and expectations of inflation, so that a currency appreciation reduces inflation on three fronts: it directly lowers domestic production costs, it reduces the pressure of demand for labour by its adverse effects on the demand for UK output, and by reducing inflation in this direct fashion it has the indirect effect of lowering the anticipated rate of inflation, thus moderating money wage demands and possibly increasing the viability of attempts to directly control money wages. The effectiveness of such a policy must, however, be questioned not least because of the ambiguity over whether any persistent change in the exchange rate is a cause of or an implication of domestically generated inflation. On more practical grounds, since imports represent only 20% of total expenditure it would seem that the impact effect of, say, a 5% appreciation would at most lower the retail price index by 1%. Furthermore, to have any direct effect on the rate of inflation would require a sustained appreciation of sterling, not a once-for-all change in its value.

So far we have taken for granted the view that the exchange rate can be managed to achieve either balance of payments or inflation rate effects. Such a view may prove excessively optimistic outside the short period. First, one has to recognize that in a world where all the major currencies are floating, governments may follow mutually inconsistent exchange rate targets and find themselves in a situation of competitive exchange rate management in which one country's policies are nullified by the actions of others. Second, experience, gained with sterling and other currencies during the 1960s, shows that it becomes increasingly difficult for the authorities to

---

1 The average import content of UK manufacturing output is currently 21%. On the wage inflation effects of devaluation see 'Some Aspects of the Present Inflation', *NIER*, no. 55, 1971. Further discussion of the effects of the 1967 devaluation may be found in the 6th edition of this volume.

2 Cf. *TER*, March 1978, no. 96. It is particularly important that the money supply is not allowed to expand and negate the effects of devaluation in reducing real money balances and absorption.

maintain an exchange rate substantially different from its equilibrium value without inducing disruptive flows of speculative short-term capital which ultimately force a change in policy. This happened to the UK as recently as October 1977, when the government was forced to abandon its attempts to hold sterling down in the face of substantial capital inflows. Third, and more fundamentally, there are strong arguments to suggest that any attempt to maintain an exchange rate other than that dictated by purchasing parity must be a failure in the long run. This argument simply takes account of the fact that any artificial, disequilibrium exchange rate will be associated with a non-zero TCF and thus with changes in the stock of foreign exchange reserves and the domestic money supply.[1] If the exchange rate is notionally devalued, for example, this will reduce the real value of monetary assets and induce a temporary trade surplus as agents attempt to restore real asset holdings to their equilibrium levels. This surplus will expand the reserves and the money supply until balance sheets are returned to equilibrium and the pre-devaluation structure of relative prices regained. The only permanent effect of the devaluation will be an equal proportionate increase in the price level and an increase in the stock of foreign exchange reserves. It must be stressed that this is a long-run argument, that the links between changes in the reserves and the domestic money supply can be offset by domestic monetary policy and that reserve changes can be isolated from the TCF by official foreign borrowing. However, despite these qualifications it throws into perspective the point that management of the exchange rate is only likely to prove successful in the short run.

Unresolved Issues: Two major issues are likely to dominate future discussion of exchange rate management in the UK: the uses of the NS oil benefit and the effects of a return to full employment.

We have described in section I.4 the way in which NS oil will relax the balance of payments constraint imposed on the UK by the 1974 oil price increase. Several options now face the government. One is to argue, correctly, that the UK has already had some of this benefit in advance by maintaining output and real incomes above their levels consistent with external balance, and that it is foreign borrowing which has made this possible. The first charge on NS oil revenues is therefore to repay some of the accumulated foreign debt. One further factor reinforcing the option is that some of the borrowing was at much higher interest rates than currently exist in world capital markets, so that there are advantages in clearing existing debts and reborrowing more cheaply if necessary. Thus in January 1977 the government announced the early repayment of $1bn of the UK's debts to the IMF, and further announcements have also been made of repayment of public sector foreign currency borrowing. However, with the OPEC surpluses still maintained, it is neither necessary nor desirable to make the repayment of debt the primary use for NS oil revenues. The chief alternative option is to use the oil revenues to stimulate the economy and run a greater import bill. Again, there exist several options. One is to allow sterling to appreciate and allow the stimulus to consumption provided by higher real wages and a lower inflation rate to reduce domestic employment. The

---

1 For useful accounts of the links between external transactions and the domestic money supply, see 'The Domestic Financial Implications of Financing a Balance of Payments Deficit on Current Account', *BEQB*, March 1975, and 'Of DCE, M₃ and Similar Mysteries', *MBR*, February 1977.

obvious objections to this policy lie in its adverse effects on exports and import penetration and in its failure to directly promote the creation of productive capital assets in the UK. Indeed it is the latter option, use of the NS oil revenues to reconstruct the UK's industrial base for when the oil benefits are exhausted in the 1990s, which seems to command most attention at the moment.[1] Greater public and private investment in infrastructure, alternative energy sources and industrial plant and equipment will, it is argued, create more employment and raise productivity so that the decline in the UK's industrial competitiveness will be reversed.

The second related issue is that of persistent unemployment in the UK and the view that in order to eliminate this and at the same time revive UK industry, some substantial protection in the form of import restrictions will be required. The argument here is complex but the broad issues are clear enough. To the extent that unemployment in the UK is a reflection of the general world recession, subsequent to the oil price increase, then there is little to commend import restrictions; to adopt such a policy would be in the worst traditions of beggar-thy-neighbour diplomacy. However, to the extent that the UK's unemployment and lack of competitive edge in world markets reflect structural problems unique to UK industry, then general import restrictions, provided they are linked to a policy of investment and industrial reconstruction, merit at least a hearing, if only because the alternative policy of a sterling depreciation may not prove viable for the reasons outlined above.[2] In response to the argument that foreign retaliation will be provoked, it should be remembered that any policy which improves the UK's trade balance and competitive strength, whether it be import restriction, export subsidy or devaluation, must 'harm the foreigner' so that the precise way this is achieved should be a relatively minor matter dictated by the net advantages of each policy for the UK. It should also be remembered that the purpose of such a policy is primarily to stimulate the demand for UK output so that its final effect on imports will be smaller than its impact effect, the difference reflecting the induced increase in imports as domestic incomes and employment increase.

During the 1960s the UK resorted to import restrictions on two occasions. In November 1964 an import surcharge of 15% was imposed on imports of most manufactured commodities, amounting to approximately one third of the import bill, and this is estimated to have reduced the 1965 import bill by £130m and the 1966 bill by £80m relative to what they would otherwise have been.[3] However, the imposition of the surcharge led to a marked display of annoyance by other members of GATT and EFTA, and as a result the surcharge was reduced to 10% in April 1965 and eliminated completely in November 1966.

The second time import restrictions were employed was in November 1968 when an import deposit scheme was introduced to reinforce the effects of the 1967 devaluation. Importers were obliged to deposit 50% of the value of imports with the government, before the goods could be cleared from Customs. The deposits earned no interest, were repayable in full after 180 days and, as with the import surcharge, they only applied to imports of manufactures. At the then ruling rates of

---

1　Cf. *The Challenge of NS Oil,* Cmnd. 7143, HMSO, 1978.
2　The most persistent advocates of this view have been the Cambridge Economic Policy Group, see e.g. their 'Economic Policy Review', no. 4, March 1978.
3　Cf. Caves, op. cit., p. 167.

interest, and assuming that all importers had equal access to credit facilities, the scheme was equivalent to an import surcharge (tariff) of 2% to 2½%. It is doubtful whether this had much effect in reducing imports, especially as the required deposit proportion was twice reduced and finally abandoned in December 1970. It is worth noting that such a scheme has recently been employed in Italy, in 1974 and more recently from May 1976, with a 50% deposit for three months being applicable to all imports. Clearly, and within the spirit of the IMF rules of the game, it is not impossible for a country with severe balance of payments difficulties to resort to general import restrictions. At the moment, however, the policy climate is such that general import restrictions are ruled out for the UK, indeed the IMF standby negotiated in 1976 was associated with a specific commitment to this effect. Exchange rate management and import restrictions aside, the government may still resort to a variety of *ad hoc* measures to change the balance of autonomous transactions. Since 1964 a variety of these have been employed; for example, restrictions on overseas military and diplomatic activities and minor changes in exchange control, most recent of which was the elimination of the practice of financing trade between third countries in sterling, announced in November 1976. Most of these policies are cosmetic and have only a minor effect on the balance of payments.

In conclusion there is little doubt that, with unemployment at 6% of the labour force and with substantial spare capacity in UK industry, the UK balance of payments remains in a state of fundamental disequilibrium. NS oil aside, there seems little prospect of resolving this situation by internal policy alone; only a sustained expansion of the world economy will provide the conditions for a return towards full employment without a slide into external deficit.

III.6 Short-Term Capital Flows and Balance of Payments Policy

Short-term capital movements have traditionally played an important role in the overall UK balance of payments situation. Their importance is the joint result of the UK position as an international financial centre and of the role of sterling as an international reserve asset and medium of exchange. Thus some short-term capital movements reflect changes in the sterling balances which foreign governments and individuals have acquired as matters of commercial and financial convenience. The remainder reflect the role of London as a centre for the Eurodollar and other financial markets, with banks in the UK lending and borrowing extensively in dollars and European currencies.

The significance of short-term capital flows for the conduct of UK policy, arises from their magnitude relative to the official reserves and from their volatility. It is convenient to divide the capital flows which influence the UK balance of payments into two broad classes; speculative and non-speculative. The motive behind speculative capital flows is one of making a capital gain from anticipated movements in exchange rates. A currency speculator would be indifferent between holding sterling or dollar denominated assets, for example, if the interest rate on sterling assets equalled the interest rate on dollar assets plus the anticipated depreciation of sterling relative to the dollar. If the anticipated sterling devaluation exceeds the sterling interest advantage, holders of sterling assets, to the extent that exchange controls permit, will switch their assets into dollars while UK importers will accelerate (lead) dollar payments for imports and UK exporters will try to delay (lag) dollar payments due from foreigners. Non-speculative activities are undertaken to avoid capital gains or losses associated with exchange rate movements, and involve simultaneous transactions in both spot and forward currency markets so that the risks associated with currency transactions may be shifted onto speculators.[1]

In sum, short-term capital movements depend on a complex set of interactions between national interest rates, spot and forward exchange rates and expectations of future changes in spot rates. Nor surprisingly, with expectations such an important factor, short-term capital flows are highly volatile and not necessarily responsive to official attempts at their control.

The implications of short-term capital flows for external and internal policy depend upon the exchange market framework in operation. Under the par-value system the first impact of a short-term capital outflow falls upon the exchange reserves, this being true of both speculative and non-speculative flows. Given the poor reserve/short-term liability situation of the UK, any such loss of reserves, if heavy, almost invariably provoked a change in demand management policy. A 'run on sterling' was normally followed by a policy to contract domestic demand and restore 'confidence', frequently in conjunction with foreign borrowing by the government. With a freely floating exchange rate however, the impact effect of a change in capital flows falls not upon the reserves but upon the exchange rate. A capital outflow will now work to depreciate sterling and an inflow to appreciate sterling. However, any such change in the exchange rate acts upon the current account in the same way as a policy-induced parity change. Hence, a capital outflow has similar effects to a devaluation; encouraging exports, discouraging imports and increasing the rate of circular flow of income. It will be clear that large and sudden capital flows can provide difficult policy problems for fully employed economies operating with floating exchange rates.

An important development since 1958 has been the increasing integration of European and American capital and money markets, and the emergence of London as a focus of Eurodollar activities. This has increased the sensitivity of international capital flows to interest-rate differentials and expectations of exchange rate changes, and allowed the mobilization of an increased volume of funds for switching between currencies.[2] In particular, in times of rapidly diverging national rates of inflation, such as experienced since 1972, interest differentials between different countries and expectations of exchange rate changes will be greatly influenced by expectations of differences in national inflation rates. In a world of high capital mobility, the short-term capital flows induced by the expectation of divergent national inflation rates can exert a dominant influence on the actual movement of the exchange rate, as the depreciation of sterling during 1976 illustrated so graphically.

What can the UK authorities do to influence short-term capital flows? A broad answer would be very little apart from the following considerations. In the first instance some restraint is provided through exchange control regulations. Residents of the UK are denied the opportunity to purchase foreign currency except for authorized purposes. In addition, direct limits are placed on the foreign exchange

---

1   See the 6th edition of this volume for a discussion of forward market transactions. More detailed treatments will be found in Grubel, *International Economics*, Irwin, chapter 12, and Kindleberger, op. cit., chapters 17 and 24.

2   Estimates put the total amount of privately held international assets available for switching between currencies at some $268bn, twice OECD member country reserves, in 1972. Even allowing for double counting, the magnitude of assets is alarming since they constitute a permanent threat to the stability of any currency.

positions which banks and other exchange dealers may undertake.[1] However, this still leaves untouched the activities of non-resident holders of sterling who tend to be the most active in switching funds between currencies.

Two alternatives remain. Manipulation of domestic interest rates is a powerful weapon in current circumstances, given the increasing integration of financial markets. Its use is subject to two limiting provisos: international retaliation and conflict with the level of interest rates needed to attain internal objectives. The remaining policy option is official manipulation of the forward exchange rate, which would allow the authorities to create for the UK a risk-free interest-rate advantage on short-term investments, as circumstances dictate. Between 1962 and 1967 the UK achieved some success with this policy, effectively counteracting pressure on the reserves on several occasions. Although such a policy may be run at a modest profit for the UK authorities, technical losses arise if the spot rate is changed while official forward contracts are outstanding. This occurred with the 1967 devaluation, when the sum of £366 million had to be paid out to foreigners who at the time held forward contracts to sell sterling. Since that episode, there has been little indication of official forward activity.

It must be noted that neither interest-rate policy nor forward intervention may prove of much avail if the spot value for sterling comes under severe speculative pressure. In these circumstances, an active interest-rate policy may merely signal to the foreign exchange market the seriousness with which the authorities view the situation, thus accentuating fears of an exchange depreciation and accelerating the capital outflow.

For the conduct of UK economic policy, the behaviour of the sterling balances is of prime importance and will continue to be as long as the authorities wish to manage the sterling exchange rate. One reason for this is that the UK reserves cannot be treated solely as a buffer stock to finance payments deficits. The reserve function of sterling places the UK in the position of an international banker with the gold and the currency reserves as backing for the short-term external liabilities. As pointed out in section I, the UK's external problems in the 1960s stemmed partly from a grossly inadequate ratio of reserves to liabilities. The result was a general lack of confidence in the ability of the UK to maintain its banking role, which grew particularly sharp whenever the reserves were used or threatened to be used to fulfil their function of financing a deficit.

Until 1968 the short-term external liability situation of the UK exhibited two important features. First, the overall stability, even in times of sterling crisis, of the sterling balances held as part of the exchange reserves of the OSA countries. Second, and in contrast, the marked volatility of the balances held by NSA governments and residents. It was the latter category which contributed most to the pressure on sterling, particularly after the return to convertibility in December 1958. As it transpired, the more volatile balances diminished in absolute and relative importance in the 1960s, forming 42% of total sterling liabilities in 1962 and 32% in 1967. It is possible to argue from this that sterling balances were becoming more stable in total, and thus that the sterling problem was diminishing. Unfortunately, 1968 saw a fundamental change in official OSA attitudes towards their sterling balances.[2]

---

1 For details see the article, 'Limits on UK banks' foreign exchange positions', *BEQB*, December 1975.
2 To some extent, reserve diversification had been taking place throughout the 1960s, but mainly via the process of overall growth in OSA official reserves. For a valuable discussion see the article, 'Overseas Sterling Balances 1963-1973', *BEOB*, June 1974.

The 1967 devaluation had the side effect of reducing the capital value of OSA reserves in terms of other currencies and gold. As a result, fears of a second devaluation in 1968 led to widespread attempts by OSA countries to liquidate their sterling holdings and diversify their reserves. In the second quarter of 1968 alone, official OSA sterling balances declined by some £230m. For the OSA countries this simply reflected their weakening economic links with the UK. For the UK, however, it represented the demise of a basic ground rule of the sterling payments system, viz., that OSA countries pool their official holdings of gold and foreign currency in London in exchange for sterling balances. Naturally, this development caused much official concern in the UK and inspired negotiations to obtain international support for sterling, the upshot of which were the Basle arrangements of September 1968. Under the Basle arrangements twelve central banks, together with the Bank for International Settlements, extended a credit of $2 billion to the UK, the facility to have a life of ten years. The finance was provided on several conditions, the two most important of which were as follows. First, the credits could only be used to cover the liquidation of private and official balances of the OSA countries and could be activated when the total of such balances fell below an agreed level. Second, to minimize the reserve diversification activities of the OSA countries, each had to negotiate a minimum proportion for the sterling component of its exchange reserves, which varied according to the circumstances of each country. Provided the minimum sterling proportion was at least maintained then, as a quid pro quo, the UK would guarantee the dollar value of that part of each country's official sterling reserves (excluding equity holdings) that exceeded 10% of that country's total reserves. The initial arrangements with OSA countries were for three to five years, all three-year agreements being renegotiated in 1971 and extended until 1973. In October 1973 the agreements were extended for six months with, from the UK point of view, an unfavourable change in the dollar rate of exchange at which the balances are guaranteed. The agreements were renegotiated in March 1974 for the duration of the year, an important development being to guarantee the balances in terms of a basket of currencies and not simply in terms of the dollar, and were finally terminated at the end of 1974. With the benefit of hindsight it is clear that the Basle arrangements helped to perpetuate the reserve role of sterling, contrary to official pronouncements that this role should be terminated. In every year between 1968 and 1974 the total of official sterling balances increased and by end 1974 they accounted for 65% of total sterling balances.[1] Perhaps paradoxically, in the light of the weakened trade and investment links between the UK and the OSA, total sterling liabilities to OSA governments were 68% greater at end 1973 compared to their value at end 1968. The sharp increase in sterling balances which took place in 1974, of course, reflected the increased oil revenues accruing to OPEC states in the wake of the oil price increase; indeed the proportion of reserve sterling balances held by the oil producers has risen from 28% at end 1973 to 48% at end 1977.

The drawings the UK was obliged to make on the Basle facility were repaid at the end of 1969 and the subsequent growth in sterling balances eliminated any further recourse to this line of credit. But the guarantee left the UK with an uncertain contingent liability, which in the fifteen months to March 1974 cost some £140m in writing up the dollar value of the relevant sterling balances.

The precarious nature of the UK's position over the sterling balances became

---

1   For detailed figures, consult Statistical Appendix, table A-8.

abundantly clear during 1976. In March 1976 the sterling exchange rate against the dollar began a rapid slide from approximately $2.00 to a low of $1.59, reached at the end of October. In the absence of the guarantee arrangements on sterling balances, official holders, and in particular the oil producers, began to diversify out of sterling on a large scale, the total of official balances falling by 38% between the end of March and the end of November to a value of £2.48bn. This reduction occurred despite the fact that the Treasury bill rate in the UK rose over the same period from 8.6% to 14.9% and at a time when non-official sterling balances actually increased. Faced with this drain upon its foreign exchange reserves, the UK government was obliged to seek a new Basle facility in which eleven central banks provided a two-year standby facility of $3bn, to cover any withdrawal of official sterling balances below a value of $2.16bn, subject to the proviso that UK official reserves be not greater than $6.75bn. As part of the agreement the UK was to 'fund' part of the official sterling balances by offering their holders medium-term bonds in exchange for their sterling holdings.[1] In the event the arrangements proved to be superfluous. The prospect of a strengthening UK payments position, as NS oil began to flow and as the UK inflation rate declined, relative to the weakening US payments position, greatly increased the attractiveness of sterling relative to the dollar. The associated increase in UK reserves and the keeping of official sterling balances above the £2.16bn mark has meant that the 1976 Basle arrangement has never been activated.

Important questions on the future of sterling balances remain as yet unanswered. As part of the 1976 Basle arrangement the UK agreed to negotiate with official sterling balance holders with the aim of reducing future growth in these balances, and to pursue a long-run policy of terminating the reserve role of sterling in line with prior commitments to the EEC. One option would be to employ NS oil revenues to effect this; another, less likely, possibility would be to arrange an international funding operation for the sterling balances and their replacement by long-term debt of the UK. Whether this would be in the UK interest, or, more to the point, within the realms of practical international politics, is not clear.[2]

In conclusion it is worth remembering that the management and performance of the UK economy has suffered considerably as a result of the sterling balance problem.[3] Official sensitivity to the country's short-term liquidity position repeatedly forced demand management policy to respond to changes in the reserves rather than to changes in the internal state of the economy. For similar reasons, governments have proved more than willing to incur substantial short-term and medium-term debt to the IMF and central banks in order to maintain confidence in sterling. Perhaps most damaging, is the argument that perceived 'moral

---

1   Arrangements for the sale of the bonds were completed by April 1977, with fifteen countries taking up bonds to the value of £394m. A choice of bonds was offered with a denomination in terms of four 'hard' currencies with maturities between five and ten years and carrying interest rates between $5\frac{7}{8}\%$ and $8\frac{7}{8}\%$. The bonds do not carry an exchange guarantee.

2   The funding of sterling balances is discussed in B. J. Cohen, 'The Reform of Sterling', *Princeton Essays in International Finance*, no. 77, December 1969.

3   For an account of the internal costs, see S. Strange, *Sterling and British Policy*, Oxford, 1971, chapters 9 and 10.

obligations' towards holders of sterling led to a persistent official discounting of devaluation as a policy option. For as we have discussed above, sterling balance holders have been adequately recompensed for any devaluation losses. In sum it appears difficult to avoid a conclusion that maintenance of the international role of sterling has seriously weakened the long-term competitiveness of the UK economy.

Moreover, events since then have demonstrated that swings in the exchange rate, over and above those required for the maintenance of purchasing power parity, are likely to pose serious economic problems for the UK as long as the total of sterling balances remains such a high proportion of total official exchange reserves.

III.7   Long-Term Capital Flows and Balance of Payments Policy

The purpose of this section is to discuss the balance of payments and other consequences of overseas investment and to outline the various measures adopted to control overseas investment flows.

Any additional flow of overseas investment by the UK will have immediate and continuing implications for the current and capital accounts of the UK balance of payments. With a fixed or managed exchange rate the impact effect is to reduce foreign exchange reserves, as UK investors acquire the foreign exchange needed for their overseas investment. If we consider direct investment, it is likely that the construction of new capital equipment overseas will involve some increased demand for UK exports of goods and services so that the UK current balance will improve and the charge on the official reserves is reduced accordingly. Should the new flow of foreign investment be associated with a reduction in UK home investment there will be a reduction in the level of economic activity in the UK, and activity will increase abroad if the foreign investment leads to additional investment there. There will then be further repercussions on the UK current balance which stem from the multiplier process at home and abroad and the linkage between changes in activity and imports. In practice, the linkage between the capital account and current account transactions is likely to be such that the current account improves but not by a sufficient amount to finance the capital outflow without loss of reserves.[1] The total increase in net external assets is therefore smaller than the direct investment outflow. If the capital outflow takes the form of portfolio investment, the impact on the current account is likely to be negligible and such investment will be matched by an equivalent reduction in other net overseas assets.

In addition to the linkages between the trade balance and the flow of direct foreign investment, account must also be taken of the return flow of profit and interest income from overseas investment. In the simplest case, in which the overseas assets are acquired without direct resort to foreign borrowing, the return profit inflow will exceed or fall short of the capital outflow according as the rate of return on the foreign investment exceeds or falls short of the percentage rate of growth of the stock of overseas assets. It is not necessarily the case, therefore, that

---

1   The theoretical mechanism which underlies this argument is known as the transfer mechanism, and explanations of it may be found in standard textbooks on international economics.

the investment outflow produces a deterioration in the overall balance of payments position, even when we ignore trade linkage effects.[1]

As long as the government aims to maintain a fixed exchange rate, the case for and against control of foreign investment involves balancing the short-term gain to the official reserves from limiting the capital outflow, against the cumulative loss through time of the forgone income from the foreign investment. When a floating exchange rate is adopted this particular problem ceases to be relevant. Any short-term cost to the reserves may be eliminated by an appropriate depreciation of the currency, and this will increase net exports so that the capital outflow may be transferred in real rather than in monetary terms. If full employment is to be maintained by government policy, the final increase in net exports will have to be matched by a reduction in domestic investment or consumption. It is then possible to evaluate the costs and benefits of alternative levels of foreign investment by direct comparison of the estimated yields of the foreign investment flows with the forgone yields as resources are moved out of alternative home uses so as to accommodate the real transfer.

This last argument is subject to the qualification that interest and profits earned overseas generate tax revenues that accrue to overseas governments, whereas home investment generates such revenues for the UK government.[2]

A country may wish to influence the inflow and outflow of long-term capital for a variety of reasons, not least among which relate to the resource allocation effects of foreign investment and the political and economic implications of an increase in the proportion of domestic capital controlled by foreign residents. In the UK the dominant motives for restrictions on overseas investment have been protection of the exchange reserves and improvement of the balance of payments, motives which were approved under the IMF par-value rules. Policy has aimed at encouraging the finance of overseas investment by foreign borrowing and the plough-back of profit earned in existing foreign operations.

Limitations on the outflow of UK capital to the OSA countries may be dealt with quickly. Until 1966 both direct and portfolio investment flows to the OSA were free from exchange restriction. This freedom was a quid pro quo to the OSA for their (unwritten) obligation to pool their foreign exchange reserves in London. In April 1966 a policy of voluntary restraint on UK investment in Australia, New Zealand, South Africa and the Republic of Ireland was introduced. The object of

---

1   For a quantitative investigation of the balance of payments effects of UK direct investment overseas, see W. B. Reddaway and Associates, *Effects of UK Direct Investment Overseas : Interim Report* (1967) and *Final Report* (1968), Cambridge University Press. For every £100 of foreign assets acquired, it was found that the current account improves by £11 in the first year (extra exports) and by £4 in every subsequent year (comprising extra exports and profit receipts, net of foreign taxation, and interest payments on accommodating foreign borrowing. These figures suggest that it would take roughly twenty-two years before a steady capital outflow of £100 per annum becomes self-financing. With 40% foreign borrowing the time period is reduced to twelve years. These figures well illustrate the short/long-run dilemma with respect to direct investment and the desire of the UK authorities to encourage the finance of investment by foreign borrowing.

2   A further qualification is that any depreciation designed to accommodate an additional flow of foreign investment will probably involve the UK in a worsening of its net barter terms of trade which raises the opportunity costs of that investment. Against this, however, must be set any future appreciation of the currency which follows from the return inflow of profits and interest.

this was to encourage firms to postpone existing investment plans in these more advanced OSA countries, and to encourage discussion of future investment proposals with the Bank of England. This policy was abandoned in March 1972. However, the respite proved to be short-lived. The floating of sterling in June 1972 resulted in the majority of OSA countries being assigned external account status, and thereby becoming subject to the same limitations on portfolio and direct investment as the former NSA countries.

As far as portfolio investment in the NSA is concerned, this has been subject to rigorous exchange control since 1945. UK residents are not permitted to buy quoted foreign currency securities with official exchange, nor are they allowed to dispose of the foreign currency proceeds of liquidated direct and portfolio NSA investments at the official exchange rate. Instead, all such transactions must pass through the separate investment currency market, at a price which balances the desire to purchase foreign currency securities with the desire to liquidate existing holdings of NSA assets. Typically the investment currency rate stands at a premium[1] relative to the spot exchange rate, the magnitude of the premium providing some indication of the degree of restriction on foreign investment.

Operation of the investment currency system has meant that the UK effectively maintains a two-tier foreign exchange market, so that portfolio investments to and from NSA countries are self-balancing and make no claim on the exchange reserves. In April 1965 an important modification was introduced, whereby 25% of the foreign currency proceeds from the sale of NSA securities had to be transferred to the authorities at the official exchange rate. It has been estimated that this 'tax' on the investment currency premium added some £1.07bn to the reserves in the period from its inception to end 1977. Since June 1972, the granting of external account status to the OSA countries meant that portfolio investment in the OSA must pass through the investment currency market. At first, liquidations of OSA securities were not subject to the 25% surrender rule, but this privilege was terminated in the 1974 Budget. It is clear that the investment currency system has provided an effective method for isolating the reserves from portfolio investment flows. The 25% surrender rule was, however, abolished at the beginning of 1978 in accordance with broad commitments to the EEC capital market harmonization programme.

From 1961 onwards, restrictions on direct investment in the NSA took the form of treating proposed investments in terms of three categories. The least restricted category consisted of so-called super-criterion projects, which were expected to bring matching returns to the balance of payments within eighteen months and which could be financed with official foreign exchange up to an effective limit of £50,000. All other projects had to be financed through the investment currency market or by overseas borrowing.[2] These restrictions have been alternatively strengthened and relaxed according to the underlying state of the basic balance. The more important changes occurred in June 1972, when direct investment in the OSA was brought within the same network of limitations, and in the Budget of

---

1 The premium is the percentage difference between the investment currency price of sterling and the price of sterling in the spot market. During 1977 the effective premium varied between a high of 48% and a low of 24%. See also the article 'The Investment Currency Market', *BEQB*, September 1976.

2 For further details, see the COI pamphlet, *Britain's International Investment Position*, HMSO, 1971.

1974, which resulted in foreign investment in the OSA, NSA and EEC being treated on an equal footing, with official foreign exchange only available for super-criterion projects. It is worth noting that these changes, together with the application of the portfolio surrender rule to OSA securities mean the end of all elements of discrimination in favour of investment in the OSA and hence the effective termination of the special economic relationship between the UK and OSA countries. The most recent change occurred in December 1977 when the limit for super-criterion investments was raised to £500,000 and the maximum payback period increased to three years, these provisions applying only to investments in the EEC.

It appears that the restrictions had little impact on the total outflow of direct investment from the UK, nor did the discriminating element in favour of the OSA prevent the swing in the geographic location of direct investment towards the EEC and North America. The most important effect of the restrictions appears to have been in saving foreign exchange. Over the period 1965-71, foreign borrowing financed 56% and internally generated profits financed 47% of all UK private investment in the NSA, so leaving a small balance to be added to the exchange reserves.[1]

At present, the UK places no legal restrictions upon inward investment, apart from those contained in the 1947 Exchange Control Act which apply to all UK residents. However, inward direct investment is subject to Treasury approval and the criteria upon which permission is granted are aimed at maximizing the contribution which the investment inflow makes to the reserves.[2]

From table 3.2 (line 7) we can see how the period 1972-7 was marked by a quite remarkable reversal of the UK's traditional role as a net exporter of long-term capital. It should be noted that this shift did not imply that UK direct investment overseas was reduced; indeed the outflow during this period averaged £1.61bn per annum, a figure twice as great as the corresponding figure for the period 1968-71. Rather, the chief proximate sources of this change comparing the periods 1968-71 and 1972-7 were an increase of 140% in direct foreign investment in the UK, roughly half of which was associated with the exploration of NS oil, and a 980% increase in foreign investment in the UK public sector, a disproportionate amount of this increase occurring during 1977.

Associated with the stocks of assets built up by overseas investment are return flows of interest profits and dividends. In this respect it is interesting to note that over the period since 1961, remitted profits and dividends have exceeded the total outflow of direct investment from the UK by a small margin – e.g. the average profit inflow from direct foreign investment for 1972-7 being £1.62bn per annum – and that the net foreign income of the UK is now less than 2% of GDP.

III.8   The UK and the European Economic Community

The subject of UK membership of the EEC has always been controversial and the controversy has shown little tendency to abate since the UK became a full member in January 1972. On gaining office the Labour government of 1974 declared its

---

1 For further discussion, see A. K. Cairncross, *Control of International Long-Term Capital Movements,* Brookings Institution, 1973, pp. 68-77.
2 M. D. Steuer *et al., The Impact of Foreign Direct Investment on the UK,* HMSO, 1973, chapter 9. Since 1972, this condition has been waived for EEC companies and investors.

firm intention to renegotiate the original terms of entry,[1] completed the renegotiations in March 1975[2] and then settled the question in favour of membership with a referendum in July 1975. In this section we shall comment only upon the balance of payments implications of membership; other implications are treated in Chapters 2 and 4 of this volume.

It was apparent at the time of the pre-entry negotiations that the full effect of entry into the EEC would imply a deterioration in the current account and possibly a deterioration in the long-term capital account of the balance of payments. To offset this, the UK would have to depreciate the exchange rate or employ direct policies of expenditure reduction in order to achieve the cut in real income and expenditure necessary to eliminate the adverse balance of payments effects of entry. Against this 'real resource cost' could be set the dynamic benefit of selling in a greatly enlarged market: a benefit which, it was argued, would result from greater economies of scale in production and which would be manifested in an increase in the UK growth rate.[3] Improved growth performance, it was thought, would possibly yield some offsetting dynamic gains to the basic balance. Unfortunately, while it proved possible to provide plausible estimates of the balance of payments cost, measurement of the potential dynamic gains has so far eluded any precise assessment. At the time of writing, belief in the benefits of entry remains an act of faith.

The effects on the UK current account can be discussed under three headings: changes in the pattern of trade in manufactures; adoption of the common agricultural policy; and contributions to the Community budget.

The main implications for trade in manufactures follow from the customs union aspects of the Community, all tariffs on trade between the UK and other members having been reduced to zero in 1977 as the UK adopted the final stages of the common external tariff (CET) on trade with non-Community countries.[4]

It is impossible as yet to say what the final effects on the UK's pattern of trade will be. Adjustment to the tariff changes will not be immediate and we must also take into account the discrimination which is now imposed against former Commonwealth countries (excluding signatories of the Lomé convention) and the associated loss of UK export preferences in the same countries. We have already shown, in section II.1, that the direction of UK trade in the 1950s and 1960s swung progressively towards Western Europe and away from the traditional markets in North America and the OSA. It seems clear that entry into the EEC has accelerated the process. Over the years 1969 to 1973 UK exports to the EEC increased at an average annual rate of 12.5%, while imports from the EEC increased by 17.7%. However, between 1973 and 1977 these average annual growth rates increased

---

1 *Renegotiation of the Terms of Entry into the European Economic Community,* Cmnd. 5593, April 1974.
2 *Membership of the European Community : Report on Renegotiation,* Cmnd. 6003, March 1975.
3 *Britain and the European Communities: An Economic Assessment,* Cmnd. 4289, February 1970.
4 The necessary tariff changes were to be achieved in stages, for details see *The United Kingdom and the European Communities,* Cmnd. 4715, July 1971, paras 79-80. The average final level of CET on UK imports of manufactures was estimated to be 8%.

dramatically with exports to the EEC increasing by 25.7% and imports from the EEC increasing by 28.5%.

Assessments of the balance of payments cost of entry for the UK have tended to concentrate upon the effects of adopting the CAP system of agricultural support in place of the deficiency payments method formerly used by the UK. Under the deficiency payments method, the UK imported foodstuffs at world prices, free of any import duty. Under the CAP system the UK is obliged to import all foodstuffs at the common EEC prices and to impose import levies on imports from non-EEC sources, to bring their prices up to EEC levels. At the time of negotiation for entry it was estimated that EEC prices were between 18% and 26% higher than world market prices and that, given an inelastic demand for imports of foodstuffs, the UK import bill would be increased accordingly.

Finally, the UK is obliged to contribute to the budget of the Community and this involves a transfer of funds across the foreign exchanges, the gross contribution of the UK being assessed with reference to the share of the UK in the total GNP of the Community. The net contribution will be smaller than the gross contribution to the extent that the UK receives reverse transfers from the EEC, for example, in the form of regional aid and industrial development aid.[1]

Estimates of the static balance of payment cost of entry produced widely varying results, although most suggested a substantial balance of payments burden[2] and thus an implicit real resource cost of UK entry to be imposed by a devaluation or other means. It was in the light of the assumed adverse balance of payments implications that the UK government renegotiated the original terms of entry. The most concrete results of the renegotiation were the creation of a mechanism for reducing the gross budgetary contribution of the UK in line with the UK's share in the total GNP of the Community, and the guarantee of continued access to the Community for Commonwealth sugar and dairy products from New Zealand.[3]

It is remarkable how inaccurate the initial estimates of the balance of payments cost have proved to be. Three factors are relevant here. First, and most important, the rise in world prices up to the level of EEC prices between 1971 and 1973 eliminated the immediate potential cost of CAP on the UK's import bill for foodstuffs. Second, the attempt to offset the effects of the depreciation of sterling on CAP prices has led to a substantial net transfer of funds from the EEC budget to the UK. The reason for this is as follows. EEC food prices are set in terms of units of account and are then translated into national currencies at representative exchange rates, determined by administrative decision. Since June 1972, the depreciation of sterling relative to the dollar has not been matched by an equivalent depreciation of the representative exchange rate for sterling, the so-called green pound, the percentage gap between the two rates reaching as much as 20% in July

---

1   Cf. Cmnd. 4715, paras 91-96 and Annex A.

2   The 1970 White Paper, Cmnd. 4289, suggested a balance of payments cost ranging between £100m to £1.1bn per annum. For a comparison with other, less extreme estimates see J. Pinder (ed.), *The Economics of Europe*, Charles Knight, 1971, chapter 6, by M. Miller. For a more optimistic assessment see R. L. Major and S. Hays, 'Another Look at the Common Market', *NIER*, November 1970.

3   Cmnd. 6003. For additional details of the convention which grants tariff preferences on exports to the EEC of industrial products, and some agricultural products from signatory developing countries, see. P. Coffey, 'The Lomé Agreement and the EEC : Implications and Problems', *TBR*, No. 108, December 1975.

1975.[1] The effect of such a sterling depreciation is to raise the sterling price of food imports into the UK above CAP levels and to create the possibility for profitable arbitrage between commodities, sterling and other EEC currencies. To prevent these disruptions to CAP, subsidies are paid to the UK to keep down the sterling price of imported foodstuffs to the level dictated by the representative exchange rate, while, at the same time, the UK is obliged to tax any agricultural exports in order to maintain their representative prices in terms of other EEC currencies. Since the UK is a large net importer of foodstuffs it has received more in the form of import subsidies than it has had to levy in export taxes and subsequently transfer to the Community budget. Third, and finally, the UK has begun to benefit in the form of payments from the regional and social funds, receiving a total of £305m in aid between January 1973 and November 1977.

The net effect of these reverse transfers has been to substantially reduce the net budgetary cost of entry below the amounts estimated in 1971. Over the five years to 1977, for example, the actual gross contribution was £2.04bn, while the estimated net contribution for the same period has been put as low as £111m. These figures take account of borrowing by UK bodies from EEC institutions, e.g. the sum of approximately £1.56m borrowed from the European Coal and Steel Community and the European Investment Bank between accession and November 1977.

It is entirely another question whether the UK will be so fortunate in future years. It does not seem possible that world food prices can be maintained at EEC levels — indeed for cereals, butter and beef they are currently well below Community levels; nor is it likely that the system of monetary compensation will continue unchanged. In the light of this it would appear to be in the UK's interest to press for a more flexible approach to CAP and to try and force EEC food prices to fall in line with productivity gains in the most advanced farming units. Failure on these fronts will simply raise again the potentially formidable cost of UK membership.

Although the CAP and budgetary contribution questions have tended to dominate practical discussion on EEC membership, it is important to recognize that the issue of monetary unification is potentially of greater significance to the UK. In 1971, the European Commission, following guidelines laid down in the Werner Report of 1970, adopted the goal of full monetary union to be achieved by 1980. In its fullest form this would involve the irrevocable fixing of the parities of EEC currencies one to another, full currency convertibility for current and capital account transactions and the creation of a Community central bank with full powers to determine monetary policy in each region of the EEC. In many respects the case for monetary union is an integral part of the case for a common market in commodities. Creation of a single currency (*de facto* by fixing exchange rates, or by the adoption of a new currency unit) reduces transactions costs and promotes exchange and the division of labour which, it could be argued, is necessary if the dynamic gains from membership are to be maximized. Furthermore, it can be argued

---

1   For a time series of the percentage premium of the green pound over the official sterling exchange rate, see R. W. Irving and H. A. Fern, *Green Money and the Common Agricultural Policy*, Wye College, Occasional Paper No. 2, 1975. The latest of a series of green pound devaluations (7½%) was announced in January 1978. A careful account of these problems is contained in C. Mackel, 'Green Money and the Common Agricultural Policy', *NWBR*, February 1978.

that once the members of the EEC develop intensive trade and investment links with one another then adoption of a fixed pattern of exchange rates is the only foreign exchange market policy consistent with price stability. Stable EEC parities are, of course, a very necessary part of the operation of CAP and other Community-wide policies. Whatever the merits of these arguments it should be realized that the costs of monetary unification are considerable.[1] As part of a monetary union, the UK would abandon the right to change its parity unilaterally against other currencies, having already surrendered the ability to impose import restrictions and export subsidies for balance of payments purposes by adopting the CET. Expenditure-switching instruments are therefore eliminated from the armoury of feasible economic policies. Adjustment to payments deficits must then be by domestic deflation and the creation of unemployment, with the harmful and ultimately self-defeating implications noted in section II.2 above. At best, a high degree of labour mobility to the other EEC countries may mitigate the effects on unemployment, while it is possible that sustained financial support from other Community members may ease, but not eliminate, the burden of adjustment. Equally, the commitment to capital market integration would rule out restrictions on capital transactions in order to improve the basic balance.

Progress to date has been non-existent and, one could say, illustrates the folly of the whole conception. The most concrete move, taken in March 1972, was to limit the margin of fluctuation between the strongest and weakest of the EEC currencies to a maximum of 2.25%.[2] The scheme proved to be ill-fated. Sterling defected in June 1972, the lira is floating independently, and the French franc has been forced out of the snake twice, the most recent occasion being in March 1976. The lesson from this is that it is pointless to fix exchange parities between countries with divergent rates of inflation, and that uniformity of inflation rates will not come about without the prior emergence of national rates of wage increase which exactly offset national differences in productivity growth. To some extent the adoption of a common central bank and co-ordinated fiscal policies may assist in this regard but such developments are likely to fall foul of the fundamental issue of national sovereignty in the formulation and implementation of economic policy.

III.9   The Reform of the International Monetary System

If the quarter century since 1945 has any one dominant characteristic in the international economic arena, it is that of the integration of national commodity and capital markets into a unified and rapidly growing system of world trade and investment. A key role in this process has been played by the international financial rules established at the Bretton Woods conference of 1944, the supervisory

---

1   The interested reader may consult Y. Ishiyama, 'The Theory of Optimum Currency Areas : A Survey', IMF *Staff Papers,* vol. 22, 1975, pp. 344-83. For a discussion of the monetary union between the UK and Eire, see O. Whitaker, 'Monetary Integration : Reflections on Irish Experience', *Moorgate and Wall St,* Autumn 1973.

2   This scheme was known as the 'snake in the tunnel', the 'snake' representing the closely linked EEC currencies which, under the pressure of market forces, is free to move up and down relative to the dollar in the 'tunnel' defined by the Smithsonian exchange rate limits. (See section III.9.) The 'tunnel' disappeared in March 1973 when the EEC currencies engaged in a joint float against the dollar.

institution of which is the International Monetary Fund (IMF).[1] The principal
features of the Bretton Woods system were, in brief, its emphasis on mutual
international cooperation and its creation of a system of fixed but, in principle,
adjustable exchange rates, the par-value system, together with the provision of
temporary and conditional balance of payments finance by the IMF to supplement
reserve media in the form of gold and foreign exchange.

Throughout the 1960s it became clear that the IMF system suffered from
potentially lethal inconsistencies and that, in particular, it placed the US in an
economic position which the European industrial nations became increasingly
unable to accept. The first weakness was the general unwillingness of the main
industrial countries to adjust par values in the face of obvious fundamental
disequilibria until the force of events, aided by currency speculation, forced
governments into belated action. The case of sterling in the mid-1960s and of
Germany and Japan in the late 1960s are obvious examples of this failure to use
the par-value adjustment mechanism in the way originally intended by the architects
of Bretton Woods. Not unrelated to this was the asymmetry between deficit and
surplus countries, in that the pressure of reserve losses bore far more heavily on the
deficit countries than did the converse phenomena of reserve gains in the surplus
countries. In practice the 'scarce currency' provisions of Article 7 of the IMF
Agreement, which were meant to act as a sanction against persistent surplus
countries, were never invoked.

The second weakness involved the supply of global reserve media, which under
the IMF system consisted mainly of gold and foreign exchange holdings, and in
particular, of course, of US dollars. The problem was that the supply of monetary
gold depended on the vagaries of mining and speculative activity, and the supply of
foreign exchange depended upon the balance of payments deficits of the US, which
could prove to be temporary and, more important, unrelated to global reserve needs.
In the light of this there was considerable discussion in the 1960s of the alleged
inadequacy of world reserves which took as its basis the observed decline in the ratio
of world reserves to world imports, from a value of 68% in 1951 to one of 30% in
1969; the latter being less than the equivalent ratio for the depressed years of the
1930s. The problem with this type of discussion was that it failed to make clear
that the demand for foreign exchange reserves is a demand to finance balance of
payments *disequilibria,* not a demand to finance the volume of trade. It failed,
therefore, to recognize that the demand for reserve media will be smaller the more
frequently exchange rates are adjusted in line with economic pressure, the more
co-ordinated are national policies of demand management, and the greater the
willingness of national governments and private capital markets to engage in mutual
international borrowing and lending to finance payments imbalances. In the limit,
for example, with a perfectly freely floating system of exchange rates the demand
for official reserves would be zero.

Finally, there was the so-called 'confidence' problem, which followed from the
increasing degree of dependence of world reserve growth on foreign exchange in the
form of the dollar and to a lesser extent sterling. The problem was simply that by
1964 the total of outstanding dollar liabilities exceeded the gold reserves of the US
and from then on this disparity between dollar liabilities and gold 'cover' increased.
By December 1971 the US gold stock amounted to only 16% of the total of US

---

1   Cf. R. N. Cooper, *The Economics of Interdependence,* McGraw-Hill, 1968.

short-term dollar liabilities held by overseas monetary authorities. *De facto* this
meant that the dollar was no longer convertible into primary reserve assets and so
the willingness to hold dollars in official reserves decreased and the danger of a
dollar crisis increased. As R. Triffin pointed out in 1958, the gold-exchange standard
contained an automatic self-destruct mechanism,[1] with the potential risk of a severe
liquidity crisis in which dollar and sterling reserves were liquidated and destroyed,
while a given total of gold reserves was redistributed between countries. It is
important, when trying to understand recent events, to realize that the Bretton
Woods system had the effect of placing the US and the dollar in a unique position
in the international monetary system. Opponents of the US have argued that the
reserve currency status of the dollar enables the US to conduct internal policies
independently of its balance of payments position and to finance an outflow of
direct overseas investment on advantageous terms. In contrast, it has been argued
that the US has no choice but to adopt a passive balance of payments policy and
run a payments deficit of sufficient magnitude to satisfy the global demand for
dollars as an international reserve asset. Whatever the merits of these viewpoints,
two aspects of the situation are clear. First, because the dollar was extensively used
as the intervention currency for stabilizing exchange rates, the US had no need to
concern itself with supporting the external value of the dollar. Second, the one
option open to the US to cure its deficit, namely a devaluation of the dollar
relative to gold and therefore relative to other currencies, was steadfastly ruled out
on political grounds, until, that is, the events of December 1971.

   Throughout the 1960s the strains inherent in the system manifested themselves
in a variety of ways. Most significant, perhaps, were the *ad hoc* measures taken by
the industrial countries to supplement the existing sources of balance of payments
finance. At one level were the General Arrangements to Borrow, organized in
October 1962, in which the Group of Ten countries (UK, France, Germany,
Belgium, Netherlands, Italy, US, Canada, Sweden and Japan) agreed to lend their
currencies to the IMF should the latter run short of one of their respective currencies.
These arrangements have been renegotiated on several occasions, most recently in
October 1975, and the amount of support now totals SDR 6.2bn. Recent years have
seen increasing use of the GAB, indeed 76% of the finance for the standby arrangements negotiated by the UK in 1976 come from eight of the GAB countries. In
addition to this there are the currency swap arrangements between the US and the
central banks of other countries, whereby each agrees to lend or acquire currency
balances for an agreed time period. Several such arrangements exist between the US
and other countries and currently total $20bn. The UK has benefited considerably
from the availability this short-term financial aid, the UK–US swap facility being
increased to $3bn in March 1974. The UK has also been able to draw upon credits
provided by European central banks from 1961 onwards. A second important
manifestation of strain related to the official price of gold and the clear possibility
that its price might have to be increased to boost world reserves and improve the
asset:liability ratio of the US. Attempts to stabilize the free market price of gold by
the major central banks which had begun in 1961 had to be abandoned in March
1968 following the loss of $3bn in monetary gold stocks, sold in an attempt to hold
down the free-market price in the previous five months. The Washington agreement
of that time created a two-tier market for gold and effectively prevented national

---

1   R. Triffin, *Gold and the Dollar Crisis,* Yale, 1958.

monetary authorities from using monetary gold stocks to finance payments disequilibria in the face of an ever widening differential between the free market and the official price of gold. This two-tier system was abandoned in November 1973.

The final, and some would say most significant, manifestation of strain was the increasing volume of speculative capital flows which from 1967 onwards repeatedly disrupted the working of foreign exchange markets and threatened the parities of the deutschmark, the yen and the dollar. It became increasingly clear that the par-value system could not survive unless more effective methods for adjusting exchange rates in line with changing economic circumstances could be devised and unless some means could be found for absorbing an increasing volume of short-term capital flows.

Not surprisingly, in the face of such obvious strains, many proposals for reforming the system were put forward during the 1960s. On the fundamental question of the adjustment mechanism, proposals ranged from the adoption of freely floating exchange rates to mechanisms for ensuring the gradual and automatic adjustment of par values to payments disturbances, the crawling peg proposal. However, the response of the IMF to such proposals was lukewarm; a study by the executive directors concluded by reaffirming faith in the viability of the par-value system, with the only concessions to flexibility being the suggestion of wider margins of fluctuation around par values and the temporary abrogation of par-value obligations.[1]

By far the most important development of the 1960s was international agreement on the creation of a new reserve asset, the Special Drawing Right. The outcome of several years of discussion, this scheme came into operation in 1970.

Special Drawing Rights: SDRs are book entries in the Special Drawing Account of the IMF by means of which countries can give and receive credit on a multilateral basis to finance balance of payments deficits. At the moment, SDRs are held only by those national monetary authorities which participate in the IMF arrangements and which agree to accept the provisions of the SDR scheme. The total of SDRs is agreed collectively by the members of the IMF, so that the supply of this new reserve asset is agreed by international decision; the basis for their creation being the provision of an adequate, but not inflationary, long-term rate of growth of world reserves. SDRs are thus superior to gold and foreign exchange in that their supply is not arbitrary but is, in principle, the outcome of rational discussion. The total of SDRs is revised on a five-year basis with the first allocation of $9.3bn being made in three stages between 1970 and 1972.[2] Each country is assigned a net cumulative allocation of SDRs, in proportion to its quota in the general account of the IMF, and can treat this allocation as 'owned reserves' to finance payments imbalances. A country in deficit, for example, may use its SDR quota to purchase needed foreign exchange from other countries. One of the most ingenious features of the scheme is that utilization of a country's SDR quota is subject to the supervision of the IMF, the object being to ensure a balanced and widespread activation of the SDR facility. Use of SDRs is thus subject to three provisions:

---

1 *The Role of Exchange Rates in the Adjustment of International Payments: A Report by the Executive Directors,* IMF, 1970.

2 The revised Articles of Agreement to incorporate SDRs may be found in the IMF *Annual Report* for 1968, or in the book by F. Machlup listed at the end of this chapter.

(i) they must be used for legitimate balance of payments purposes and not, for example, to diversify exchange reserve portfolios; (ii) a country need not accept SDRs in excess of twice its net cumulative allocation; and (iii) a country's average holding over a period of five years must not fall below 30% of its net cumulative allocation — essentially to prevent the persistent, as distinct from temporary, financing of a deficit with SDRs. To give effect to these provisions two types of transactions in SDRs are allowed: designated transactions and non-designated transactions. With designated transactions, the IMF decides the countries that will add to their SDR holdings and so provide the currencies required by the country running down its SDR holdings, the choice of countries for designation being decided on the basis of their balance of payments strength and the adequacy of their reserve holdings. In contrast, non-designated transactions involve the transfer of SDRs between countries without recourse to the IMF where the objective is to redeem the currency liabilities of the transferer.

It is perhaps too early to say whether the scheme is successful but initial indications are promising. At the end of the first five-year reconstitution period, no participant had violated the 30% minimum average holding rule and a balanced utilization of SDRs had been achieved. As one would have expected, the industrial countries, with the exception of the UK and US, had been net recipients of SDRs and the less developed countries had been heavy net users of their SDR allocation.[1] More interesting questions relate to the future status of SDRs relative to gold and foreign currencies, especially the dollar. At end 1977, SDRs provided 3.6% of total world reserves compared to gold which accounted for 16% and the dollar which accounted for 69%. The question is, are SDRs simply to co-exist with other reserve assets or are they to be developed as a replacement for either or indeed both?

In the initial arrangements SDRs were effectively a gold substitute; they had a gold guarantee and carried a low rate of interest on net holdings of 1½%. On the understanding that the dollar is not devalued relative to gold, then SDRs are inferior to the dollar as a reserve asset because of their lower interest yield and lesser convenience of usage. However, the dollar devaluations of 1971 and 1973 upset this situation, as did the resort to a general floating of the important currencies relative to gold. In response to these changed circumstances the IMF announced, 1 July 1974, that the value of the SDR would be computed as a weighted average of sixteen currencies, that the link with gold would be terminated, and that the interest rate on net holdings of SDRs would be increased to 5%.[2] These changes provided scope both for the elimination of gold as a reserve asset and for the replacement of the dollar and other reserve currencies by SDRs.

The 1971 Crisis and a Forum for Reform: Any illusions that the creation of the SDR scheme had inaugurated a new period of stability for the par-value system were quickly shattered. Following a period of considerable uncertainty in foreign exchange markets and massive short-term capital outflows from the US, the US

---

1 For details consult IMF, *Annual Report 1975*, Washington, tables 1-3 and 1-6.
2 Details of the composition of the currency basket and of the formula for changing the interest rate on SDRs in line with commercial rates in international money market are in the article, 'The New Method of Valuing Special Drawing Rights', *BEQB*, September 1974. For further analysis of SDRs see F. Hirsch, 'An SDR Standard Impetus, Elements and Impediments', *Essays in International Finance, No. 99*, Princeton, 1975. For latest details of the SDR currency basket and SDR interest rates see IMF *Survey*, 3 April 1978.

government announced in August 1971 that the dollar was no longer convertible
into gold and that to eliminate the disequilibria in the international economic
system other countries must revalue their currencies relative to gold. To add
pressure toward this end a 10% surcharge was imposed on US imports of manufactures and the US proclaimed its intention to obtain trade concessions from Japan
and the EEC. Detailed and intensive official decisions culminated in a meeting of
the finance ministers of the Group of Ten countries at the Smithsonian Institute
in Washington in December 1971. The main points agreed were: (i) a new set of
values of exchange rates which involved a revaluation of the deutschmark and the
Japanese yen; (ii) that 'pending agreement on longer-term monetary reforms' the
permitted IMF margins of fluctuations around par values would be increased to
± 2.25%; (iii) that the US would devalue the dollar in terms of gold by 7.89% so
creating a new official price for gold of $38 per oz and that this would form the
new par value of the dollar; (iv) that the 10% import surcharge would be abolished;
(v) that new discussions should be undertaken, under the auspices of the IMF, to
consider the long-term reform of the international monetary system in all its major
aspects.

The forum for discussion of international reform was set up in June 1972 and
became known as the Committee of Twenty, holding meetings between September
1972 and June 1974 when the final report was presented. Three items dominated
the deliberations of the C-20. Firstly, methods of absorbing and re-cycling short-term
capital flows. Secondly, the creation of an exchange rate system with stable but
adjustable par values and with recognized and widely acceptable criteria for
instigating changes in par values. Thirdly, the future reserve base of the international
monetary system and in particular the role of the SDR in any reformed system. The
deliberations of the C-20 could hardly be described as successful; the final report
made clear that substantial differences of view existed on fundamental issues.[1] The
most concrete outcome of the C-20 activities has been its perpetuation in the form
of an Interim Committee which continues to discuss proposals for reform. However,
it would have indeed proved remarkable had any concrete reform proposals emerged,
for the reform discussions were overtaken by two important events: the adoption
of generalized floating by the major industrial countries in March 1973 and the
massive increase in the price of oil in December 1973.

Managed Floating and the Oil Price Issue: Confidence in the Smithsonian exchange
parities proved to be short-lived and in the period to March 1973 frequent
speculative crises disturbed the international monetary system, the only effective
counter to which was the adoption of floating exchange rates by the major industrial
nations. By April 1973, the par-value system had collapsed, perhaps the predictable
outcome of the drift of the Bretton Woods system into a reluctant dollar standard.

The experiences of 1972 and 1973 have underlined a major problem faced by an
exchange rate system in current circumstances, viz., coping with the massive volume
of short-term funds which can be switched very rapidly between financial centres.
Short-term capital flows forced the abandonment of Smithsonian parities and have

---

1 The final report of the C-20 'Outline of Reform' was published in IMF *Survey*, June 1974.
   See also *International Monetary Reform, Documents of the Committee of Twenty*, IMF,
   1974. For a valuable account of the activities of C-20 and its failings, see J. Williamson,
   The Failure of World Monetary Reform, 1971-74, Nelson, 1977.

played an important part in the fluctuations experienced by floating rates. Various measures have been adopted to limit such flows; for example, a two-tier foreign exchange market by Italy, direct controls on overseas borrowing by Germany, and an extension of inter-central bank currency swap arrangements, but these are of a somewhat *ad hoc* and inadequate nature.

The inception of a period of managed floating raises several difficulties for the international monetary system, in particular those of mutually inconsistent exchange rate stabilization policies, the possibility of competitive, beggar-my-neighbour, exchange rate management and the problem of exchange instability in the face of speculative pressure. To help avoid these problems the IMF issued guidelines for exchange rate management in June 1974.[1] The guidelines emphasized the point that exchange rate policy is a matter for international consultation and surveillance by the IMF and that intervention practices should be based on three principles: (i) exchange authorities should prevent sudden and disproportionate short-term movements in exchange rates and ensure an orderly adjustment of exchange rates to longer-term pressures; (ii) in consultation with the IMF, countries should establish a target zone for the medium-term values of their exchange rates and keep the actual rate within that target zone; (iii) countries should recognize that exchange rate management involves joint responsibilities. The experiences of the period of managed intervention have been mixed. On the one hand, short-term movements in exchange rates have been more volatile than advocates of flexible rates would perhaps condone while, on the other hand, exchange rates have been managed without any overt clashes of national interest and have changed to compensate substantial national differences in inflation rates.[2]

More damaging to the reform movement is the increase in the price of oil which created an unprecedented imbalance in the international economic system, in the form of a massive payments surplus for the oil producers and a corresponding deficit for the oil-importing countries. The problem is simply that the ability of the oil producers to spend their oil revenues on imports of goods and services has not so far matched the increase in revenues. Thus the oil producers enjoyed aggregate payments surpluses of $56.4bn in 1974 and an average surplus of $33bn in the three years 1975 to 1977, and it is estimated that by 1980 their cumulative payments surpluses could total as much as $300bn, expressed in terms of 1974 dollars.[3] Too much weight should not be placed on such estimates but it is salutary to note that the figure of $300bn is almost twice the total of world reserves at the end of 1975. Since, as is generally agreed, the OPEC countries have no serious alternative but to invest their surplus revenues in the advanced industrialized nations, so returning on capital account the purchasing power extracted from the current accounts of the oil-importing nations, the oil problem raises three serious issues for the stability of the international monetary system. First, there is the potential havoc which would be wrought to foreign exchange markets if surplus oil funds are invested in liquid

---

1 Cf. IMF *Survey,* 17 June 1974, pp. 181-3.
2 IMF *Annual Report, 1976.* On the volatility of exchange rates see F. Hirsch and D. Higham, 'Floating Rates–Expectations and Experience', *TBR,* June 1974, and P. A. Tosini 'Leaning Against the Wind : A Standard For Managed Floating', *Essays in International Finance,* No. 126, Princeton, 1977.
3 A compendium of widely differing estimates of OPEC financial accumulation by 1980 is in T. D. Willett, 'The Oil-Transfer Problem and International Economic Stability', *Essays in International Finance,* No. 113, Princeton, 1975.

assets and switched between currencies in search of interest return and the expected capital gain from exchange rate alterations. Clearly some means must be found of placing the funds in less liquid investments and/or creating sufficient central bank co-operation to undertake large scale re-cycling operations. Second, and more important, is the fact that the attractiveness of different oil-importing nations as havens for OPEC investment need bear no relation to the way in which their respective current account balances have been affected by oil price increases. The possibility is therefore reinforced that individual countries will try to eliminate their deficits by deflation or currency depreciation, the only outcome of which would be a worsening of the world recession. Finally, there are the problems faced by the developing nations which have seen the real values of aid inflows virtually eliminated by the increase in oil prices.[1]

One immediate response to these problems was the IMF's proposals to borrow from the oil-exporting nations and those industrial nations in a relatively strong payments position and to make the proceeds available to the countries most severely affected by the oil price increase. Two such oil facilities were negotiated, the second expiring in April 1976, and in total they channelled approximately SDR 7bn to countries in balance of payments difficulties. Borrowing from the second oil facility had to be repaid within three to seven years and a country could borrow up to a maximum amount, the smaller of 125% of the IMF quota or 85% of the increase in its oil import bill, all borrowing being conditional on IMF approval of the medium-term policies adopted by the borrowing country. The UK borrowed SDR 1bn from the facility in 1975.

As a replacement for these temporary arrangements, the IMF announced a new supplementary financing facility in 1977, of not less than SDR 7.75bn to assist members in balance of payments difficulties, the solution to which is thought to be long term.[2]

The Jamaica Agreement: The final report of the C-20 advocated an evolutionary approach to the problems of world monetary reform and, despite the problems noted in the previous section, it seems substantial progress has been made. During 1975 the Interim Committee held several meetings, and agreement on four important issues was reached in January 1976 at a meeting held in Jamaica. It was first agreed to increase the global quotas in the general account to SDR 39bn, an increase of 32.5%, and within this total to double the quotas of the oil-producing nations. Furthermore, as a temporary measure, until the increase in quotas was ratified, the size of each credit tranche at the IMF was to be increased from 25% to 36.25% of quota, so raising the size of each country's borrowing facility from 100% to 145% of its quota. This provided some $1.5bn to $2bn extra conditional finance to cover payments deficits. As a further aid to developing countries, the compensatory financing facility, established in 1963 to assist primary producing countries facing fluctuations in export receipts, was relaxed so that countries could make maximum drawings of 75% of their IMF quota, instead of the previous 50% limit. This facility has been heavily used in the past two years.

---

1 For discussion of the adverse effects on developing countries and possible means of easing their problems, consult C. Michalopoulos, 'Financing Needs of Developing Countries: Proposals for International Action', *Essays in International Finance*, No. 110, Princeton, 1975.
2 For details see IMF *Survey*, 5 September 1977.

Also agreed at the 1976 meeting were some longer-term measures of considerable consequence which relate to the role of gold and the permissible types of future exchange rate regime. On gold it has been agreed that countries need no longer supply 25% of their quotas in gold, nor are they obliged to use gold in other transactions they may undertake with the IMF. The IMF was also to sell one sixth of its gold stock on the free market over the next four years and use the proceeds to establish a Trust Fund, the object of which will be to provide balance of payments assistance on concessionary terms to the poorer countries, i.e. those with per-capita income not greater than SDR 300 in 1973. A further one-sixth of the IMF gold stock was also to be transferred to IMF members at the official price. The object of these moves is clearly to eliminate gold from the international monetary system and to establish the SDR as the principal reserve asset.[1] To date, the auctioning of gold has added the net amount of 1.17bn to the Trust Fund and has not shown any tendency to depress the free-market price of gold. The second of the four planned sales of gold to members was completed in January 1978.

Without doubt the most fundamental outcome of the Jamaica meeting was the agreement to amend Article 4 of the IMF agreement. The main points are as follows:[2] (i) a general return to stable but adjustable par values can take place with the support of an 85% majority in the IMF; (ii) par values may not be expressed in terms of gold or other currencies but can be expressed in terms of SDRs, the margins of fluctuation around par values remain at ± 2.25%; (iii) with the concurrence of the IMF, any country may abandon its par value and adopt a floating exchange rate; (iv) the exchange rate management of a floating currency must be subject to IMF surveillance and must not be conducted so as to disadvantage other countries; (v) the agreed practices with respect to floating rates will operate until such time as a general return to par values is attained. In effect, floating exchange rates have been legalized within the framework of the IMF system and without any diminution of the powers of the IMF.

Finally, the Jamaica meeting argued that the SDR should evolve into the major reserve asset of the international financial system.

The Jamaica reforms, which became operative in April 1978, are undoubtedly important and reflect well on the IMF as a forum for effective international co-operation, especially at a time of substantial short-term disruption of the international monetary system. However, the reforms fell well short of the ideals outlined by the C-20 and their long-run effect may be questioned.[3] On adjustment, criteria for exchange rate surveillance and management have yet to be agreed and the question of whether surveillance should extend beyond exchange rate policy

---

1 The Group of Ten also agreed that they would not attempt to peg the price of gold or to increase the stock of gold in their reserves for a two-year period. These proposals have now been terminated. IMF *Survey,* January 1976 and January 1978.

2 The text of the proposed new Article 4 is contained in IMF *Survey,* 19 January 1976, pp. 20-1. Full details of the revised articles of agreement may be found in *The Second Amendment to the Articles of Agreement of the International Monetary Fund,* Cmnd. 6705, HMSO, 1977.

3 For somewhat jaundiced views of the Jamaica agreement see E. Bernstein, *et al.* 'Reflections on Jamaica', *Essays in International Finance, No. 115,* Princeton, 1976, and A. Kafka, 'The IMF : Reform without Reconstruction?', *Essays in International Finance,* No. 118, Princeton, 1976.

has yet to be faced.[1] On liquidity, it is plain that the SDR is currently the least significant reserve asset in the system and that the aim of demonetizing gold is far from reached. Indeed by allowing the revaluation of monetary gold in line with the free-market price it has strengthened the role of gold and made it highly likely that central banks will attempt to stabilize the free-market price. The questions of asset settlement and the role of the dominant foreign exchange component of world reserves also remain unresolved. Until answers to these issues are provided there seems little prospect of re-creating a stable international monetary system.

1   Details of the latest proposals on exchange rate practices are given in IMF *Survey*, 3 April 1978.

REFERENCES AND FURTHER READING

Sir Alec Cairncross (ed.), *Britain's Economic Prospects Reconsidered,* George Allen and Unwin, 1971.

Sir Alec Cairncross, *Control of Long-Term Capital Movements,* Brookings Institution, 1973.

R. E. Caves and Associates, *Britain's Economic Prospects,* Brookings Institution and George Allen & Unwin, 1968.

H. G. Grubel, *International Economics,* Irwin, 1977.

H. G. Johnson and J. E. Nash, *UK and Floating Exchanges,* Hobart Paper 46, Institute of Economic Affairs, 1969.

C. P. Kindleberger, *International Economics,* Irwin, 1973.

F. Machlup, *Remaking the International Monetary System,* Committee for Economic Development and Johns Hopkins, 1968.

C. McMahon, *Sterling in the Sixties,* Oxford University Press, 1964.

J. E. Meade, *UK, Commonwealth and Common Market : A Reappraisal,* Hobart Paper 17, Institute of Economic Affairs, 1970.

W. B. Reddaway, *Effects of UK Direct Investment Overseas : An Interim Report,* Cambridge University Press, 1967; *Final Report,* Cambridge University Press, 1968.

B. Tew, *International Monetary Cooperation 1945-70,* Hutchinson, 1970.

B. Tew, *The Evolution of the International Monetary System, 1945-77,* Hutchinson, 1977.

S. J. Wells, *British Export Performance,* Cambridge University Press, 1964.

J. Williamson, *The Failure of World Monetary Reform, 1971-74,* Nelson, 1977.

OFFICIAL PUBLICATIONS

Bank of England Quarterly Bulletin

Economic Trends (regular analyses of balance of payments in March, June, September, and December issues).

IMF *Annual Report* and IMF *Survey* (twice monthly).

NEDC reports, especially *Export Trends* (1963) and *Imported Manufactures* (1965).

Report of Committee on the Working of the Monetary System, Radcliffe Report, Cmnd. 827, 1959.

Trade and Industry (weekly) (previously *Board of Trade Journal*).

UK Balance of Payments Pink Book (CSO annually).

4

Industry and commerce

J. R. Cable

I   INTRODUCTION: SOME THEORETICAL BACKGROUND

Whenever we attempt to analyse the behaviour of firms and industries we have, at some stage, to rely on theoretical models. Orthodox theory has it that firms behave as if their objective was to maximize profit. The theory offers us many insights and can lead to important policy implications for the government and others. But there are alternative models which will be drawn upon in this chapter for additional insights.

One strand of recent theoretical development has resulted in a group of 'managerial' models. These recognize that in modern, large firms there has been a divorce of ownership (by shareholders) from control (by salaried executives).[1] In this situation profit remains important to policy makers within the firm both for survival and also because it may be directly linked to executive salaries through incentives such as stock-option schemes and bonuses linked to profits. But it is argued that where top management exercises the degree of control over policy that it appears to do in practice, firms are most likely to behave as if maximizing the value of variables yielding utility to managers, subject to some profit or other financial constraint. The variables in question vary from model to model. In Baumol's model the firm is assumed to maximize sales revenue, subject to a profit constraint.[2] Marris has developed an alternative, growth maximizing model, with a security (stock market valuation) constraint.[3] Williamson put forward a more general model of managerial utility, in which the objective function incorporates salary, the number and quality of subordinates, control over discretionary investment and expenditure on managerial perquisites.[4]

Firms pursuing such objectives would usually arrive at equilibrium outcomes which differ from those of a profit-maximizer, e.g. in terms of price and output levels. In some cases they would also adjust decision variables in the opposite direction to a profit maximizer, in response to changes in the business environment, e.g. changes in tax rates. Hence in analysing firms' behaviour and in assessing the

1   See A. A. Berle & G. C. Means, *The Modern Corporation and Private Property*, revised edition, Harcourt, Brace and World, N.Y. 1968; P. Sargent Florence, *Ownership Control and Success of Large Companies*, Sweet and Maxwell, 1961; R. Marris & A. Wood, *The Corporate Economy*, Macmillan, 1971; A. Wood, *A Theory of Profits*, CUP, 1975, and M. King, *Public Policy and the Corporation*, Chapman and Hall, 1977.

2   W. J. Baumol, 'On the Theory of Oligopoly', *Economica*, Vol. XXV, No. 99, August 1958, pp. 187-98, and *Business Behaviour Value and Growth*, Macmillan, 1959.

3   R. Marris, 'A Model of the Managerial Enterprise', *Quarterly Journal of Economics*, May 1963, and *The Economic Theory of Managerial Capitalism*, Macmillan, 1964.

4   O. E. Williamson, 'Managerial Discretion and Business Behaviour', *American Economic Review*, December 1963, and *The Economics of Discretionary Behaviour: Business Objectives in the Theory of the Firm*, Prentice Hall, 1964.

effects of government policy we may reach different conclusions depending on which theoretical model of behaviour we apply. Unfortunately there is at the moment no clear way of telling which model should be adopted. Empirical testing of the hypotheses so far has produced some evidence in support of each, but none of the theories – including profit maximization – has yet been accepted as demonstrably superior. In this situation perhaps the most we can do when looking at the behaviour of firms and industries is to be very clear on the theoretical assumptions we make and, especially when appraising public policy issues, consider the various responses which might be expected under different theoretical assumptions.

Alongside the managerial theories is another, somewhat more radical, new theoretical departure. The 'behavioural' theory emphasizes the organizational aspects of firms and the limited amount of knowledge available in decision-making.[1] In the behavioural theory the firm is seen to pursue a number of goals in the form of independent, aspiration-level constraints, e.g. a particular sum of profits, or level of sales, or a target rate of return on capital, which firms attempt to 'satisfice'. Goals are imperfectly rationalized, may conflict, and receive sequential rather than simultaneous attention. Over time, aspiration levels for a particular goal will change according to past achievements in relation to past aspirations. The firm is seen as an adaptive organism, solving pressing problems rather than attempting to apply plans leading to optimal equilibrium values or growth paths of decision variables, as in more conventional approaches. In a situation of imperfect knowledge, search (the acquisition of information) is neither continuous nor determined optimally as an investment decision. Rather, search is 'problemistic', requiring to be motivated e.g. by adverse feedback on goal fulfilment or by some external event or evidence of failure. Search is 'limited' or 'narrow'; solutions are sought at first in the neighbourhood of problem symptoms and current alternatives and search widens only as satisfactory solutions fail to be found. In choosing among alternative strategies 'satisficing' procedures are adopted, the first acceptable strategy being selected. The firm's behaviour is constrained by standard procedural rules governing search, choice, etc., and these are abandoned only under duress. However, in the long term organizational learning occurs, and search and choice rules are adapted in the light of experience. Typically, firms exhibit organizational slack in the form of excess resources within the organization.

In order to derive quantitative predictions of firms' behaviour from the behavioural model it is necessary to develop specific computer simulation models. However, the theory does permit of some qualitative analysis without this. Like the managerial theories, the behavioural theory is important because it may lead us to conclusions about firms' behaviour which are different from those of other models. However, one distinguishing feature of the behavioural model is that it specifically sets out to embody the decision process. Thus, unlike all the other models so far mentioned, the behavioural model *does* attempt to tell us how various outcomes are arrived at as well as what the outcomes will be.

The theoretical approaches to firms' behaviour so far discussed have generally been conceived with the private sector of the economy in mind, and especially

---

1 H. A. Simon, 'A Behavioural Model of Rational Choice', *Quarterly Journal of Economics,* February 1955; R. M. Cyert and J. G. March, *A Behavioural Theory of the Firm,* Prentice Hall, 1963, and H. A. Simon, 'Theories of Decision Making in Economics and Behavioural Science', *American Economic Review,* June 1959.

'secondary' manufacturing industry rather than the 'primary' sector (agriculture and extractive industries) and the 'tertiary' sector (transport, distributive trades, professional and other services, government administration, etc.). Nevertheless there are some insights which they can give in all areas of industry and commerce, whether public or private, and the scope of this chapter is not limited to the private manufacturing sector. Some of the issues we shall consider do mainly concern the private sector (e.g. the question of monopoly control). But in another section we also consider the public sector issue of pricing and investment criteria for nationalized industries. And a number of the issues considered are common to both the public and private sectors and all industry and commerce, e.g. the whole question of efficiency, productivity and technical progress.

II   THE SIZE STRUCTURE OF INDUSTRIES AND TRADES

An idea of the size structure of UK industrial groupings is given in the second column of table 4.1. Size is measured in terms of output. Alternative measures

TABLE 4.1

Size Structure and Growth of UK Industries, 1957-77

Industry	Annual rate of growth, 1957-77 (%)	GDP by industrial origin, 1976 (£m)[3]
Agriculture, forestry and fishing	1.74[1]	3,116
Mining and quarrying	−1.14	2,458
Manufacturing:		
Food, drink, tobacco	2.37	3,433
Chemicals, oil products	5.39	2,892
Metal manufacture	−0.27	2,296
Engineering and allied industries	1.93	12,477
Mechanical	2.07	3,434
Electrical	4.20	2,744
Vehicles	1.01	3,235
Textiles, leather, clothing	1.10	3,123
Printing, paper, publishing	2.09	2,436
Total Manufacturing	2.24	30,464
Construction	1.38[1]	7,793
Electricity, gas, water	4.52	3,905
Transport and communications	2.85[1]	10,315
Distributive trades	2.33[1]	10,379
Insurance, banking, finance and business services	4.87[1]	7,717
Miscellaneous services	1.88[1]	13,417
GDP[2]	2.4	109,080

Sources: *NIBB* and *NIER.*
Notes: 1 1957-76.
     2 Includes public services and administration, defence, ownership of dwellings, adjustment for financial services and residual error.
     3 Contribution of each industry to GDP before providing for depreciation but after providing for stock appreciation. Figures for individual manufacturing industries are estimates.

would be employment and capital stock. In some cases these would produce a rather different picture, because of inter-industry differences in capital/labour ratios. For instance, in 1974 the UK coal, petroleum and chemical industries together accounted for 18.2% of total capital employed in manufacturing but only 7.4% of manpower and 9.0% of output. Evidently there is need for some care in choosing the most appropriate size measure for any particular given purpose.

Industry boundaries are based on the Standard Industrial Classification for the UK. The SIC groups the UK economy into Orders, which are subdivided into Minimum List Headings. The latter are generally the nearest one can get in official statistics to what we would normally mean by an 'industry', although even these subdivisions are too broad in some cases.[1] The industry groups in the table are mostly Orders, or even groups of Orders, and it must be remembered that they may be composed of a very large number of sub-trades, often quite disparate. Although there may be quite strong technological links among the industries concerned, it is by no means certain that their various products necessarily have high cross-elasticities of demand. In general, industrial classifications tend to be product-orientated.

In comparison with other major European countries the UK has a relatively small agricultural sector, reflecting a greater reliance on food imports in the past (see below, p. 175), but some larger tertiary industries, notably finance, insurance, etc. The manufacturing sector as a whole is not large in relation to GDP by

TABLE 4.2

Relative Importance of Manufacturing Industries, UK and Selected European Countries, 1970[1].

| | Percentage of Manufacturing Output | | | |
	UK	France	W. Germany	Italy
Food, drink and tobacco	11.52	9.99	12.45	11.80
Chemicals	11.29	18.50	16.23	13.45
Basic metals	7.98	9.53	7.79	7.06
Iron and steel	6.15	7.04	6.60	5.84
Non-ferrous metals	1.82	2.50	1.19	1.21
Metal products	42.30	41.09	40.80	31.53
Non-electrical machinery	15.05	15.21	11.26	11.58
Transport equipment	11.52	11.46	10.17	7.94
Textiles, clothing, leather	9.35	7.60	7.47	16.98
Other manufacturing	17.56	13.28	15.26	19.18
All manufacturing	100.00	100.00	100.00	100.00
Manufacturing output in thousand millions of I.U.A.[2]	34.3	49.9	79.2	23.9

Sources: *Industrial Production: Quarterly Supplement to Main Economic Indicators 1977-4,* OECD, and *General Statistics 1977,* Statistics Office of the European Commission.

Notes: 1   The figures have been extracted from tables containing weights for mining, electricity and gas, as well as manufacturing.
2   International Units of Account: an EEC monetary unit based on the gold content of the US dollar prior to its devaluation in December 1971.

---

1   For example, see p. 196 below.

international standards, and certainly accounts for a much smaller share of all economic activity than in West Germany.

Table 4.2 enables more detailed comparisons to be made among the major West European countries for the manufacturing sector. This shows a comparatively small UK chemicals sector, and somewhat larger metal products group, which includes the engineering and allied industries. The UK textiles and clothing industry is larger than in France and West Germany, but much smaller than in Italy.

Changes in the size distribution will obviously occur when industries grow at different rates. As the next section will show, there have been considerable differences in growth experience among individual UK industries since the early 1950s. These have produced some significant changes in the proportion of GDP originating in broad sectors of the economy. In particular, the share of manufacturing fell from 36.7% in 1955 to 27.9% in 1976, and that of other 'industrial' production (agriculture, mining and construction) also declined, from 14.1% of GDP to 12.3%. Public utilities and commerce (distribution, transport, insurance, etc.) increased their share of GDP from 26.6% up to 29.6% and the share of miscellaneous services, public administration and defence also rose.[1]

III   INDUSTRIAL OUTPUT GROWTH 1957-77
III.1   General Output Trends

The growth of UK industrial output over the past two decades, at a rate of approximately 2.3% per annum, has been extremely modest by international standards. Table 4.3 compares the annual growth rates for total industrial production (manufacturing, mining, electricity and gas) between the UK and the six original EEC members. Most of the other countries grew at around twice the UK rate or

TABLE 4.3

Output Growth and GDP per head in the UK and EEC, 1957-76

Country	Annual growth of industrial production[1] 1957-76 (%)	Total growth of industrial production, 1957-76 (%)	GDP per head (in IUA) 1960	1976
UK	2.27	57.8	1374	2824
France	5.03	151.2	1337	4474
Germany	4.93	146.6	1298	5412
Italy	6.41	219.6	696	2449
Belgium	3.88	106.2	1253	4648
Netherlands	6.03	201.6	979	4602
Luxembourg	1.84	53.2	1568	4938
EEC (the Six)	5.32	160.4	1110	4160
EEC (the Nine)	–	–	1168	3950

Sources: *Industrial Production,* OECD; *National Accounts of OECD Countries,* OECD; and *General Statistics 1975-12,* Statistics Office of The European Community.

Note: 1 Includes manufacturing, mining, electricity and gas.

1 For a stimulating and controversial discussion of Britain's alleged structural malaise, with too few resources committed to marketed goods, see R. Bacon and W. Eltis, *Britain's Economic Problem: Too Few Producers,* Macmillan, 1976.

more, except for Belgium and Luxembourg, and of these two the Belgian rate was also well above the UK's. If differences in growth rates such as these persisted for only short periods there would be little change in relative output levels and, ultimately, living standards among the various countries. When they persist for a time period as long as that covered in table 4.3 the differential impact is large. Whereas UK industrial production grew by a little under 60%, that for the EEC as a whole rose to over two and a half times the original level, while the Italian and Dutch production more than trebled. At the beginning of the period (and indeed up

TABLE 4.4

Degree of Self-Sufficiency in Agricultural Products in the UK and EEC, 1974/75 (Value of Domestic Consumption as % of Domestic Production)

	1974/5 (%)	
	UK	EUR-9
Wheat (soft)	67	116
Wheat (hard)	–	82
Rye	38	100
Barley	102	107
Oats	101	99
Potatoes	99	101
Sugar	22	87
Vegetables	76	94
Fresh fruit	35	79
Whole milk	100	100
Cheese	68	104
Butter	11	100
Eggs	97	100
Meat	73	96

Source: *Yearbook of Agricultural Statistics, 1976,* Eurostat.

to 1967) national income per head was higher in the UK than in the EEC as a whole, although the French and German GDP per head had exceeded the UK's since 1961. By 1972 the UK had become one of the poorer European nations.

Table 4.1 shows a fair measure of diversity among the growth rates for various industry sectors in the UK over the same period, with the chemical industry and the public utilities expanding at around twice the average rate, and with two industries actually declining. Yet even the faster-growing sectors have scarcely matched the average performances in the EEC countries previously discussed. As one would expect, examples of more impressive expansion do emerge upon further disaggregation, e.g. plastics, electronics and man-made fibres. The physical quantity of synthetic resin production increased more than eight-fold between 1950 and 1973, and total production of man-made fibres more than trebled between 1958 and 1973. In both cases, however, output has either levelled out or declined since then.

What the eventual effects of EEC membership on individual UK industries will be is hard to say. Various forecasts were made at the time of UK entry. One of the most comprehensive produced a ranking of some 230 manufactured products in order of those most likely to benefit from entry.[1] The products belonged to nine industrial sectors: chemicals; manufactures of leather, wood, rubber, paper, etc.; textiles and clothing; iron and steel; non-ferrous metals and metal manufactures; mechanical engineering; electrical engineering; transport equipment; and a miscellaneous category. The broad conclusion was that none of these industrial sectors was likely to fare much better or worse than any other across the board. Rather, each sector had its more promising and more vulnerable parts. This result accords well with previous findings that the creation of the EEC influenced the economies of the original partners mainly by a redistribution of resources within rather than between industries.[2] However, the findings for individual products did not in all cases agree with an official list of products thought likely to benefit from entry.[3] This included footwear, machine tools and food-processing equipment, all of which figured among those expected to do least well of all among the 230 products in the first study.

III.2 Agricultural Development and Policy

As in almost all other developed countries, UK agricultural production has been maintained and developed since the war at a higher level than would otherwise be the case, given the costs of domestic production and world price levels for agricultural products. The method by which support was given prior to the entry of the UK into the EEC differed in some respects from the Common Agricultural Policy (CAP) operated by the EEC.

Under the UK scheme up to 1973, farmers received assistance in two main ways: through deficiency payments and through direct grants for capital investment and farm improvement schemes. The deficiency payments scheme operated as follows. Agricultural products sold in the UK at world price levels, with more or less free access to the UK market for foreign producers, and some preferential treatment for Commonwealth producers. Where these prices were below the level of a guaranteed price, set by the government to encourage a certain level of home production taking production costs and farm incomes into account, farmers received from the government a deficiency payment equal to the difference. Thus the UK maintained open markets to foreign producers and consumers enjoyed the relatively low world food price levels, but home production was encouraged and farm incomes were stabilized and controlled. The cost fell on the Exchequer and varied inversely with the level of world prices. Early experience of the mounting cost of an open-ended support scheme, with no upper limit on quantities produced at home and hence on the liability of the Exchequer, led to a modification in the early 1960s. Around 1963 'standard quantities' were introduced for most products, and the guaranteed price fell as these were exceeded.

The farm capital grants scheme provided assistance for investment in farm buildings, fixed machinery, land drainage, hill-land improvements and remodelling works for farm amalgamations, etc. The rates of grant aid tended to differ among

---

1   S. S. Han and H. H. Liesner, *Britain and the Common Market,* University of Cambridge, Department of Applied Economics, Occasional Paper No. 27, 1971.

2   B. Balassa, 'Tariff Reductions and Trade in Manufactures among the Industrial Countries', *AER,* June 1966, pp. 466-73, and I. Walter, *The European Common Market: Growth and Patterns of Trade and Production,* New York, 1967.

3   *BTJ,* 8 July 1970, pp. 41-3.

projects, although steps were taken in 1970 towards a comprehensive scheme with a basic rate of 30%. In addition to capital grants, subsidies were offered for certain current expenditures, e.g. those associated with the use of fertilizers and lime. The guaranteed prices, grants and subsidies were reviewed annually and published in the *Annual Review and Determination of Guarantees.*[1]

One overall result of the old UK policy was certainly to make domestic production higher than it would have been without official support (and assuming other countries continued to support their own farmers). The policy also affected the composition of agricultural output and the efficiency of the industry. In the later years of the policy especially, guaranteed prices were manipulated to produce selective expansion. Similarly, selective use was made of grants and subsidies to bring about desired changes in the structure of the industry, and to mechanize and modernize it. The fact that between 1955 and 1972 output grew by 2.7% per annum and capital by 3.0% while employment fell by roughly 3.1% is some indication of the extent to which this happened.

The EEC arrangements for agricultural support under the CAP have objectives which are very similar to those of the previous UK policy. Article 39 of the Treaty of Rome mentions securing increases in agricultural efficiency, stabilizing agricultural markets, guaranteeing regular supplies, and ensuring reasonable prices to consumers and fair living standards for the agricultural population. The two policies are also similar in that support to farmers comes partly in the form of price guarantees and partly in capital and current grants or subsidies. However, the methods of operation are different, especially on the price-support side.

The CAP was designed to bring about free intra-Community trade in agricultural products, with uniform prices among the members and a common external tariff. Since the early 1960s 'target' prices have been negotiated for many products which, like the old UK guaranteed prices, make domestic production profitable. However, under the EEC arrangements consumers pay the full target price, or a price close to it. To ensure that this is so, there is a system of variable levies on imports from the outside world, broadly designed to equalize the supply price of foreign produce (including transport costs) and the target price. In addition, there is provision for support-buying of unsold produce when prices fall below an intervention-price level. In some cases the intervention price is set close to the target price. For instance, the intervention price for grain is within 5–7% of the target price. For some products, however, such as fruit and vegetables, prices can fall significantly before support buying occurs. The central authority responsible for the policy is the European Agricultural Guidance and Guarantee Fund. Price support is managed by the Guarantee wing of this authority. The fund receives its income ultimately from the Exchequers of member nations, contributions being determined partly by negotiation and partly in proportion to the size of the import levies arising from each nation's external trade in agricultural products.

Grant aid to farmers comes under the Guidance wing of the EAGGF but grants are actually made by each national government. Up to 1971 the assistance schemes of each country had not been harmonized, but over the 1960s an increasing proportion of the relevant expenditure was reimbursed by the Fund. The rate of grant aid for approved schemes varied up to a maximum of 25%, and as in the UK

---

1   Since 1977 the *Annual Review* has been published separately from the determination of prices, much of which is now decided at European level.

some grant aid was available for current expenditures (i.e. towards the cost of non-capital inputs).

The relative merits of the old and new systems are worth considering. From a world standpoint many observers have commented unfavourably on the protectionist attitude of the CAP towards non-Community produce, in contrast to the 'open door' aspect of the earlier UK policy. Secondly, the high domestic price characteristic of the CAP has been adversely compared with the former UK 'cheap food' policy, especially as food expenditure accounts for a higher proportion of total expenditure among poorer families. Thirdly, many observers would say that compared with the UK system the CAP is an inefficient scheme in a number of technical respects.

Thus one problem is that of surpluses of major products. The CAP's high prices and support-buying arrangements stimulate production and remove the normal market sanction on oversupply (i.e. downward price adjustment) while simultaneously discouraging demand. In the absence of other non-market controls on supply, such as the 'standard quantities' under the old UK system, this produces a chronic tendency towards the appearance of surpluses. At one time or another there have in fact been surpluses of butter (purchased to sustain a high target price for milk), grains, sugar, beef, fruit and wine. A second technical deficiency, which also arises from the open-ended nature of the support system, is that there is in principle no upper limit to the cost of support. Thirdly, the CAP as at present operated places much less emphasis on raising farm efficiency than did the old UK system. Despite the *Mansholt Plan* of 1968, which was designed to shift the emphasis of CAP away from price support towards structural reform, price support retains the major share of expenditure. Thus the Guidance wing of the policy accounts for only around a third of the total cost, compared with the 60% or so going on grants and subsidies under the old UK system.

The CAP has always been a source of problems among the member countries, with their differing domestic agricultural situations and interests. Setting suitable common target prices against a background of widely differing productivity levels from country to country has been a major and recurring problem. Lengthy and often heated negotiations also occur over the size of the Farm Fund and of individual member contributions to it, in a situation where West Germany in particular, and also Britain and Italy are net losers in terms of budgetary contributions and receipts, and the remaining countries either benefit or receive roughly what they give. In the 1970s currency problems have also loomed large: since agricultural prices are fixed in IUA, changes in official parities within the Community create a need for adjustments to maintain agricultural price uniformity in real terms. In the case of Britain, the 'green pound' — the exchange rate between sterling and IUA for agricultural purposes, which does not float — was devalued by a total of 15% in 1974 and 1975, and a further 7.5% in early 1978. However, at the time of writing the total devaluation since 1973 is only 21.4%, compared with a decline of nearer 40% in sterling against major trading currencies over the same period.

III.3   Energy[1]

The growth of total energy consumption, at less than 1% p.a. over the past fifteen years (table 4.5), has clearly been much less than the expansion of GDP over the

---

1   See also the government consultative document *Energy Policy*, Cmnd. 7101, HMSO, February 1978.

same period. The introduction of technical economies in fuel use, and relatively slow growth in some fuel-intensive industries such as iron and steel and rail, are among the factors which explain this differential growth. In addition energy demand has been reduced due to the sudden large price increase, particularly in petroleum prices, in 1973; between 1973 and 1975 total energy consumption actually fell by 8.5%, followed by a rise of 2.5% in 1976.

The discovery of natural gas and then oil in the North Sea, together with the quadrupling of world petroleum prices by OPEC countries in 1973-4, have produced dramatic changes in the pattern of UK energy procurement. Gas was the first industry to be affected, moving from stagnation to resurgence in the mid-1960s as cheap, imported gas became available to replace town gas. Growth then accelerated under the impact of even cheaper and growing North Sea supplies in the 1970s. From 1969 to 1976 sales rose at over 16% p.a. and by the later date 95% of gas used was natural. However, on present indications a further significant increase in the share of gas in total energy use seems unlikely.

Direct use of coal was in very sharp decline over the period 1960-74. (The reduction in coal output was much less rapid however (cf. tables 4.5 and 4.1)

TABLE 4.5

Total UK Inland Energy Consumption, 1960-76, by Type of Fuel – Heat Supplied Basis (million therms)

Type of fuel	1960	(%)	1965	(%)	1970	(%)	1976	(%)	% Change 1960-76
Coal (direct use)	23,433	(46.4)	17,409	(32.4)	11.839	(20.4)	6,022	(10.5)	−74.3%
Gas	3,187	(6.3)	3,868	(7.2)	6,182	(10.7)	13,827	(24.1)	+333.9%
Electricity	3,372	(6.7)	5,022	(9.4)	6,567	(11.3)	7,358	(12.8)	+118.2%
Petroleum (direct)	12,385	(24.5)	19,820	(36.9)	27,198	(46.9)	26,193	(45.7)	+111.5%
Other fuels[1]	8,154	(16.1)	7,568	(14.1)	6,167	(10.6)	3,928	(6.9)	−51.8%
Total	50,531	(100.0)	53,687	(100.0)	57,953	(100.0)	57,328	(100.0)	+13.5% (= 0.8% pa)

Source: AAS.
Note: 1 Includes coke, breeze, solid smokeless fuel and liquid fuels derived from coal.

because coal has been retained, by a deliberate act of government policy, as a primary energy source in electricity generation. Up to the mid-1970s there was rapid growth of electricity demand, and the electricity industry's share in total coal sales rose from 21.8% in 1957 to 62.9% in 1976.) The reason for coal's decline over the period was primarily that after 1956 petroleum had become relatively much cheaper. The 1973-4 oil price rises, however, restored coal's price competitiveness, and the industry's prospects have also been improved by the discovery of large reserves at Selby and in Warwickshire, and by technical developments in mining technology. Re-expansion of coal production was planned to provide an extra 42 million tons p.a. by 1980 (a 37% increase on the 1975 production level) of which 10 million tons was expected from a new pit at Selby. However, by early 1976 much of coal's price advantage over oil had been lost, and the *actual* development of coal up to 1980 will depend very much on trends in UK inflation rates, mining productivity and the level of world oil prices. So far the most that can be said is that the long-term decline of coal has, for the time being at least, been halted. In the period 1971-2 to 1976-7 production has fluctuated around an average level of just over 110 million tons per annum, compared with an average of around 180 million tons during the 1960s.

Large-scale production of North Sea oil began in 1976, production rising from 12.0 million tonnes in that year to 38 million tonnes in 1977. Present forecasts are for further rapid expansion to 104 million tonnes in 1980, and a maximum 146 million tonnes in 1984, after which output is expected to level off or decline. Once again, however, these estimates should be treated with caution. North Sea oil, though of high quality, is expensive and economically viable only if world price levels are high. (Production costs in the North Sea are approximately ten times those of the most accessible Middle East sources.) As with coal, actual future production will depend on the trend of extraction costs, the price of imported oil, and world political developments which affect the strategic value of a secure, domestic source of supply.

Because North Sea oil is unlikely to be significantly cheaper to the consumer than imported supplies, its availability is not expected to lead to dramatic changes in the future pattern of fuel use. In fact, oil consumption in 1980 is expected to be not much different from the 1974 level. The main benefits from North Sea oil lie elsewhere, in particular in the form of a significant increase in the growth of GNP,[1] and favourable effects on the balance of payments and government revenue.

Energy consumption per head in the UK is higher than in Europe, by 8% in total than the average in the nine EEC member countries, and 9.5% higher in the household consumption sector.[2] However, even without the effect of North Sea oil, UK dependence on imported fuel is much less, 43% as against 57%. This is the result of an even more rapid rundown of coal production and switch to petroleum on the continent than in the UK. In 1950 coal supplied nearly 75% of energy needs in the Six, and petroleum only 10%. In 1975 the proportions of coal and oil among the different primary fuels in gross inland consumption in the UK and in the Nine were:

	UK	EEC-9
Hard Coal	35.3%	19.3%
Crude Petroleum	44.7%	55.1%

Comparatively speaking, therefore, the 1973 oil crisis was less serious for the UK than for the European countries.

Like agriculture, energy is the subject of a common policy in the EEC. However, the energy policy is rudimentary compared with the elaborate CAP. It is also very different in that the Community opted for a cheap energy policy during the 1960s based on imported crude oil, with some subsidies to internal coal producers. These characteristics typify the UK agricultural support system rather than CAP. One reason for the rather limited agreement over energy policy which has been achieved

---

1 A recent estimate suggests that, taking into account the oil price increases of 1973-4, total growth of GDP from 1975-85 is temporarily raised by about 4%, about half this increase coming in 1977-9, when the annual measured growth rate is on average 0.7% higher due to oil. See *NIER*, February 1978.
2 *Source:* Eurostat, *Quarterly Bulletin of Energy Statistics, 4-1976*. Figures are for 1975. The gap is closing however: comparable figures for 1971 are 15.6% and 19.7% respectively.

is that before 1967 responsibility for the various fuel industries was divided. Coal was the responsibility of the European Coal and Steel Community (ECSC); oil, natural gas and electricity were covered by the EEC; and nuclear power was the province of the European Atomic Energy Community (Euratom). After the merger of the three communities in 1967 the full extension of the Treaty of Rome to the energy sector was agreed; i.e. a common market in energy was created. Since then the European Commission has undertaken short- and medium-term forecasts of energy demand and supply, analysed the problems likely to occur up to 1985, and identified various policy options. A number of directives, orders, regulations and decisions have also been made. Through these, members have agreed to maintain certain levels of oil stocks (ninety days by 1 January 1975) and to supply regular information on oil and natural gas imports and on certain investments in oil refineries, oil and gas transport and storage facilities, and in electricity production. Support of coal production by member governments had been authorized, e.g. by financing stocks, and a subsidy introduced for EEC production of coking coal and coke. Other proposals not yet adopted at the time of writing include harmonization of fuel taxes (at a proposed level lower than the present UK fuel-oil tax) and a detailed package containing forty-six measures, proposed in 1972, covering such things as environmental protection; developing relations between petroleum-exporting and -importing countries; and defining medium-term guidelines for the coal industry.

In the nuclear energy sector Euratom was set up to promote and co-ordinate research; help disseminate technical information; facilitate capital investment; establish a common market in specialized material and equipment; free movement of capital and manpower in the nuclear field; and maintain links with other countries and international organizations. Some progress has been made in each of these areas, but generally less than was envisaged originally. In particular Euratom has not been successful in co-ordinating the national nuclear R and D programmes of members.

III.4 Transport

Provision of transport services has grown faster than the output series for the transport and communications sector suggests, at least on the passenger side (cf. tables 4.6, 4.7, and 4.1). This is mainly because the output series takes no account of private motoring, which is where the main increase in passenger mileage occurred, until checked in 1974 by the very sharp increase in fuel costs. The impact of rising incomes on car ownership has been a major factor. (The number of private cars currently licensed rose from 4.2 m. in 1957 to 14.0 m. in 1976). Before 1974 relative price movements would have also been a reinforcing factor; both rail and bus fares rose very much faster over the period than did private motoring costs. In the inland freight sector the two growth rates are much more nearly in line, but there too there has been a major re-allocation of traffic towards road services (table 4.7).

Because so much of public transport is nationalized, developments in the transport sector are more than usually subject to government policy.[1] A consultative document published in April 1976 highlighted a number of problems.[2] One was the lack of a

---

1 See also section IV.
2 'Consultative Document on Transport Policy', Department of the Environment, 13 April 1976. See also N. Lee, *A Review of Current Transport Policy and Objectives in Britain, TBR*, March 1977.

proper framework for the co-ordination of transport policy, at both the national and local levels. A second was the problems facing certain vulnerable groups, in particular the 50% of households without a car, whose mobility has been reduced as the growth of private motoring adversely affected the revenue base of public transport and

TABLE 4.6

GB Inland Passenger Mileage, 1960-76[1] (000m passenger–miles)

			Road		
	Air	Rail	Public service vehicles	Private transport	Total
1960	0.5 (0.3%)	24.8 (15.6%)	43.9 (27.7%)	89.4 (56.4%)	158.6 (100.0%)
1965	1.0 (0.5%)	21.8 (10.6%)	39.2 (19.0%)	144.7 (70.0%)	206.7 (100.0%)
1970	1.2 (0.5%)	22.2 (8.7%)	34.8 (13.7%)	196.2 (77.1%)	254.4 (100.0%)
1976	1.4 (0.5%)	20.8 (7.5%)	32.9 (11.8%)	223.1 (80.2%)	278.2 (100.0%)
% Change 1960-76	180%	−16.1%	−25.1%	149.6%	75.4% = 3.6% per annum

Source: *AAS.*
Note: 1   % figures in brackets show respective contributions to the total in any one year.

the level of services provided. This problem is especially severe in rural areas (where the proportion of households without cars is 30%). Thirdly, environmental problems were listed as requiring a greater degree of priority in the future. Finally, the document stressed the problem of transport subsidies, which rose from £300m in 1968 to £630m in 1975. The bulk of this money has gone to the railways; despite the writing off of more than £3,000m debt over twenty years, the annual rail support (excluding current subsidies) has risen to £327 in 1977-8. The document stressed that these subsidies, especially to rail users, do not necessarily represent

TABLE 4.7

GB Inland Freight Transport, 1960-76[1] (000m ton–miles)

	Road	Rail	Coastal shipping	Inland waterways	Pipelines[2]	Total
1960	30.1 (49.3%)	18.7 (30.6%)	11.9 (19.5%)	0.2 (0.3%)	0.2 (0.3%)	61.1 (100.0%)
1965	42.1 (57.1%)	15.4 (20.9%)	15.3 (20.8%)	0.1 (0.1%)	0.8 (1.1%)	73.7 (100.0%)
1970	50.0 (60.6%)	16.4 (19.9%)	14.2 (17.2%)	0.1 (0.1%)	1.8 (2.2%)	82.5 (100.0%)
1976	58.5 (67.3%)	14.1 (16.2%)	12.2 (14.0%)	0.1 (0.1%)	2.0 (2.3%)	86.9 (100.0%)
% Change 1960-76	94.4%	−24.6%	2.5%	−50.0%	900.0%	42.2% = 2.2% per annum

Source: *AAS*
Notes: 1   % figures in brackets show respective contributions to the total in any one year.
    2   Excludes the movement of gases by pipeline, and pipeline less than 10 miles long (prior to 1965).

transfers to the poorer sections of the community; thus the richest 20% of households account for 50% of rail travel, whereas the poorest 40% are responsible for only 15%.

The document did not detail specific proposals, although some suggestions and probable directions of future policy were intimated. The idea of switching freight from road to rail was rejected, mainly on the ground that the impact would be slight. Thus, even if all journeys over a hundred miles were transferred to rail, only a 2% to 4% reduction in road traffic would result. Also the document did not suggest that any drastic measures to curtail private motoring were being contemplated. Continued subsidies to rail transport were described as unjustifiable, and further rail fare increases are clearly to be expected, especially as the document claimed that 1975 experience showed that demand for rail services is price-inelastic.[1] On the other hand, subsidies for bus operations may increase, these being more likely to find their way to poorer people and those without cars. Other forms of encouragement for buses and local transport are also envisaged, perhaps including some relaxation of the licensing system. Heavier taxes on lorries were mooted, especially heavy lorries with few axles for which current tax levels do not cover resource costs, let alone environmental costs. In road building environmental considerations may lead to more investment in bypasses around sensitive and congested areas. Finally, the document proposed that a National Transport Council be set up as a forum for policy formulation.

Specific policy proposals were outlined in a 1977 White Paper.[2] Total planned expenditure, £2.2bn in 1980 (at 1976 prices), represents a significant reduction from the £2.6bn spent in 1976-7 and compares with £2.0bn in 1971-2. The main emphasis of current policy is to remain on public transport. Expenditure on roads is reduced in absolute terms, but will remain at about 51% of total expenditure, as in 1976-7, compared with 76% in 1971-2.[3] No subsidies will be given to rail freight and inter-urban passenger services. But major cuts in the rail network are ruled out, and support for passenger services is to continue, though at a level of £295m in 1980, compared with £325m in 1976-7. Bus services are also to continue to receive support, especially in rural areas, via concessionary fares, grants and fuel-duty rebates.

EEC transport policy originates from a European Commission memorandum of 1961 (the Schaus Memorandum) and an Action Programme of the following year. One of the general aims was to prevent transport from blocking the development of an effective common market for other goods and services. Transport is an important element in the cost of many commodities. If, for instance, transport undertakings in one country gave preferential treatment to certain industries or firms, this would frustrate attempts to secure competition among member states on equal terms. A second general aim was the more positive one of fostering transport developments which would stimulate trade and the opening up of markets, e.g. in the development of transport networks. Thirdly, the Community was to endeavour to create in the transport sector (as elsewhere) 'healthy competition of the widest scope'.

Subsequent detailed agreements have gone only part of the way towards

1 Prices rose by 50% and traffic fell by 5%, implying a price-elasticity of demand of 0.1.
2 *Transport Policy,* Cmnd. 6836, June 1977.
3 See also the first annual White Paper on the road programme promised in Cmnd. 6836: *Policy for Roads,* Cmnd. 7132, April 1978.

achieving these objectives. Prohibitions have been introduced on discrimination in the transport sector on grounds of nationality, and on tariffs designed to give the kind of preferential treatment outlined above. An inquiry was held into the way costs of infrastructural investments were met in the member countries, in the first instance to see whether the costs fell broadly on those to whom the benefits accrued, or whether, on the other hand, infrastructural developments tended to result in tariff structures not truly reflecting the costs of providing the relevant services. There has also been harmonization of the regulations governing lorry-drivers' ages, qualifications, hours, rest periods, etc. Some agreement has been reached whereby bilateral arrangements between members for quotas for public service licences would be replaced by Community-wide agreements. Some uniformity in tariffs has also been agreed, e.g. in the form of maximum and minimum road haulage rates, between which any rate negotiated between contractor and customer should settle. It has been established that the EEC rules of competition apply to the transport sector. Finally, agreement has been reached on the 'normalization' of railway accounts to take account of any social burdens placed on the systems, with common rules for granting subsidies in such cases and a common definition of obligations that could be imposed in return for such subsidies.

IV   POLICY TOWARDS THE NATIONALIZED INDUSTRIES
IV.1   Background

On a wide definition, public enterprise exists where there is an undertaking which is publicly owned and directed by a branch of the government, or a body especially set up for the purpose by the government. This would include all public administration and defence, and the public health and education services, together with a number of government agencies such as the British Tourist Authority, the Forestry Commission, the Herring Industry Board, etc.[1] Our present concern is with the narrower area of the nationalized industries, which in general are distinguishable from the rest of the public sector by the fact that the goods and services they supply are marketed.

The nationalized industries have for a long time dominated four strategic sectors of the economy: energy, public transport, communications and iron and steel. In 1976 the involvement in the energy field was extended by the formation of the British National Oil Corporation, and in 1977 the areospace and shipbuilding industries were added to the nationalized industry sector. Together the nationalized industries employ around 1.7 million people (7% of the total workforce) and in 1976 they accounted for 14% of total fixed investment in the economy and for 10% of output.[2]

In EEC countries, it is fairly general for there to be some form of state control of electricity, gas and water, postal services, railways and parts at least of broadcasting and the national airlines. Steel, however, is generally in private hands. The French have a particularly large public sector and own among other things the

---

1   See R. Maurice (ed.), *National Income Statistics: Sources and Methods,* Central Statistical Office, HMSO, 1968.

2   See *The Nationalised Industries*, Cmnd. 7131, HMSO, March 1978. These figures do not include the activities of companies within the responsibility of the National Enterprise Board, such as British Leyland and Rolls-Royce. See below, p. 218.

Renault car manufacturers. The Italians have two giant state companies, IRI – a wide-ranging holding company – and ENI, an oil and chemicals firm. There is also the uniquely continental phenomenon of a state monopoly in certain goods for taxation purposes; that is, the state retains a monopoly profit as part of its fiscal revenue. The match industry (in France, West Germany and Italy) and the tobacco industry (in France and Italy) are examples.[1]

IV.2   Price and Investment Policy: Theory

The economists' prescription for nationalized industry pricing is that prices should be set equal to marginal cost.[2] The overall objective is to ensure an efficient allocation of resources as between these industries and the private sector. A simple rationale can be given for such a policy. On the one hand the demand curve for a nationalized industry product tells us how much consumers will pay per unit for different quantities supplied, and so we interpret the demand curve as consumers' evaluation of the good or service as output is varied. On the other hand the marginal cost curve tells us the incremental cost of producing each unit, and if we can equate the money costs actually incurred by the undertaking with the true opportunity cost of diverting extra resources from alternative uses to the undertaking in question, we can construe the marginal cost curve as recording consumers' evaluation of the foregone alternative product. If consumers value the public enterprise good more than the alternative (demand price exceeds marginal cost) then welfare can be increased by diverting more resources to the public enterprise, so increasing output, and vice versa. Hence, for an optimum level of output, price should equal marginal cost.

Unfortunately, this apparently straightforward principle raises many difficulties in practice. Firstly, an optimum is reached only if a large number of other conditions are met, including the equality of all other prices with marginal cost. Otherwise the 'second best' solution will very likely require a price not equal to marginal cost.[3] A modification of the marginal cost pricing rule which takes some of this into account is to set price equi-proportional to marginal cost. Thus if price is on average, say, 10% above marginal cost in the economy, this same margin should be included in public enterprise prices. So long as we are concerned only with the relative output levels in commodity markets this has some merit. But it will not produce an overall optimum, since income/leisure preferences will be affected and the supply of labour (and hence also total output) will be less than is consistent with an ideal; that is, optimum conditions will be fulfilled in commodity markets but not in factor markets.

Secondly, even if all necessary conditions are met, the ensuing resource allocation is optimal only within the existing distribution of income among consumers. If this distribution is not accepted as being ideal, it would be perfectly justifiable for the government to modify some or all nationalized industry prices in the name of social

1   See D. Swann, *The Common Market*, 3rd edition, Penguin Books, 1975, and Stuart Holland, *The Unequal Mix: European Public Enterprise*, Martin Robertson, 1978.
2   For a fuller discussion, see Ralph Turvey, *Economic Analysis and Public Enterprise*, Allen and Unwin, 1971, and *Public Enterprise*, Penguin Books, 1968.
3   See R. G. Lipsey and K. Lancaster, 'On the General Theory of Second Best', *RES*, Vol. XXIV, 1956-7, pp. 11-32.

justice. (It could be argued that this is precisely what the government does in not charging or making only token charges for some public sector goods and services, e.g. health and education.)

Thirdly, price must be set equal to marginal social cost, rather than marginal private cost. Where, for instance, increased output in one industry confers external benefits by reducing production costs in other industries, marginal private costs in that industry will exceed marginal social costs, and vice versa for an industry imposing net external costs. Therefore, even if all other necessary conditions for a welfare maximum were met, a nationalized industry equating price with marginal private cost would be producing too much, from the community standpoint, if it gave rise to net external costs and too little if it conferred net external economies. Hence, for maximum welfare, external effects of this sort must be taken into account in both the nationalized sector and elsewhere.

Fourthly, economists are themselves divided as to whether price should be equated with short-run marginal cost (the rate of change of total costs in the short run, i.e. when some factor or factors are fixed) or with long-run marginal cost (the rate of change of total costs in the long run, when there are no fixed factors). Finally, except where there are constant returns to scale, neither short-run nor long-run marginal cost pricing will automatically ensure that total costs will be recovered from revenue. Marginal and average costs are equal only at that output at which average costs are at a minimum. Hence marginal cost pricing will exactly equate total costs and revenues only if, by chance, the output level which results happens to be this one. Otherwise, either a deficit (marginal cost is less than average cost) or a surplus (marginal cost exceeds average cost) will result. In practice, most of the nationalized industries are thought to be ones where average costs decline continuously over the relevant range of outputs, so that marginal cost is less than average cost and a deficit is likely to result. Since there is no agreed method of financing deficits (or distributing surpluses) in a way which will not affect resource allocation, there is a basic conflict between financial rectitude and pricing policies designed to optimize resource allocation.

For optimal investment by public enterprises, the two main requirements are that the costs and benefits of any project over its life are correctly evaluated, and that estimates of future costs and benefits are correctly related to the present decision-making period.[1] In evaluating costs and benefits, due account must be taken of external effects on other producers and consumers. Moreover, since market-determined prices in a 'second best' world will not necessarily reflect the true worth of inputs and outputs to the community, it will usually be necessary to attempt the difficult task of adjusting these on a socially desired basis.[2] The method of relating together costs and benefits in different periods that is generally thought best is to express the returns to an investment project in terms of net discounted

---

1 For a description of the methods used to evaluate investment in nationalized industries see R. Pryke, *Public Enterprises in Practice*, MacGibbon and Kee, 1971, chapter 15.

2 For an extended discussion of cost–benefit analysis, see A. R. Prest and R. Turvey, 'Cost Benefit Analysis: A Survey', *EJ*, December 1965.

present value.[1] Generally speaking, the rate of time discount used in evaluating public sector projects should be the same as is used elsewhere (and any allowance made for uncertainty should also be the same). Otherwise the relative merits of private and public sector projects will be distorted.[2]

Even if public sector projects were treated scrupulously in the desired manner outlined, the maximum benefit would not be derived from the total of funds available for investment in the economy unless private projects were treated in exactly the same way. In practice, private sector investments will almost invariably be evaluated with no regard for external effects; various ways of treating uncertainty are likely to be used; and a substantial amount of decision-making will be undertaken by rule-of-thumb methods.[3] In so far as the government is unable to regulate all private sector investment appraisal appropriately, the best that can be hoped for is a form of sub-optimization, the correct principles being applied in the public sector only.

IV.3   Price and Investment Policy: Practice

The post-war nationalization Acts merely required the industries to break even, taking one year with another. Later, in 1961, the financial responsibilities of the industries were tightened in a number of ways, and financial targets were introduced, usually expressed as a rate of return on assets employed.[4] However, up until 1967 explicit guidelines on pricing and investment policy were lacking. Then long-run marginal cost pricing was introduced as the official policy, together with the net-present-value approach to investment decisions.[5] A test discount rate (TDR) of 8% was laid down, later raised to 10%.[6] The 1967 policy focused very much on the pricing of individual goods and services, and on individual investment projects. Arbitrary cross-subsidization amongst different groups of consumers was to be avoided, and the need to distinguish social as distinct from purely commercial operations was stressed. The government undertook financial responsibility for non-commercial operations, e.g. by specific subsidies or grants. The existing system

---

1   Net discounted present value (R) for any project with a life of n years is given by

$$R = \sum_{t=1}^{n} \frac{B_t - C_t}{(1+r)^t} - I$$

where B_t, C_t are benefits and costs respectively in the year t, r is the rate of discount and I is the initial cost. The main merits of this method over its chief rival (internal rate of return or marginal efficiency of capital) are that it always gives a unique solution and always ranks projects correctly.

2   A discussion of the implications of using different rates of time discount appears in R. Pryke, op. cit., ch. 16.

3   See NEDO, *Investment Appraisal*, HMSO, 1967.

4   *The Financial and Economic Obligations of the Nationalized Industries*, Cmnd. 1337, HMSO, April 1961.

5   *Nationalized Industries: A Review of Economic and Financial Objectives*, Cmnd. 3437, HMSO, November 1967.

6   The rate chosen was expressly intended to match the return looked for by private industry on marginal, low-risk investment. Because of differences in financing methods and tax liability the equivalent private sector rate will be higher than any given nationalized industry rate; the original 8% was held to be equivalent to 15% to 16% in the private sector.

of financial targets was retained, as a measure of expected performance against which to compare actual achievements.

For a year or two after 1967 there was some progress towards revising pricing methods, especially in the Post Office and British Rail. However, in the early and mid-1970s macroeconomic and financial considerations had become of overriding importance once more, as they had tended to be before 1967. Up to 1974 severe price restraint was applied by the government, and investment programmes were cut. This led to mounting deficits, indiscriminate subsidies to the consumer from taxpayers, and in some cases sharp reductions in investment and employment. Then followed a period of very rapid price increase, with the prime objective of first holding and then eliminating Exchequer support. By 1978 significant improvement in financial performance had occurred in most cases, though with some exceptions, including the much-publicized steel industry.[1]

This 'interference' with the nationalized industries' price and investment policies did not contravene the 1967 White Paper's recommendations, which explicitly reserved the right of the government to intervene on national economic grounds. In the event, however, the price restraint of the early 1970s and its subsequent correction led to suspension of both the financial targets and attempts at economic pricing policies which the White Paper sought to introduce. The most recent White Paper on nationalized industry policy,[2] whose publication follows an earlier report by the Select Committee on the Nationalized Industries,[3] and an independent review by NEDO,[4] seeks to reintroduce and reinforce the 1967 White Paper, and avoid repetition of the 'mistakes' of the early 1970s.

The 1978 White Paper shares with its 1967 predecessor the objective of optimal resource allocation, reiterates the need to avoid cross-subsidization amongst consumers and to distinguish social from commercial services, and retains the use of marginal cost pricing policies and of TDR in investment decisions. However, the limitations of the latter two in practice are recognized, and they no longer occupy the forefront of policy. The government recognizes that in many cases prices are 'market determined' and that even where this is not so, the difficulties of practical application of marginal cost pricing can be severe. It is admitted that TDR has not lived up to expectations, in part because much investment which is undertaken forms part of an existing system, or is 'necessary for safety or security'. The main focus of current policy is therefore shifted from these matters affecting individual services and projects to the opportunity cost of capital in the industry as a whole. A 'real rate of return on assets' (RRR) is defined which is to be achieved by the industries on new investment as a whole. The RRR is principally related to the real rate of return (and its expected trend) in the private sector, taking into account questions of the cost of finance and of social time preference. It is set initially at 5%, and is to be reviewed every three to five years. The RRR is not the same as the financial target rate of return for each industry, which varies and takes into account the earning power of existing assets, sectoral and social objectives and so forth.

Thus the main matters over which the government will in future seek to exercise

---

1 See *British Steel Corporation: The Road to Viability*, Cmnd. 7148, HMSO, March 1978.
2 *The Nationalized Industries*, Cmnd. 7131, HMSO, March 1978.
3 *Ministerial Control of the Nationalized Industries*, H. of C. 371-I, II and III, 1968.
4 *A Study of the UK Nationalized Industries: Their Role in the Economy and Control in the Future*, NEDO, November 1976.

control are the RRR and the financial target together with the 'general level of prices'. Individual prices and investment priorities are left largely up to the industries themselves, subject to the vague admonition to 'pay attention to the structure of prices and its relation to the structure of costs' and to the need to consult sponsoring departments on certain major investment proposals.

In some ways current policy represents a retreat from the ambitious 1967 position. Although a commitment to marginal cost pricing is retained even the White Paper exhibits at points a certain resignation over how much is to be expected in this direction. More important, though, is the fact that the latest White Paper contains no policy change or promise that macroeconomic considerations will not again overrule questions of nationalized industry policy *per se*. Indeed, current policy if anything increases this possibility in that it is proposed to introduce powers for Ministers to give specific directives in addition to the general directive presently provided for. Given the large size of the nationalized industries it is easy to see how governments are tempted to use them directly to help manage the economy. While this possibility remains open, so also does that of current policy going the way of its predecessor.

IV.4 Organization, Control and Productive Efficiency in the Nationalized Industries

Many of the problems of internal organization and efficiency which arise in the nationalized industries are of the same kind as those encountered in private industry. There are, however, differences in degree. Because of the extremely large scale of the operations under one administrative control, the organizational problems exceed those of all but a few, giant private firms. Moreover, in seeking solutions to these problems the nationalized industries are inevitably subject to much more publicity and outside criticism than private enterprises.

Several important organizational developments have taken place in recent years. A number were embodied in the 1968 Transport Act which, *inter alia*, eliminated the regional divisions of British Rail; set up a National Freight Corporation and Freight Integration Council; created Passenger Transport Authorities for four major conurbations (now increased to five) and transferred the London Transport Board to the GLC making, effectively, a sixth, and established a National Bus Company for England and Wales, and a Scottish Transport Group. Then from October 1969 the Post Office, previously a government department, became a public corporation, to be run on more commercial lines. The British Steel Corporation was reorganized into a system based on product divisions[1] (four steel-making, one for constructional engineering, and one for chemical activities). Formerly there were four large groups, under which system most products fell within more than one group. Finally, there has been a major reorganization of the gas industry. The Gas Council and the area boards have been replaced by a single authority, the British Gas Corporation. A recurring theme in these organizational changes was clearly to provide for better co-ordination and planning throughout the whole of the particular industries concerned.

Where the problems of running the nationalized industries do differ from those of private industry is over the need to reconcile operating efficiency on the one hand

---

1 See British Steel Corporation, *Third Report on Organization*, H. of C. 60, 1969-70.

with public accountability on the other. The one arguably requires maximum autonomy, delegation and decentralization in nationalized industries; the other inhibits this. In the latest White Paper this conflict is recognized, but the government stresses that it must be concerned with strategy in such basic industries; with their efficiency in the absence of a bankruptcy sanction and (in some cases) significant market pressures; and with securing an acceptable return.

Many difficulties have arisen in this area in the past. In 1968 the Select Committee on the Nationalized Industries concluded that Ministers have tended to do the opposite of what Parliament originally intended.[1] Whereas they were supposed to lay down policies, but not intervene in management, they have in practice given very little policy guidance but been closely involved with many aspects of management. The NEDO report proposed a formal two-tiered structure as a solution to this problem, the industries to be run by Corporation Boards but under the strategic direction of Policy Councils. However, this was rejected in the White Paper on grounds of likely confusion of responsibility between the Policy Councils, Ministers and sponsoring departments, and a consequent slowing down of decision making.

No major structural alternative was offered in the White Paper, though a number of procedural changes were proposed. As we have seen, the RRR and financial targets are to form a central focus of government-nationalized industry relations, within the corporate planning context. In addition, the industries are to be asked to select and publish an appropriate set of other performance indicators, to supplement the financial targets which could, of course, otherwise be met in various antisocial ways, e.g. monopoly pricing. The introduction of powers for Ministers to make selective directions is regarded as superior to the present system of informal persuasion, not least because it makes for greater clarity of accountability. It is proposed that a civil servant be appointed to corporation boards, to improve the understanding by sponsoring departments of industry problems. In line with its general policy in the area the government has asked chairmen for proposals concerning the implementation of industrial democracy.[2] Finally, the industries remain open to the quasi-independent sanction on their efficiency represented by the Price Commission, which since July 1977 has discretion (subject to ministerial veto) to investigate most nationalized industry price increases.

Throughout the White Paper there is a recurring emphasis on the need for more publication of nationalized industry affairs; actual versus target performance in Annual Reports; historical series of other performance indicators; the extra costs due to Ministerial intervention; and so on. The aim seems to be to satisfy the public accountability requirement directly, by making the performance of the industries, the intervention by government, and the scope for the Price Commission, more obvious and publicly available. The intention is wholly admirable provided it does not make the task of running the industries unattractive to managers who can otherwise work in private industry, not subject to the same exposure. The ability of the nationalized industries to attract highly qualified management in any case tends to be reduced by the levels of remuneration offered. In 1969 the NBPI found that top salaries and retirement pensions were substantially lower in nationalized industries than in comparable private sector jobs, and large increases for Chairmen of the main

1 *Ministerial Control of the Nationalized Industries,* H. of C. 371-1, II and III, 1968.
2 A two-year experiment with a mixed management, union and independent Board is already under way in the Post Office.

undertakings were subsequently implemented.[1] However, the government did not implement the increases recommended in a further, independent study published at the end of 1974, though at the time of writing it seems inclined to implement further recommended increases to an average 31% above the proposed 1975 level.[2]

IV.5   EEC Provisions

The EEC members have not so far devised a common policy on the control and financing of public enterprise. On the other hand the publicly owned industries and firms are, of course, affected by Community policies towards industry, such as the competition and regional policies, and the common policies towards energy and transport. All of these are discussed elsewhere in this chapter. Two other issues are of relevance for the UK in this context.

The first concerns the use of subsidies by member governments. As we have seen, these are an important feature of the UK policy, but they are contrary to the spirit and rules of the Community. This is because if one particular member government subsidizes a loss-making industry of its own the free play of competition within the Community-wide industry would be inhibited. However, in practice it can be hard for the Community to apply meaningful sanctions on such behaviour. Moreover, it could be that UK subsidies for the strictly non-commercial activities taken by the nationalized industries would be sanctioned, e.g. under the 'harmonization of accounts' procedure agreed for railways.[3] On the other hand some limitations could be set on the precise nature of the social obligations placed upon the industries. More difficulty is likely to arise over any remaining annual revenue supports to cover operating deficits after allowance for social obligations is made, and cases where, from time to time, the accumulated deficits of UK industries like coal and rail in particular are written off, or interest payments suspended.

Secondly, two of the UK nationalized industries come within the sphere of influence of the ECSC, the history and role of which is of some importance.[4] The ECSC is the oldest of the three communities (ECSC, EEC and Euratom) and was the first step towards European integration, i.e. the first common market. Among other things, the 1951 Treaty of Paris abolished duties and quotas on trade in coal and steel among member states; discrimination in prices, delivery terms and transport rates; and restrictive practices leading to collusive sharing or exploitation of markets. Up to 1967 the ECSC had separate institutions but the relevant bodies are now those of the three merged communities, the European Commission and Parliament, the Council of Ministers and the European Court of Justice. One additional body which survived from the earlier period was a high-level consultative committee, composed of producers, consumers, workers and dealers.

The ECSC maintains a policy of free trade in coal and basic iron and steel products. Producers are required to publish all prices at selected basing points, and transport charges also have to be published or notified. Levies are made upon coal and steel producers, currently equivalent to around 0.2% of production value but

---

1   NBPI Report No. 107, *Top Salaries in the Private Sector and Nationalized Industries*, Cmnd. 3970, March 1969.

2   *Report on Top Salaries*, Cmnd. 5846, December 1974; Cmnd. 7253, July 1978.

3   See above, section III.4

4   See P. M. Topley, 'The E.C.S.C.: the oldest of the Communities', *TI*, 17 January 1974.

with some variation according to product. Various kinds of central benefits are paid out, in the form of assistance to redundant or transferred coal and steel workers (provided this is at least matched by the member government); contributions to technical research projects; and loans at attractive rates for investment projects capable of employing redundant ECSC workers in the declining coal and steel areas, housing for ECSC workers and investment projects to facilitate the capital investment programmes of the coal and steel industries. At the time of writing, redundancy assistance has been agreed for UK steel workers and is under negotiation for coal workers. Also, contributions have been received for steel industry research undertaken in 1973, and other discussions are in progress. As in most EEC affairs, it seems that much depends on the process of negotiations, in this case between the European Commission and the UK government.

The ECSC regulations obviously provide an additional set of considerations for the industries, affecting pricing in particular. In steel and to some extent coal and transport, modifications of existing practices have been required. In principle, however, there is no reason why the ECSC requirements should clash with the basic marginal cost pricing rules and investment procedures which are still recommended practice in the UK nationalized industries.

V COMPETITION POLICY AND CONSUMER PROTECTION[1]
V.1 The Case for Policy Measures

Whichever theory of the firm we take, monopolistic market structures and practices raise questions of public policy. The precise criticisms, however, vary somewhat according to our choice of theoretical model.

Under profit-maximizing assumptions monopoly price exceeds marginal cost, with consequential resource misallocation and reduced consumers' welfare. Secondly, supernormal profits will be earned (if price also exceeds average cost), so that income is redistributed in favour of producers. Thirdly, possession of market power permits firms to undertake practices such as price discrimination among consumers and cross-subsidization among activities. These can also reduce welfare and, furthermore, can be used to protect a monopoly position. A fourth argument is that monopolists will tend to be inefficient, costs being higher than they need be because the presence of excess profits blunts the desire to seek out and apply cost-minimizing techniques. However, this argument is not strictly consistent with profit maximization, since it implies pursuit of some other objective, e.g. leisure, at some point.

The main significance of monopoly under the managerial theories is that the existence of market power is likely to increase the tendency for firms to pursue managerial objectives other than profit. The criticisms of monopoly derived from the profit-maximizing model may not apply, but managerial behaviour need not lead to genuine cost minimization (e.g. in Williamson's model organizational slack is typically present)[2] and, in general, a part of the stream of resources being generated by the firm is diverted for the satisfaction of managerial aims (sales, growth, discretionary investment, staff, slack, etc.) and away from consumers'

---

1 See also J. D. Gribbin, 'Recent Anti-Trust Developments in the UK', *Antitrust Bulletin*, Vol. XX, No. 2, Summer 1975; Alex Hunter, *Competition and the Law*, Allen and Unwin, 1966, and *Monopoly and Competition*, Penguin Books, 1969.
2 See above, p. 170.

welfare. The behavioural principle of 'satisficing' behaviour suggests that although monopoly potential may exist it will not necessarily be exploited. Whether the type of market structure will affect efficiency under the behavioural theory would depend on the effect on search and decision procedures, and little is known about this at present. In general, if the behavioural theory is adopted, the whole basis for discussing monopoly in terms of resource allocation and supernormal profits is lost.

There are many alternative, and often conflicting, theoretical models of why firms merge. But clearly one effect may be to create monopoly situations, even though this need not be the sole objective, with consequences as outlined above under the different theories. Official thinking on mergers[1] emphasizes the potentially anti-competitive effects of both horizontal and vertical mergers, but recognizes that there may be substantial efficiency gains from scale economies, rationalization of production, etc.[2] Conglomerate mergers are seen as a special category. Both the anti-competitive effects and the potential for increased efficiency are considered likely to be smaller than for horizontal and vertical mergers, but there is concern that many may take place for purely financial reasons, and yield very little benefit in terms of increased efficiency, but at some anti-competitive risk. Moreover, it is argued that conglomerate mergers could lead to substantial losses in operating efficiency.[3]

Under profit maximization the argument against restrictive trade practices is, broadly, that by concerted action a group of firms may achieve the same result as a single-firm monopolist. Thus the formal model explaining joint profit maximization by two or more firms is identical with the one explaining multi-plant monopolist behaviour.[4] Moving away from the formal model, it is also argued that if prices are set at a level which allows the least efficient to survive many firms will earn abnormal profits without difficulty, the inefficient will not be eliminated, and the general competitive spur to efficiency will be lost; and that restrictive agreements may also provide a base for collusive action to forestall the entry of new competition, suppress new techniques and developments, etc. How the managerial

---

1 See *Annex* to Monopolies Commission, *The Rank Organisation Limited and De La Rue Company Limited*, 298, H. of C. 1968-7, and Board of Trade, *Mergers: A Guide to Board of Trade Practice*, HMSO, 1969. (A revised version of the latter was prepared by the OFT in 1977 for publication in 1978).

2 Horizontal mergers are between competitors in the same market, vertical mergers are between customer and supplier. The first will, other things being equal, increase market concentration (the share of supply in the hands of a few large suppliers). Vertical mergers threaten competition where, for instance, a manufacturer takes over the firm supplying raw material both to himself and to his competitors, and would be able to charge disadvantageous prices to them, or where a manufacturer secures control over the sales outlets for both his own and his competitors' products.

3 Conglomerate mergers are those where there has previously been neither a vertical nor horizontal link between the parties. Efficiency gains would probably be mainly financial and managerial; efficiency losses might arise because of the complexity of operations under one control. Competition might be harmed if the conglomerate firm, by virtue of its size, became accepted as a price leader in a particular market, or fought its way to a monopoly position in that market via a price war, accepting temporary losses in that market, compensated for by profits earned elsewhere. See also J. D. Gribbin, 'The Conglomerate Merger', *Applied Economics*, 1976, 8, 19-35.

4 See, e.g., K. J. Cohen and R. M. Cyert, *Theory of the Firm*, Prentice-Hall, 1956, p. 235. In practice the degree of co-ordination of activities required is greater than would normally occur under a restrictive agreement between firms.

theories might qualify these arguments has yet to be shown. In a behavioural analysis we should probably be much less suspicious of the motives underlying restrictive practices than if we assume profit maximization. Assuming profit maximization, restrictive practices would not exist unless profits were thereby raised; under behavioural analysis this need not be so. Moreover, restrictive practices fit fairly easily into the behavioural concept of the 'negotiated environment', the implication being that they are primarily uncertainty-reducing phenomena, perhaps with advantages in facilitating forward planning, etc.

Clearly the criticisms of monopoly and monopolistic practices do vary somewhat according to our choice of theoretical model. Moreover, one of the problems confronting policy-makers is that whichever model we take, monopoly or monopolistic practices may confer advantages as well as disadvantages. For instance, against adverse effects of monopoly on resource allocation and income distribution under the profit-maximization hypothesis is the fact that, if scale economies are to be exploited, there may be room for only one firm of minimum optimal scale in some markets. Moreover, it has been vigorously argued (though not universally agreed) that the security and profitability of monopoly is an important enabling condition for technical progress.[1] It has also been pointed out[2] that an active merger market may make firms more efficient than they would otherwise be, for the companies most likely to be taken over are those which are operating at a high level of slack, have a correspondingly low level of profit, and so are poorly rated on the stock market. A 'take-over raider' who hopes to make the firm more efficient will thereby make a capital gain. However, such a threat, presumably accompanied by threatened displacement of management, may well serve to keep the present management 'on its toes'.

A further problem confronting policy-makers, though one arising only if profit-maximizing assumptions are retained, concerns the 'second-best'. Where competition does not prevail in every other market, removal of an individual monopoly or monopolistic practice cannot be relied upon to increase welfare (as a result of the ensuing change in resource allocation), and may indeed reduce it.[3]

The control of anti-competitive market structures and practices is itself a form of consumer protection, since the exercise of market power is typically at the expense of the consumers' interests. This aspect apart, economic theory does not place much emphasis on the need for consumer protection. In the theory consumers are assumed to have a complete ordering of their preferences for different goods and services based on full information about the characteristics of the commodities and the utility to be gained from consuming them. Consumers then attempt to maximize their utility, faced with their income and market-determined prices. Provided these prices (including the price of labour and hence income) are competitively determined, the theory implies that all is well with the consumer. In practice the consumer is not fully and costlessly informed, and may not be able to

---

1 See section VII below, and J. Schumpeter, *Capitalism, Socialism and Democracy*, Allen and Unwin, 1943; J. K. Galbraith, *American Capitalism*, Hamish Hamilton, 1956 (revised edition) chapter 7; J. Jewkes, D. Sawyers and R. Stillerman, *The Sources of Invention*, Macmillan, 1969; and C. F. Carter and B. R. Williams, *Industry and Technical Progress*, Oxford, 1957, chapter 11.

2 See B. Hindley, 'Capitalism and Corporation', *Economica*, November 1969.

3 See above, p. 185, and R. G. Lipsey and K. Lancaster, op. cit.

judge the utility he will derive from a certain good. He may not, for example, realize that a drug may be unsafe under certain conditions, or that food may be too old for use and he may be faced by confusing packaging or subject to misleading claims by advertisers or retailers. Lastly, he may not be able to choose how much or how little service he obtains with a good.

There is nothing to guarantee that it is in the manufacturers' best interests for consumers to exercise a totally free and informed choice. It is this potential divergence of interests which creates the need for policy measures.

V.2   Structural Conditions in UK Markets

According to orthodox micro-theory the main structural characteristics of markets which determine market conduct and performance are the degree of actual competition, measured by seller concentration; the degree of potential competition, reflected in the height of barriers to the entry of new competition; the extent of product differentiation in the market; and the rate of growth or decline of demand.[1] All of these have a bearing on the degree of market power enjoyed by firms in a market, and it is control over the exercise of such power that competition policy attempts. Unfortunately, systematic information on structural conditions in the UK is limited to the first characteristic only, seller concentration.

The most comprehensive source of concentration data is the Census of Production. The latest available figures are for 1972 and refer to Minimum List Headings (MLH) which are rather broad industrial categories from an analytical point of view. A frequency distribution of 120 MLH industries by concentration class (range of five-firm concentration ratio) is given in the right-hand column of table 4.8. From a number of published studies it emerges that concentration has been increasing over time, and at a much faster rate since the late 1950s than previously. One pioneering study found that in 41 out of 200 industries for which accurate comparisons were possible, concentration increased in 27 trades over the period 1935-51 and fell in only 14.[2] Between 1951 and 1958 there was apparently a somewhat similar tendency, concentration increasing in 36 of 63 industries and falling in 16, with two showing no change and nine undetermined.[3] A more recent analysis of the period 1958-63 reveals that the unweighted average concentration ratio for 214 market or product areas rose from 55.7% to 58.6% (in terms of the average weighted by total sales in each market, the rise was from 65.8% to 69.0%).[4] Analysis of a sample of 30 markets out of the 214 suggested that merger activity had been responsible for around one third of the net change in concentration overall and one half of the total change in those cases where concentration had increased. Between 1963 and 1968 there was a further and more rapid increase in concentration levels, especially pronounced where concentration levels were already high.

---

1   See J. S. Bain, *Industrial Organization,* 2nd edition, Wiley, 1968, and R. Caves, *American Industry: Structure, Conduct and Performance,* 2nd edition, Prentice Hall, 1967.
2   R. Evely and I. M. D. Little, *Concentration in British Industry,* CUP, 1960.
3   See W. G. Shepherd, 'Changes in British Industrial Concentration 1951-58', *OEP,* 1966, and K. D. George, 'Changes in British Industrial Concentration 1957-58', *JIE,* July 1967
4   P. E. Hart, M. A. Utton and G. Walshe, *Mergers and Concentration in British Industry,* CUP for the NIESR, 1973.

While the analysis of MLH data gives an indication of the way concentration has increased over time, because MLH categories span more than a single market, the level of concentration at a given time tends to be underestimated. This is brought out clearly in table 4.8 which also includes a frequency distribution by concentration

TABLE 4.8

Seller Concentration in Selected UK Markets

Concentration class[2] (range of five-firm concentration ratio, %)	Product Group Basis 1968[1] Number of product groups in class		MLH Basis 1972	
	(Number)	(%)	(Number)	(%)
0 – 9	0	0.0	1	0.8
10 – 19	8	2.4	11	9.2
20 – 29	20	5.9	13	10.8
30 – 39	28	8.2	15	12.5
40 – 49	34	10.0	24	20.0
50 – 59	47	13.8	10	8.3
60 – 69	36	10.6	14	11.7
70 – 79	38	11.2	13	10.8
80 – 89	46	13.5	10	8.3
90 – 100	83	24.4	9	7.5
TOTAL	340	100.0	120	100.0

Source: Census of Production, 1968 and 1972

Notes: 1   The markets included are sub-Minimum List Heading product groups in mining and quarrying and manufacturing, for which five-firm concentration ratios are available.

   2   The meaning of this column is that, taking the 1968 column, there are no product groups in which the largest five firms account for less than 10% of total sales, eight in which they account for 10% to 19%, and so on.

class for 340 more narrowly defined markets, or product groups. The striking feature here is that in almost one quarter of the 340 markets five firms held 90% or more of total sales, while in only 16.5% of markets was the top five firms' share under 40%. In comparison, the MLH statistics for the later year 1972 show only 7.5% of industries with concentration ratios over 90%, and 33% with ratios under 40%.

From an analytical viewpoint the main question is how far UK markets fall into the 'atomistic', oligopolistic or monopolized categories, for which theoretical models exist. Since concentration ratios tell us nothing about the size distribution among the largest firms, Census data can tell us only about the division between atomistic and non-atomistic markets, the latter including both oligopoly and monopoly. Without supplementary information even this division is not easily made. The first two concentration classes are almost certainly atomistic, but when the five firm ratios exceed 30% the possibility of some recognized interdependence among the market leaders, or of one firm among the five exerting some form of leadership, must be recognized. When the ratio exceeds 50%, the probability of this must be reckoned very high. Thus, on the basis of the more disaggregated, market level data in table 4.8 no more than 8.3% of the 340 markets can safely be assumed atomistic. An alternative approach is to base the division on previous empirical results relating seller concentration in different markets to their performance and especially to differences in profit rates, which we should expect from neoclassical theory to be higher in non-atomistic markets. One pioneering study for the US found systematic differences according to whether or not the seven-firm concentration ratio exceeded 70%.[1] Making a notional adjustment for the fact that table 4.8 has five-firm ratios, we might guess that at least 40% to 45% of the 340 markets came above the critical line in 1968.

An indication of the incidence of single, dominant firms was contained in a Parliamentary answer in 1970. This suggested that in 1965 there were 156 product areas where one firm had 50% or more of the market.[2]

Alongside the trend towards a higher degree of seller concentration in individual markets there has been a similar, accelerating increasing in overall concentration, as measured by the share in net output of the hundred largest firms in the economy. Before World War I this was less than 20%, rising to 33% in 1958. Over the next twelve years the rate of increase roughly trebled, and in 1970 the hundred largest firms accounted for nearly 50% of net output.[3] The precise connection between overall concentration and seller concentration in individual markets is not well documented. But a recent source indicates that of the hundred largest manufacturing companies between 1968 and 1974 approximately half were known to have two or more 'monopolies' (25% shares in particular markets) and of these twenty companies had five or more monopolies.[4]

The inescapable conclusion is that UK economic activity is relatively highly concentrated in the hands of a fairly small number of firms, and that this concentration is increasing. Less up-to-date data suggest the level of market concentration is much higher than in at least two of Britain's major European partners, France and Italy (table 4.9). Concentration in Belgium and the Netherlands is much the

TABLE 4.9

Seller Concentration in Selected Markets, UK and some EEC countries, 1963[1]

Concentration class (range of four-firm concentration ratio, %)	UK No. %	France No. %	Italy No. %	Netherlands No. %	Belgium No. %
0 – 9	7 5.98	42 43,39	36 36.73	13 13.40	13 13.83
10 – 29	47 40.17	43 44.33	43 43.88	44 45.36	34 36.17
30 – 59	43 36.75	11 11.34	18 18.36	23 23.71	32 34.04
60 – 100	20 17.08	1 1.03	1 1.02	17 17.52	15 15.96
Total number of industries	117 (100.0)	97 (100.0)	98 (100.0)	97 (100.0)	94 (100.0)

Sources: M. C. Sawyer, 'Concentration in British Manufacturing Industry', *OEP*, November 1971, pp. 352–78 for the UK figures and Louis Phlips, *Effects of Industrial Concentration, A Cross Section Analysis for the Common Market*, North Holland, 1971.

Note: 1 The markets are roughly equivalent to Minimum List Heading level for the UK and the other countries. The figures are derived in very similar ways.

1 J. S. Bain, op. cit.

2 *Hansard,* April 1970. Reprinted as Appendix A in G. Walshe, *Recent Trends in Monopoly in Great Britain*, CUP, 1974.

3 S. J. Prais, *The Evolution of Giant Firms in Great Britain: A Study of Concentration in Manufacturing Industry in Britain 1909-70*, CUP, 1976.

4 J. D. Gribbin, 'The Conglomerate Merger', *Applied Economics*, 1976, 8, 19-35.

same as in the UK, but high concentration in these countries is to be expected in view of the much smaller total markets; if firm size is governed at all closely by minimum efficient scale of production, which varies little from country to country, seller concentration is bound to be higher where total market size is less. Comparable West German data are unavailable.

V.3   Policy Measures

Legal powers to promote competition derive from a number of enactments beginning with the 1948 Monopolies and Restrictive Practices Act. The principal pieces of legislation on which current policy rests are, however, the Fair Trading Act of 1973, the Restrictive Trade Practices Act of 1976, and the Resale Prices Act of 1976.

The Fair Trading Act is now the basis of the law dealing with dominant-firm monopoly and merger.[1] It also codified and extended previous legislation offering a variety of safeguards to consumers. Thirdly, it introduced important organizational changes in the application of the policy, providing for the appointment of a Director General of Fair Trading to centralize the application of competition and consumer protection policies. Previously this responsibility had been rather widely shared.

On the monopoly front, the 1973 Act repealed the earlier Monopolies Acts of 1948 and 1965, which had created powers of control over dominant firm monopolies. However, the 1973 Act contained provisions similar to but more wide-ranging than those enacted in the earlier legislation. Monopolies in the UK are not presumed illegal *per se,* as they are in the US, but there is provision for review of monopoly situations by the Monopolies Commission (MC), which is an independent administrative tribunal, supported by a research staff. Monopoly references may be made either by Ministers or the Director General (subject to veto). The latter is expected to provide a broader-based view of the state of competition in the economy, to which end he has a responsibility to collect data on market structure and the behaviour of firms, on which the MC may draw. An economic information system has now been set up in the Office of Fair Trading for this purpose. Merger references are the sole prerogative of the Secretary of State.

Dominant-firm situations may be referred if the firm holds at least one quarter of total sales in the relevant market (prior to 1973 the figure was one third). The market share rule also applies to reference of proposed merger cases, which may alternatively be referred if the gross assets are £5m or more. One new feature introduced by the 1973 Act is that the market share test may be applied to sales in a particular local area, rather than at the national level only. Responsibility for acting upon the recommendations of MC reports rests with the appropriate Minister, whose task it is to make the necessary statutory orders. In practice the Director General of Fair Trading has been asked by the Secretary of State to discuss the recommendations with the firms concerned and, when appropriate to secure undertakings to implement them.

Anti-competitive practices of firms are now subject to constraints imposed under the 1973 Fair Trading Act, and the 1976 Restrictive Trade Practices and Resale Prices Acts. Under the Fair Trading Act, uncompetitive practices adopted by firms in their capacity as employers, uncompetitive practices adopted by nationalized

---

1   A useful summary of the Act appears in *TI,* 9 August 1973, pp. 301-5.

industries and restrictive labour practices are liable to investigation by the MC. In the latter case, however, the intention is to stimulate informed discussion only, and there is no power to make orders based on the MC's conclusions.

Other types of anti-competitive practice are dealt with by the Restrictive Practices Court, originally set up under the Restrictive Practices Act of 1956. At that stage the scope of the legislation was limited to the supply of goods: specifically it embraced agreements under which two or more persons accept restrictions relating to the price of goods, conditions of supply, quantities or descriptions, processes, or areas and persons supplied. In 1968 'information agreements' were also included; that is, agreements under which no restrictions are accepted, but information concerning prices, conditions, etc., are exchanged. The 1973 Act permitted the extension of the legislation to cover the supply of services, and action implementing this provision was taken in early 1976. The 1976 Act merely consolidated the legislation contained in previous Acts.[1]

The general procedure with restrictive agreements is that they must be registered, and it is the Director General's responsibility (formerly that of the Registrar of Restrictive Practices) to bring them before the Court. This has the status of a High Court, and consists of five judges and ten other members appointed for their knowledge and experience of industry, commerce or public affairs. Agreements are presumed contrary to the public interest, and the onus is on the parties to prove the reverse by seeking exemption under one or more of eight escape clauses or 'gateways'. Valid grounds for exemption may be found if it can be shown that the restriction gives protection from injury to the public; benefits consumers; is necessary to counteract measures taken by others to prevent competition, or to counter-balance a monopoly or monopsony; avoids local unemployment; promotes exports; is required to maintain some other restriction which the Court finds to be not contrary to the public interest; or does not directly or indirectly restrict or discourage competition to any material degree. If a case is made out on one or other of these grounds, the Court has to be further satisfied that, on balance, benefits to the public outweigh detriments. Otherwise the agreement is declared void, and continuation would be in contempt of court.

There is a time limit for the registration of agreements,[2] and penalties for non-registration, and interim orders may be made on registered agreements, while a final decision on them is being made. The relevant Minister may exempt certain agreements which he deems to be in the national interest or intended to hold down prices.

One particular restrictive practice is the subject of its own act. This is 'resale price maintenance' which is not dealt with by the Resale Prices Act of 1976. Prior to 1964, when individual RPM was first controlled,[3] it was the manufacturers' general practice to specify actual (as opposed to maximum) prices at which their product should be retailed with sanctions for non-compliance. Procedure with resale price maintenance is very similar in form to that for restrictive practices in general,

---

1 A further Restrictive Practices Act was introduced in 1977 primarily to exempt agreements involving restrictions accepted in loan-finance agreements that were caught by the extension of the legislation to cover services.

2 The 'call up' for registration of agreements relating to commercial services specified a three-month period from 22 March to 21 June 1976.

3 Collective RPM (i.e. RPM maintained by the sanction of a group of firms withholding supplies) was prohibited by the Restrictive Practices Act of 1956.

involving a general prohibition and 'escape clauses'. Although resale price maintenance remains in a few trades, for instance in the supply of books, it has in many
cases been superseded by the device of 'recommended' retail prices, which are in
effect maximum prices. This device has been investigated by the MC which concluded
that it operated with different effects in different industries, not always contrary to
the public interest.

Monopoly and restrictive practice legislation is now both comprehensive and
detailed, after more than a quarter of a century of modifications to remedy
shortcomings and fill in perceived gaps in the earlier Acts. By contrast, the concept
of overall government responsibility for consumer protection (as opposed to
piecemeal responsibility) is quite new. Under the 1973 Act the Director General
of Fair Trading is again assigned a key position.

He has a duty to collect and assess information about commercial activities, in
order to seek out trading practices which may affect consumers' economic interests.
If he finds areas in which there is cause for concern, he then has two options. The
Director General may either make recommendations to the relevant Minister as to
action which might be useful in altering the malpractice, whether it concerns
consumers' economic interests or their health, safety and so on. Or, presumably
where more severe action is demanded, he may set in motion a procedure which
could lead to the banning of a particular trade practice. To do this he makes a
'reference' along with proposals for action to the Consumer Protection Advisory
Committee (CPAC), which considers whether his proposals are justified, given that
the practice is covered by the legislation. This body, after taking evidence from
interested parties, reports to the relevant Minister, who then makes an Order, when
appropriate, with the agreement of Parliament.

Another of the Director General's main functions in the area of consumer
protection is to make sure that those who are persistently careless of their existing
legal obligations to consumers mend their ways, either by his seeking written
assurance or, failing this, in the courts. Lastly, the Director General has obligations
to pursue an informal dialogue with industry; to publish information and advice
for consumers; and to encourage trade associations to use voluntary codes of practice
to protect consumers.

V.4   Policy Impact[1]

A total of over sixty monopoly situations had been investigated by the Monopolies
Commission by the end of 1977. In addition, several hundred merger cases had been
screened since 1965. However only a small proportion were actually referred to the
Commission. For instance, between November 1973 (when the Fair Trading Act
came into force) and the end of 1977 around seven hundred merger cases were
screened, of which only twenty-three were referred. The total number of restrictive
practices registered by end 1976 was 3,150, of which 2,800 had been abandoned.
Of course, not all these cases were heard by the Court. Many were terminated
voluntarily after the results of key cases became known, and others were simply
left to expire. By end 1977 206 cases relating to the supply of services had
accumulated on the register of restrictive practices. .

On the consumer protection side, a number of references have been made to the

---

1   See also the *Annual Reports of the Director General of Fair Trading*, HMSO, 1974-7.

CPAC. By end 1977 a total of twelve voluntary codes of practice had been introduced, including the servicing of electrical appliances, package holidays, the sale of new and used cars, the sale and repair of shoes, laundering and dry cleaning, and so on. The Office of Fair Trading has also investigated various other practices (e.g. bargain offer claims, party-plan and door-to-door selling, and one-day sales) and reviewed the conduct of a large number of individual companies, of which nineteen subsequently gave assurances about their future business practices. The working of the 1968 Trades Description Act has been reviewed, and the Office of Fair Trading issued nine consultative documents concerning the implementation of the 1974 Consumer Credit Act, and carried out the licensing provided for under the Act.

In very bare outline, these are the results of competition policy as developed in the UK over thirty years. Bearing in mind the comparatively small number of single-firm monopoly cases investigated, reservations about the quality of the analysis in some cases,[1] and an unaggressive approach in applying remedial measures, it seems unlikely that this particular strand of the policy has had a marked general effect on seller concentration levels or on the behaviour of dominant firms. In the merger field, a small number of proposals have been stopped, or allowed to proceed only after certain assurances had been given. Again, in purely numerical terms the impact of policy can hardly be said to have been widespread.

The control of restrictive practices has undoubtedly done away with a great mass of overt price-fixing that had existed before 1956. But this is not necessarily conclusive evidence of success. Firstly, both the escape clauses in the 1956 Act and the quality of the Court's reasoning and decisions have been adversely criticized.[2] Indeed, doubts have been expressed over the suitability of judicial practices for resolving complex economic issues. Secondly, it is questionable how far the abandonment of restrictive practices has actually affected behaviour in the markets concerned. Especially where the practices abandoned are in fairly concentrated, oligopolistic markets, they may merely formalize the mutually accommodating behaviour which would in any case occur. Removal of an agreement in these circumstances would not touch the underlying, structural cause of this behaviour.[3]

The variety and detail of the consumer protection activities undertaken since 1973 is in some ways impressive. As expected, the overwhelming emphasis has been on voluntary solutions: negotiated codes, assurances and the like. The advantages of this approach, its flexibility, cost-effectiveness and constructiveness, are heavily stressed by the Director General of Fair Trading in his first two Annual Reports.[4] Its main drawback is perhaps that voluntary cooperation is most likely to be forthcoming and effective where it is least needed.

Misgivings over the effectiveness of competition policy as a whole led to the setting up of an inter-departmental review, announced in November 1977. A subsequent consultative document suggested a number of procedural changes in the way mergers are reviewed, but it failed to propose shifting the onus of proof to the parties,

---

1 See C. K. Rowley, *The British Monopolies Commission,* Allen and Unwin, 1966; and A. Sutherland, *The Monopolies Commission in Action,* CUP, 1970.
2 See e.g. R. B. Stevens & B. S. Yamey, *The Restrictive Practices Court,* Weidenfeld and Nicolson, 1965, and D. Swann *et al., Restrictive Practice Legislation in Theory and Practice,* Allen and Unwin, 1974.
3 See J. B. Heath, 'Restrictive Practices and After', *MS,* May 1961.
4 H. of C. 370, 21 May 1975 and H. of C. 288, 7 April 1976.

so that mergers in future would be allowed only if the companies can demonstrate positive benefits.[1] If implemented, this change would have resulted in a drastic reduction in merger activity.

V.5   EEC Provisions[2]

Articles 85 and 86 of the Treaty of Rome set out EEC regulations dealing with monopolies, mergers and restrictive practices. The European Commission is the body responsible for applying the policies and investigating breaches in them.

The most fully developed parts of the regulations are those relating to restrictive practices. These prohibit all agreements, such as price fixing and market sharing, which prevent, restrict or distort competition in the EEC and extend over more than one member country. As in the UK however, exemption may be gained via a 'gateway' if the agreement improves production or distribution or promotes progress. There is also provision for block exemptions. At present these apply in two narrowly defined cases: one deals with certain types of exclusive dealing agreement between a supplier and a distributor, and the other with certain arrangements for specialization of production. Finally, the Commission has indicated that certain general areas of agreement are not caught by the regulations, mainly because of their limited impact on inter-member trade, or because they deal with rather peripheral or partial cooperation between firms. Firms wishing to test whether their agreements conflict with the legislation are invited to apply for 'negative clearance' while their cases are being investigated.

EEC monopoly regulations are less clear-cut since, although any abuse of a dominant position within the EEC is prohibited if it affects trade between member countries, it is not clear as yet what sort of market share criterion constitutes dominance, or what abuses will be covered by the regulations. Even less clear up to 1971 was the position of mergers. Until the case of Continental Can (an American firm) in that year it was unsettled whether Articles 85 and 86 could be applied to merger cases. Although this particular merger was allowed on appeal to the European Court of Justice, the implicit extension of the legislation to mergers was accepted. Since then a proposed regulation concerning mergers has been approved by the European Parliament.[3] This empowers the European Commission to prohibit mergers involving combined assets of 200 million IUA or 25% of a national market where the merger in question creates or strengthens a position of the parties 'to hinder effective competition in the common market or in a substantial part thereof', and to exempt such anti-competitive mergers in particular cases where this is 'indispensable to the attainment of an objective which is given priority treatment in the common interest of the Community'. It further provides for a compulsory system of advance clarification in cases of large mergers involving combined assets of 1 billion IUA unless the acquired firm has assets of less than 30 million IUA.

It is perhaps appropriate that EEC competition policy should focus rather more on restrictive practices than monopolies, given the lower seller concentration levels

1 *A Review of Monopolies and Mergers Policy,* Cmnd. 7198, May 1978.
2 For a useful summary of the Community's competition policy see D. W. McKenzie, 'Fair Competition in the EEC', *TI,* 13 December 1973. See also D. Swann, op. cit., pp. 55-68 and 159-75, and K. D. George and C. Joll, 'EEC Competition Policy', *TBR,* March 1978.
3 For a discussion of the regulation, which is under consideration by a special working party of experts from member states, see Kurt Market, 'EEC Competition Policy in Relation to Mergers', *Antitrust Bulletin,* Vol. XX, No. 1, spring 1975.

in at least some EEC countries, and given the long history of cartelization in countries such as Germany. Besides, economic integration of the member countries obviously involves breaking down many such restrictive agreements. Even in the area of restrictive practices, however, it is only comparatively recently that the Commission has been shown to have any teeth in dealing with severely anti-competitive cartel practices, by imposing fines on such groups as the 'Aniline Trust' which negotiated more-or-less simultaneous price increases in the Market, and on a group of firms fixing prices and market shares in the market for quinine. Some agreements between UK firms may well fall foul of the EEC regulations. For example, the agreement by which Imperial Tobacco and British American Tobacco shared common brand names, but only sold cigarettes in certain specified agreed markets, has undergone extensive modification.

EEC case-law on monopoly is virtually non-existent as yet. This is partly due to the concern in the Community that EEC industry should be competitive in world markets with US industries, and the arguments that this needs large firms, in order to obtain full economies of scale. It could be argued, however, that some of these scale economies, such as economies of scale in Research and Development, might better be achieved by means of common research work, since this particular kind of restrictive agreement is not proscribed in the treaty.

VI   REGIONAL POLICY AND THE LOCATION OF INDUSTRY
VI.1   The Regional Problem and the Rationale for Government Action

According to one writer a regional problem might be said to exist when there is somewhere a sense of regional grievance.[1] This could arise over regional discrepancies in unemployment and activity rates, average income per head, output growth, net emigration and so on. Statistical information on some of these disparities will be found in Chapter 5, section 1.3. A major influence on the character of the UK regional problem since the mid-1950s has been the decline of certain staple industries, especially coal, cotton textiles and shipbuilding, and falling agricultural employment. However, the UK regions are nearly all mixed urban-rural areas with a fair spread of activities and by international standards the imbalance between them is fairly slight.[2] For instance there is nothing to compare with the 'southern problem' in Italy, where income per head was estimated to be just over half the national average (in the mid-1960s) and only one quarter of that in the richest part of the EEC (in the late 1950s). Other main aspects of the EEC regional problem are some low-income agricultural areas in France and the Irish Republic, and certain older industrial areas developed around iron ore and coal – the Ruhr, Saar and Lorraine.[3] The industrial centres of the EEC outside the UK lie mainly along the Rhine-Rhône valleys, from

1   A. J. Brown, 'Surveys of Applied Economics: Regional Economics, with Special Reference to the United Kingdom', *EJ*, vol. LXXXIX, no. 316, December 1969. See also the same author's *The Framework of Regional Economics in the UK*, CUP, 1972; G. McCrone, *Regional Policy in Britain*, Allen & Unwin, 1969; H. Richardson, *Elements of Regional Economics*, Penguin, 1969; and *MBR*, November 1975, pp. 11-19. For an official treatment see *Regional Development in Britain*, COI Reference Pamphlet 80, HMSO, 1976.
2   The standard regions of the UK are: Northern, Yorkshire and Humberside, E. Midlands, E. Anglia, S. East, S. West, Wales, W. Midlands, N. West, Scotland and N. Ireland.
3   D. Swann, op. cit.

the Netherlands to northern Italy. These are estimated to have accounted for some 60% of the Gross Product of the EEC before its enlargement in 1973.

The original objective of UK regional policy was to reduce the very high unemployment rates in the regions in the 1930s. Although there are now other policy considerations, such as securing economic growth, the efficient utilization of national resources and demand management, concern over regional unemployment is still very much to the fore. Persistent regional unemployment indicates a continuing labour market disequilibrium, with excess supply of labour at the ruling wage levels. One justification for government intervention is that such disequilibria have proved themselves non-self-curing through normal market mechanisms. Presumably this has been due to the immobility of capital and especially housing, and of labour for various reasons, including social ties, imperfect knowledge of job opportunities elsewhere and, perhaps, downward rigidities in wage rates.

A second justification for government regional policy is the likely divergence of social and private costs and benefits in firms' location decisions. Thus, left to their own devices firms might choose locations which permitted minimum cost production (or at least a satisfactorily low level of costs) when the costs actually entering their accounts are the only ones considered. But when the social costs are taken into account (e.g. arising from increased congestion and differential effects on unemployment as between high and low employment areas) we might find that the most desirable location was a quite different one.

VI.2   Regional Policy Measures

These have been implemented by the Special Areas Act 1934, the Distribution of Industry Acts since 1945, the local Employment Acts since 1960 and various Finance Acts. Current policy is laid down by the 1972 Finance Act and also the 1972 Industry Act, which gave effect to the White Paper Industrial and Regional Development (Cmnd. 4942) published in that year. The history of regional policy since 1945 is one of repeated experiment. The following description looks first at the types of area designated to receive assistance, and then at the forms this assistance has taken.

Up to 1966 the criterion used for designating areas for assistance was simply the level of unemployment. Since then the criterion has been widened to 'all circumstances, expected and actual' which allows, for example, population migration to be taken account of as well. The first areas to be selected were the pre-war 'special areas' (South Wales, North-East England, West Cumberland, and the Clydeside-North Lanarkshire area). In 1945 these were extended to produce fairly large 'development areas'. These were replaced in 1960 by some 165 smaller development districts, based on local employment exchange areas, the idea being to channel assistance to the most severely affected centres of unemployment. But this change in the policy gave rise to considerable uncertainty about the continuing status of individual districts, and in 1966 there was a reversion to the policy of specifying broad development areas. This remains the basis of current policy, although two other types of area have been designated, in addition to the development areas. These are the 'special development areas' and the 'intermediate areas'. Special development areas, lying within the development areas, were first created after 1967 in areas affected by colliery closures because of the imminence there of high and persistent unemployment, but were later extended to other areas. Intermediate areas were designated after the Report of the Hunt Committee in 1969,[1] being areas outside development areas suffering problems similar in kind if not in acuteness, and likely to decline relative to areas which either had natural advantages or were already receiving assistance.[2]

The geographical extent of the assisted areas at the time of writing is as follows: development areas cover all of Scotland and the Northern Region of England; Wales (except for its eastern fringes, both north and south); Yorkshire and Humberside; and North Devon and Cornwall. Special development areas exist in West Central Scotland, (centred on Glasgow); the Tyneside–Wearside area and West Cumberland in the North of England; Merseyside; part of North Wales including Anglesey and a large area of South Wales around Cardiff. Intermediate areas cover those parts of the North West and Wales not already mentioned, as well as the Chesterfield area and part of Devon. Altogether, the assisted areas account for 43% of total employment in Great Britain. Northern Ireland is treated as an additional, special, case.

In looking at the assistance measures which have been adopted at one time or another it is convenient to distinguish between measures designed to prevent expansion in areas considered to be sufficiently developed, and financial assistance designed to encourage expansion in the regions. The principal member of the first group is the Industrial Development Certificate (IDC), required for factory building or extension. Up to 1972 they were required in all areas for projects above a certain minimum size, and after 1966 their issue was strictly controlled in the Midlands and South East. From 1972 IDCs have not been required in development areas, and since 1974 a three-tier system has applied to the rest of the country, the maximum size limit for exemption being 15,000 sq. ft in the intermediate areas, 5,000 sq. ft in the South-East planning region and 10,000 sq. ft elsewhere. The 1974 change represented a tightening of the system in the non-assisted areas, although in the recession situation which followed IDC control has apparently not been applied strictly.

In some ways similar to IDCs are the permits required for office development. This control began in London in 1964, and was later extended to certain other areas, although it subsequently lapsed in some. In February 1969 the exemption limit in outer London was raised from 3,000 sq. ft to 10,000 sq. ft. This form of control was retained in 1972 in view of the planning pressures in the South East. However, control of office development has never been regarded as a major policy instrument for dispersing jobs to the regions, and has tended to operate more with regard to intra-regional considerations.

Up to 1963 the financial inducements offered to firms moving to or located in the assisted areas were mainly in the form of discretionary grants and loans which were conditional upon the creation of sufficient employment (at a capital cost not exceeding certain limits, albeit flexible ones). In addition, there was government provision of 'advance factory units' for sale or lease to firms at attractive rates. From 1963-6 these measures were supplemented by a system of tax allowances favouring firms in development areas. In January 1966 the tax allowances were

---

1 *Report of the Committee on Intermediate Areas,* Cmnd. 3998, HMSO, 1969.
2 A fourth type of area, the North Midlands 'Derelict Land Clearance Area' received certain subsidies to encourage the modernization and construction of industrial buildings from 1972 to 1974.

replaced by a system of cash grants on plant and machinery, combined with initial allowances[1] on industrial buildings. From September 1967 to 1976 manufacturers in development areas also received a regional employment premium (REP) the value of which was doubled in 1974. For a time they also benefited relatively to firms elsewhere under Selective Employment Tax. In October 1970 cash grants gave way once more to differential tax allowances in the regions, but in 1972 these latter benefits were made nationwide. Extra assistance for the regions was then added in the form of grants. In 1973 a special scheme was introduced to assist removals to the assisted areas by firms in service industries, offering fixed grants per employee transferred and rent-free periods in the new premises.

The last major reshaping of regional policy was in 1975. The incentives offered since then include regional development grants for buildings, new plant and machinery; selective assistance loans or interest relief grants; removal grants; advance factories; tax allowances on machinery and industrial buildings; finance from European Community funds (e.g. from the European Investment Bank of the European Coal and Steel Community); REP, until later 1976; manpower training assistance; help for transferred workers; and contract preference schemes relating to contracts placed by government departments and nationalized industries.[2] Obviously not all of these will apply in every case. Some are conditional on the amount of employment created and the rates of benefit vary among the different types of area, Northern Ireland generally offering the highest rates. No major changes in the approach to regional policy have occurred since. But the measures taken in July 1976 to reduce planned public expenditure included unification of REP for men and women (with a reduction for men) and postponement of payments of regional development grants. Later in 1976 REP was finally phased out.

In terms of both the size of the areas covered and the variety of scope of the assistance measures, regional policy could hardly be more comprehensive. However, the regional measures described so far have existed alongside another, to some extent competitive, policy. Under the New Towns Act 1946 and Town Development Act 1952, some twenty new towns have been established and rather more enlarged. The principal objective here has been to relieve congestion and assist urban renewal in large conurbations. But this policy impinges on regional policy since the new and enlarged towns have by no means all been in development areas, and their creation may have been a counter-attraction to firms which might have moved to development areas.

VI.3   Some Issues in Regional Policy

One criticism that has been made of government intervention in the location of industry is that it will give rise to an efficiency loss in the form of higher real costs of production.[3] This real cost must be set against the social benefits of regional policy, and might overwhelm them. The argument makes two assumptions. The first

---

1   An initial allowance is an additional proportion of the cost of an asset which may be written off for tax purposes in the year in which the capital expenditure takes place. See chapter 2, section IV.6.

2   For full details see Department of Industry, *Incentives for Industry in the Areas for Expansion*, HMSO, 1978 and *Regional Development Incentives*, HMSO, Cmnd. 6058, May 1975. See also A. Whiting (ed.), *Economics of Industrial Subsidies*, HMSO, 1976.

3   See, e.g., A. C. Hobson, 'The Great Industrial Belt', *EJ*, September 1951.

is that firms will locate at cost-minimizing sites if left alone, and the second is that location significantly affects costs.

There is some evidence, on the first of these, that firms do not approach location as a cost-minimizing exercise, but, in practice, more as is predicted by the behavioural theory of the firm. Thus, apparently, firms do not seek an optimum location but rather an adequate site which satisfies certain minimum requirements. Choice is usually from among a very limited number of alternatives, perhaps no more than two or three. The decision to move is usually stimulated by some problem such as expiry of a lease or a cramped, physically constrained site, rather than by the attractions of alternative locations alone. Search for a new site is 'narrow' in the literal sense of not spreading far from existing operations. By itself this evidence does not enable us to dismiss the argument that interference necessarily results in an efficiency loss. For the sites selected might be lower-cost locations than ones to which government policy directs firms, although not optimal ones. On the other hand, they might be higher-cost locations. Thus, once cost-minimizing assumptions are abandoned, it becomes impossible to predict whether intervention will on balance lead to an efficiency gain or loss, assuming that location significantly affects cost.

On this second question there is some evidence to suggest that location may not significantly affect costs, at least for the majority of manufacturing. One study estimated that some 70% of manufacturing is 'footloose', i.e. not critically affected by costs at different locations.[1] Another writer suggests that some two-thirds of manufacturing is probably footloose with respect to transport costs, which are obviously an important consideration in this context and have always received much attention in location theory.[2] A third, very comprehensive, study found little evidence of continuing excess costs in plants which had moved in relation to the levels in parent or original plants, although it could take five years for initial excess costs to disappear.[3] Thus it appears that a serious efficiency loss would not be inevitable if at least a good deal of manufacturing industry were relocated, though there could obviously be specific exceptions.

A second criticism of UK regional policy has been over its capital bias. Prior to 1967 the various grants, loans and tax allowances offered as financial incentives related exclusively to capital expenditures. As a result the policy was especially attractive to firms with capital-intensive operations, and this was clearly not helpful to the policy objective of creating new employment. Moreover, by lowering the relative price of capital inputs, the policy would tend to increase capital/labour ratios of firms receiving the assistance, perhaps causing this ratio to depart from what it should be for efficient utilization of resources. However, while in force, REP (and, for a short time, SET subventions) would have worked in the opposite direction.

A number of other issues have arisen concerning the nature of the policy instruments used at various times.[4] Firstly, the widening of financial incentives

1   R. J. Nicholson, 'The Regional Location of Industry', *EJ*, 1956. But see A. J. Brown, op. cit., on the reliability of this result.
2   L. Needleman, 'What are We to do About the Regional Problem?', *LBR*, January 1965.
3   W. F. Luttrell, op. cit.
4   See also T. Wilson, 'Finance for Regional Industrial Development', *TBR*, September 1967.

after 1963 to include tax allowances or cash grants for investment and the REP etc. has been criticized on the ground that a larger and larger proportion of the aid given has become unconnected with the creation of new jobs; it is available to firms already in development areas as well as to those moving in. As this has happened, it is argued, the cost-effectiveness of the policy in creating new jobs must have fallen. However a profit-maximizing firm, with reasonably full information and already situated in a development area, would presumably now find it profitable to expand output and employment and seek to do so, and even satisficing firms with only limited perception would tend to do so in so far as aspiration levels adjust to what is attainable and if there is sufficient publicity surrounding the new measures. Secondly, it has been argued that where tax allowances give way to cash grants assistance is paid to the inefficient as well as the efficient, since their receipt does not depend on profits being earned, as do the benefits through tax allowances. Thus a policy including grants may result in propping up ailing firms. On the other hand, the arguments in favour of grants carry some force. Broadly, these are that grants are more likely to be taken into account in decision making, since there is evidence that returns in investment are often calculated pre-tax;[1] that grants are more conspicuous and the benefits offered easier to calculate; and that the longish time-lag in the 'payment' of tax allowances can be avoided, as can the uncertainty of benefits under the allowance system, since these depend on future, unknown, profitability. Especially if firms' location policy is on behavioural lines, it could well be that a system of grants is necessary for incentives to be effective, even if on other grounds tax allowances might be preferable. Thirdly, it could be argued that the use of a negative prohibition like the IDCs as a policy instrument may be less acceptable than positive financial incentives. For, if rigidly applied, IDCs could do harm by choking off investment and expansion altogether in some cases (e.g. in non-footloose trades). Financial incentives on their own would not entail this risk and, moreover, footloose industries would presumably select themselves, thus automatically minimizing the real costs of, e.g., achieving a given reduction in regional unemployment. This argument is quite strong so long as profit maximization is assumed. On a behavioural analysis, however, the IDC comes off rather better in some respects. If firms 'satisfice', financial incentives on their own are unlikely to succeed, or will work only sluggishly. For although higher profits are made attainable in development areas, the response (especially from existing firms) may well be slight if adequate profits can still be earned elsewhere. On the other hand, failure to secure an IDC, like expiry of a lease, is exactly the kind of problem to which firms are stimulated to respond in the behavioural theory, and the obvious response is to move. Two pieces of empirical evidence may be cited in this context: the conclusion that the stimulus to move comes from the 'exporting' area not the 'importing' area[2] and the belief among the administrators of the policy that at least up to the mid-1960s it was the IDC rather than the financial incentives which had most effect. Thus, like cash grants, the IDCs may be necessary for an effective policy, even if there could be other drawbacks. Moreover, on a behavioural analysis the IDC or similar controls may have other merits. Thus, we no longer assume cost-minimizing location decisions and, by promoting wider search than would otherwise occur, the IDC could increase the chances of lower-cost locations being found. Indeed, it could

---

1   See NEDC, *Investment Appraisal*, HMSO, 1965.
2   B. J. Loasby, op. cit.

even be that the IDC is a necessary adjunct to financial incentives because it plays an attention-focusing role in bringing their existence to the notice of firms.

Finally, let us look at two rather contentious issues in regional policy. One is that offering incentives to individual firms is not an effective way of inducing them to move to areas which are otherwise unattractive to them. More effective would be to create positive, real attractions like new towns or other 'growth points', and by the government undertaking more infra-structural investment in roads, docks and other items of social capital stock.[1] Resolution of this argument requires a good deal more knowledge than we have at present about firms' motivation.

Secondly, there has been some dispute over the respective merits of the present 'work to the workers' policy and of the alternative solution of encouraging migration ('workers to the work'). The alternative policies may be thought of as eliminating unemployment (excess supply of labour) by shifting the demand curve to the right (work to the workers) and shifting the supply curve to the left (workers to the work). The migration solution, even if successful in eliminating regional unemployment, would not necessarily remove all inter-regional differences. In particular it would increase net emigration from some areas. Arguments against the migration solution would be that the most mobile workers are probably also the fittest and most skilled, so that the areas they leave become even less attractive to firms; that social overhead capital might be wasted; that congestion in receiving areas would intensify; that the community life and culture in the emptying regions would deteriorate, and so on. However, some limited sorts of migration might avoid these effects (e.g. marginal population movements from large, old, industrial centres to expanding towns outside major conurbations in the prosperous regions). It is very unlikely that a thorough comparison of the costs and benefits of migration and of existing policy would indicate that present policy should be scrapped. But it may be that the two policies are not mutually exclusive and, especially in view of the very small scale of assistance towards migration at present,[2] it could be that some readjustment of the relative weight given to the two policies is desirable. The 1972 policy changes did include more financial help for workers moving house in search of work, but did not go very far in this direction.

VI.4   The Effectiveness of Regional Policy

The statistical evidence shows that, despite the existence of regional policy, the regional problem is still with us. There has been no long-term trend for regional disparities in unemployment to disappear. None of the depressed regions acquired rates of output-growth significantly faster than the UK average, though regional policy has undoubtedly helped Scotland to equal, and occasionally overtake, the overall rate in the 1960s, after a period of very slow relative growth in the late 1950s. Except for Northern Ireland and the South West, the 'problem' regions all had higher personal incomes in relation to the UK average in 1954-5 than in the subsequent ten years. Finally, although the drift to the South East was checked in the later 1960s, net emigration from Scotland, the worst affected region in this respect, increased markedly in the 1960s.

Yet studies do suggest regional policy has had some impact. Two studies of

---

1   See, e.g., *Report on the Scottish Economy, 1960-61* (The Toothill Report), Edinburgh, 1962.
2   See chapter 5, section I.3.

investment grants in the period 1966-8 concluded that planning regions showing predominantly 'development area' status enjoyed a greater level of investment of plant and machinery per employee than the other planning regions,[1] with the marked exception of the South East in the case of one study. A third study analysed patterns of relocation of manufacturing over the period.[2] From 1945-51 about two-thirds of all moves in manufacturing were to development areas. But this was largely because in this period of postwar reconstruction the chief factor stimulating moves was the availability of factory space, which was under government control and mainly in development areas. Between 1952-9 this control had disappeared, the shortage eased, financial inducements under regional policy were not yet strong and IDCs were not too difficult to get outside development areas. As a result the proportion of moves to development areas fell below 25%. But stricter control over IDCs and larger financial incentives subsequently raised this figure to 50% by the mid-1960s. More recently published studies tend to confirm that regional policy had had a significant effect, suggesting that the strengthening of the policy in the 1960s may have increased the number of moves to development areas by 70 to 80 per annum (in relation to a maximum of around 160 per annum) with a total employment effect of about 220,000 jobs by 1970. Apparently all three major policy instruments – IDCs, financial incentives and REP – exerted a separate significant influence.[3]

If the regional problem remains, but regional policy has had some mitigating effects, there is only one conclusion. But for the existence of the policy, the regional problem would now be worse than it is.

VI.5   EEC Provisions

Subsidies given to assist the development of backward regions are explicitly permitted by the Treaty of Rome. In the early development of the EEC and up to 1969 the member governments gave a variety of regional aids with very little supervision or guidance from the central EEC institutions. As a result there was very little harmonization of attitudes towards regional problems and of types and rates of assistance. There is even some evidence of competition among member governments to attract foreign investment to their own problem regions. However, there was some activity at Community level. The European Investment Bank, provided for in the Rome Treaty, financed projects in less developed regions and made loans to firms for rationalization required because of the creation of the Common Market; these loans were at commercial rates of interest and intended to top-up funds raised from other sources to the required level. Also, some of the activities of the ECSC and Agricultural Guidance and Guarantee Fund contributed to the Community regional policy effort, especially as the EEC regional problems

1   See A. Beacham and T. W. Buck, 'Regional Investment in Manufacturing Industries', *Yorkshire Bulletin of Economic and Social Research,* May 1970; and C. Blake, 'The Effectiveness of Investment Grants as a Regional Subsidy', *Scottish Journal of Political Economy,* February 1972. The former relates to 1966, and the latter to the 1967-8 period.

2   R. S. Howard, 'The Movement of Manufacturing Industry in the UK 1945-65', *Board of Trade,* 1968.

3   B. Moore and J. Rhodes, 'Evaluating the Effects of British Regional Policy', *EJ,* vol. 83, 1973, pp. 87-110; and 'Regional Economic Policy and the Movement of Manufacturing Firms to Development Areas', *EC,* 43, pp. 17-31, February 1976.

have much to do with agriculture and the coal and steel industries. Finally, the Social Fund financed training schemes for unemployed workers, though mainly on an industry-by-industry rather than regional basis.

In 1969 a memorandum from the European Commission expressed the need for a more cohesive policy and made certain proposals. These included annual examination of each nation's regional problems; the establishment of a standing committee to review aid schemes; and a Regional Development Rebate Fund to give financial aid to member governments from Community sources (in the form of abatements of interest) for approved aid schemes.

Lengthy and inconclusive negotiations over EEC regional policy measures took place in late 1973 and early 1974, ultimately being suspended because of elections in Britain and France. The size of the Regional Fund was a major source of disagreement, the UK originally proposing a large sum of £1,500m over three years compared with the £250m proposed by West Germany when negotiations broke down. Agreement was finally reached at a Meeting of Heads of Government in December 1974. The Fund was established from 1 January 1975 at a level of £540m for the three years 1975-7. The UK share was set at 28%, second largest after Italy (40%) with a net gain to the UK of about £60m after deducting our contribution through the EEC budget. This figure compares with a total of around £500m spent on regional aid within the UK in 1975. Moreover, receipts from the Fund go to the government rather than to the promoters of individual projects, and so form part of the UK total spending rather than an addition to it.

At one time there were some doubts about the compatibility of UK regional measures with overall EEC policy, but this issue has now been resolved. In general the EEC philosophy appears to favour selective rather than automatic aids, and aids directed towards investment rather than operating costs. Thus automatic aids like the UK Regional Development Grants do not find favour, while the REP which was both automatic and related to operating costs was positively disliked. Nevertheless, the existing UK measures have been accepted in the EEC, albeit after a certain amount of rewording of the Community's principles during the re-negotiation of the UK's terms of entry.[1] EEC policy distinguished between 'central' and 'peripheral' areas, with 20% and 30% ceilings on the level of assistance respectively. In the UK non-assisted and intermediate areas have been classified as central, and development and special development areas as peripheral, with Northern Ireland being treated as a special case.

VII INDUSTRIAL EFFICIENCY
VII.1 Introduction

In earlier sections of this chapter we have seen that industrial growth in the UK has proceeded at a very modest rate by international standards, to the point that in terms of GDP per head Britain has now to be regarded as one of the poorer countries in Western Europe. In the search for explanations various questions have been asked. Has Britain fallen behind because of a lack of technical progressiveness and R and D spending? Are UK firms too small to compete with those of other countries in world markets? Does UK management and workforce exhibit inefficiency to an

---

1 See *Membership of the European Community: Report on Renegotiations,* Cmnd. 6003, March 1975, pp. 9-10 and 20-1.

unusually large degree? There are no complete answers to these questions, but in the following pages we shall consider some of the evidence relevant to them and especially the role of the government.

In the following sections five aspects of the problem and their accompanying strands of policy are isolated and discussed. These are R and D performance; industrial structure (in particular the size distribution of plants and firms); problems of financing investment; the role of planning and of information exchange; and the micro-level significance of price control.

When considering these matters we should, of course, bear in mind the view that industrial growth may not be unambiguously beneficial. For many people it is an open question how long the richer industrialized countries can continue to grow with little regard for the position of developing nations. Moreover, some would argue that the current pursuit of industrial expansion will lead to its own downfall, and to the breakdown of society, by irreversibly disrupting the life systems on the planet.[1]

VII.2   R and D and Technical Progressiveness

The latest available statistics show that in 1972-3 total UK R and D expenditure was £1,310m.[2] This represents about 2.3% of GDP, and a slight fall from level of 2.6% in the 1960s. Private industry carried out most of the work but provided only 37.5% of the funds. 48.9% was financed by the government. The league table of industries undertaking most work is headed by electrical engineering (26.5%, with electronics and telecommunications alone contributing 18.3%) followed by aerospace (25.2%) chemical and allied industries (16.7%), motor vehicles (6.9%) and mechanical engineering (6.5%). Other industries had less than 4%. R and D activity is known to be very much the preserve of large firms. A survey in 1959 of nearly 5,000 firms showed that 350 large firms (employing over 2,000 workers) accounted for about 85% of the total R and D expenditure, with medium and small firms contributing only a minor share, and small firms virtually nothing.[3] Although the data are now twenty years old, they would undoubtedly still give a fair idea of the present situation.

UK spending on R and D is creditably high by international standards. Historically, Britain and especially America have been regarded as international 'creditor' countries in R and D, while Europe is in deficit.[4] However, more recent data, although restricted to public spending only, give a somewhat different impression (table 4.10). In relation to GNP, UK spending falls slightly below that of West Germany and only just above that of France. And while America still spends most, relative to GDP, the lead has been cut significantly since 1970, especially relative to West Germany, where spending has increased markedly.

A high level of R and D effort does not necessarily go hand in hand with rapid growth of GNP. Thus America and Britain, which research most, have grown less

---

1 'A Blueprint for Survival', *The Ecologist*, vol. 2, no. 1, January 1972, and E. Goldsmith (ed.), *Can Britain Survive?*, Sphere Books, 1972. For a criticism of this standpoint see 'The Case Against Hysteria', *Nature*, vol. 235, no. 5333, 14 January 1972.

2 *Source: AAS.*

3 See C. Freeman, 'R and D: A Comparison between British and American Industry', *NIER*, May 1962.

4 See C. Kennedy and A. P. Thirlwall, 'Technical Progress: A Survey', *EJ*, March 1972.

rapidly in recent years than has Europe, which invests less in R and D. Nevertheless, encouragement of research activity is a longstanding element in government policy. The large share of R and D which is government-financed has already been mentioned. The benefit to private industry from this work would not be as great as if, for instance, grants of equivalent value were made for firms' own projects. Nevertheless, a substantial overspill of new developments into the firms' other operations does occur, especially in such fields as aircraft, electronics, metallurgy, engines and machine tools. In some cases, notably computing, aircraft and machine tools, the

TABLE 4.10

Public Sector R and D in Relation to GDP, in UK, USA and Major European Countries, 1970 and 1975

	R and D as a percentage of GDP				
	UK	West Germany	France	Italy	USA
1970	1.25	0.96	1.24	0.46	1.56
1975	1.18	1.22	1.16	0.40	1.33

Source: Eurostat, *Public Expenditure on Research and Development,* 1974-6.

government has provided funds for the development of firms' own projects. Additionally, the government sponsors work on behalf of industry in its own research establishments; funds research through various Research Councils; gives grants to cooperative research associations in various industries; and via the National Research and Development Council (NRDC) finances development of inventions made in government laboratories and by private individuals, where this is in the public interest.

All of the measures impinge directly on R and D activity. Two other strands of government policy may have had an indirect bearing: policies to encourage larger firm size, and competition policy. These policies are discussed elsewhere.[1] Here we consider only the reasons for their connection with R and D.

As we have seen, R and D activity is heavily concentrated in large firms in Britain and America, and one school of thought is that large firm size is a necessary condition for technical progressiveness, primarily because of the large financial requirements.[2] However, not all stages of the innovation process are expensive. Invention itself can still involve only negligible expenditure. It is the subsequent stage of development up to the point of commercial application, and the actual introduction of the new product or process, which are typically expensive. In the past, many important inventions have been the work of individuals or small firms. This sort of evidence puts the contributions of large firms, as measured by R and D inputs, into a different perspective. There is some evidence that in Britain and

1 See sections VII.3 and V respectively.
2 See J. K. Galbraith, *American Capitalism,* Hamish Hamilton, 1956; and Lord Blackett's evidence to the Select Committee on Science & Technology, Minutes of Evidence, 14 March 1968, *Defence Research,* HCP 139-V, 1967/8.

elsewhere large firms are a comparatively minor source of fundamental break-throughs,[1] and that the R and D resources they commit are devoted mainly to relatively minor product improvements and modification.

The question of large absolute size and technical progressiveness intertwines with the argument that market power (large size relative to market supply) is an important facilitating condition.[2] Empirical tests of this hypothesis and its rival — that competition is conducive to technical progress — have so far proved very inconclusive.[3] It is difficult to say why this is so. It might be because of practical difficulties in measuring technical progressiveness, of which there is no direct measure. Alternatively, the explanation could be that both competition and market power carry with them both advantages and disadvantages from the point of view of securing technical advances, and the balance between them is either roughly equal or varies from case to case. Thirdly, it may be that there are other important factors at work.

VII.3   Scale, Unit Cost and Structural Reorganization

The ideas that there are widespread and large economies of scale in production, and that they fairly frequently fail to be exploited, are recurring themes in discussions of UK industrial growth. The extent of potential scale economies can be gauged by either observing the physical relationship between inputs and output in production (i.e. by estimating production functions) or by direct observation of long-run average costs as scale is varied. To assess how fully such scale economies as exist are exploited we would need to relate additional information on the actual size distribution of plants and firms to these estimates of potential scale economies. There is a fair amount of information on the first of these questions. The second has received very little attention in the literature, but certain limited conclusions can be drawn from Census of Production data.

In general, empirically estimated production functions in both the UK and most other countries have revealed remarkably few results that are inconsistent with a constant returns hypothesis.[4] By contrast, empirical cost functions have suggested that average costs decline rapidly at first as scale increases, but that the rate of decline lessens as scale is increased further, the cost curve tending to flatten out until it is virtually horizontal. Thus an 'L'-shaped long-run average cost curve is observed, indicating substantial economies to increases in scale over smaller size ranges; further, but less substantial, economies at higher size levels; but with no evidence of eventual diseconomies of scale.[5] According to the evidence there is much inter-industry variation in the magnitude of scale economies. One study shows

---

1 See e.g. J. Jewkes, D. Sawers and R. Stillerman, op. cit., and F. M. Scherer, op. cit.

2 See also section V above.

3 The evidence is mainly for the US. Scherer, op. cit., after providing an excellent summary, notes 'that market concentration has a favourable impact on technological innovation in certain situations. How much concentration is advantageous remains to be determined. Obviously there is no general answer . . . ' (p. 376).

4 See A. A. Walters, 'Production and Cost Functions: An Econometric Survey', *Econometrica*, 1963.

5 Ibid.; see also J. Johnston, *Statistical Cost Analysis*, McGraw-Hill, 1960; C. F. Pratten, *Economies of Scale in Manufacturing Industry*, CUP, 1971; and Z. A. Silberston, *EJ*, March 1972.

the percentage increase in total cost per unit faced by plants producing at only 50% of estimated minimum efficient scale (m.e.s.) for various industries;[1] in brick production, for instance, costs would be some 25% above the level of m.e.s. whereas for a sulphuric acid plant the increase would be only 1%. In view of this inter-industry variation, only very rough generalizations can be made. But from the

TABLE 4.11

Distribution of Manufacturing Establishments[1] by Employment Size, UK, 1972

Employment size Category	No. of units	%	Total employment (000s)	(%)	Total net output (£m)	(%)
1–10	37,878	43.5	194.5	2.6		
11–24	22,261	25.6	378.2	5.0	3.460.5	15.8
25–99	15,122	17.4	797.3	10.6		
100–199	5,027	5.8	691.3	9.2	1,850.6	8.4
200–499	4,050	4.7	1,269.8	16.9	3,623.8	16.5
500–999	1,459	1.7	1,021.3	13.6	3,007.5	13.7
1,000 and over	1,157	1.3	3,168.6	42.1	10,000.7	45.6
TOTAL	86,954	100.0	7,521.9	100.0	21,942.8	100

Source: *Census of Production, 1972.*

Note: 1   An establishment is the smallest unit capable of supplying census information, usually a factory or plant at a single site or address.

available evidence it seems that scale economies in most trades are likely to have been secured by plants five times as big as the smallest and even where economies continue to be enjoyed at larger size levels, they will almost certainly have been exhausted by plants ten times the size of the smallest.

This tentative conclusion enables us to draw from Census data some equally tentative inferences about the degree of exploitation of scale economies. Table 4.11 shows the size distribution of plants in 1972. It shows that small plants are numerically predominant. This can mean one of several things. Either these plants are all in industries, or subsections of industries, where there are few, if any, economies of scale; or the larger plants are run inefficiently, so that there is room for small efficient plants which nevertheless fail to exploit scale economies fully; or the owners of these small plants are content to accept a very low rate of return on their investment; or, finally, scale economies are of very little importance, so that the size distribution is the outcome of purely random effects.[2] Attempting to allow for the first suggestion, we might say that the smallest plants which generally exist in an industry employ 100 workers. Then, if we take plants employing 500 workers

---

1   C. F. Pratten, op. cit., m.e.s. is the point on the L-shaped long-run average cost curve at which average costs cease to fall.

2   It has been pointed out that the configurations we observe are similar to those one might expect if firms, initially of equal size, were subjected over a longish period to a succession of pieces of good or bad luck, each having a proportionate effect on firm size. For a discussion of this idea see: H. A. Simon and C. P. Bonini, 'The Size Distribution of Business Firms', *AER*, September 1958; P. E. Hart, 'The Size and Growth of Firms', *EC*, February 1962, and F. M. Scherer, op. cit., on Gibrat's law.

Industry and commerce

TABLE 4.12

Distribution of Manufacturing Enterprises[1] by Employment Size, UK, 1972

Employment size category	No. of enterprises (No.)	(%)	No. of establishments (No.)	(%)	Total employment (000s)	(%)	Total net output (£m)	(%)
1–99	66,119	91.4	71,249	82.2	1,133.7	16.0	2,815.6	13.6
100–499	4,675	6.5	5,999	6.9	959.6	13.5	3,537.4	12.2
500–999	686	0.9	1,654	1.9	478.5	6.7	1,317.8	6.3
1,000–4,999	635	0.9	3,597	4.1	1,340.7	18.9	4,051.2	19.5
5,000–9,999	101	0.1	1,247	1.4	703.8	9.9	2,375.3	11.4
10,000–49,999	72	0.1	1,888	2.2	1,374.2	19.3	4,323.3	20.8
50,000–99,999	9	0.01	553	0.6	523.8	7.4	1,535.6	7.4
100,000 and over	4	0.006	515	0.6	590.7	8.3	1,804.5	8.7
TOTAL	72,301	100.0	86,702	100.0	7,104.9	100.0	20,760.5	100.0

Source: *Census of Production, 1972.*

Note: 1 An enterprise means one or more establishments under common ownership or control.

or more and apply the conclusion of the previous paragraph, we find from table 4.11 that nearly 60% of total output is produced in plants in which the bulk of scale economies can fairly safely be assumed to have been exploited. On the same basis, around 45% of total output is in fact accounted for by plants at least ten times the size of the smallest. The same general picture emerges for manufacturing enterprises (groups of establishments under common ownership) (table 4.12). Without close study at the individual industry level, firm conclusions should not be drawn. But it could be that the efficiency loss believed to arise from the existence of sub-optimal scale has been exaggerated.

Over time, there has certainly been a marked trend towards larger plants and firms. Plants with over 1,500 workers accounted for 15.2% of total employment in private sector manufacturing industry in 1935, and for over 30% in 1972; those with under 100 employees accounted for 25.6% in 1936 and for 18.2% in 1972. Perhaps, therefore, the importance of plant scale economies is increasing, but if so the evidence indicates it is being taken up to some extent. Also, it is interesting to observe that the number of establishments (plants) per enterprise is quite small, 1.33 in 1968,[1] so that if firms *are* efficient then economies of multi-plant operation must be very limited in most industries.

As a means of securing greater efficiency and growth, structural reorganization has tended to receive emphasis under Labour governments, particularly from 1964-70. Thus an Industrial Reorganization Corporation (IRC) was set up, which initiated and aided a number of mergers including some spectacular ones such as Leyland-BMC and GEC-AEI-English Electric. The 1968 Industrial Expansion Act was also designed to provide government support for schemes which would improve economic efficiency, expand productive capacity and promote technical improvements, and a specific

1 *Census of Production 1968.* On this point see F. M. Scherer *et al., The Economics of Multi-Plant Operation,* Harvard University Press, 1975.

programme of grant-aided help was provided to reorganize the shipbuilding industry under a 1967 Act.

Under the 1970-74 Conservative government emphasis tended to swing away from 'structural' solutions to industrial problems in favour of a greater reliance on the pressure of competition, and the IRC was dissolved in May 1971. The main emphasis on current government policy is described in section VII.5.

VII.4 Finance for Investment

Orthodox economics suggests two possible reasons for government intervention in private sector capital formation. One would be that, for some reason, the social returns on investment projects undertaken by firms are greater than the private returns. If so it is legitimate to reduce the cost of capital services to the firm in order to raise the level of investment in capital goods from the privately optimal to the socially optimal level. The divergence between social and private benefits might arise from the impact of investment on unemployment or on the balance of payments or even on national prestige. Secondly, intervention would be justified if there was evidence of 'market failure' in the supply of funds for investment: that is, if shortcomings in the organization of financial institutions, or in the information flows on which they base their decisions, left firms unable to borrow at 'appropriate' interest rates given the profitability and degree of risk of their investment plans.

Alternative explanations, implicitly drawing on rather different theoretical models of the firm, might be that firms facing an uncertain future simply tend to under-estimate the private returns to investment, or that investment policies resulting from the gradual adjustment of firms' aspirations to their past achievements would result in growth rates that were unacceptably low to the government.

In practice, the rate of investment in UK manufacturing is widely regarded as being too low. Also, new investment tends to earn relatively poor returns, and capital market imperfections are believed to exist, mainly affecting the supply of medium- and longer-term funds. A number of measures to improve investment performance were embedded in a broader government industrial strategy, outlined in a White Paper published in November 1975.[1] The investment measures themselves stem from the Industry Acts of 1972 and 1975. The 1972 Act affirmed the (Conservative) government's determination to provide a substantial and lasting impetus to profitable industrial expansion, modernization and a higher growth-rate by increasing the government's incentives to investment in all regions of the UK. The main investment incentive was the allowance of free depreciation (whereby firms set capital expenditure against tax at whatever rate suits them best)[2] on new plant and machinery and an initial tax allowance of 50% on industrial buildings and structures throughout the UK, measures which had previously applied only to the assisted areas.[3] Further, there was a system of grants to industry for capital expenditure in the assisted areas and in some cases elsewhere. A special provision of the Act was a system of short-term tapering grants to shipbuilders until a longer-term solution for this industry had been worked out.

---

1 *An Approach to Industrial Strategy*, Cmnd. 6315, HMSO, November 1975.
2 In most cases free depreciation amounts to a 100% initial allowance.
3 See also section VI and chapter 2, section IV.6.

One other provision of the 1972 Act was that grants might be given only in exchange for state shareholdings in the companies concerned. This provision was not used by the Conservative government, but has been used subsequently by the Labour government, for example in its rescue of British Leyland in 1975.

The 1975 Act greatly increased the emphasis on extending state ownership in the provision of assistance to industry. Part I of the Act set up the National Enterprise Board,[1] with initial finance of up to £1,000m to assist firms, or the reorganization of industries, exercising the powers of selective financial assistance under the 1972 Act. A controversial feature of the NEB is that it is empowered to extend public ownership not only to companies asking for help (as Upper Clyde Shipbuilders, Rolls-Royce and British Leyland had earlier done) but also into profitable companies. The NEB is required to promote industrial democracy in the undertakings controlled by it, and to hold and manage securities and other property in public ownership which is transferred to it (including Rolls-Royce, Alfred Herbert, Ferranti, and BL). The Act required the NEB to earn an 'adequate' return on its capital, and made acquisitions exceeding £10m in a company or 30% of a company's share subject to the consent of the Secretary of State.[2]

At one time there was optimism in left-wing circles and apprehension elsewhere that the NEB would lead to a major extension of public ownership, to include at first a hundred and then twenty-five of the biggest UK companies. It is now clear that the NEB as presently organized and financed cannot and is not intended to attempt such a task. As and when fixed investment in manufacturing recovers from the recession levels of the mid-1970s it seems likely that the generous tax incentives under the 1972 Act will provide more of a stimulus than will the NEB.

The question of possible institutional shortcomings in the private sector supply of investment funds to industry is one of the issues being reviewed by the government-appointed Committee set up under the chairmanship of Sir Harold Wilson on The Functioning of Financial Institutions. More generally, the financial problems of smaller companies have recently received considerable public discussion and attention, notably in the April 1978 budget.

VII.5   Information Exchange and Planning

In most textbook descriptions resource allocation takes place in market economies without the need for economic agents to meet, exchange information and co-ordinate their behaviour in any direct way. Planning is effected via the price mechanism. In the UK, especially under Labour governments, steps have been taken to supplement the impersonal price signals in the market with other types of information, and to create a measure of non-market planning in the resource-allocation process.

The first major effort in this direction was the National Plan of 1965. As a planning exercise this was short-lived. However some of the institutional structure associated with the Plan survived, in particular the Economic Development Committees for different industries. Twenty-one EDCs were set up, under the *aegis*

---

1   Other parts of the Act dealt with planning agreements and information disclosure, which are discussed in section VII.5.

2   Guidelines published in 1976 restricted the NEB's freedom of action without reference to the Secretary of State to £0.5m in cases of share purchases contested by shareholders.

of the central National Economic Development Council, and they undertook a wide range of activities. These have included regular demand and supply forecasts and publication of information on export performance, sales opportunities in particular markets, and import trends. Other topics which have been covered include manpower problems; standardization; stockholding procedures; factors affecting investment; R and D; and the effect of decimalization, taxation and devaluation. The information has been disseminated within industries via newsletters and reports, and there has also been some exchange of information between industries.

A 1974 White Paper introduced a different type of policy instrument, the planning agreement.[1] These were intended as a means of exchanging information between the government and individual companies on long-term objectives and medium-term expectations and plans.[2] Agreements would be concluded annually, though subject to revisions, and they would also be voluntary. However, companies could find themselves under considerable pressure to volunteer, in order to secure maximum benefits from government assistance measures. Thus, for instance, the 1975 Industry Act provided safeguards to firms with Planning Agreements over the rates of grant and qualifying conditions for regional development grants and selective financial assistance. Moreover part IV of the same Act provided a procedure – albeit a cumbersome and lengthy one – whereby companies could be compelled to disclose information of a planning nature. (In return it obliged the government to publish 'in due course' a model of the economy so that the public could make forecasts using their own assumption about GDP, unemployment, the balance of payments, retail prices, average earnings and other matters.)

More generally, government philosophy on planning was described in a 1975 White Paper, *An Approach to Industrial Strategy*.[3] The White Paper described itself as not a strategy but a programme for developing a strategy. It proposed as a first step the provision of a systematic statistical and analytical framework, embracing the past performance of thirty or so individual sectors of manufacturing, and the implications for each of alternative medium-term growth assumptions. The sectors chosen would be industries 'intrinsically likely to be successful', or with the potential of being so (together with industries 'whose performance (as in the case of component suppliers) is most important to the rest of the industry'). The White Paper then envisaged government–industry consultations at three levels: national, industry and company. Frequent references were made to the role of the EDCs, the NEB and Planning Agreements. The whole exercise was intended as an annual 'rolling-plan' procedure.

Amongst non-involved observers (including economists) there is often marked disagreement about the relative merits of market solutions versus planning, and there is a dearth of objective theoretical knowledge and empirical evidence to help resolve the issues. Moreover, it is particularly hard to evaluate mixtures of planning and the market mechanism such as present policy in the UK implies, as distinct from 'ideal' stereotypes.

On the one hand, it is possible that the government, if it succeeds in discovering more about the micro-implications of its macro policies, could avoid some of the

---

1 *The Regeneration of British Industry*, Cmnd. 5710, HMSO, 1974.
2 For a description of the possible contents of such agreements, see *TI*, 8 August 1975, pp. 338-42.
3 Cmnd. 6315.

past errors which the White Paper listed: unduly sharp and frequent changes of economic regulators; pre-emption of resources for the public sector and personal consumption; and intervention in the nationalized industries. It is possible also that companies, if better informed about government intentions and less prone to suffer from the errors listed above, could improve their own planning and resource utilization. On the other hand, the White Paper made little effort to conceal that the government is only feeling its way towards a planning system, and the eager cooperation of companies is unlikely to be forthcoming. The process of finding the policy is thus bound to be a slow one. At the time of writing very little progress appears to have been made.

VII.6 Some Microeconomic Implications of Price Controls

Statutory price controls were first introduced by the Labour government in 1966, after a period of voluntary control. Applications for increases were reviewed by the now disbanded National Board for Prices and Incomes (NBPI). Subsequently, statutory controls gave way to voluntary arrangements until November 1972. In the first stage there was a virtual standstill on most prices other than food for five months. Stage II of the policy saw the creation in 1973 of a Price Commission (PC). About 200 of the largest firms (later increased to around 1,400) were required to give prior notice of price increases to this body. Smaller firms had to report prices intermittently, and the smallest to keep records for inspection. Increases were accepted only on the basis of 'allowable' cost increases; that is, a rise in the price of materials, fuel, rents, transport, etc., and a proportion of labour costs, and as long as profit margins did not exceed a 'reference level' — the average level in the best two of the previous five years. The PC as originally constituted remained in being until 1977, during which time the basic nature of price-control policy was unaltered, though many detailed changes were made, mainly towards relaxation of the 'Price Code', especially in December 1974 and August 1976. Over the period some 8,000 notifications were received each year, together with a total of 350,000 inquiries or complaints about pricing matters. From July 1977 a reconstituted PC has been in operation, operating what is in practice a somewhat looser and more flexible policy.[1]

The primary objectives of price-control policies are macroeconomic ones. The final periodic report of the original PC[2] suggests that at the last peak of economic activity (in 1973-4) it may have kept prices 3—4% lower than they would otherwise have been. In the subsequent recession however, its effect was minimal, and the binding constraint on price levels was almost certainly depressed trading conditions rather than price control.

Our present interest is less in the macroeconomic significance of price controls than on their incidental microeconomic effects, especially their impact on industrial efficiency. On orthodox theoretical arguments, we should expect these to be small or non-existent. If firms are already maximizing profits and pursuing cost-minimizing policies, the extra sanction of price control will be on output and employment levels

---

1 See *Quarterly Reports of the Price Commission,* and for a first-hand account of the original PC's role Sir Arthur Cockfield, 'The Price Commission and the Price Control', *TBR,* March 1978.

2 HC 459, 1977.

and on investment. Thus, if costs increase but prices do not adjust to the same extent, the profit-maximizing output and employment levels will generally fall. If current and expected future profit levels fall, the incentive to invest is weakened, while at the same time the surplus available for re-investment is less.

Other models lead to somewhat different conclusions. As was noted earlier, in section I, the managerial and behavioural theories suggest that there is generally some discretionary expenditure and/or slack in the firm's operations. In the behavioural theory in particular, firms do not generally operate at or close to maximum efficiency, in the sense of choosing cost-minimizing factor ratios and obtaining the maximum output it is possible to get from any given bundle of resources. One set of empirical estimates of the degree of technical inefficiency – or X-inefficiency in the writer's own terms – suggests that it may amount to 25% of output in many cases and up to 80% in some.[1] If these estimates are anywhere near the mark, the scope for raising efficiency is clearly considerable, and the sanction of price controls is one possible way of achieving it. Thus, in the Williamson model, the introduction of price controls could result in a more adverse business environment, causing discretionary expenditures to contract. In behavioural terms, price control could be exactly the kind of 'problem' to which firms will respond by cutting slack and widening the search for new and better production methods. However, the gains will not always be unambiguous ones. For instance, where firms are forced to abandon managerial objectives there will be some loss of managerial utility to offset the social gain arising from cost savings, and organizational slack may serve a useful social function to some extent as a form of contingency reserve. Moreover, cutting slack will tend to have employment implications, with the attendant social costs especially at times when unemployment is already high.

What the actual effects of price control have been in this area is hard to assess. The NBPI reports contained a good deal of specific recommendations for improved efficiency and long-term productivity benefits. Similarly, the PC uncovered important areas of 'administered pricing' policy where significant improvements could be made to the benefit of the community, especially where competitive pressure is lacking. In its first periodic report the new PC tended to see its role to lie in investigating pricing in monopoly or imperfect competition situations.[2] The question which then arises is whether there is scope for a second agency in this area, additional to the Monopolies Commission. Especially in view of the earlier plan to merge the MC and NBPI in 1970, it would not be surprising if the committee reviewing the working of competition[3] policy were to propose a similar union of the MC and PC.

REFERENCES AND FURTHER READING

F. M. Scherer, *Industrial Market Structures and Economic Performance*, Rand McNally, 1970.

B. S. Yamey (ed.), *Economics of Industrial Structure*, Penguin, 1973.

R. Turvey, *Economic Analysis and Public Enterprise*, Allen and Unwin, 1971; and *Public Enterprise*, Penguin, 1968.

---

1 H. Leibenstein, 'Allocative Efficiency vs. X-Efficiency', *AER*, 1966.
2 HC 117, 1977.
3 See above, p. 201.

R. Pryke, *Public Enterprise in Practice,* McGibbon and Kee, 1971.

R. Rees, *Public Enterprise Economics,* Weidenfeld and Nicolson, 1976.

The Nationalised Industries, Cmnd. 7131, HMSO, March 1978.

S. J. Prais, *The Evolution of Giant Firms in Britain,* CUP, 1976.

L. Hannah and J. A. Kay, *Concentration in Modern Industry,* Macmillan, 1977.

A. Hunter, *Monopoly and Competition,* Penguin, 1969.

A. J. Brown, *The Framework of Regional Economics in the UK,* CUP, 1972.

H. W. Richardson, *Regional and Urban Economics,* Penguin, 1978.

C. F. Pratten, *Economies of Scale in Manufacturing Industry,* CUP, 1971.

C. Freeman, *The Economics of Industrial Innovation,* Penguin, 1974.

D. Swann, *The Common Market,* 3rd edition, Penguin, 1975.

For information on current developments in industry and commerce:
Trade and Industry
National Institute Economic Review (especially February issue).

5

Labour

David Metcalf and Ray Richardson

I THE LABOUR FORCE

I.1 Total Employment

In September 1977, the working population (or labour force) in the UK was estimated to be 26,542,000[2]. This aggregate was composed of employees in employment (22,719,000), employers and self-employed (1,886,000), HM Forces (328,000) and the registered unemployed (1,609,000). Since 1971, when a new method of estimating the number of employees in employment was introduced, there has been a continual rise in the mid-year estimates of the working population. On the face of it, this implies a re-establishment of the pattern which prevailed from 1950-66, during which period the working population fell only in 1958, and a break with the sustained fall in working population that is estimated for the period 1966-71[3].

To some extent, these changing labour force patterns over time may reflect measurement and estimation difficulties. For example, it is difficult to estimate accurately the number of self-employed workers, and it has been suggested that certain tax and National Insurance changes have given substantial incentives for people to switch into (and more recently, out of) self-employed status. If this has happened it is quite possible that the estimated changes in working population are misleading because they would capture the change in employees but not that in the self-employed. Here, however, we will assume that the official estimates are broadly correct and discuss what determines the size of and changes in the labour force.

One influence is the size and demographic composition of the population. For example, younger and older males are less likely to be in the labour force than are males aged between twenty-five and fifty-five. In order to abstract from demographic changes it is convenient to discuss these issues in terms of activity rates (sometimes called labour force participation rates). These express, for any age and sex group, the proportion of working to total population. There are two influences on male activity rates to consider here: first, the trend in economic growth and secondly, fluctuations around that trend.

Economic growth tends to reduce male activity rates. In particular, younger males stay in the educational system longer and older males retire earlier, especially when growth is accompanied by improved retirement pensions. Thus, between 1961 and 1976, the proportion of boys who stayed on in school rose from 23% to 51% for sixteen year olds and from 13% to 21% for seventeen year olds.[4] The reported

---

1 David Metcalf has worked as a Special Adviser in DHSS in 1977-8. He is writing here in his personal capacity.

2 *DEG*, March 1978, p. 350

3 *BLS*, p. 220 and *DEG*, March 1977, pp. 250-2.

4 *AAS*, 1977, p. 131, and *AAS*. 1971, p. 106.

activity rates for older males have fallen in each successive Census of Population; for example, from 48% to 31% for sixty-five to sixty-nine year olds over the period 1951 to 1971.[1] These changes predominantly reflect the fruits of economic growth.

Superimposed on this inverse relation between growth and the male labour force is a complex reaction to fluctuations in growth. The dominant reaction to fluctuations in growth has generally been a positive one; the male labour force has tended to contract (or grow less rapidly) during economic recessions, and grow (or contract less rapidly) during periods of economic expansion. There are exceptions to this general pattern, notably in the recession which began in 1974. Between 1974 and 1977, the number of male employees (either in employment or unemployed) rose by nearly 300,000; this is in contrast to a corresponding fall of 300,000 during the recessionary period 1969-72. Fully convincing reasons for the recent apparent change in labour force behaviour have not so far been offered.

The two typical relations between growth and the size of the labour force, the negative and the positive, are not contradictory, as they might seem at first sight. The first concerns people's responses to a permanent increase in wealth levels; the second concerns people's responses to what is presumed to be a temporary fall in employment prospects. This is an application of the fundamental notions in economics of income and substitution effects. If a worker is not planning to supply the maximum amount of labour at all times, he can choose the most advantageous periods when the supply is to be offered. On many calculations the most advantageous periods occur when wages are high and jobs are easy to find; that is, in expansionary conditions. Consequently, a recession is a period during which there is less point in offering one's services. This view therefore predicts that over the business cycle the size of the labour force will be positively related to the state of the economy. It is usually termed the 'discouraged worker effect', meaning that as the economy contracts, the number of people in employment falls by more than the increase in the number counted as unemployed.

There is an alternative and opposite view to the one just described, labelled the 'added worker effect'. It suggests that as 'primary' (i.e. permanent) members of the labour force are made unemployed in recessions, 'secondary' (i.e. temporary) workers are drawn into the work force so as to provide an additional source of income for the family; the result is that the number of unemployed rises more than the number disemployed. This view obviously has some validity but it is basically a qualification to the 'discouraged worker' hypothesis. It stresses that many households plan imprecisely, that unpredicted events are important and force changes even in carefully laid plans, and that savings, credit and social welfare payments may be inadequate to maintain family living standards for more than a relatively short period. These and other factors are all of obvious practical importance, but they should not be taken to imply that the 'discouraged worker' hypothesis, with its emphasis on rational calculation, is thereby unrealistic and likely to be misleading. In fact, when careful statistical analysis is carried out, the evidence strongly suggests that it is the 'discouraged worker' effect which dominates the 'added worker' effect.[2]

---

1   *ST,* 1975, p. 84.
2   B. Corry and J. Roberts, 'Activity Rates and Unemployment: the experience of the UK 1951-66', *Applied Economics,* vol. 2, no. 3, 1970.

I.2 Female Employment

For many years now there have been substantial differences between male and female employment changes. Concentrating on the estimates of employees in employment, it can be seen that the number of male workers in the UK rose fairly consistently from 13,722,000 in June 1950 to 14,999,000 in June 1966;[1] by June 1977, the figure had fallen, again fairly consistently, to 13,383,000.[2] The net result over the twenty-five years was a fall in the number of male employees in employment. Female employees, on the other hand, have not had prolonged periods of decline and have risen in number from 7,036,000 in June 1950 to 9,281,000 in June 1977, a rise of more than 30%. Around that long-run trend there have been years of increases and occasional falls but over the period as a whole the female percentage of the working population has risen from 32 to 38.

It should be noted that by far the most dramatic rise in participation has come from married females, at all ages. Comparing 1951 with 1971, wives' activity rates have risen by about 35% for younger wives, by more than 100% for middle-aged wives and by more than 300% for older wives.[3] The corresponding figures for single females and for widowed and divorced females are more mixed. Activity rates of the younger groups have tended to fall, a development that may be explained by educational trends and the increase in one-parent families. Those of the older groups have tended to rise, albeit much less dramatically than those of wives. Despite these differing trends, however, it is still the case that in absolute terms female activity rates are highest for single women and lowest for married women.

Given that the experience of the two groups, married and unmarried, has been different, it seems likely that the major explanation of the increase in the number of working wives is not something that affects women generally, such as a decline in anti-female discrimination. Whether or not such discrimination, usefully defined, is extensive, there have been no conclusive studies showing changes in its extent.

Concentrating, therefore, on influences primarily affecting married women, we can point first to the fact that the average number of children per family has fallen over time. Whether this is a cause or effect of higher participation is not known. What is known, for the US, is that activity rates have also risen for married women with young children. This suggests that declining family size is, at best, only a partial explanation of rising activity rates.

A second possibility is that, due to the introduction of new products, there has been a rise in the productivity of the housewife, effectively allowing her to produce the same amount of housewifely services as before but in less time. By itself this improved productivity does not necessarily make for greater participation by the wife in the labour force because, at the same time, everyone's income has risen. With the rise in income one might expect both the family's demand for housewifely services and the housewife's demand for personal leisure to increase, thereby decreasing the incentive to join the labour market. Only if the domestic productivity effect is strong will the net effect be to release housewives for market work. With this possibility there is again the question of whether the product improvements were cause or effect. That is, did they appear autonomously or were they induced

1 *BLS*, p. 221.
2 *DEG*, March 1978, p. 350.
3 *ST*, 1975, p. 84.

and hurried along by the independent effect of a rise in working wives caused by some other factor? To our knowledge, no study has given a satisfactory answer to this question.

A third possible explanation of the rise in activity rates for married women is that social attitudes have become increasingly tolerant of wives, even mothers, working. This explanation is probably the most popular of all of the explanations and there is certainly no doubt that attitudes have changed. Again, however, there is the difficulty of deciding the extent to which changes in attitudes were an independent cause or were themselves a response to changes in practice. It does seem plausible that the two world wars were very influential in this matter. They were, as far as the labour market was concerned, exogenous events inducing many women to join the market for the first time. This process surely changed social attitudes, encouraging working wives. It is also notable that over the last twenty years the largest increases in activity rates for married women are associated with older women, who experienced to the full the turmoil of wartime. However, one note of caution is worth sounding as to the impact of wartime exigencies. The available data are very sketchy, but they suggest that the increase in the proportion of wives who work in the market is very much an international phenomenon, extending even to countries for which the impact of the wars was quite modest.

The above explanations all run in terms of supply influences, implying that progressively more married women are willing to work in the market. Demand influences may also have been important. One possibility is that the attempts by successive governments to induce greater regional evenness of employment have been successful in bringing some work to women who previously had very limited job opportunities. Related aspects of this view are discussed in section I.3 below, but there are two qualifications to be noted. First, if this argument has much weight one would expect that, region by region, more or less equal increases in activity rates for married and unmarried women would have occurred. It is not clear that this has happened. Second, if the point were merely that there has been a geographical redistribution of jobs one would expect a decline in female activity rates in the prosperous, job-losing regions. This has certainly not happened in absolute terms, but it is true that female activity rates have tended to rise more rapidly in areas where they have traditionally been low.[1] In fact there has not been merely a redistribution of jobs. Since the end of the 1930s, the UK economy has been run at unprecedented and persistent tightness. It seems most plausible to us, in the absence of hard statistical confirmation, that it is this influence rather than deliberate geographical dispersion that explains a major part of the rise of women in the labour force.

A second, structural argument relating to demand influences could be made. It might be suggested that female activity rates have risen because expansion has been particularly marked in industries employing a high proportion of female to male workers. It is shown below, in section I.4, that these female-intensive industries have indeed enjoyed a relative expansion, certainly since the Second World War. However, most of these sectors are not inherently female intensive and we should again put principal stress on the general expansion of the economy when considering demand influences which account for the rise of female participation in the

---

1   J. Bowers, *The Anatomy of Regional Activity Rates,* Regional Paper 1, NIESR, 1970, chapter 3.

labour market. Essentially what has been happening here has been the tapping of a labour reserve.

Recently there has been some interesting research in this area, specifically in explaining the variation in married females' activity rates between towns and cities in Great Britain.[1] It was shown that wives' activity rates were greater, the higher were female wage rates and the lower were male wage rates; wives' activity rates were also higher for the foreign born, for those with little wealth, for those who lived in the larger cities and for those who lived in towns with low male unemployment rates.[2] In general where labour markets are tight, as judged by unemployment or wages, married women are more likely to be in the labour force.

I.3   Spatial Employment Patterns

The national pattern of jobs and workers in Great Britain is changing rapidly both within regions and between regions.

For example, the resident labour force in the seven British conurbations fell by more than 650,000 between 1961 and 1971.[3] During the same period, Greater London lost more than 25% of its jobs in manufacturing, many of them to other parts of the country, particularly to the rest of the South East region. This reduction in workplace and labour force densities, together with shifts between the standard regions, has sometimes been a response to natural market forces and sometimes a result of deliberate planning policy. Thus, in the period since the Second World War there has been a great planned expansion of new towns that ring many of our major cities. Often, firms have wished to expand their operations around their existing inner city sites but have been denied planning permission. They have therefore been obliged to move either to a nearby new town or to a more distant depressed region. Of course, many firms have moved for reasons other than planning difficulties, for example because suitable nearby land was not physically available, or because labour was increasingly scarce locally or because local transportation facilities were deteriorating.

The loss of workplaces in many of the major cities may or may not imply higher urban unemployment. For example, in London there has been no obvious change in unemployment, relative to other areas, during the period of major job loss. This implies either that the population is leaving London at the same rate as jobs or that commuting patterns are changing. Clearly some cities are suffering from the loss of jobs (Glasgow is often said to be in this category), while others benefit from the reduction of congestion that decline implies.

Until recently, when specific urban problems became more acutely perceived, the most noticed national aspect of employment was the inter-regional one. In the latter context the pattern of unemployment across regions was of most concern but attention was also paid to variations in activity rates by region.

In considering the activity rates of different regions a certain degree of care must be taken. The calculation of activity rates for adult, male employees by region produces a significant variation, from a high of 81% in the Midlands to a low of 67%

---

1   C. Greenhalgh, 'Labour Supply Functions for Married Women in GB', *EC,* August 1977.

2   Somewhat similar, but not identical, results can be found in R. McNabb, 'The Labour Force Participation of Married Women', *MS,* September 1977.

3   J. Corkindale, 'The Decline of Employment in Metropolitan Areas' *DEG,* November 1977.

in Northern Ireland. However, with the inclusion of the self-employed, family
workers and the armed forces, the variation is much reduced, from a high of 89%
for the Midlands to a low of 83% for the south west. Refining the computations
further to take account of students and the aged, the regional variation virtually
disappears, to give the familiar result that nearly all prime age males are economically
active. Nevertheless, it is not without significance for the efficient allocation of
resources that as many as 16.4% of male workers in Northern Ireland were estimated
to be self-employed. The greater importance of agriculture in that region is unlikely
to account fully for such a high figure, and the suspicion exists that so much self-
employment represents considerable under-employment of labour resources.

For females the picture is more complicated. First, the variation in activity rates
between regions is much more pronounced. In 1961 rates for married female
employees varied from 34% in the north-west to only 17% in Wales.[1] An adjustment
for the self-employed, the aged and students does not, as with all female groups,
appreciably affect the picture. For unmarried females the rates are much higher and
have a smaller regional variation; nevertheless in 1961 they varied from 54% in both
the Midlands and Scotland to 41% in Wales. A second feature of the pattern of
regional employment for females is that the rise in activity rates has been particularly
pronounced in those regions with very low rates initially. Consequently, regional
variation is being progressively reduced.

I.4   Employment by Industry and Occupation

In September 1977, the manufacturing sector of the British economy employed
only 33% of all employees at work.[2] Adding the number of employees in agriculture,
mining, construction and gas, electricity and water we still get only 43% of all
employees, implying that the service sector now accounts for well over half of the
employment in the country. The tendency for the service sector labour force to
grow relative to the whole labour force began in the mid-1950s when the manufacturing and service sectors each employed about 42.5% of the total number of
employees. The marked absolute decline in manufacturing employment began in
1966. In that year, manufacturing employment stood at 8.4 million; subsequently
it has fallen in nearly every year (1969, 1973, 1974 and 1977 are the exceptions)
and in nearly every individual manufacturing grouping, so that in January 1978
there were only 7.2 million workers employed in manufacturing.[3]

Within the service sector the main growth areas have been professional and
scientific services, particularly in education and medical and dental services. In the
ten years to June 1976, the numbers employed in education and medicine rose by
nearly one million. Some service sectors have become smaller over this period, for
example, transport and communications (due mainly to the rapid decline in railway
employment) but the general tendency is for growth.

Another way of examining the composition of the labour force is to examine
the division between the private and the public sectors. Over the period 1959 to
1975, there was an increase in the proportion of the labour force in the public

---

1 Bowers, op. cit., p. 22.
2 *DEG,* March 1978, p. 352.
3 Ibid.

sector from 25% to 29%. Within that aggregate figure there has been a substantial increase in the number of local authority workers (from 7.5% of the employed labour force in 1959 to 12.0% in 1975), a small decline in the number in public corporations (i.e. roughly, the nationalized industries) and a recent rise in the proportion of civilian employees working for central government.[1]

These structural changes are also reflected in the relative growth of female employment, referred to above, because much of the service sector has made intensive use of female labour. Thus, approximately 70% of the employees in professional and scientific services are female, as against 20% in agriculture and only 5% in mining and shipbuilding. It is true that the textile and clothing industries are also female-intensive, but their decline has not been great in comparison to the expansion of the service sector. It is also worth emphasizing that a significant number of females, particularly in the rapidly expanding service sectors, work only part-time. Thus, in June 1976, more than half of the 1.25m females working in education and 40% of the nearly 1m in medical and dental services were part-time workers.[2] This compares with only 24% for manufacturing and it may suggest that some of the sectoral shifts that have occurred are not a purposeful move away from manufacturing but the use of a previously unused labour reserve that would not be available for full-time work, or perhaps even for part-time work in other sectors.

I.5   Hours Worked

To clarify discussions of hours of work one should distinguish between normal basic hours, normal hours and actual hours of work. The first term relates to the number of hours a person is expected to work at basic rates of pay; the second includes any guaranteed overtime paid at premium rates; the third, and for most purposes much the most interesting notion, includes all overtime, guaranteed or not. Actual hours are typically in excess of normal hours, but by including absenteeism and sick days in the picture the situation may be reversed.

As with activity rates, two lines of enquiry can be distinguished for hours worked by the labour force as a whole. First, one wants to explain the trend; second, one wants to explain temporary variations around it. Further, it is revealing to examine the structure of hours worked, e.g. by occupation or wage level.

Over a long period average actual hours of work have fallen, from around sixty hours per week in the early part of the century to approximately forty-one hours by 1976. Initially, the fall was in hours per day; subsequent reductions have been first in days worked per week and second in weeks per year. There is therefore a clear tendency for extra leisure to be bunched, there being 'economies of scale' in leisure activities.

For many years, normal hours fell more rapidly than actual hours, implying an increase in the number of overtime hours. Thus, between 1948 and 1968 normal weekly hours of male manual workers fell from 44.5 to 40.1.[3] Actual hours in the same period tended to rise until the mid-1950s and fall thereafter. Since the late-1960s, however, normal hours have been relatively constant[4] but actual hours have

---

1   *ET*, February 1976, pp. 119-27 and *ET*, February 1977, pp. 78-81.
2   *DEG*, November 1977, pp. 1208-10.
3   *BLS*, p. 160.
4   *DEG*, March 1978, p. 381.

continued to fall, so that the gap between the two has fallen from over 6 hours per week in 1968 to 4 hours per week in 1976.

Hours of work fluctuate a good deal from year to year. The changing tempo of the economy is the principal explanation of these variations, with the length of work weeks falling in recessions and rising in expansions.

In the recession that began in 1974, the reduction in the work week, as measured by the percentage of operatives in British manufacturing who worked overtime,[1] was somewhat smaller than might have been expected. A possible explanation for this relative buoyancy in overtime working is the increasing burden of hiring and firing costs felt by employers, which makes them economize on the number of workers they employ.

There are wide variations between industries in actual hours worked. In 1975 the average annual hours worked per employee in Great Britain was 2,165 in construction as against 1,616 in mining.[2] Within manufacturing the range was from 1,995 in the bricks and pottery sector to 1,582 in clothing and footwear. It is also clear that operatives work more hours than white collar workers and males more than females.

Some of the variation observed in such a cross-section is due to the different industries being at different stages in their own business cycle. Additionally, some industries have relatively old labour forces whose work weeks are naturally shorter. Nevertheless, there are persistent real variations across industries and occupations in hours worked and these certainly affect the attractiveness of the different jobs. Some research work is beginning to explain such variations. In a recent study[3] it was shown for a sample of ninety-six industries in Britain that the number of hours offered by the average manual male worker was positively affected by the hourly wage rate and low skill levels and negatively affected by the number of fellow workers employed in the factory, residence in the south east and Midlands and residence in conurbations. Further, the number of work hours demanded from the male worker was greater when the worker was more skilled, aged between twenty-five and fifty-four and working in industries that were fast growing or highly concentrated; fewer hours were demanded from young males and from those who tended to work alongside females.

I.6   The Quality of the Labour Force

As time goes on, the average skill level of members of the labour force rises. This is one component of the increased quality of the working population, implying that, from a given number of workers and a given quantity of supporting factors of production, potential output grows over time. Other important sources of higher quality are better health levels, an improved spatial distribution of employment and, up to a point, shorter working weeks. In quantitative terms the increase in skill levels has had much the largest impact on productivity of any of these sources.

There is no precise, independent measure of the increase in average skill level in the UK over any period and no comprehensive indication of the allocative efficiency

---

1   *DEG*, March 1978, p. 370.
2   *DEG*, September 1977, p. 937.
3   D. Metcalf, S. Nickell and R. Richardson, 'The Structure of Hours and Earnings in British Manufacturing Industry', *OEP*, July 1976.

of labour between various skill levels. In recent years, however, a number of studies have been made, mainly of the educational system. The formal education sector is not the only source of skill augmentation but the model testing its efficiency has general applicability. The problem at issue may be described as follows. If the sector is organized efficiently the net social value of the marginal pound's expenditure will be the same for all types and levels of education. What we must do, therefore, is to equalize the social profit rate on all educational activities.

The terminology employed here may be disagreeable to some people. However, as long as account is taken of all sources of cost and benefit, whether they be material or psychic, there can be no real objection. It is true that some sources may not be measurable in practice and that others may be measured only imperfectly. These defects do not suggest that no measurement should take place, merely that decisions and judgements should not be based solely on what is measurable.

In fact the measurement of the profitability of education and training pro-grammes is decidedly imperfect. The usual measure of benefits is some estimate of the expected increase in monetary earnings enjoyed by the trainee, i.e. his expected full earnings minus the earnings he would otherwise expect were he not to undertake the training under consideration. To take a concrete example, in estimating the profitability of a university degree a comparison is made between the observed earnings of people already graduated and those of people who stopped just short of going to university. This provides an earnings differential for each age group which stands for the earnings increase expected by the current trainee at each stage of his working life.

This estimate is extremely crude and a number of adjustments can be made to improve upon it. For example, not all of the crude differential can be attributed to education because ability and motivation levels differ between the two groups from which the data are drawn. Consequently, an effort should be made to estimate the independent effect of ability differences.

Once the estimate of benefits has been obtained it is necessary to estimate the costs of the training. The principal cost is the output that could have been produced by the trainee had he been in full-time work. Its value is usually measured by the monetary earnings he forgoes while being trained or educated. Added to the forgone earnings are the direct costs of instruction, represented by salaries of teachers, cost of buildings, etc.

The two most substantial research efforts for the UK are by Blaug[1] and Morris and Ziderman[2] and both contain a clear account of the procedures and difficulties involved. The latter was more comprehensive and among its conclusions were (1) that postgraduate qualifications were not very profitable for society and (2) that higher national certificates were very profitable indeed. If these calculations are correct they imply that society would be better off if there were more resources involved in HNC work and less in postgraduate work. At present, these calculations suggest, the UK educational system is inefficiently structured and is turning out the wrong mix of graduates.

The importance of adequate supplies of skilled labour has been increasingly

1   M. Blaug, 'The Rate of Return on Investment in Education in Great Britain', *MS*, September 1965.
2   V. Morris and A. Ziderman, 'The Economic Return on Investment in Higher Education in England and Wales', *ET*, no. 211, May 1971.

recognized in public discussion in the last ten to fifteen years. In 1964 the Industrial Training Act was passed in an attempt to increase the quantity of skilled manpower and improve the quality of training. Under the Act, Industrial Training Boards were set up for a number of industries. The Boards impose a levy on the firms in the industry and with the proceeds approved training schemes are financed. More recently the government has set up the Training Services Agency with substantial funds to provide a wide range of training programmes. None of these attempts to improve the skill structure has yet been evaluated very thoroughly.

I.7 Unemployment

On 9 February 1978, there were 1,509,000 persons registered as unemployed in the UK, or 6.3% of all employees.[1] The male unemployment rate was 7.6%, the female unemployment rate was 4.4%. Unemployment has grown considerably in recent years. From the end of the Second World War to the mid-1960s the unemployment rate rarely exceeded 2.0%; since 1967, it has never been below 2.0% and has averaged more than 3.5%.

It has become a major focus of labour market analysis to explain and assess these increases as well as the structural changes that have accompanied them. In order to do this it is first necessary to understand some institutional details. The monthly count of the registered unemployed refers to those who have reported to an Employment Office or 'Jobcentre' during the month and are, on the day of the count (now the second Thursday of the month) classified as 'being capable of and available for' full-time work. There are two principal reasons for registering: (i) to become eligible for cash benefits (e.g. unemployment benefit and supplementary benefit) and to be excused National Insurance contributions while out of work, and (ii) to obtain help in finding a job.

It is known that the register includes some who are, in practice, not capable of or available for work, and excludes others who are. The usual indicator of unemployment is therefore an inaccurate measure of those who wish to work at current wages and its degree of bias is quite likely to change over time and between areas.

Those who are on the register but are not capable of and available for work include (i) those committing fraud by simultaneously being in work (perhaps on a self-employed or casual basis) and claiming cash benefits, (ii) the 'workshy', (iii) older persons in receipt of occupational pensions who wish to have their National Insurance contributions paid for them so as to be eligible in the future for the full state retirement pension, (iv) some of those classified as partially disabled, and (v) the truly 'unemployable'. There are few pieces of reliable information on the extent of these categories, but the official view is that they are not likely to be numerous or volatile.[2] One indication is given in the annual General Household Survey, which reported for 1972 (1973) that 7% (11%) of males and 18% (28%) of females on the register described themselves as economically inactive, i.e. would presumably not take a job if one were offered.

In addition to these 'registered non-unemployed', there are many non-registered unemployed. It is thought that the latter are usually ineligible, or think themselves

---

1 *DEG,* March 1978, p. 335.
2 *DEG,* March 1975, pp. 179-83.

to be ineligible, for cash benefits, and so do not bother to register. The largest group here have been those wives who have chosen not to pay the full National Insurance contribution when previously at work. (This option is being phased out from April 1978, on the introduction of the new pension scheme. Unregistered female unemployment will therefore tend to decline in future.) In addition, there are young people and, perhaps, the formerly self-employed. Some idea of their numbers can be gained from the Censuses of Population and the General Household Surveys. These suggest that unregistered male unemployment was nearly 30% of total male unemployment in 1966, and had fallen to under 10% in 1971; the corresponding figures for females were 57% and 33%. From the GHS it is estimated that unregistered male unemployment, as a percentage of the total, rose from 9% in 1972 to 17% in 1973; for females, the change was from 52% to 66%. This further suggests that the relative importance of unregistered unemployment varies positively with the business cycle, so that when the economy contracts, a higher percentage of the total unemployment appears on the register.[1]

Why, then, has registered unemployment tended to be high in recent years? It is quite clear that the dominant reason for the high unemployment has been the relatively depressed state of aggregate demand in the economy. The latter can be measured directly by growth rates in real income or indirectly by unfilled job vacancies. It is, however, unlikely to be the only reason and there are many who question the consistency of the unemployment figures over time. The discussion may best be summarized by considering the observed relationship between unemployment and job vacancies.

For many years, the unemployment/vacancy relationship was thought to be reliable, stable and inverse; as unemployment rose, vacancies fell, and vice versa. Starting at the end of 1966, it has seemed to many observers that the relationship has disintegrated, with much more unemployment being associated with a given level of vacancies. A number of explanations for the changed relationship have been advanced but many of them are suspect because they apply equally to both sexes, whereas the unemployment/vacancy relationship has changed *only* for males and *not* for females (at least until 1975).[2] The most popular surviving explanations of the changed relationship are (i) that increased unemployment benefits, primarily affecting male workers, have raised the duration of unemployment, by relieving the pressure on workers to take an early job offer, and (ii) that incomes policies have tended to erode wage differentials and have tended to price younger and unskilled workers out of jobs. These possibilities are difficult to quantify and there is no agreement on how much of the changed relationship they explain. The official view, as expressed by a working party in the *DEG*,[3] is that the relationship has not in fact changed very much. Their argument, illustrated in figure 5.1, is that since 1966 we have explored a new part of the always existing relationship; the reason we have done this is that since the mid-1960s, the economy has tended to grow relatively slowly, so that we have had relatively few vacancies more or less continuously (with the exception of 1973-4, which remains, on this view, highly problematical). Apart

1 A. Evans, 'Notes on the Changing Relationships between Registered Unemployment and Notified Vacancies', *EG*, May 1977, pp. 179-96.
2 For a discussion of some of the alternative explanations see *DEG*, October 1976, pp. 1093-9.
3 Ibid.

from the experience of 1973-4, when there were relatively many vacancies but, by historical standards, quite heavy unemployment, the principal weakness of this interpretation is the absence of similar developments in the female unemployment/vacancy relationship.

To summarize, there is still controversy as to why, and even whether, the unemployment/vacancy relationship has changed. If it has changed, it may be unwise to see the unemployment figures as a structurally stable series, pointing to an unchanged attainable level of unemployment that is consistent with economic stability.

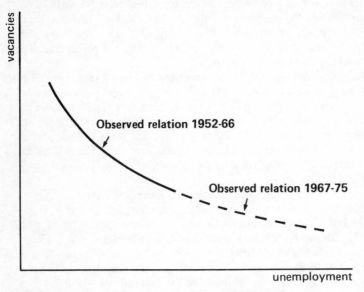

Figure 5.1   Male unemployment/vacancy relationship for GB, 1952-75

Apart from attempts to analyse the unemployment/vacancy relationship, there has been some work done in trying to measure the impact on unemployment of changes in the unemployment benefit and supplementary benefit levels. The most convincing, but doubtless not the final, analysis of this question concludes that higher benefits have clearly raised registered unemployment, but not by very much.[1] Specifically, on the basis of the empirical findings, we would expect a 20% rise in unemployment from 1964 to 1971 and a 3% rise in unemployment from 1966 to 1973 due to benefit effects. Since the percentage of males registered as unemployed rose by 270% in the first interval and 50% in the second, we, clearly, have not explained very much of the change. In addition, it was estimated that the introduction in 1966 of Earnings Related Supplement (an addition to the flat rate unemployment benefit for the relatively highly paid) raised registered unemployment by a further 10%.

1   S. Nickell, 'The Effect of Unemployment & Related Benefits on the Duration of Unemployment', *EJ*, 1979.

At any given time, unemployed workers are likely to have certain characteristics. Thus, in a recent study of male unemployment rate differences between seventy-eight English towns in 1971[1] it was found that unemployment rates were higher in those towns with relatively many unskilled workers and older workers and lower where there are relatively large numbers of married workers and immigrants. In the current recession the structure of the unemployed has changed in certain respects. Thus, in January 1978 there were nearly twice as many unemployed males below the age of thirty as there had been five years earlier; for the over-thirties the increase over the same period was only about 40%.[2] Also, there has been a very much larger increase in female unemployment than in male unemployment; between October 1973 and February 1978, female unemployment grew by nearly 350%, while male unemployment grew by 130%.[3] Some observers have suggested that this latter difference might be a result of equal pay and opportunities legislation (see section II.6 below). While these acts might have played some part, it must also be noted that during the same period the ratio of female to male *employment* continued to grow, albeit at a slightly reduced pace, which might itself be fully explained as a typical reaction in a contracting economy.

The recent rise in unemployment is largely caused by the increase in the average duration of unemployment experienced by each individual. For example, between October 1974 and October 1977, the proportion of male unemployed workers who had been out of work for more than twenty-six weeks rose from 35% of the register to 42%.[4] However, it remains true, even during the current recession, that the gross flows joining and leaving the register each month are very large. In the second half of 1975, when registered unemployment was increasing rapidly (by more than 40,000 per month), the number joining the register each month averaged about 375,000 and the number leaving the register, most of them to go to jobs, averaged about 335,000. These flow figures emphasize that the unemployed are not an unchanging group but are rapidly changing, even in recessions.

In the face of the great increase in unemployment after 1974, the UK government, in common with many governments abroad, introduced and has progressively widened the coverage of a whole range of specific measures designed to alleviate the situation.[5] Some of the measures have focused on the supply of labour, others have focused on demand.

The first of these schemes, starting in August 1975, was the Temporary Employment Subsidy (TES). Under the initial terms of this, a subsidy was paid of £10 per week, for a three-month period, for every full-time job maintained by firms who were prepared to defer planned redundancies involving fifty or more workers. Thus, the scheme was designed to keep in work some of those who would otherwise have been made redundant. Subsequently, the scheme was extended from the assisted areas (i.e. areas of high unemployment) to include the whole of Britain, and the amount and duration of the subsidy was increased. It was officially estimated that

1 D. Metcalf, 'Urban Unemployment in England', *EJ*, September 1975.
2 *DEG*, March 1978, p. 362.
3 *DEG*, March 1978, p. 354.
4 *DEG*, November 1977, p. 1303.
5 Details and occasional evaluations of the schemes are given in a number of issues of the *DEG* after August 1975.

the operation of TES took 132,000 workers off the unemployment register in 1977.[1]
It is notable, however, that the greater part of the total expenditure on TES went to
the textile, clothing and footwear industries. This raised opposition from fellow
EEC countries, who claimed that the scheme led to unfair competition from these
industries, and the scheme was modified in March 1978.[2]

In September 1975, other specific measures were announced. The Job Creation
programme was initially designed to provide labour-intensive projects, particularly
for young people, in areas of high unemployment. The aim was to develop projects,
like cleaning beaches, that would not be undertaken in the absence of the scheme;
in this way it was hoped that Job Creation projects would not displace other
workers.

In addition, there was a recruitment subsidy scheme to raise the demand for
school leavers, expanded training programmes (again with an emphasis on the
young), and an expanded employment transfer scheme, designed to increase worker
migration from the high unemployment areas.

In September and October 1976 two further schemes were announced. The first
was the Job Release scheme, under which workers in assisted areas and near to
retirement age would be paid a tax-free allowance of £23 per week until they
reached retirement age providing they left their job and were replaced by a younger
registered unemployed worker. The second scheme was the Youth Employment
Subsidy, under which employers who hired young persons who had already been
unemployed for at least six months received £10 per week per worker hired, for a
period of up to twenty-six weeks.

In June 1977 the Youth Opportunities Programme was announced. This was
designed to consolidate and expand existing schemes and was focused on both
employment provision and training and education. More recently, consideration has
been given to further early retirement measures and to work-sharing schemes. Some
pressure has built up, but no official action seems likely, to discourage the use of
overtime.

Evaluating any or all of these schemes is difficult. Broadly, the accepted view is
that in comparison with an equivalent amount of money being spent on general
reflation (e.g. by cutting taxes) these schemes provide somewhat more jobs somewhat sooner. This conclusion is based on the facts that the programmes are
explicitly labour-intensive and direct. They also allow the government to focus on
groups thought to be particularly badly hit by the recession, e.g. the young. The
principal disadvantage of the schemes is that the output produced, e.g. under Job
Creation, may not be particularly worthwhile compared to that which would come
from an equivalent general reflation.

II   WEALTH, INCOME AND PAY

The distribution of wealth, income and earnings are topics which excite great
controversy. In this section we describe the (unequal) distributions of wealth,
income and pay and discuss some of the theories advanced to account for these
distributions. Our analysis of labour earnings looks at the pay-structure by industry,
occupation and sex, wages in local labour markets and poverty and low pay.

---

1   *DEG*, December 1977, p. 1378.
2   For details see *DEG*, March 1978, p. 275.

II.1   Distribution of Wealth[1]

The measurement of personal wealth, and its distribution, is notoriously difficult. There are three main methods by which the distribution of personal wealth can be estimated. First, a sample survey could be undertaken of individuals' assets and liabilities to determine net wealth (sometimes referred to as net worth). Such a survey is desirable in principle but would be difficult to execute because of such problems as a low response rate and the difficulty of determining the composition and valuation of items to be included in wealth. Second, the investment income method works backwards from statistics on investment income to determine the distribution of capital from which this investment income is derived. Third, under the present British tax system the only time an individual's wealth becomes known is at death when a return is filed for capital transfer tax. These estate returns to the Inland Revenue form the basis of most of our knowledge on the distribution of wealth. The calculations assume that the wealth of the individuals who die comprises a sample of the assets of the living. Some problems with this approach will be elaborated below.

The Inland Revenue wealth data based on estate returns demonstrate the inequality in the distribution of wealth. In 1975 this conventional measure showed that the richest 1% of the adult (aged eighteen and over) population owned 23% of the personal wealth and the richest 10% owned 63% of the wealth. In absolute terms the Inland Revenue estimated personal wealth in 1975 to be £190 billion, which implies an average holding of about £9,000 per head of the adult population identified as having any wealth; or £4,500 per head of the total adult population (see table 5.1). There were 29,000 individuals with assets worth £200,000 or more, and on average these people possessed wealth valued at £420,000 − some fifty times the overall average. These figures refer to individual wealth. Clearly, if wealthy men marry wealthy women the distribution of wealth among families is likely to be yet more concentrated.

The main items comprising the 1975 figure of personal wealth (£190 billion) are dwellings (43%), securities and shares (10%) and life assurance policies (15%). The relative importance of each item varies according to the range of net wealth. For example, National Savings and household goods account for a relatively high proportion of the wealth of the poorest groups while shares and land are more important for richer people.

One graphic method describing the extent of some wealth holdings is to compare such holdings with lifetime earnings. This comparison below ignores taxes and inflation: it merely brings out some rough orders of magnitude. In 1975 adult manual earnings were approximately £3,000 p.a. If an individual entered the labour force in 1975, worked for fifty years and received £3,000 per year plus real growth in earnings of 1% per year his (undiscounted) earnings after a lifetime of work would total about £200,000. In contrast we see (table 5.1) that in 1975 29,000

---

1 The three main sources for the discussion contained in this section are A. B. Atkinson, *The Economics of Inequality*, Oxford University Press, 1975; Royal Commission on the Distribution of Income and Wealth (Chairman Lord Diamond), *Initial Report on the Distribution of Income and Wealth*, Cmnd. 6171, HMSO, 1975 and *Report No. 5*, Cmnd. 6999, HMSO, 1977. These are referred to as Atkinson, RC(1) and RC(5) respectively. See also A. B. Atkinson and A. J. Harrison, *Distribution of Personal Wealth in Britain*, Cambridge UP, 1978.

individuals had personal wealth of at least £200,000. These individuals comprise the richest 0.1% in Britain. If their wealth brought no annual return these people could nevertheless sustain a consumption level equivalent to that of the typical worker even if they opted for a life of leisure. In fact, most forms of wealth do

TABLE 5.1
Inland Revenue Estimates of Personal Wealth, UK, 1975

Range of net wealth (lower limit) (£)	Total		Males		Females	
	Number (000)	Amount (£000m)	Number (000)	Amount (£000m)	Number (000)	Amount (£000m)
Nil	3,463	1.9	1,767	0.9	1,695	1.0
1,000	4,849	8.9	2,719	5.2	2,129	3.7
3,000	2,514	10.0	1,429	5.7	1,085	4.3
5,000	4,707	34.6	3,050	22.5	1,657	12.1
10,000	2,688	33.0	1,762	21.7	926	11.3
15,000	1,038	18.4	605	10.5	433	7.9
20,000	603	13.8	350	8.0	253	5.8
25,000	809	28.1	462	16.9	347	11.2
50,000	252	18.2	131	10.6	120	7.5
100,000	69	11.1	40	6.6	29	4.5
200,000	29	12.2	18	7.3	12	5·0
Under 10,000	15,533	55.4	8,965	34.3	6,566	21.1
10,000 and over	5,488	134.8	3,368	81.6	2,120	53.2
Total	21,020	190.3	12,333	115.9	8,687	74.3

Source: RC(5), p. 69.

bring an annual return and there are around 100,000 people who could sustain such a consumption level without ever working by virtue of the return of their holdings and the gradual erosion of their wealth over their lifetime.

These data also show a trend towards greater equality in the distribution of wealth at particular points in time. The share of the richest 1% (10%) has declined from 69% (92%) in 1911-13 to 23% (62%) in 1975.

Share of personal wealth owned by top percentage of adult population		
	Top 1%	Top 10%
1911-13	69	92
1924-30	62	91
1936-38	56	88
1954	43	79
1960	38	77
1966	32	72
1972	30	72
1975	23	62

Source: RC(1) and RC(2), p. 76.

There are a number of reasons why the degree of inequality in the distribution of wealth measured at particular intervals has lessened over this century. First, the rates of estate duty have risen steeply: Atkinson states that in 1911 an estate of £1 million paid duty of 14% while in the early 1970s the rate was 75%; it seems likely that such an increase in tax liability has sharpened the incentive to avoid the duty by distributing the estate among heirs prior to death. Second, the proportion of owner-occupied dwellings has risen from around 10% in 1900 to over 50% in the 1970s and this, coupled with the rise in house prices, has caused a sharp narrowing in the distribution of (net) wealth. Third, it is likely that some of the reduction in top wealth holdings between 1972 and 1974 is attributable to the decline in share prices in 1973-4. It cannot be assumed that the trend towards a more equal distribution of wealth will automatically persist in the future: if the rate of increase in the proportion of householders who are owner-occupiers declines, or if house prices fall significantly, or if share prices rise dramatically people will have to look at alternative measures, such as the proposed wealth tax or the capital transfer tax, to ensure that the trend towards a more equal distribution of wealth is sustained.

The Royal Commission have made a number of corrections to the Inland Revenue data. In particular if we treat wealth in terms of its income-yielding characteristics, the imputed value of the future stream of benefits locked away in occupational and state pension schemes can be allowed for. This modification causes the share of personal wealth accounted for by the richest 1% (10%) to decline to 14% (40%) while the share of the bottom 80% is calculated to rise from 28% on the Inland Revenue basis to 46% on this adjusted basis. This is because all members of the adult population are counted as having accrued rights to state pensions.

It is an open question whether wealth in the form of future pension rights should be included in these calculations and, if they should be included, the method by which they should be calculated. Unlike wealth held as stock, land, houses, etc., this (anticipated future) wealth is not marketable (if it were marketable, ownership of one individual by another would be implied). Further, if we are prepared to impute a value to the stream of future pension benefits why not also impute the (non-saleable) wealth associated with being a member of a powerful craft union or that which occurs because of individual investment in education or health?

The attempts to explain the current (cross section or snapshot) distribution of wealth have concentrated mainly on the pattern of wealth accumulation over the life cycle and on inheritance.[1] Polanyi and Wood emphasize the role of the life-cycle pattern of savings and asset accumulation. Even if income and inheritance were equal, some inequality in wealth would occur because older people would have saved absolutely larger amounts than younger people. This factor is important (on reasonable assumptions it can generate a situation where 10% of the population in this egalitarian society hold 30% of the wealth) but it is far from the whole story. In particular, the distribution of wealth within age groups is itself concentrated and similar to the overall wealth distribution, yet if the life-cycle explanation is correct we should find higher wealth holdings occurring disproportionately in the older age groups.

The Royal Commission undertook a survey of 238 estates of £15,000 or more receiving probate in 1973 in order to assess the workings of inheritance. It showed

---

1 For a discussion of life-cycle accumulation, see G. Polanyi and J. Wood, *How much Inequality?* Institute of Economic Affairs, London, 1974 and J. S. Flemming and I. M. D. Little, *Why we need a Wealth Tax,* Methuen, 1974. For an analysis of the role of inheritance, see C. D. Harbury and P. C. McMahon 'Inheritance and the distribution of personal wealth in Britain', *EJ,* vol. 83, 1973, and RC(5), chapters 5, 8 and 9.

that in most estates, irrespective of size, the major part of disposable property is bequeathed to relatives. The pattern of accumulation of savings based on lifetime earnings was much less than wealth holdings at the top of the wealth distribution. This confirms the view that rich people inherit a disproportionate amount of their wealth.

II.2   Distribution of Income

The distribution of total income from all sources (i.e. from employment, pensions, dividends, etc.) is less concentrated than the distribution of wealth. This is because earnings from employment are the main source of total personal income and these earnings are more equally distributed than the investment income provided by personal wealth.

The composition of total personal income in the UK may be seen from the following figures:[1]

Source of Income	Percentage distribution	
	1966	*1976*
Employment	71.6	70.9
Self-employment	8.4	9.2
Rent, dividends, interest, etc.	11.4	9.0
Social security benefits, etc.	8.6	10.9
Total personal income	100.0	100.0

The main change which has occurred in the last decade is the increased importance of social security and other state benefits in total personal income. This mainly reflects the higher unemployment levels prevailing in the 1970s and the larger number of pensioners and higher pensions.

The distribution of personal incomes is shown in table 5.2. The data are derived from the Inland Revenue supplemented by information from the Family Expenditure Survey on incomes which are not taxable (for example, unemployment benefits) or are below the tax threshold. The data refer to tax units, i.e. generally treat a married couple as one unit. It will be seen that in 1974-5 two-thirds of pre-tax incomes were between £1,000 and £4,000 and only 10.9% of the 28m tax units had incomes over £4,000. The fact that there are relatively few people with high incomes makes the redistribution of income, and greater provision of desirable health and education services, difficult. While it may be possible to squeeze many thousands of pounds out of a rich individual, there are not many of them so that the extra revenue raised by squeezing them harder is quite small.

The bottom part of table 5.2 provides information enabling us to compare the distribution of incomes and wealth. The top 10% (1%) of *individual* wealth holders accounted for 62% (23%) of conventionally defined wealth in 1972 (section II.1). In contrast the top 10% (1%) of the income distribution of *tax units* accounts for only 26.6% (6.2%) of total income before tax and 23.0% (4.0%) after tax. Thus income distribution is much less concentrated than the distribution of wealth.

---

1 *Source: ST,* No. 8, 1977, table 6.2.

TABLE 5.2

Distribution of Personal Incomes before and after Tax UK, 1974-5

	By range of income before tax			By range of income after tax		
	Numbers of tax units (000s)	Income before tax (£m)	Income after tax (£m)	Numbers of tax units (000s)	Income before tax (£m)	Income after tax (£m)
Income ranges						
Lower limit of range (£)						
Under 625	2,073	1,122	1,122	2,077	1,126	1,122
625	1,591	1,145	1,139	1,706	1,234	1,219
750	2,919	2,593	2,539	3,489	3,246	3,092
1,000	2,682	3,027	2,841	3,304	4,093	3,723
1,250	1,976	2,719	2,454	2,506	4,004	3,447
1,500	1,663	2,705	2,341	2,322	4,519	3,779
1,750	1,807	3,381	2,861	2,126	4,775	3,982
2,000	3,452	7,730	6,472	3,874	10,469	8,680
2,500	3,067	8,409	6,949	2,865	9,537	7,833
3,000	3,966	13,635	11,099	2,806	11,971	9,528
4,000	1,681	7,432	5,834	658	3,852	2,905
5,000	623	3,374	2,573	285	2,179	1,538
6,000	435	2,953	2,167	177	1,979	1,204
8,000	148	1,313	893	55	948	487
10,000	66	719	449	16	394	172
12,000	53	708	397	5	181	69
15,000	39	650	342	2	99	32
20,000 and over	33	1,060	356	1	69	16
All ranges	28,274	64,675	52,828	28,274	64,675	52,828

	Pre-tax income (Percentages)			Post-tax income (Percentages)		
Quantile shares						
Top 1%	6.2			4.0		
2–5%	10.6			9.7		
6–10%	9.8			9.5		
Top 10%	26.6			23.2		
11–20%	15.8			15.8		
21–30%	13.1			13.2		
31–40%	11.0			11.4		
41–50%	9.3			9.4		
51–60%	7.6			7.6		
61–70%	5.8			6.4		
71–80%	4.6			5.3		
81–90%	3.6			4.4		
91–100%	2.6			3.1		
Median (£)	1,913			1,604		

Source: ST, No. 8, 1977, table 6.6.

TABLE 5.3

Redistribution of Income through Taxes and Benefits, UK, 1975

Average in each range of original income (£ per year)	Range of original income (£ per year)										Average over all income ranges
	under 381	381–	557–	816–	1,194–	1,749–	2,561–	3,750–	5,490–	8,038 and above	
Original income	102	470	687	995	1,480	2,185	3,176	4,561	6,505	10,569	3,386
Direct benefits in cash: (+)	930	806	853	771	543	361	200	145	131	125	377
Original income and cash benefits	1,032	1,276	1,540	1,766	2,023	2,546	3,376	4,706	6,636	10,694	3,763
Direct taxes: (−)											
National insurance, employees contributions	—	—	5	13	44	86	143	192	252	296	130
Income tax and surtax	1	26	60	100	172	289	497	803	1,273	2,671	617
Disposable income	1,031	1,251	1,475	1,653	1,807	2,171	2,736	3,712	5,111	7,727	3,016
Indirect benefits (housing and food subsidies) (+)	149	132	105	107	112	119	107	90	91	79	109
Indirect taxes (−)	203	281	295	350	413	514	594	763	1,004	1,388	619
Income after all taxes and transfers	977	1,102	1,285	1,410	1,506	1,776	2,249	3,039	4,198	6,418	2,506
Direct benefits in kind: (+)											
Education	74	218	87	135	172	250	288	343	375	345	258
National health service	200	205	228	210	195	228	234	217	230	246	220
Welfare foods	8	6	6	10	14	16	18	20	16	15	16
Income after all taxes and benefits	1,259	1,531	1,606	1,765	1,887	2,270	2,789	3,619	4,819	7,024	3,000

Source: ST, no. 8, 1977, table 6.22.

Nevertheless, the share of the top 20% of the income distribution, with 42.4% of income, is seven times the share of the bottom 20% who account for only 6.2% of the total. Likewise, the top half of the income distribution has three times the share of the bottom half. It should be borne in mind that these figures refer to the current distribution: many of those in the bottom half of the distribution in 1974-5 (e.g. some pensioners and students) will be in the top half at other points in their life. The inequality in lifetime incomes is less than the inequality of the income distribution observed at any particular point in time.

The government attempts to redress some of the inequality in income via taxes on income and expenditure and benefits in cash and in the form of services such as education and health. The relationship between taxes paid and income, and benefits received and income, is given in table 5.3. All taxes combined (rows with minus signs) are only modestly progressive (with a progressive tax system the ratio of tax paid to income received rises as incomes rises; the reverse is true for a regressive system). This is because although income tax is progressive, National Insurance contributions by employees and indirect taxes are regressive.

Social service benefits as a whole are very progressive (rows with a plus sign). The direct cash benefits consist mainly of social security payments. Other social service benefits include the National Health Service, education and housing and food subsidies.

It should be noted, however, that richer groups get the largest direct benefits from education and the NHS. Those households with incomes over £3,750 in 1975 received education services worth around £350, some £100 greater than the average. This reflects in part the greater likelihood of their children staying at school beyond the age of sixteen.

Atkinson and the Royal Commission provide evidence on trends through time in the distribution of income. The biggest change in recent years occurred between 1938 and 1949 when the pre-tax share of the top 1% fell by one third and the share of the top 10% fell from 40.5% to 32.1%. Subsequently the share of the top 10% has continued to fall but at a very modest and decelerating pace.

It is interesting to note (table 5.4) that the decreased pre-tax share of the rich has not resulted in an *equivalent* gain for the poor. The middle income groups have also

TABLE 5.4
Distribution of Income before and after Tax UK, 1959 and 1974-5

	Percentage share of total income (by tax unit)			
	Before tax		After tax	
	Top 10%	Bottom 30%	Top 10%	Bottom 30%
1959	29.4	9.7	25.2	11.2
1974-5	26.6	10.8	23.2	12.8

Source: RC(5), table 5.

increased their share in pre-tax total income. The increased pre-tax income share of the middle 60% is probably due to two important postwar features of the labour market. First, the pre-1975 full-employment policy ensured that there was not a large number of workers forced into the lower tail of the distribution by prolonged unemployment. Second, the increased labour-force participation rates of married women have boosted the family incomes of those of labour-force age.

The income figures presented and discussed in this section should be treated cautiously for the following reasons: (i) the data ignore income in the form of imputed rent from owner-occupied houses, fringe benefits, home production and capital gains; (ii) the data are uncorrected for tax evasion and misreporting; (iii) the data refer to money but not real incomes. This is important because inflation affects people differently according to the basket of goods they consume. For example over the last twenty years the prices of housing, food and fuel have risen faster than the overall index of retail prices. As pensioners and low-income families spend relatively large amounts of money on these items the changes in the distribution of real incomes will be different from those in the distribution of money incomes; (iv) income alone does not capture other aspects of welfare such as leisure, security and job satisfaction; (v) family composition has changed over time such that there are now more old and young people living alone; this will tend to increase the dispersion in income observed over time; (vi) the data refer to current and not lifetime income distributions.

II.3   Distribution of Earnings

The distribution of earnings, like the distribution of income, is positively skewed (median earnings are less than mean earnings). However, the earnings distribution is more equal than the distribution of income because the latter includes a return on wealth which, as we have seen (section II.1), is very concentrated.

The dispersion of earnings in April 1977 (full-time workers, men aged twenty-one and over, women aged eighteen and over, whose pay for the survey week was not affected by absence) was as follows.[1]

	Median earnings per week (£)			As a % of median		
		Lowest decile	Lower quartile	Upper quartile	Highest decile	Mean
Men	72.3	68.1	81.4	125.6	157.6	108.8
Women	46.9	68.6	82.1	124.7	162.1	108.6

Both men and women towards the bottom of the distribution (specifically those at the lowest 10% point) earned two-thirds of median pay while the best-paid 10% earned around half (men) or two thirds (women) more than the corresponding median.

There are two particularly important and interesting facts concerning the

---

1   DE, *New Earnings Survey 1977 DEG,* October 1977. (See also *DEG,* June 1977.) The data discussed in this section refer to individuals, not families or Inland Revenue income units. Many people only work part time or only work part of the year and therefore the distribution of annual earnings of those who worked at any time during the year is different from the distribution above because the annual earnings distribution has a concentration of people in the lower tail.

distribution of gross weekly earnings of male manual workers. First, the dispersion
of the distribution has been quite stable for almost a century:[1]

| | *Distribution of weekly earnings, manual men (% of median)* | | | |
	1886	*1938*	*1965*	*1977*
Lowest decile	68.6	67.7	69.7	70.6
Lower quartile	82.8	82.1	82.9	83.1
Median	100.0	100.0	100.0	100.0
Upper quartile	121.7	118.5	121.4	120.3
Highest decile	143.1	139.9	143.9	144.4

This stability suggests that we might seek to explain the distribution of earnings by
factors such as differences in ability, motivation and luck, which might be expected
to remain fairly stable from one generation to the next, rather than by appeal to
institutional factors such as the growth of unions, or social forces such as the
extension of public intervention, which have changed dramatically in the last
century.

Second, the position an individual occupies in the distribution changes from year
to year. Evidence on the gross weekly earnings of all full-time adults who were in
the New Earnings Surveys in 1970 to 1974 (*DEG,* January 1977) indicates that the
lowest-paid workers received by far the largest percentage increase in earnings
between one survey and the next, while the higher-paid workers tended to experience
much smaller percentage increases. Such movements are known as 'regression
towards the mean'. Between 1970 and 1974 21% of male manual workers were in
the lowest paid tenth in at least one of the five surveys, but only 3% were in this
tenth in all of the surveys. These movements refer to weekly earnings of full-time
workers and therefore reflect the variable nature of many components of manual
workers' earnings (e.g. overtime, short-time bonuses, piecework), the effects of job
changes and the incidence of wage settlements. Movements in individuals' hourly
earnings, which may more nearly reflect skill and motivation, or in annual earnings,
which may reflect the incidence of unemployment, could be more or less dramatic
than the fluctuations in weekly earnings.

One important explanation of the skewed distribution of earnings relates to the
coupling of natural ability and training. In a smoothly functioning, competitive
labour market, earnings will reflect productivity at the margin. Among all the
determinants of marginal productivity we may concentrate here on a worker's
'natural ability' and training. If, for a given level of formal training, a man comes
to the labour market with relatively great motivation, ability and drive he will tend
to earn more than the average worker. Further, it is established that on average the
more naturally gifted man tends to undertake more than average amounts of

---

1 *Social Trends,* No. 6, 1975, table 5.15. 1977 data refer to GB, other years refer to UK. A
   very full discussion of the evidence on the distribution of earnings and evaluation of theories
   seeking to explain this distribution is contained in A. R. Thatcher, 'The New Earnings
   Survey and the Distribution of Earnings', in A. Atkinson (ed.), *The Personal Distribution of
   Incomes,* Allen and Unwin, 1975. E. H. Phelps Brown, *The Inequality of Pay,*
   Oxford UP, 1977, contains much evidence on this topic.

training. An unskewed distribution of ability combined with a skewed distribution of training produces a skewed distribution of productivity. The last, in an approximately competitive market, produces a skewed earnings distribution.

This simple picture is only a partial explanation of the actual earnings distribution. First, not everyone has equal access to the educational and training sectors, even where natural ability is the same for all. One implication is that relatively bright working-class children have difficulty in getting sufficient secondary and advanced education. This means that ability is not properly harnessed with education, thereby reducing the degree of earnings inequality.

Second, in some activities, including many of the professions, free entry of labour is restricted and earnings are pushed above the competitive level. This will raise inequality, at least as measured by comparing the bottom 20% of wage-earners with the top 20%, because the low paid can only rarely restrict entry.

Third, luck plays a significant part in determining earnings, particularly in any one year. The last qualification is important because a more valid measure of material well-being than current earnings is the discounted sum of lifetime earnings. If a man is lucky one year but unlucky the next we would have a misleading view of his well-being by looking at either year in isolation. Similarly, if a man is receiving a low wage currently because he is training, but expected to do well when he is trained, it would be mistaken to view him as a poverty case. The same may apply to people approaching retirement. When measured by lifetime earnings the distribution of material rewards is substantially more equal than when measured in cross-section by current earnings.

There has recently become available in Britain a rich new data source, the General Household Survey, which provides each year information on individual earnings and related individual characteristics such as age, schooling, work experience, race and family background. Some research has been undertaken analysing this data.[1] Approximately one-third of the variation in the annual earnings of the 7,000 or so male employees in the survey is explained by years of schooling (for which the individual receives a compensating wage differential to make up for his forgone earnings while undertaking extra schooling) and work experience; these two variables measure the human capital embodied in the individual. A further third of the variance in earnings is explained by differences in the number of weeks worked in a year by each individual (which may itself be explained by human capital factors: for example, skilled workers experience less unemployment than unskilled workers).

One particularly important finding concerns the influence of colour and country of birth on pay. Other things being equal (i.e. holding constant age, experience, weeks worked, years of schooling, marital status, etc.), West Indian-born workers receive hourly earnings 14% lower than whites. Other non-whites receive, on average, some 30% less than whites. These differentials occur because black and brown workers tend (like women) to be crowded into low-paying occupations and industries. Thus while 58% of Pakistani males and 32% of West Indian males working in Britain are unskilled or semi-skilled, the corresponding figure for whites is 18%. Further, virtually no whites with degree-level qualifications do manual work but

1　Mark Stewart, 'The determinants of earnings in Britain', Centre for Labour Economics, LSE Discussion Paper No. 4, 1976; D. Piachaud, R. Layard, M. Stewart *et al.*, *The Causes of Poverty*, Background Paper to the Royal Commission on the Distribution of Income and Wealth, Report No. 6 on Lower Incomes, Cmnd. 7175, 1978.

around one fifth of such men from minorities do manual work, and minority men with high qualifications are much less likely than whites to be in professional and management occupations.[1]

This occupational structure discourages them from undertaking extra schooling or training because the pay-off to such investment is lower than it is for whites. Further, their occupational status may lead potential employers to conclude that non-whites are feckless when in fact their higher average turnover rate or higher average absenteeism rate are characteristics of their occupations and industries and not inherent racial characteristics. For example, a study of labour turnover at London Transport[2] showed that, other things being equal, blacks had a longer duration of employment than whites. It seems clear that the occupational composition of black and brown workers, as compared to white workers, will shortly (quite rightly) become a pressing policy issue. The problem is in many ways analogous to that facing women (see section II.6).

A nice contrast to the inferior economic status of non-white workers in Britain occurs if we examine the pay of the chief executives (i.e. highest-paid director) in UK companies in 1971. The highest-paid director in every industrial order was paid over £32,000 and the top man in the Green Shield Trading Stamp Company received £282,035. This executive pay information is quite new and has recently been analysed to determine the extent to which economic forces are important in explaining the pay structure of these top earners.[3] The main influence on pay is company size (measured by assets or sales) which alone explains half of the variance in chief executive salaries. The relationship between profitability and pay, while positive, is much weaker. Further, *ceteris paribus*, executives in monopolistic or oligopolistic industries (as measured by industrial concentration) do not receive higher rewards than those in other industries. The Confederation of British Industry and other employers' groups continually bemoan the low level of profitability of British industry. It would appear that some part of the remedy for this low profitability lies in their own hands; why not reward chief executives more on the basis of their company's profits and less on the basis of their size?

The Royal Commission on the Distribution of Income and Wealth has investigated the pay of very high earners.[4] In 1974-5 there were 65,000 individuals who earned £10,000 or above. They comprised 0.3% of the labour force and accounted for 2.1% of the total employment income received by all persons. Only one in fifty of these high earners were women. These people were disproportionately represented in London and the South East and tended to work in managerial occupations. The evidence shows that the inequality in the distribution of earnings has declined modestly since 1959. For example the pay of the highest millile (i.e. top 0.1%, implying in turn that the pay of 99.9% of males fell below the following figures) rose from £5,854, or ten times median earnings, in 1959-60 to £12,590 or eight

1 D. Smith, *Racial Disadvantage in Britain,* Pelican, 1977. See also DE (Unit for Manpower Studies), *The Role of Immigrants in the Labour Market,* 1976, for a comprehensive discussion.

2 J. Smith, *Labour Supply and Employment Duration in London Transport,* Greater London Paper No. 15, 1976.

3 A. Cosh, 'The remuneration of chief executives in the UK', *EJ,* vol. 85, no. 337, March 1975.

4 Royal Commission on the Distribution of Income and Wealth (Diamond Commission) Report No. 3, Cmnd. 6383, HMSO, January 1976.

times the median, in 1972-3. Further, the real disposable earnings (i.e. after allowing
for income tax and the increase in the retail price index) of those in the top 0.1% of
the distribution actually fell a little in the decade prior to 1973-4 while median
earnings rose some 18%. Nevertheless, despite this trend towards greater equality in
the distribution of earnings it should be remembered that, post tax, the earnings of
the top 1.0% of males in 1973-4 were over three times median earnings while those
in the top 0.1% earned over seven times the median.

We now turn to examine some more narrowly defined aspects of the distribution
of earnings. The next four sections analyse the pay structure by occupation, industry,
sex, and in local labour markets. The lower tail of the income distribution is studied
in the final sections on poverty and low pay.

II.4   Wage Structure by Occupation

The foundations of wage theory are contained in two famous principles. First, Adam
Smith's principle of net advantage states that when competition exists in the labour
market the 'whole of the advantages and disadvantages' of different occupations
will continually tend towards equality. Note that this principle does not imply that
wages will tend towards equality, but that (suitably discounted) lifetime returns to
one occupation will tend to equal those in another occupation. The returns that
make an occupation attractive or unattractive are both pecuniary and non-pecuniary.
Second, we have the principle of non-competing groups, which evolved from the
work of John Stuart Mill and Cairnes; this states (broadly) that certain non-
competitive factors may inhibit the tendency towards equality in net advantages.

Linked to these two principles are two sets of reasons for the existence of
occupational wage differentials: compensatory wage differentials and non-
compensatory wage differentials.

Compensatory wage differentials are those differentials which are consistent
with competition in the labour market.[1] If individuals were not compensated for
the factors listed below (in the form of higher wages when at work) then the supply
of labour to those occupations would tend to be deficient. All other things being
equal, individuals will tend, for example, to be compensated in the form of higher
wages for entering occupations that (1) require long periods of education and/or
training, (2) are dangerous or dirty, (3) are subject to lay-offs or have a relatively
short working life. (4) Also if they are risk averters, they will desire to be compensated in terms of the mean earnings of the occupation if the dispersion of the
earnings around the mean is very large. (5) Differentials will also accrue to wholly
exceptional workers, such as professional sportsmen and entertainers, this being an
example of economic rent applied to the labour market.

Non-compensatory occupational wage differentials are different. They occur for
institutional or economic reasons inconsistent with perfect competition. For example,
ceteris paribus: (1) legislation which raises the school-leaving age will tend to raise
the wages of teenagers relative to non-teenagers; it reduces the supply of teenagers

---

1 The extent to which the occupational pay structure is the outcome of competitive forces
   or of custom excites considerable controversy. Two good articles on the controversy are
   M. Fisher, 'The Human Capital Approach to Occupational Wage Differentials', *International
   Journal of Social Economics*, vol. 1, no. 1, 1974, and G. Routh, 'Interpretations of Pay
   Structure', *International Journal of Social Economics*, vol. 1, no. 1, 1974.

below what it would otherwise have been. (2) Minimum wage legislation will tend, at least in the short run, to raise the pay of (employed) unskilled workers relative to skilled workers. (3) Equal Pay for Women legislation will tend to raise the pay (employed) women relative to men.

Earnings by broad occupational groups are presented in table 5.5. It will be seen that earnings of non-manual workers are greater than those of manual workers. This

TABLE 5.5

Earnings by Occupation: Full-Time Adult Men, April 1977

Occupation	Average gross weekly earnings (£)	Average gross hourly earnings (p)
Non Manual		
1 General management	123.5	322
2 Professional and related management and administration	103.6	276
3 Professional and related in education welfare and health	97.6	283
4 Literary, artistic, sports	86.5	219
5 Professional and related in science, engineering and technology	94.4	240
6 Managerial	88.8	225
7 Clerical and related	67.2	167
8 Selling	71.9	176
9 Security and protective service	78.5	172
Manual		
10 Catering, cleaning, hairdressing	59.2	128
11 Farming, fishing and related	55.1	118
12 Materials processing (excluding metals)	71.2	154
13 Making and repairing (excluding metal and electrical)	71.3	159
14 Processing, making, repairing (metal and electrical)	76.7	166
15 Painting, repetitive assembling, product inspection	70.4	157
16 Construction, mining	72.7	159
17 Transport operating	70.8	146
18 Miscellaneous	66.3	143
Total: Manual	71.5	154
Total: Non-Manual	88.9	228
Total: All occupations	78.6	182

Source: DE, *New Earnings Survey* 1977, *DEG,* October 1977, table 8.
Note: Both sets of figures exclude those whose pay was affected by absence. The gross hourly earnings figure excludes the effect of overtime.

reflects in some large part the relative education/training intensities of the two groups. There is also evidence of other compensating differentials. Within group 14, furnacemen earn 175.0p per hour while plumbers earn 159.0p per hour. The furnacemen are being compensated for the unpleasant conditions in which they work. Bricklayers (group 16) earn 162.0p per hour, while general labourers (group 18) earn 132.0p: the bricklayers are being compensated for their relatively low earnings while apprenticed. Within group 7, firemen earn 144.0p per hour while security guards earn 137.0p. The firemen are being compensated because their job is more dangerous.

There is also evidence of individuals being compensated for being more able, or having more alternative job opportunities, or undertaking a more skilled task, even though the length of education and training is similar to that of their less skilled colleagues. In group 3, for example, teachers in further education earn 373.0p per hour which is 40p more than secondary school teachers earn. Within group 17, the earnings of a lorry driver are positively related to the size of vehicle: drivers of heavy goods vehicles (over 3 tons) earn 13p per hour more than other goods drivers.

Trade unions are able to influence the occupational earnings structure if the demand for labour is inelastic and/or if they can control the labour supply. For example, miners (group 16) earn 202.0p, which is 32% more than postmen (group 7) earn. This reflects, in part, the strength of the National Union of Miners, conferred by the inelastic demand for domestic coal which results from the currently used methods of electricity generation, together with limitations on imports. In contrast the lengthy postmen's strike of 1972 certainly did not bring the country to a halt, partly because telephonists and other postal workers continued working and tolerable substitutes were therefore available for the postal workers' services.

II.5   Wage Structure by Industry

There are a number of reasons for studying the industrial wage structure. First, it is important to know whether labour can be allocated among industries independently of wages or whether expanding (contracting) industries must pay higher (lower) wages to get the labour they require. Such information is useful in designing a pay policy. Second, how are the gains in labour productivity distributed? They can go to labour in the form of higher wages or firms in the form of higher profits or consumers in the form of lower prices. Analysis of the industrial wage structure provides evidence on the topic. Third, it is important to know whether, independent of the characteristics of the individuals working in the industry, highly concentrated industries or industries with large plants pay higher wages; such data would be useful in, for example, designing our monopoly legislation.

Wage Changes and Employment Changes:[1] Price theory implies that in the long run, given competitive conditions, each industry will, *ceteris paribus,* pay for a given grade of labour a wage identical to that paid by other industries. The *ceteris paribus* assumption implies that there are no differences in the non-pecuniary attractions of different industries or location or in the cost of living by location. In the long run therefore the growth in industry wage levels should not be correlated with the growth in the amount of labour employed. In the short run an industry which expands its demands for labour will tend to have to raise the wages it pays because of short-run inelasticities in labour supply. Therefore the theory predicts a positive association in the short run between changes in employment by industry and changes in wages by industry.

---

1   OECD, *Wages and Labour Mobility,* 1965, pp. 85-118; W. B. Reddaway, 'Wage Flexibility and the Distribution of Labour', *LBR,* October 1959; E. H. Phelps Brown and M. Browne, 'Earnings in Industries of the UK 1948-1959', *EJ,* vol. 72, September 1962. These references also contain information on earnings and productivity cited below.

The OECD found that in all cases but one the short-run (i.e. one year) associations between changes in earnings and changes in employment were positive in the UK in the 1950s. Reddaway examined the employment changes and earnings changes in 111 minimum list heading industries between 1951 and 1955 and found a positive association ($r = +0.43$). Finally Phelps Brown and Browne made a similar calculation for 132 industries over 1948 to 1958 and found a tendency for the relative earnings of expanding industries to rise and contracting industries to fall ($r = +0.24$). These studies suggest therefore that the market labour supply curve does slope upwards in the short run but that in the long run an industry can get all the labour it requires at the going wage rate. Thus a pay policy which hoped to avoid labour shortages developing might need to permit labour shortage sectors to pay above the norm.

Wage Changes and Productivity Changes: An industry may react to an increase in physical productivity by lowering its relative product price or raising the relative wages it pays. If wage changes among industries are significantly (positively) related to movements in value productivity (i.e. variations in physical productivity and product prices taken together) this implies that non-competitive forces, such as ability to pay, determine the wage structure. In contrast, if the differential wage changes are unrelated to change in value productivity by industry this implies that competitive forces dominate in the explanation of wages. We anticipate such forces will be important because there is no reason, on equity or efficiency grounds, to expect that sectors with high labour productivity or growth in labour productivity will, *ceteris paribus,* pay high wages; working with bigger machines, if the intensity of work is unchanged, is no reason for higher pay (see also section IV.2).

Neither Phelps Brown and Browne (using observations from one hundred and thirteen industries) nor OECD (using observations from eighty-six industries) found any relationship between changes in male average hourly earnings and changes in the gross value of output per worker over the period 1948-54. The correlation coefficient (r) in the OECD study was .05. This is clear evidence in favour of the competitive hypothesis: differential inter-industry wage changes appear unrelated to differential productivity changes. A more recent study[1] also found no association between industrial capital: labour ratios and earnings. Individuals who work with a lot of capital do not receive higher pay, *ceteris paribus,* than individuals working with little capital. These findings are reassuring. They suggest that workers who cannot increase their productivity easily (such as musicians or nurses) do not find their relative position in the pay structure worsening persistently. Further, they also indicate that, after allowing for general inflation, the gains from increased labour productivity flow mainly to consumers.

Industry Characteristics and Wage Levels: There has been considerable interest recently in the idea that the labour market is segmented into two (or more) sectors, one of which is high paying, with well developed internal labour markets allowing for promotion within the firm, employing high quality labour with low quit propensities and the other with opposite characteristics. Some recent studies on

---

1 W. Hood and R. D. Rees, 'Inter Industry Wage Levels in the UK Manufacturing Industry', *MS*, 1974.

the structure of earnings in British manufacturing industry throw some light on this idea.[1]

Differences among industries in the demographic composition of their work-forces are partly responsible for inter-industry wage differentials. Industries which employ skilled prime age workers pay, on average, higher wages than other industries. What is more interesting is that even after allowing for the influence of personal characteristics, industries with large plants or which are highly concentrated tend to pay higher wages than industries with small plants or which are atomistic.

Highly concentrated industries might pay higher wages, *ceteris paribus,* for two reasons (though both appear *a priori* unlikely to us). First, if the high concentration reflects monopoly power and supernormal profits are earned by concentrated industries, the managers of those industries might attempt to purchase good industrial relations by sharing those profits with their employees. Second, the high wages paid in concentrated industries might be an attempt by the existing firms to forestall entry by new firms. Industries with large plants have a high proportion of shift work and workers on payments-by-results schemes which both boost average pay, but even after allowing for these institutional arrangements large plant industries still have relatively high pay.

This evidence provides modest support for the notion of a segmented labour market. Big firms in monopolistic industries (the so-called primary sector) pay high wages relative to small firms in unconcentrated industries (the secondary sector). This wage differential is attributable, apparently, to higher labour quality, the disutility of working in large plants, the higher profits of concentrated industries and the higher density of union membership in the primary sector. However, the policy implications of such findings are far from clear. Should we, for example, encourage unionization in the secondary sector or discourage it in the primary sector? Should we encourage small plants to merge? Further to the extent that labour quality is important the evidence does not tell us which firms will choose a low wage, low labour quality, low productivity strategy as against a high wage, high quality, high productivity strategy. Clearly, there is a lot more work to be done before we can fully understand the factors underlying the structure of earnings across industries.

II.6   Wage Structure by Sex[2]

Evidence: Females account for 40% of employees in employment in Britain, yet less than 2% of those earning over £10,000 per year in 1974-5 were females. Females

---

1   D. Metcalf, S. Nickell and R. Richardson, 'The Structure of Hours and Earnings in British Manufacturing Industry', *OEP,* July 1976; M. Sawyer, 'The Earnings of Manual Workers: A Cross Section Analysis', *SJPE,* vol. XX, No. 2, June 1973; A. Tylecote, 'Determinants of Changes in the Wage Hierarchy in UK Manufacturing Industry: 1954-70', *BJIR,* vol. XIII, No. 1, March 1975; K. George, R. McNabb and J. Shorey, 'The Size of the Work Unit and Labour Market Behaviour', *BJIR,* July 1977.

2   A useful summary of the existing literature is B. Chiplin and P. Sloan, *Sex Discrimination In the Labour Market,* Macmillan, 1976. A readable, thorough, statistical analysis is S. Nickell, 'Trade Unions and the Position of Women in the Industrial Wage Structure', *BJIR,* July 1977. For details of the equal pay and equal opportunity legislation see DE, *A Guide to the Equal Pay Act 1970,* HMSO, 1975; Home Office, *A Guide to the Sex Discrimination Act 1975.* For preliminary analysis of the impact of the legislation and of firms' response to it, see *DEG,* December 1976.

earn less than males in each broad occupational and industrial group: the data in table 5.6 show that the hourly earnings of full-time female adult workers were, on average, 74% of male hourly earnings and that the percentage differential between male and female pay is higher for non-manual workers than for manual workers.

There are two broad reasons why average male pay exceeds average female pay. First, and more important, women are crowded into the low-paying occupations and industries. Second, within occupational groups women tend to be paid less than men. In education, for example, women are disproportionately represented in the

TABLE 5.6

Male–Female Hourly Earnings, Full-Time Workers, April 1977

	Female (p)	Male (p)	Female/Male (%)
Total manual	111	154	72
Total non-manual	144	228	63
Total	134	182	74
All Wage Boards and Wage Councils			
Manual	95	124	77
Non-manual	99	160	62
Occupations: non-manual			
Professional: management	209	276	76
Professional: health, education, welfare	193	283	68
Professional: science, engineering, technology	169	240	70
Managerial	140	225	62
Clerical	130	167	78
Selling	94	176	53
Occupations: manual			
Catering, cleaning, hairdressing	108	128	84
Materials processing (excluding metals)	108	154	70
Making and repairing (excluding metal and electrical)	108	159	68
Processing, making, repairing (metal and electrical)	122	166	73
Repetitive assembling, etc.	114	157	73
Transport, etc.	113	146	77

Source: DE, *New Earnings Survey,* 1977, *DEG,* October 1977, tables 2, 3, 8, 9.
Note: Data refer to adult workers whose pay in the survey week was not affected by absence and excludes the effect of overtime.

relatively low-paying primary segment, and within primary school teaching women earn 16% less than man. It must be noted, however, that even within primary teaching the main reason for the differential is not that women are paid less than men for doing the same job but rather that women are underrepresented in the higher-paying headship and deputy headship jobs. This example could be repeated for other occupations and industries.

Reasons why women earn less than men: A major reason why women earn less than men is that their attachment to the labour force is weaker than that of men. This relatively weak attachment is in large part because it is widely believed that it is the role of women rather than men to drop out of the labour force to care for young children: the lower lifetime commitment of women to the labour force is a response to centuries of social conditioning rather than an inherent trait. Attitudes on the roles of the two sexes can certainly be influenced by economic factors; for example the two world wars, which caused the demand for female labour to rise substantially, were particularly important in raising the labour-force status of women. This suggests that the respective roles of men and women are thus amenable to change via economic and other influences. The observed weaker labour-force attachment causes females to be crowded into the lower-paying segments of the labour force and, in some cases, to be paid less than men in a given task. Some manifestations of the relative labour-force attachments of men and women, which partially determine their occupational composition, include the following.

Labour turnover is higher for women than for men. Such turnover imposes costs on the employer; at a minimum these costs will be the hiring costs incurred when replacing employees. For example, the New Earnings Survey shows that in April 1974 the number of female employees who had been with their employer under twelve months was 29% while the corresponding male figure was 19%.[1] It is often argued that these figures reflect a composition effect, i.e. that females are disproportionately represented in industries and occupations which themselves have high turnover. This appears not to be true: in every industry and every occupation except one female turnover is greater than male turnover. An alternative possibility, however, concerns the age composition of the labour force. Young workers have dramatically higher turnover rates than prime-age and older workers. Therefore some of the observed higher female labour turnover may occur because younger workers account for a higher fraction of the female labour force than the male labour force.

Females are also more prone to absenteeism. In April 1970, for example, 23.8% of full-time adult women were paid for less than their normal working hours because they were absent from work owing to sickness (certified or uncertified), late arrival or early finish, holidays or other approved absence, or unspecified reasons. The corresponding figure for men was only 15.9%. Absenteeism also causes costs to employers, for example, by disrupting production schedules.

Because women have higher turnover rates than men, employers have less incentive to pay for female training. A profit-maximizing employer will be willing to pay for his employees' training if he can get a return on his investment by paying the trainee less than the value of his services when the training is completed. Given that women are more likely to quit or to be absent from a firm than men, employers will prefer to train men. This is compounded by hours legislation prohibiting women from working over a certain number of hours per week or at certain times.

Similarly, girls have less incentive to finance their own education and training. Staying on at school or university or taking a computer programming course entails costs, for example tuition costs or foregone earnings (i.e. earnings that could have been received if working). If a woman has children this will involve a period out of the labour force; further, women retire at a younger age than men. Thus the time over which she will receive benefits (in the form of higher earnings) from the training is less than for a man. Thus, of those young persons entering employment in 1974, 44.3% of the boys entered apprenticeships to skilled occupations or

---

1 *DEG*, January 1975, pp. 25-6.

employment leading to recognized professional qualifications, while only 8.3% of girls followed this route. In contrast 40.0% of the girls are immediately segmented into clerical employment. The contrast is even clearer if we consider highly qualified people (i.e. those holding an academic or professional qualification of degree standard). The DE estimates[1] that in 1971 the stock of such highly qualified males was 1,060,000, compared with 352,000 females.

If females go out of the labour force for a period in their twenties or thirties they will accumulate less experience and seniority (on the job training, learning by doing) than males. On all these grounds, females will tend to be less productive than males. They will therefore earn less within a given occupation and will be less likely to progress up the occupational hierarchy.

Females will also tend to be paid less than men if the firm draws them from a limited geographical area: they will incur lower transport costs on average than men. Also, women may tend to work in more pleasant conditions.

The structure of the industries in which females work is a further element in the explanation of the sex differential. Females are disproportionately represented in small plants and atomistic industries, which tend to pay less and offer poorer career prospects than larger plants and concentrated industries; also a relatively low proportion of the female labour force is unionized, which reflects in part the higher costs of organizing in industries consisting of small plants.

Discrimination: It is frequently alleged that the main cause of the pay differentials is that discrimination exists against women. However, it seems unlikely that discrimination *in the labour market* is an important cause of their low pay and lack of promotion. Employer discrimination means that if the net value of the woman's service is identical to that of the man the latter receives a higher wage. The only way that the woman can offset the employer's discrimination is to accept a lower wage. If *all other things are equal* yet firms pay, because of discrimination against women, higher wages to men than to women, then higher profits will accrue to the firm that replaces men with women. Male sales assistants are paid 130p per hour whilst females are paid 90p per hour. It is unlikely that if both males and females were equally productive, firms would not substitute female labour for male labour.

It should be noted that none of the above discussion implies that women are not discriminated against in society at large — they obviously are. The crucial question is how that discrimination can be ended, and the problem here concerns the causal relationship. We believe that if females could be given greater incentives than they have at present to remain in the labour force, accumulate experience, undertake training, travel longer distances, etc., then this will cause the distinction between the traditional roles of men and women to be eroded fairly speedily.

The equal pay and equal opportunity legislation which effectively came fully into force in 1976 should provide some incentive to stronger female labour force attachment. However, should this legislation prove too frail other policies exist to improve the lot of women in the labour market and these will be considered below.

The purpose of the Equal Pay Act is to eliminate discrimination against women in connection with wages and fringe benefits. A woman is to receive equal treatment when she is employed (a) on work of the same or broadly similar nature to that of men; (b) in a job which, though different from those of men, has been given an equal

---

1 DE, *Employment Prospects for the Highly Qualified*, Manpower Paper No. 8, HMSO, 1974.

value to men's jobs under a job evaluation exercise. Thus the act is designed to ensure that if the net value of a woman's services is identical to that of a man both will receive identical wages and conditions.

If discrimination does exist it is based on hostility to women employees or lack of information (e.g. employers think that women will be more likely to be absent or to quit and therefore pay them less than men or refuse to promote them). The Equal Pay Act by itself is likely to lead to a reduction in information about the relative performance of men and women both because of segregation and because female unemployment may rise on account of the higher costs of employing women.

On two grounds, at least, the Act may result in reduced employment of women, especially where men and women are doing the same job. First, if employers do discriminate against women then the legislation will protect men's jobs by reducing the possibilities of women replacing men by accepting lower pay. Second, female employment may fall if the cause of the pay differentials is not discrimination but lower female productivity or the higher costs of employing females. If this is the case then female labour costs per unit of output may rise and women be replaced by machines or men.

Further, the intentions of the Act can be overcome in a number of ways. Men and women can be segregated by job. This has already happened. The standard occupational classification lists over two hundred occupations but the 1975 New Earnings Survey reports only thirteen occupations with sufficient men and women to provide comparisons of their earnings. It seems possible that this Act will therefore compound rather than reduce occupational segregation. If women believe that they are nevertheless doing work of equal value the jobs can be subjected to a job evaluation scheme. But the employer can give a relatively high weight in such a scheme to attributes such as physical strength where men have a relative advantage, and a low weight to manual dexterity where women have the advantage (although there is a right of appeal on the 'fairness' of the job evaluation scheme). Legislation precludes women from night work and limits the number of overtime hours women may work; an employer may therefore pay large shift work or overtime supplements.

The Sex Discrimination Act will probably be more important in overcoming the current underrepresentation of women in high-paying sectors. It covers education and the supply of goods and services as well as employment. The Act says that women must be given equal treatment in the arrangements for selecting a candidate for a job, in the terms on which a job is offered, on access to promotion, transfer and training or any other aspects of the job and on dismissal. The Act established the Equal Opportunities Commission with fairly wide powers: it can help individuals to bring cases if it considers them of wider interest; it can conduct formal investigations compelling people to give evidence; it can serve non-discrimination notices and seek injunctions against persistent discriminators. Unfortunately the EOC has so far done little to raise the status of women.

Average hourly female earnings rose from around 65% of male earnings in 1974 to 74% in 1977. This is a large compression of the wage differential in a short time period. It could have occurred for many reasons. For example, the occupational composition of females may have changed so that females are increasingly represented in higher-paying occupations. Pay differentials within narrowly defined occupations may have been reduced or eliminated. The Equal Pay Act requires that in collective agreements female hourly earnings must not be set below the lowest male hourly earnings. The flat rate element (e.g. cash increases of £6 a week rather than percentage increases) in the 1975-77 pay policy may have worked to narrow the sex differential.

Although the narrowing of the pay differential is to be welcomed it is not without offsetting disadvantages. It is noticeable that in 1976 and 1977, the first two years of the full operation of the Act, female unemployment rose around 60% while male unemployment rose by only around 10%. The disproportionate rise in female labour costs surely contributed to this rise in relative female unemployment. Nevertheless female *employment* continued to rise during this period.

The Employment Protection Act (1976) should also favourably influence women's labour-force commitment. It provides for six weeks' paid maternity leave and twenty-nine weeks' unpaid leave with no loss of seniority or status. This legislation is of particular significance for women in highly skilled sectors.

The government could consider a number of alternative strategies to improve the labour-force status of women. First, it might encourage them to join unions: the male—female wage differential is, *ceteris paribus,* smaller in those industries which are highly unionized. Second, more girls could be encouraged to take apprenticeship or college training by providing them with differentially large training grants. Third, female quotas, especially in the higher occupational grades, could be enforced. Finally, women's pay could be forced up relative to men's pay by subsidizing women's employment.

II.7 Local Labour Markets

A local labour market may be defined as 'the geographic area containing those actual or potential members of the labour force that a firm might induce to enter its employ under certain conditions, and other employers with which the firm is in competition for labour'.[1] Evidence suggests that, for a given occupation, substantial dispersion of earnings exists within the local labour market. For example Robinson, examining earnings in ten occupations in engineering plants within an (unspecified) local labour market, finds that the range in pay between the highest and lowest paying plants is never less than 55% and is over 100% on two occasions. It is possible that this wage dispersion indicates the existence of healthy competition in the labour market, in contrast to an institutional domination of wage determination which would establish a common rate across all plants. It may also reflect the fact that information about wages and conditions in other plants is costly to obtain, thus allowing inter-plant wage differentials to persist for a long time.

Evidence from another source shows that earnings in local labour markets in engineering are positively related to plant size.[2] The rank correlation coefficients

1 D. Robinson, 'External and Internal Labour Markets', in D. Robinson (ed.), *Local Labour Markets and Wage Structures,* Gower Press, 1970, chapter 2. This book contains a wealth of evidence on earnings within local labour markets and within individual plants. See also D. Mackay, D. Boddy, J. Brack, J. Diack and N. Jones, *Labour Markets under Different Employment Conditions,* Allen and Unwin, 1971. This book contains precise summaries of previous literature on local and internal labour markets and synthesis of theory and facts. It also contains a full discussion of factory (i.e. intra-plant) wage structures and labour turnover, which pressure on space forces us to omit here.
2 S. Lerner, J. Cable and S. Gupta, *Workshop Wage Determination,* Pergamon, 1969, p. 32.

found between earnings and plant size by industry were:

Electrical machinery	+0.85	Radio and telecommunications	0.00
Motor vehicles	+0.78	Mechanical engineering	+0.19
Insulated wires	+0.65	Metal working	+0.37
Scientific instruments	+0.73		
Miscellaneous electrical	+0.73		

The rank correlation coefficients for the industries on the left-hand side are statistically significant. Before such evidence is used to refute the hypothesis that wages are determined by competitive factors, it is necessary to show that the quality of labour is the same in all plants; it could be that the large plants pay high wages to get superior-quality labour. Indeed, in their conclusions the authors stress the importance of competitive conditions in determining engineering wages: 'There was recurring evidence in all studies of the need for earnings to conform in some degree to prevailing local levels. In engineering it was found that if the average earnings in a works were below the modal level for a district this was usually sufficient grounds for securing a wage increase from the local employers' association.' Firms which paid less than the going rate in an area tended to find that they experienced problems recruiting and retaining adequately qualified labour. One particularly interesting strand of local labour market analysis concerns how long workers stay with their firms. For individual employers quits are usually costly, for a number of reasons. First, they either disrupt production and delivery dates or require the employer permanently to take on excess labour in order to minimize the impact of such disruption. Secondly, they directly raise costs by increasing the number of employees dealt with in any year, thereby raising total training costs, personnel department costs and orientation costs. Thirdly, they affect the stability of the work group and lower its morale. Apart from raising costs, the instability associated with frequent quits may have an additional social cost in inhibiting a number of valuable manpower practices. Thus, an employer facing a high quit rate often feels less concern for the welfare of his workforce and may, for example, be less inclined to provide the best training facilities.

Quit rates have been examined in detail recently for London Transport, British Road Services, the Metropolitan Police and the Department of the Environment.[1] For London Transport (LT) three cohorts — drivers, male conductors and female conductors — were studied. Their respective mean employment duration at LT was thirty, twenty-one and twenty-one months.

A number of influences had a clear impact on lengths of stay. Workers younger than thirty spent considerably less time with London Transport than did older workers; five months less in the case of drivers, nine and eight months less in the case of conductors. Colour also had a marked association with length of stay. Non-whites consistently stayed longer: ten months more for drivers and up to twelve months more for conductors. Those who were willing and able to work overtime, and hence had relatively high earnings, also tended to stay longer, so that a 1% increase in earnings raised length of stay by between 1.1% and 2.6%. A fourth variable that was associated with length of stay was the number of quits in the

1 R. Richardson, C. Robinson and J. Smith, 'Quit Rates and Manpower Policy', *DEG*, January 1977.

three years prior to joining London Transport. For each of the three cohorts, the larger the frequency of previous quits the shorter the stay with London Transport.

The results of analyses like this have important pointers for firms' manpower planning and for overcoming labour shortages in particular occupations. When selecting new recruits it should be possible, while considering all applicants on their merits as individuals, also to take account of what is known about the average effect of various factors on quit rates.

II.8   Poverty[1]

One aspect of income distribution which causes widespread concern is the problem of poverty. Low earnings from work are only one part of the poverty problem, which also encompasses hardship faced by, for example, old people, sick or disabled people, families with large numbers of children, fatherless families, and the unemployed.

In this section we discuss measurement problems, the characteristics of low-income families, and the role of the social security system. Low pay is discussed more fully in the next section.

Measurement

Poverty can be defined as an absolute or relative standard. Absolute standards are based on consumption of necessities. The quantity of necessities consumed is valued at current prices to obtain a monetary poverty standard. Relative standards are normally related to some measure of income in the general population. So, broadly, absolute standards attempt to estimate subsistence needs which do not vary with social progress, while relative standards relate poverty to rising living standards.

If poverty is defined on the basis of the *absolute* living standard in 1971, numbers in poverty declined from about a fifth of the population in 1953 to about a fortieth in 1973. In twenty years, on this absolute standard, the numbers in poverty declined dramatically — by a factor of eight. But in *relative* terms there was little change. The net income of the poorest 5th percentile was about the same proportion of median income in both years.[2]

Recent practice in Britain has been to base poverty standards on the current values of the supplementary benefit scale rates. This defines poverty in the *relative* sense because the scale rates are set in such a way that they increase broadly in step with general standards of living.

At the end of 1975 the number of families (counting single persons without children as a family) with incomes normally below their supplementary benefit (SB) level were:

before social security benefits added to income	7.3 million
after social security benefits added to income	1.1 million

1   For a full discussion of the issues see A. B. Atkinson, *The Economics of Inequality*, Clarendon UP, 1975; Royal Commission on the Distribution of Income and Wealth, Lower Incomes Report No. 6, Cmnd. 7175 HMSO, 1978; R. Layard, D. Piachaud, M. Stewart *et al.*, *The Causes of Poverty*, Background Paper to Cmnd. 7175.

2   G. Fiegehen, P. Lansley and A. Smith, *Poverty and Progress in Britain 1953-73*, Cambridge UP, 1977.

Over two thirds of the 7.3m figure are pensioners. The remainder consist of sick and disabled people, the unemployed and the low paid. Naturally, once social security benefits are taken into account the number of families with incomes below SB levels falls, but it is still very worrying that over a million families have incomes below SB. This occurs mainly because some people who are eligible for SB do not claim it.

A number of problems exist in measuring living standards. Should the income unit, for example, be the individual, the family or the household? How are we to control for household size and composition? Presumably larger households need more income than smaller households to get a similar standard of living. Likewise older children cost more to maintain than younger children. Therefore to measure comparative living standards sensibly, normal net household income must be adjusted for these size and composition effects. The adjustment factors are known as *equivalence scales.* The effects of adjusting the distribution of normal net household income for household size and composition are substantial. The 'equivalent income distribution' is considerably more equal: fewer households have low or high incomes and more have intermediate levels of income.

Characteristics of Low-Income Households[1]

Van Slooten and Coverdale define a household in the lowest quintile (fifth) of the *equivalent income distribution* as a low-income household. Such households have incomes less than or equal to approximately 120% of the supplementary benefit scale. Low incomes are most prevalent in pensioner and one-parent family households. Pensioner households account for over half of all the low-income households, and nearly half of the pensioner households have low incomes (50% of households for single pensioners and 41% for married pensioners). The incidence of low income becomes more severe at age seventy-five and above. Over half of the one-parent families have low incomes but, because there are few of them relative to other households, they account for only 6% of all low-income households.

Low pay is one important factor in low income. If we exclude pensioner households and consider only those households headed by a man, 62% of those with low incomes are working full time (16% as self-employed and 46% as employees). The remainder are working part-time, unemployed, sick or retired early. Two thirds of these low-income men are manual workers.

The incidence of low-income households is much lower in the southern part of Britain than elsewhere. Public housing is particularly important in looking after the needs of low-income families. Almost a half of low-income households are council tenants whereas less than a third of households in the top 80% of the income distribution live in local authority housing.

Social security benefits provide over half the income of low-income households. Social security benefits account for 88% of gross income in low-income pensioner households, 74% in low-income one-parent households, but only 17% in low-income two-parent households. The main forms of social security received by this group of low-income households are supplementary benefits, pensions and rent and rate rebates.

Low-income households spend proportionately more of their income on food,

---

1   R. Van Slooten and A. Coverdale, 'The characteristics of low income households', *ST*, No. 8, 1977.

housing, fuel and light than other households. And, not surprisingly, they have markedly fewer durable goods than the better-off households.

Role of Social Security

The Current Position: Currently, poor or disadvantaged people are aided by the state in six ways. (i) National Insurance benefits, mainly retirement pensions, unemployment and sickness pay; these benefits are available as a right to those satisfying the statutory conditions. Payments vary according to marital status and number of children. (ii) Supplementary benefits to persons over sixteen who involuntarily fall below a prescribed 'tolerable' level of income laid down by Parliament below which it is felt to be wrong that any family's income should be allowed to fall. These benefits are paid only after investigation of the individual's family circumstances. (iii) Child benefits are paid for all dependent children up to a maximum age of nineteen. (iv) An array of benefits in kind exists in housing (e.g. rent and rate rebates), education (e.g. school milk and meals), health (e.g. wigs, spectacles, prescriptions and dental services) and legal aid. (v) Family income supplement (FIS) aids very low wage earners with large families who claim the benefit. FIS is discussed in the next section. (vi) Some benefits are paid without a means test but also without National Insurance conditions, e.g. attendance allowance, mobility allowance, non-contributory invalidity pension. In 1976-7 social security spending was £12,717m, equivalent to 22% of all public spending.

It was originally hoped that the National Insurance system as proposed by Beveridge in 1942 would provide a level of benefits equal at least to the official poverty line, and that supplementary benefits (then called national assistance) would wither away except as a last resort for the few people who fell through the National Insurance net. This hope has not been realized. The number of people receiving supplementary benefit in 1976 was 2.9m, double the figure for 1951.

The increase in recourse to SB is because there are more old people now and many must top up their National Insurance pension to meet their needs; there is now less reluctance to apply for SB. Also, as unemployment has risen the number of unemployed who have exhausted their entitlement to National Insurance unemployment benefit has risen.

It should be remembered that the figure of 2.9m refers to benefit recipients at a point in time, i.e. they are stock data. During the course of 1976 many more than 2.9m people received supplementary benefit at some time: the annual flow of recipients is greater than the stock because, for example, in the course of a year some single parents with dependent children will marry, some unemployed will find jobs and some pensioners will die.

Criticisms: The current system has been criticized on a number of grounds, although some of the criticisms are contradictory. First, the growth in the number receiving supplementary benefits demonstrates that some groups are not adequately catered for by the other anti-poverty measures. Important groups here include the long-term unemployed and fatherless families. Unemployment and sickness benefits include an earnings related supplement to the flat rate benefit. This supplement is paid only for the first six months of unemployment or sickness. When unemployment rises rapidly this is partially because more individuals register as unemployed but mainly because the duration of unemployment increases, leading to the loss of earnings related supplement for many workers. Further, higher overall levels of unemployment imply that many individuals may have more than one bout of unemployment in a year and may thus exhaust their National Insurance unemployment benefit. Fatherless families may have no income sources other than supplementary benefit. This group of benefit recipients has grown substantially recently.

The second criticism of the current arrangements is that, despite a battery of measures to alleviate poverty, a substantial number of people still exist below the poverty line defined by the supplementary benefit level. Some 1m families or 2m people lived below the official poverty line in November 1975. There are two main reasons for this. First, many people, especially pensioners, while eligible for supplementary benefit do not claim it. Second, many individuals are poor despite working: their weekly earnings are below the official poverty line. The Family Income Supplement was introduced in 1971 to mitigate poverty associated with low earnings.

The third criticism concerns the income-related nature of many benefits. The core of the problem is whether benefits should be related to income or whether the National Insurance system should be designed to ensure that everyone has a tolerable minimum income, with the tax system taking back some benefits from those who do not need them. (It must be recognized that, for the time being, there are severe technical difficulties to making short-term National Insurance benefits taxable under the PAYE system.) The criticism has a number of strands. (i) Benefits which are related to means are traditionally unpopular and discourage a full take-up. Many of those eligible for supplementary benefit do not claim; the take-up rate of rent and rate rebates appears only to be around 50% of those eligible. (ii) It may result in absurd marginal tax rates for those with low incomes. This is known as the poverty trap: as the earned income of the family rises it loses not only monetary supplementation such as FIS but also benefits in kind such as free school meals or prescriptions. DHSS estimates that at the end of 1975 50,000 families with children might have been liable to receive no increase in net income from a £1 rise in earnings and a further 40,000 might have received less than 25p.[1] Given the government's belief that high marginal tax rates discourage proper work effort this is clearly anomalous. (iii) The discretionary nature of the SB system makes it difficult for clients and officials to understand fully. There may also be indirect administrative costs such as social workers.

The final criticism concerns the benefits in kind. These distort the price system, the consumer paying less than the cost of providing the service (e.g. 'free' school meals or milk). Critics argue that individuals should be assured of some minimum money income and then left to spend it as they wish, with the purchases priced according to cost. This raises much wider issues than poverty relief and will not be pursued here.

Reform of Social Security: A number of important reforms are taking place in the social security system. These affect the National Insurance system (especially pensions), family support, supplementary benefit and new benefits for the disabled.

National Insurance contributions are earnings related. Employees in the full state pension scheme pay 6½% of their pay as National Insurance contributions (up to a ceiling, equal to £120 in April 1978) and employers pay 10%. These contributions include components to help finance the National Health Service, Redundancy Fund, and Unemployment and Sickness Insurance as well as Old Age Pensions.

The benefit side is changing too. Although unemployment and sickness benefit

---

1   *ST,* No. 8, 1977, p. 114.

will continue as now for the time being (i.e. with flat rate and earnings-related components), pension benefits are gradually to be substantially improved.

The New Pension Scheme operating from April 1978 consists of two components. The *basic* flat rate pension continues as at present and will be uprated annually in line with the earnings index (or, if higher, the prices index). The *additional* pension is earnings related. The employee will get one-eightieth of his earnings (between a specified floor and ceiling) for each contribution year after 1978, subject to a maximum of twenty eightieths. The average married couple will, when the scheme is fully mature in 1999, receive a total pension equal to at least two thirds of the man's real take-home pay. So this scheme will help to eliminate poverty in old age. If an employer runs an occupational scheme which is at least as good as the state scheme he can opt out of the additional segment of the state scheme and he and his employees pay correspondingly lower contributions.

The system of family support is also being reconstituted. Child benefit, a universal tax-free weekly amount per child, is replacing the old system of child tax allowances (CTAs) and family allowances. The new system has three important advantages. First, individuals who had low incomes and paid no tax gained no advantage from CTAs, but they do get child benefit. Second, child benefit is paid for all children whereas family allowances were paid only for second and subsequent children. Third, child benefit is paid to the mother whereas the benefit of CTAs went to the father.

It should be noted that child benefits – £4.00 per week per child from April 1979 – are primarily designed to achieve horizontal equity rather than vertical equity. They help ensure that, at given income levels, families with children do not have wildly different living standards from families without children. While they may incidentally help low-income families, this is a secondary consideration. If relief of poverty were the main reason for child benefits, there would be little point in paying a tax-free universal benefit which costs over £600m per year extra public expenditure for each £1.00 per week per child increase. It is an open question whether or not family support should be more concerned with relief of poverty and less with horizontal equity. The government will also have to decide shortly whether to index child benefit to earnings or prices so that it is automatically uprated annually; and whether to stick with a flat amount per child or to vary the amount by age of child, family size or some other factor.

The system of supplementary benefits is also being reviewed with a view to simplification. The discretionary nature of the system makes it inevitable that it becomes complicated and, possibly, anomalous over the years. Special needs payments, heating additions, rent allowances, children's rates varying by age, etc., all make the system difficult to understand. The aim of the review is to reduce discretion and produce a simpler system.

A number of new benefits have been introduced for disabled people in the 1970s. These include attendance allowance for people who need looking after constantly or nearly constantly; mobility allowance to help disabled people offset the costs of getting around (previously only those with invalid trikes received such help); non-contributory invalidity pension (NCIP) to provide a weekly income as a right to disabled people of working age, including a special NCIP for housewives. The Pearson Report[1] has also recommended a new benefit for disabled children. It

---

1 Pearson Report, *Report of Royal Commission on Civil Liability and Compensation for Personal Injury,* Cmnd. 7054, HMSO, March 1978.

seems probable that this patchwork of benefits will shortly be ripe for review to see whether they could be integrated into a unified benefit for the disabled which would vary according to degree of disability.

Alternative Reforms

Despite the progress in reforming the social security system many other suggestions for reform continue. This is not surprising because the present system still has a number of problems. These include (i) the fact that many people still have incomes below SB level. (ii) Some individuals both receive benefits and pay income tax (this is mainly because in recent years income tax allowances have not kept pace with inflation but social security payments have done). (iii) It is widely believed that many people have little incentive to work because payments when out of work are greater than or approximately equal to payments in work. This problem is real but exaggerated. It occurs primarily in the case of individuals with large families who receive large earnings related supplements and tax rebates (which last only for a limited period) on becoming unemployed. (iv) The poverty trap is held to reduce incentives to earn more money.

There have been three main sets of suggestions concerning the direction of reform.[1] They have a superficial similarity, in that under each scheme individuals will be guaranteed a minimum income at around supplementary benefit level and the need for supplementary benefits will be substantially reduced. In fact, however, the schemes are very different.

The first suggestion is for a 'new Beveridge Plan'. Under the original Beveridge proposals it was proposed that social *insurance* should guarantee everyone a minimum standard of living. This subsistence income was to be provided as a right, without a means test; the part played by national assistance was to be virtually phased out. In the postwar period, however, National Insurance benefits have usually been below the prescribed minima laid down by national assistance (now supplementary benefits). The suggestion is therefore to implement fully the original Beveridge proposals. One of the aims of the new pension scheme (discussed above) is to ensure pension benefits of sufficient size virtually to eliminate the need for pensioners to turn to supplementary benefits to augment their income. Higher child benefits are also held to be important. Advocates of this universalistic approach to curing poverty generally qualify it by suggesting that the benefits from raising social security payments could be taxed and thereby directed towards those with lower incomes. However, many benefits (e.g. unemployment benefits and child benefit) are not taxable and therefore could not be clawed back at present.

This policy would obviously be successful in raising the incomes of non-employed disadvantaged individuals. It does not involve high marginal tax rates and is therefore less likely to have disincentive effects on working harder. Further it would

---

1 See F. Field, *Poverty: the Facts,* Child Poverty Action Group, 1975, for the general case for the 'back to Beveridge' proposals. See A. Cristopher *et al., Policy for Poverty,* Research Monograph 20, IEA, 1970, for the general case for a negative income tax. See J. Meade, 'Poverty in the Welfare State', *Oxford Economic Papers,* November 1972, for the case for the Social Dividend Scheme. Meade has recognized the impractical nature of the Social Dividend Scheme and now advocates a 'new Beveridge Plan'. See Meade Report, *The Structure and Reform of Direct Taxation,* IFS, 1978. Chapter 13 of the Meade Report has a clear exposition of the Social Dividend and New Beveridge Schemes.

not involve any major administrative problems. It does have two disadvantages. First, it would be costly. However, this is merely another way of stating the seriousness of the poverty problem. Second, the problem of the employed with low incomes remains. This problem would be moderated if income tax thresholds were raised. But minimum wage legislation – the policy most frequently advocated to raise earnings by the back-to-Beveridge protagonists – may result in unemployment among the very groups it is designed to help.

The second scheme for reform, the Social Dividend, is the boldest. Under this scheme a non-taxable flat rate sum would be paid weekly to every individual irrespective of income. This would be accompanied by a proportional personal income tax. All other elements of the social security system (insurance contributions and benefits, supplementary benefits and family allowances) would be abolished. This system has the advantage that the benefit paid is insensitive to income. Work incentives may nevertheless be impaired because it is generally agreed that the proportional tax rate would have to be over 50%. The scheme also has the administrative drawback of extending income tax to everyone, however small his income.

The third alternative, which has many variants, is the Negative Income Tax. This scheme involves a minimum income guarantee and a break-even income. If an individual is employed and earns between the minimum and the break-even income his earnings are supplemented (by the negative income tax); beyond the break-even income he pays positive income tax. The FIS is thus a prototype NIT. This scheme could be all-embracing, covering the whole range of government welfare programmes, or could be oriented towards particular problems such as poverty caused by large families. The essential problem with this scheme is that a choice must be made between high marginal rates of negative income tax and low minimum levels of payments. For example, from 1978 the point at which a single individual starts paying income tax is £985. If the NIT is operated with a rate of 50% this means that 50p is payable to an individual for every £1 by which his income is less than £985. Thus the basic minimum payment is only £493. If this basic minimum is too low the tax rate could be raised to 75% giving a minimum of £739. Such a high marginal tax rate is likely to have disincentive effects on labour supply. Further problems with the NIT, which could be overcome with time and ingenuity, are (i) that the unit to which it applies, the individual, the family or the household, must be determined; (ii) that the NIT must be on a weekly basis, but (positive) income tax has always been assessed yearly; (iii) that people not in employment have to claim the NIT; (iv) that assets may be difficult to incorporate into the NIT scheme.

II.9   Low Pay[1]

Low pay is one part of the poverty problem. Industries which rank at the bottom of the earnings structure tend to be characterized by high proportions of small plants, of women workers, of unskilled workers and of falling demand for labour. It is also clear that low-paid workers are heavily represented in the service sector. In the five main service sectors (distributive trades; insurance, banking and finance; professional and scientific services; miscellaneous services; public administration)

---

1   For a general survey of the problem of low pay see NBPI, *General Problems of Low Pay*, Report No. 169, Cmnd. 4648, 1971 and F. Field (ed.), *Low Pay*, Arrow, 1973.

Labour

7.4% of full-time male manual workers earned under £40 a week in April 1977 while the corresponding figure for manufacturing industry was 1.2%.

Low pay is also related to age and skill. Teenagers, workers in their early twenties and workers over fifty are disproportionately represented. Older and unskilled workers not only tend to have relatively low earnings, but also to suffer higher rates of unemployment. Unemployment rates referring specifically to unskilled workers are at least three times the national average unemployment rate. The annual earnings differential between them and other workers is therefore greater than apparent from a comparison of the earnings of those in work.

Two important features of the structure of the low-pay problem are worth noting. First, if the low paid are described as those in the lowest tenth of the distribution of manual earnings, we observe considerable movement across the boundary of this lowest tenth. 21.4% of manual men were in the lowest-paid tenth at least once in the five years 1970 to 1974, but only 2.9% were in this tenth in each of the years.[1] Second, low pay must be seen as part of a general problem of labour market disadvantages in that it is associated with a high incidence of job instability, ill-health and lack of fringe benefits.[2] The low-paid worker is more vulnerable to the interruption of earnings power, cannot save for old age or emergencies, and can only borrow at very high interest rates such as through HP. Thus low pay is an important element in the cycle of poverty.

In Britain we approach the problem of low pay in two main ways. First, the FIS is a form of negative income tax. Second, the wages councils provide a form of minimum wage legislation.

FIS was introduced in August 1971 to help mitigate poverty caused by low pay. When family income falls short of a prescribed level (from November 1977 £43.80 per week for a one-child family plus £4.00 for each additional child) the family is paid a benefit equal to one half of the difference between its total gross income and the prescribed level (with a maximum supplement of £9.50 for a one-child family and £1 for each additional child). This is a potentially powerful policy to raise the welfare of the low paid. Even though it is necessary to claim this income related supplement, the take-up rate is over 90% in cash terms. Further, families who receive FIS are also automatically entitled to certain other benefits including free school meals, free milk and vitamins for expectant mothers and children under school age and exemption from NHS charges for prescriptions, glasses and dental treatment.

An oft-cited cure for low pay is a national minimum wage. Elements of a minimum wage policy exist via the wages councils which set minimum rates in certain industries. Direct state intervention in fixing minimum wages first occurred in 1909 with the Trade Boards Act. In 1945 trade boards were renamed wages councils. There are forty-seven wages councils. They are generally believed to be ineffective in helping low-paid workers and are thought to inhibit the development of voluntary collective bargaining arrangements.[3]

---

1 *DEG*, January 1977. The great fluctuations in individuals' pay from year to year occur throughout the earnings distribution. This implies that there is less inequality in career earnings than there is in annual earnings.
2 See Susan Owen, 'Do the faces in the dole queue change? The concentration of unemployment within the British male labour force 1970-74', DHSS Working Paper, 1977.
3 NBPI, op. cit., para. 124.

A national minimum wage (assuming it is set above the existing wage for low-paid workers) will raise the money earnings of those who remain employed, but will cause some unemployment. Recall that the old and unskilled, the people the minimum wage is designed to help most, already have the highest unemployment rates. It may also give only a temporary boost to the low paid. Overseas evidence suggests that the original wage differentials are quickly restored. Proponents of minimum wage legislation also argue that it raises the productivity of labour. So it will if capital is substituted for labour, but this is an inefficient substitution and unemployment will also result. It is sometimes said, however, that the minimum wage legislation will have a 'shock effect' and thereby raise productivity without any loss in employment. This is unlikely to be widespread in that it implies that firms currently have a careless attitude towards profits. Further, many of the low-paying industries are competitive and are therefore unlikely to need a national minimum wage as a spur to efficiency. Thus 'no false hopes should be attached to a national minimum wage . . . our main conclusion therefore has to be that there is no single remedy for low pay'.[1]

This suggests that provision of more training facilities, better information about wages and opportunities both locally and nationally, inducements to labour mobility, wage subsidies, and running the economy with lower, more evenly distributed unemployment levels, are likely to be more effective solutions to the problem of low pay than is a national minimum wage.

III   TRADE UNIONS AND INDUSTRIAL RELATIONS

III.1   Trade Unions

At the end of 1976 there were estimated to be 12,376,000 trade union members in the UK.[2] This implies that over half the nation's employees (in employment plus unemployed) were trade union members, a significant expansion from the corresponding figure of 42% for 1964.

The number of unions is still tending to fall, down from 630 in 1965 to 462 in 1976, in spite of a small increase in 1973 that was probably the result of the 1971 Industrial Relations Act. Nevertheless, in 1976 there were still 68 trade unions with less than a hundred members each.

In addition to those in formal trade unions many workers belong to other associations that engage in collective negotiations and bargaining; for example, many individual business concerns have what are sometimes called 'company unions'. Other workers are in industries that have wages councils, public bodies that are designed to reproduce many of the features of collective bargaining where trade union growth is inherently difficult.

In 1973 the *New Earnings Survey* for the first time gave disaggregated estimates of the number of workers covered by various types of collective agreement.[3] It was suggested there that 17% of full-time male workers and 28% of full-time female workers were not party to a collective agreement. For both sexes the service sectors, particularly the distributive trades and personal services, were heavily characterized

1 NBPI, op. cit., paras 124-5.
2 *DEG*, November 1977, pp. 1203-5.
3 *New Earnings Survey*, 1973, pp. 176-83.

by individual negotiation, and in the manufacturing sector, clothing and footwear had relatively little collective bargaining.

Formal unionization is particularly extensive among male workers, manual workers, semi-skilled workers and workers in the manufacturing and public sectors. There are no absolutely reliable figures, but one recent study[1] suggests that membership by industry varies from 100% of workers in coal mining and the railways to around 20 to 25% in food and drink and clothing.

Unionization is more limited in newer industries and in the expanding white collar trades.[2] Where unions have been involved in the latter sectors they have traditionally differed from those in the blue collar sectors in their aims, attitudes and militancy. Recently, however, the extent of white collar organization has been growing, and with it has come more aggressive union behaviour.

It is interesting to know which factors are associated with year-to-year changes in total union membership. It appears that price inflation, changes in money wages, unemployment and the size of the potentially unionizable labour force are all related to movements in aggregate unionization.[3] What is now required is a theoretical rationale for such associations.

III.2 Economic Analysis of Unions

Economists tend to analyse unions by their impact on resource allocation and wages. Other observers might argue that what is more important about unions is their impact on work rules, consultation procedures, worker representation and so on.[4] Even if the latter view is true, the effect of unions on wage levels and wage structures is still an interesting problem.

The conventional view is that unions will be most effective (i.e. will secure for their members large wage gains at only a small cost of reduced employment opportunities) where two conditions hold: (1) when the demand for labour is wage inelastic; (2) when the costs and difficulties of organization are low. Following Marshall, the demand for labour is seen to be less wage elastic: (a) the lower is the price elasticity of demand for the labour's output, (b) the more modest are the technical possibilities of substitution between labour and other factors, (c) the less available are substitute factors and (d) the lower is the proportion in total costs of labour costs. On these grounds it is often asserted that 'craft' unions, i.e. unions of selected artisans like printers or boiler-makers, will be more successful in securing large wage increases for their members than will 'industrial' or 'general' unions.[5]

The costs of successful organization are less frequently analysed but they are highly influential in determining union strength. It is usually said that such costs are low when the workforce in question is (a) stable and so not subject to high rates of quits or lay-offs, (b) concentrated among relatively few employers, (c) concentrated geographically, and (d) possessed of certain attitudes, sometimes labelled 'class consciousness'.

---

1 J. Pencavel, 'Relative Wages and Trade Unions in the UK', *EC*, May 1974.

2 G. Bain, *The Growth of White Collar Unionism*, Oxford, 1970.

3 G. Bain and F. El-Sheikh, *Union Growth and the Business Cycle*, Basil Blackwell, 1976. See also the review by R. Richardson in *BJIR*, July 1977.

4 See W. J. McCarthy (ed.), *Trade Unions*, Penguin, 1972.

5 For some valuable qualifications to this view, see L. Ulman, 'Marshall and Friedman on Union Strength', *REST*, November 1955.

So much for a sketch of the principles of effective unionization. A number of recent studies have attempted to measure the impact of collective bargaining on the structure of relative wages.[1] It appears that average hourly pay in an industry whose labour force is completely covered by a collective agreement is around 20% greater than the average wage in a completely uncovered industry.

In the 1960s many industrial relations specialists became concerned at the apparently haphazard nature of local bargaining which was often superimposed on official bargaining and which, it was claimed, contributed to strike activity and inflation. For example, the Donovan Report[2] suggested that many sectors of British industry had two systems of collective bargaining with informal workplace-bargaining between shop stewards and plant management existing simultaneously with formal company or industry-wide bargaining, and the Report expressed its distaste for the informal element. It is interesting therefore to examine how the wage premium associated with union coverage varies by type of agreement. It appears that in manufacturing industry the wage premium associated with a national agreement is, at best, small, while those covered by district, local and company agreements have a wage advantage in excess of the overall average union mark-up of around 20%. Remember, however, that many such supplementary agreements have a national flavour. The industrial relations literature is rich in descriptions of institutional mechanisms whereby local bargains struck in one plant are transmitted to plants of the same firm in other areas or to plants of different firms. Thus even supplementary district, local or company agreements may have national dimensions.

It is not clear at whose expense unions extract this wage premium. For much of this century the share of wages in national income was broadly constant.[3] This would imply union members gain at the expense of non-union members. Such unorganized workers tend either to be relatively low paid or relatively high paid but it is not known which of these two sets of workers loses from unionizat on.

Further, in the last decade or so labour's share in national income appea s to have risen.[4] Indeed, between 1968 and 1970 union membership and the share of wages in manufacturing national income both rose by 10%. In this case unions may have secured their wage gains at the expense of profits rather than at the expense of their fellow, non-union, workers. This may, in turn, result in lower investment and a slower growth in real wages in the future.

III.3 Strikes and Industrial Relations

Strikes: In 1976 3.2 million working days were lost through industrial disputes,[5] roughly one hour per year per member of the labour force. Put this way the

---

1 See J. Pencavel, 'Relative Wages and Trade Unions in the UK', *EC*, May 1974; C. Mulvey, 'Collective Agreements and Relative Earnings in UK Manufacturing in 1973', *EC*, November 1976; articles by J. Pencavel, D. Metcalf, A. Thompson *et al.* and S. Nickell in *BJIR*, July 1977.

2 *Report on the Royal Commission on Trade Unions and Employers' Associations 1965-1968* (Chairman Lord Donovan), Cmnd. 3623, HMSO, 1968.

3 E. H. Phelps Brown, *Pay and Profits*, Manchester UP, 1968.

4 A. Glyn and R. Sutcliffe, *British Capitalism, Workers and the Profits Squeeze*, Penguin, 1972; M. King, 'The UK Profits Crisis: Myth or Reality', *EJ*, March 1975.

5 *DEG*, June 1977, p. 579.

phenomenon of strikes may seem less important than many newspaper headlines suggest. After 1967 the number of days lost rose from the 1-2 million per year it had been for some time, up to nearly 24 million in 1972. Since then strike losses have tended to be smaller. It is also worth pointing out that many other industrialized countries have worse strike records than Britain. For example, over the period 1965-75 Australia, Canada, Italy and the US all lost more working days per employee from strike activity than did Britain.[1]

Strikes vary in incidence across different firms, industries and occupations. Thus, over the period 1966-73 mining lost an average 4,300 days per year per 1,000 employees; the next most strike-prone sector was vehicles with 2,100 days, followed by shipbuilding with 1,820 days; in contrast the distributive trades lost seven days per year per 1,000 workers.[2] Another feature of strike behaviour is the strong inverse relation between plant size and days lost through strikes. For manufacturing plants employing more than 1,000 workers, days lost averaged 2,050 per 1,000 workers over 1971-3 compared with fifteen days per 1,000 workers in plants employing between eleven and twenty-four workers.

It is important to note that the vast majority of plants are not affected by stoppages. For example, between 1971 and 1973 95% of plants in manufacturing industry were free of stoppages. Thus only 5% of manufacturing plants had at least one stoppage in these three years. Of these, two thirds had only one stoppage, but a small minority had a large number. Britain apparently suffers from a concentration of stoppages in the docks, coal mining and in a small proportion (between 2% and 5%) of plants in manufacturing industry, especially motor vehicles and shipbuilding.[3]

More generally, strikes seem more likely when inflation is rising and when unemployment is low and less likely when recent wage changes are high. Comparing different industries, strikes are more likely in those industries with relatively few female workers, extensive payments-by-results systems, rapid technical change and slowly growing wages.

There has been comment in recent years on payment of supplementary benefit to strikers' families.[4] It is certainly true that state support to strikers' families has increased in the 1970s compared with the earlier postwar period. This increase is associated, in part, with a change in the pattern of strikes. There has been an increase in the number of longer, official strikes, particularly in the public sector (e.g. postmen 1971, miners 1974, firemen 1977). But, in recent years, the proportion of those eligible who actually received supplementary benefit was, at most, around one third. Further, SB plays only a minor role in the budgets of those on strike. Only 15% of the postmen's income while on strike came from the state. Strikers and their families rely far more on running down their savings, deferring HP, rent and mortgage payments, living off wives' pay and back-pay and tax rebates. Gennard provides persuasive evidence that state income support does not cause or prolong strikes and that modifications in the availability of SB to strikers' families would, in some cases, cause much hardship and would probably sour industrial relations.

---

1 *DEG*, December 1976, p. 1353.
2 *DEG*, February 1976, pp. 115-23.
3 *DEG*, November 1976, pp. 1219-24.
4 For a full and non-partisan discussion see J. Gennard, *Financing Strikers*, Macmillan, 1977. The facts in this paragraph are taken from this book.

Industrial Relations system: Strike activity is the most heavily publicized aspect of industrial relations but by no means the most important one. It arouses considerable public comment and often provides dramatic situations with great political significance but in so doing it tends to obscure other aspects of the relationships between employer and employee which make up industrial relations. For at least the last ten to fifteen years there has been much concern over the British 'system' of industrial relations, sparked off by two principal worries.

First, in many sectors the traditional industry-wide collective bargaining was becoming less important. It appeared that the sustained full employment in the postwar period had made the role of shop stewards and local negotiations much more important; in many manufacturing industries local agreements were mounted on the back of industrial agreements, causing substantial wage drift. Also the majority of strikes were unofficial. Second, the postwar period has also been marked by aggregate wage settlements, substantially greater than productivity changes, leading to price inflation. It was felt that the relative strength of labour compared with employers had shifted unduly in favour of the former.

This concern, coupled with certain legal judgements particularly affecting the position of individuals, led to the establishment of a Royal Commission[1] to investigate the industrial relations system. This Commission virtually ignored the second problem, despite the fact that compatibility of collective bargaining with full employment and economic growth had by then become an open question.

The Royal Commission thought that the principal problem in industrial relations was that two systems – the formal and the informal – existed. It further believed that certain industries where the conflict between the two systems was very apparent, e.g. engineering, were industries whose bargains set a pattern for others. It saw the remedy in integrating the informal systems and stressed the desirability of both plant bargaining and full employer recognition of unions. However, it strongly believed that the reform should be voluntary rather than imposed by law. It recommended the establishment of a Commission on Industrial Relations, a form of investigatory tribunal, to facilitate this voluntary reform. It believed implicitly that if reform could be achieved in a few key sectors this would percolate through the rest of the system. The report was not well received by independent observers who felt that it merely pushed people in the direction they were already going anyway, and that it did little to change the ground rules of the industrial relations system or to get at the problem of excessive wage inflation.

Legislation: The report resulted in action from both Labour and Conservative governments. Labour established a Commission on Industrial Relations whose functions the Conservatives subsequently altered; on returning to power in 1974, the Labour government abolished the CIR. In 1969-70 the Labour government proposed additional reforms but withdrew them in the face of strong union and backbench opposition. It was left to the Conservatives to legislate substantial reform but their Industrial Relations Act (1971) had a stormy history, arousing bitter hostility in the trade union leadership, before it was repealed in an early action by the Labour government of 1974. That action, the Trade Union and Labour Relations Act, together with the associated Trade Union and Labour Relations

1 *Report of the Royal Commission on Trade Unions and Employers' Associations 1965-1968* (Donovan Report), Cmnd. 3623, HMSO, 1968.

(Amendment) Act (1976), in many ways restored the pre-1971 situation, but in some respects the position of trade unions was further strengthened. For example, under the controversial closed shop provisions, it is no longer unfair for an employer to dismiss employees for refusing to join a union in those situations where employers and unions have agreed to a 100% union membership provision.

Additional industrial relations legislation has also been introduced. The Employment Protection Act (1975) also encourages constructive union activity. Employers now must disclose certain information judged to be relevant to collective bargaining, consult with unions on the handling of redundancies and face more pressure to recognize independent trade unions when their employees wish to be represented. The legislation also gives powers to the Advisory, Conciliation and Arbitration Service and extends the legal rights of individual employees, e.g. in maternity pay and leave provision. The position of unions has also been strengthened by the passing of the Health and Safety at Work Act (1975) and the Industry Act (1975). The latter gives worker participation in an embryonic form by encouraging Planning Agreements, i.e. agreements between individual employers, union and the government relating to the operations of firms.

Worker participation in its fullest form was considered by the Bullock Committee.[1] The majority of the Committee recommended that when employees numbered 2,000 or more in a firm they should have the same number of board seats as shareholder representatives. Together these two groups would co-opt a (smaller) third group of independent directors. Worker directors could continue to act as shop stewards and would not be excluded from any boardroom discussions when, for example, the subject is wages. These proposals would affect about 1,800 private companies grouped into 738 enterprises, employing around 7 million people. Reaction to these proposals was mixed.

The Labour Government proposed a weaker form of industrial democracy.[2] The first stage is the setting up of joint union-management committees in companies with 500 or more employees to discuss strategic planning decisions. Such committees would discuss investment plans, mergers, expansions or contractions and major organizational changes. Building on the first stage, at a later date workers would be elected to board level. The government propose a two-tier board with workers initially comprising one third of the supervisory board, but not being on the (ostensibly) lower-level management board. This is a retreat from the proposals in the Bullock Report which advocated an equal number of worker and shareholder directors on a unitary board.

Industrial democracy – a share of both power and responsibility – is thought to be an important avenue to strengthen workers' commitment to their company. Another way to achieve this is by profit sharing. From April 1979 shares up to the value of £500 can be allocated annually to each employee. The shares must normally be held for at least 5 years. Income tax will not have to be paid on the initial value of the shares until they are sold – and then at a rate which tapers according to the length of time they have been held.

---

1 Committee of Enquiry into Industrial Democracy (Chairman Lord Bullock), 1977.
2 *Industrial Democracy*, May 1978.

IV WAGE INFLATION AND PUBLIC POLICY

Of all the areas of controversy and disagreement in economics, the one that is most confused and least resolved is probably that of inflation, particularly its causes and cures. It is widely agreed that the most important immediate determinant of price inflation is changes in money wages. This is because wages are the major component of production costs and, as a matter of fact, the prices of finished goods usually change only after costs have changed. There are, of course, other components of costs, and changes in these may also affect prices. Thus, the course of price inflation is additionally affected by changes in (a) non-wage labour costs, e.g. training costs or National Insurance costs, (b) productivity, (c) taxes or subsidies on goods and services, (d) the foreign currency price of imported goods, (e) the exchange rate and (f) profit margins. In the recent past, each of these has had an influence on the price level for a time but changes in wages have been even more important.[1]

The determinants of these non-wage cost components are not a matter of very great controversy, though they are usually very difficult to forecast at any given time. However, there is very little agreement as to what determines the course of wage costs, and correspondingly little agreement on how that course might be changed by policy. As a consequence, we are now unable to forecast at all accurately future changes in average wages in the UK. As wage changes are so central to many economic events, this inability makes all macro-economic forecasting extremely hazardous and conjectural. In recent years it has been necessary for forecasters to take a range of possible wage changes and to make separate calculations for each; for a year like 1977-8, the range might stretch from 10% to 20% p.a. With such large unknowns economic policy presentation becomes very difficult.

IV.1 Explanations of Wage Inflation

A traditional view is that average wage changes are largely the result of changes in the aggregate demand for labour relative to its supply. This may be true in two senses. One is that as demand increases relative to supply, people in work tend to work more overtime and hence have increased total earnings. The other, and this is what is being considered here, is that as demand increases relative to supply, earnings increase for a given number of hours and amount of effort − this may be called wage inflation. Many different types of economists believe that wage inflation is caused by tight labour markets, i.e. where the demand for labour is high relative to its supply.

At least until the mid-1960s, many economists, following the work of Phillips,[2] believed that there was a stable relationship between wage inflation and the state of aggregate demand as measured either by unemployment, or vacancies or an index of unused industrial capacity. It was not, however, thought that aggregate demand was the sole determinant of wage inflation. Phillips noted that wages also seemed to respond to a very rapid rise in import prices, and other economists felt that recent price changes, whatever their source, might influence current wage inflation.

---

1   See chapter 1, section V for further discussion.

2   A. W. Phillips, 'The Relation between Unemployment and the Rate of Change of Money Wage Rates in the United Kingdom, 1861-1957', *EC*, vol. 25, November 1958, pp. 283-99.

They also added further variables to the Phillips framework; for example, the level of industrial profits or the degree of industrial concentration. In addition to these influences it was felt that the position and shape of the Phillips Curve was the result of the institutional arrangements in the economy; for example, the collective bargaining structure. Thus, a change in these institutions might affect unemployment and inflation simultaneously.

All these additional arguments having been made, it was nevertheless widely felt that changes in the rate of wage inflation from year to year were mainly the result of changes in the level of aggregate demand relative to supply. It was also felt that the principal way the government could influence the level of aggregate demand was by varying its fiscal policy, by which was meant a change in taxes or government expenditure that produced a change in the public sector financial deficit or surplus.

After the mid-1960s, faith in the Phillips framework was reduced as wage inflation and unemployment tended to move in the same direction rather than inversely (see table 5.7). At the same time there was a revival in monetary analysis, which tended to restore to a position of importance the rate of increase in the

TABLE 5.7

Unemployment and Wage Inflation 1955-77

	% Change in hourly wage earnings	% Unemployment males, GB
1955-60 (average p.a.)	6.2	1.6
1961-9 (average p.a.)	6.7	2.3
1970	15.3	3.4
1971	12.9	4.5
1972	15.0	4.9
1973	14.1	3.5
1974	21.4	3.5
1975	26.9	5.2
1976	12.1	7.2
1977	8.4	7.4

Source: DEG, various issues.

supply of money as an explanation of the rate of inflation. Thus, an increase in the money supply was thought to raise the demand for goods and services and hence for labour; this would subsequently raise wages and prices. The transmission from changes in money supply to prices was thought to be complex, and was associated with time lags that were believed to be both long (averaging perhaps eighteen months) and varied. In addition to re-affirming a link in the short run, between aggregate demand and wage inflation, the revival of monetarism also emphasized the importance for wage inflation of expectations of future price increases. Monetarists do not believe that there is more than a temporary trade-off of any significance between wage inflation and aggregate demand (as measured, for example, by unemployment). Instead, they believe that there is a single equilibrium unemployment rate, the 'natural' rate, and that any departure from that rate can only be temporary (although 'temporary' could mean many years). Starting from a position of equilibrium, a sustained increase in the rate of monetary expansion is seen to lead to a sequence of events first lowering and then raising unemployment, to produce in the new equilibrium, the initial level of unemployment but a higher level of inflation, for both wages and prices. Thus wage inflation is seen to be heavily influenced by price expectations that are themselves a direct or indirect result of monetary expansion.

In some respects these two groups, the followers of Phillips and the monetarists, agree. Both believe that a policy of reducing the level of aggregate demand relative to supply will reduce wage inflation. One group would say that this would result in permanently higher unemployment, the other would deny this and claim that the rise in unemployment was temporary; they might therefore disagree as to whether the policy is desirable. Monetarists would say that the change in aggregate demand can be engineered only by a change in the rate of monetary expansion, whereas others would stress fiscal policy. In practice, however, there has not been much disagreement because in the UK a change in the public sector deficit has usually been followed by a change in the rate of monetary expansion. It is rare, perhaps unknown, for an increase in the deficit to be financed exclusively by greater sales of public debt, thus leaving the money supply unchanged (though with the coming of monetary targets we may see such an event).

Finally, both groups believe that other policy changes could influence wage inflation. Many of those who worked within the Phillips framework saw in incomes policy a chance to shift the whole Phillips Curve, producing less unemployment and lower inflation. Monetarists have tended to be sceptical of incomes policies, partly perhaps because the latter have often been accompanied by monetary expansion. However, a monetarist certainly could argue that an incomes policy might reduce inflationary expectations and thus make a tight money policy work more quickly and smoothly. It would, however, be difficult for a monetarist to argue that monetary control and incomes policies were alternatives. In addition, both groups could agree that a whole range of micro-economic institutional changes might affect either the position of the Phillips Curve or the natural rate of unemployment.

In contrast to those who stress changes in fiscal or monetary policy, there are many observers who believe that wage inflation is the result of the configuration of unions or of collective bargaining structures. Further, the latter group tends to believe that the course of wage inflation is largely uninfluenced by variations in such indicators as the unemployment rate. Thus, Sir Kenneth Berrill, then Chief Economic Adviser to the Treasury, remarked to a Committee of the House of Commons in June 1974 that 'we do not believe the Phillips Curve over quite a large band, but starting at the top end, when you reduce unemployment you can begin to see shortages of skilled labour, bottlenecks and so on developing which affect the balance of payments and also earnings and prices. Then there is a large flat band. What happens at the heavy levels of unemployment we do not know because we have not had that since the 1930s.'[1]

A relatively early expression of this diverse group is to be found in the work of Hines, who attributed wage inflation to trade union pushfulness.[2] Hines set out an index of trade union pushfulness $\Delta T (= T_t - T_{t-1}$, where T_t denotes the proportion of the labour force unionized, or union density, in year t). His thesis was that ΔT is a measure of union activity which manifests itself simultaneously both in increased

1 Ninth Report from the Expenditure Committee, *Public Expenditure, Inflation and the Balance of Payments*, Session 1974, HMSO, p. 136.
2 A. Hines, 'Trade Unions and Wage Inflation in the UK 1893-1961', *RES*, vol. 31, 1964, pp. 221-51.

union membership and density and in pressure on money wage rates. He tested this hypothesis with aggregate data from 1893-1961 and found, broadly, that through time excess demand for labour had become less important as a cause of inflation and that in the postwar period wage pushfulness was a key factor in the explanation of inflation. The importance of unions in industry level wage adjustment was confirmed in a subsequent article.[1]

Given the controversial nature of this topic and the originality of Hines' contribution it is not surprising that the latter has been subjected to careful scrutiny. The most wide-ranging critique is that of Purdy and Zis[2] who examines Hines' theory, data, estimation technique and interpretation.

Their main criticism is that Hines presents no theoretical underpinning for the proposition that militancy (ΔT) shows simultaneously in increased membership and in upward pressure on wage rates: 'There is a presumption in his theory that unions aim to drive up their members' real wages by exerting pressure on money wages; that unions aim to extend the organized proportion of the labour force lying within their jurisdiction and that the rate at which they succeed in carrying out this latter objective is a major determinant of their success in pursuing the former.'[3] However, none of this comes out of a formal model of union behaviour or a discussion of what unions do when conflicting objectives, e.g. higher wages associated with lower employment, occur. Even more important, theoretically, is that the pushfulness view pays little attention to the employer. Hines argues that, through time, employer resistance is of less consequence because of the wage round and because of administered prices. While this may be true it still seems likely that the secular reduction in employer resistance will have some cyclical variability superimposed on it — that in the motor industry, for example, employer resistance is related to the demand for cars; indeed there is evidence that employers initiate strikes when demand is slack — and this should be discussed in the wage adjustment model.

A second criticism of the union pushfulness model is that it is not clear what ΔT measures: it is defined as a measure of militancy but the contribution of unions to the process of inflation may depend more on their strength than on their militancy. This distinction is slippery but not trivial. If unions are strong they may get large money wage increases with a small show of militancy (indeed if they operate a closed shop ΔT, the militancy measure used by Hines, is by definition zero). Further many labour historians (Phelps Brown,[4] Ross[5]) believe unions were more powerful (militant?) in forestalling and minimizing money wage cuts in the interwar period than they are in obtaining wage increases — in the words of Phelps Brown unions are stronger when they act as the anvil than as the hammer.

Two semi-statistical problems concern (i) simultaneity between union density and wage changes and (ii) the fact that union density may not be independent of excess demand. The proportion of the labour force unionized is a function of the

1   A. Hines, 'Wage Inflation in the UK 1948-62: A Disaggregated Study', *EJ,* vol. 79, 1969, pp. 66-89.
2   D. Purdy and A. Zis, 'Trade Unions and Wage Inflation in the UK', in D. Laidler and D. Purdy (eds), *Inflation and Labour Markets,* Manchester UP, 1974.
3   Ibid., p. 296.
4   E. H. Phelps Brown, *Pay and Profits,* Manchester UP, 1968.
5   A. Ross, 'Changing Pattern of Industrial Conflict', in *Proceedings of Twelfth Annual Meeting of Industrial Relations Research Association,* edited by G. Somers, 1959.

costs of organization, as measured by factors such as the number of workers per plant, the benefits of membership and simply whether the union member can afford his dues. It is well known[1] that over long periods union membership is positively related to economic activity; for example, union membership fell steadily between 1926 and 1933 and rose steadily during the mid and late 1930s. It seems likely therefore that the level of union membership depends both on money wage changes and on the level of excess demand.

Purdy and Zis point to data problems within the union pushfulness model. One such problem is that until recently there has been little variability in ΔT in the postwar period. More important, where a closed shop exists, the basis of using ΔT as a measure of militancy is unclear because union membership will only rise or fall as employment in the closed shop sectors rises or falls. Purdy and Zis quote evidence from McCarthy,[2] who estimated that 3.75 million workers were employed in closed shop establishments and a further 1.35 million were in open shops within trades where the closed shop practice predominated, and which were therefore quasi-closed shops enforced by informal sanctions. In all, 22% of manual workers were covered by closed shop arrangements and these constituted 49% of manual trade unionists. It is clear therefore that in large numbers of plants increased union activity is unlikely to be reflected in ΔT because the employees are already completely organized.

Finally, Purdy and Zis found that when they re-estimated the union pushfulness model to take account of their various criticisms, the impact of ΔT on wage changes, although still positive, was much reduced. This is confirmed by Wilkinson and Burkitt,[3] who used carefully constructed data on unionization by industry and found that ΔT is significantly associated with wage changes in only one industry, textiles, out of the eleven they studied.

The statistical studies discussed above have neither confirmed nor rejected the central place of unions in the inflationary process and, in consequence, the debate concerning the underlying causes of inflation continues unabated. It is generally agreed that a correlation exists between the growth in the money supply and the rate of inflation and that this correlation is stronger in the long run than in the short run. What is in dispute is whether inflation is caused by excessive growth in the money supply or whether union power or some other social force causes money wages to rise which in turn induces the authorities to expand the money supply in order that unemployment does not result.

One way of getting a clearer understanding of the part played by unions in the inflationary process is to turn to micro-economic analysis. For example if it could be demonstrated that unionized sectors received large wage settlements in times of heavy unemployment or severe deceleration in the rate of growth of the money supply and that such settlements were followed, with a lag, by the non-union sectors, this would suggest that unions are not irrelevant.

Some progress has been made recently towards a synthesis of the conflicting views. For example Tobin[4] and Hicks[5] have developed similar models which

1   E. Hobsbawm, *Labouring Men: Studies in the History of Labour,* Weidenfeld and Nicolson, 1964.

2   W. McCarthy, '*The Closed Shop in Britain*', Blackwell, 1964.

3   R. Wilkinson and B. Burkitt, 'Wage Determination and Trade Unions', *SJPE,* vol. XX, No. 2, June, 1973.

4   J. Tobin, 'Inflation and Unemployment', *AER,* vol. LXII, no. 1, March 1972, pp. 1-18.

5   Sir J. Hicks, *The Crisis in Keynesian Economics,* Blackwell, 1974.

emphasize that the labour market is not one market but is composed of many markets by industry, occupation, area, etc. If one market is in disequilibrium with excess demand for labour, wages will be pulled up in that market and this wage rise will in turn, via either equity or labour supply considerations, feed into the other markets: inflation is initiated by excess demand factors and transmitted by the institutional arrangements and social pressures prevailing in the labour market. Hicks states that such social pressures 'may take the form of strikes, but that may not be necessary. Any arbitrator will agree that a rise in wages is "fair". And it will be clear to employers that they must raise wages for the sake of "good industrial relations".' This certainly seems precisely the sequence of events which has occurred in many public sector pay settlements in the last few years.

This multisector view makes clear that there is force in both the monetarist and the social force views of the inflationary process. The various markets which make up 'the labour market' tend to have at any point in time different levels of excess demand. Those with large positive excess demand experience large money wage increases (the monetarist element) whilst those with excess supply do not, as in the distant past, experience money wage cuts. An active employment policy which aims for full employment 'on average' implies that some markets will always be experiencing excess demand and the wage increases in such markets spill over into the other markets via social pressures such as arbitrators' conceptions of equity or union power (the cost-push element).

The literature which examines wage inflation by disaggregating the various components of the labour market is not large and it is too soon to say whether the *a priori* plausible hypothesis of Hicks and Tobin are acceptable. This literature is discussed next.

IV.2 Disaggregated Analyses of the Wage Inflation Process

Regional: Regional labour markets have received more attention than other narrowly defined labour markets in part because of economists' long interest in regional policy. Regional wage differentials have been remarkably stable despite persistent differences in the regional unemployment rates. This fact leads, as Mackay and Hart[1] point out, to two interesting, interrelated, lines of investigation. First, what is it that holds the regional wage structure together in view of the regions' different labour market experience? Second, if a given national unemployment rate were to be associated with less dispersion in regional unemployment, would the rate of wage inflation be lower? Thirlwall,[2] Metcalf[3] and Archibald[4] have each demonstrated that one important factor in preserving the regional wage structure is national wage bargaining.

1 D. Mackay and R. Hart, 'Wage Inflation and the Regional Wage Structure' in M. Parkin (ed.), *Contemporary Issues in Economics,* Proceedings of the 1973 AUTE Conference, Longman, 1974.
2 A. Thirlwall, 'Regional Phillips Curves', *Bulletin of Oxford Institute of Economics and Statistics,* vol. XXXII, February, 1970, pp. 19-32.
3 D. Metcalf, 'Determinants of Earnings Changes: A Regional Analysis for the UK 1960-68', *International Economic Review,* vol. XII, June 1971, pp. 273-82.
4 C. Archibald, 'Analysis of Regional Economic Policy', in B. Corry and M. Peston (eds), *Essays in Honour of Lord Robbins,* Weidenfeld and Nicolson, 1972.

A study which analysed in detail the institutional structure of the engineering industry labour market (Lerner and Marquand[1]) found that local bargaining resulting in earnings increases substantially in excess of the nationally negotiated wage rates occurs initially in regions experiencing an excess demand for labour, and that these higher earnings spread out over the other regions via the mechanism of the shop stewards combine committees. Mackay and Hart,[2] in a careful study, provide econometric support for this hypothesis using data provided by the Engineers Employers Federation disaggregated to the level of the town. Although the mechanism by which similar earnings increases get spread out around the country is complicated, 'for London itself there is a very significant relationship between earnings changes and excess demand pressure, which may be transferred to other markets whose own earnings changes show little association with local excess demand pressure . . . [further it is] possible that earnings changes in local labour markets exhibit strong associations with wage leaders in their more immediate vicinity'.

Whilst this institutional and econometric evidence relates only to engineering and does not necessarily hold for the other sectors (cf. Lerner, Cable and Gupta[3]) it prompts the question: if, for a given national unemployment rate, unemployment rates were more evenly distributed spatially would the aggregate rate of money wage inflation be lower?

There are two reasons, *a priori*, why the dispersion in sectoral unemployment and inflation might be positively related. First, if each sector has similar non-linear Phillips curves (or, under certain circumstances, linear curves with different locations) the macro Phillips Curve will lie above the micro curves. This is known as the aggregation hypothesis. Second, if the low unemployment sector is the wage leader, macro inflation is largely determined by its unemployment rate and not the economy unemployment rate. The aggregation hypothesis has been much studied, although the data show quite plainly that the sectoral Phillips curves are not identical but that those for the high unemployment sectors, which have similar wage increases to the low unemployment sectors, lie above those for the low unemployment sectors. It seems likely therefore, that if dispersion in sectoral unemployment is positively associated with inflation this is because of spillovers rather than aggregation.

The possible link between lower dispersion in spatial unemployment and a lower inflation rate was responsible, in part, for the regional policy of the mid 1960s which, for example, limited office building in the South East and subsidized employment with the regional employment premium in the high unemployment areas. A number of studies have investigated this link by including the dispersion of regional unemployment rates as an explanatory variable in models of macro wage-adjustment. The results, unfortunately, are inconclusive. A sample of the empirical work shows that Archibald[1] and Thomas and Stoney[2] (1972) both find

1 S. Lerner and J. Marquand (1963), 'Regional Variations in Earnings, Demand for Labour and Shop Stewards Combine Committees in the British Engineering Industry', *MS*, vol. XXXI, 1963.

2 D. Mackay and R. Hart, 'Wage Inflation and the Phillips Relationship', *MS*, June 1974.

3 S. Lerner *et al., Workshop Wage Determination,* Pergamon.

4 C. Archibald, 'The Phillips Curve and the Distribution of Unemployment', *AER*, vol. LIX, May 1969, pp. 124-34.

5 R. L. Thomas and P. Stoney, 'Unemployment and Dispersion as a Determinant of Wage Inflation in the UK 1925-66', *MS*, June 1971, vol. 39, pp. 83-111.

a significant positive association between the dispersion of regional unemployment and the rate of money wage inflation but Mackay and Hart do not, although they believe that there exists an underlying relationship between the dispersion of spatial unemployment and wage inflation but that this relationship is masked because the absolute dispersion and the average level of unemployment are themselves positively correlated.

Industry: A number of studies exist on the interrelationships amongst industrial wage movements. Kaldor[1] initiated a model in which the engine room of the inflationary process is the rate of increase in labour productivity in the production sector. In this model, firms in the production sector can afford to pay relatively large annual wage increases without their unit labour costs rising much because of the secular rise in their workers' productivity (this rise in productivity being caused, in general, by better organization and a higher capital: labour ratio rather than greater intensity of effort on the part of the operatives). Subsequently the wage increases gained by employees in the high productivity growth sector spill over to the service sectors causing a large rise in their unit labour costs. Thus at macro level the percentage increment to money wages is at least as large as the percentage increase in labour productivity in the production sector which, in turn, is substantially in excess of the percentage growth in aggregate real national income. The underlying mechanism has been confirmed both by Aubrey Jones[2] and by other Cambridge writers. For example Turner and Jackson[3] demonstrate that the model fits the facts about productivity increases in earnings increases in Britain. More recently, Eatwell, Llewellyn and Tarling[4] provided an ingenious test of the hypothesis using international data. They examined the growth in earnings and the growth in output per man in the industries within the manufacturing sector in fifteen countries over the period 1953-67. Within each country it was found that earnings increases were much more similar than labour productivity increases. Further, the average rise in earnings in a country over the period approximated closely to the labour productivity increase of the three industries with the fastest growth of labour productivity rather than to the average increase in labour productivity across all the industries. One problem with this explanation of inflation is that it does not spell out how the wage settlement gained in the high productivity growth sector also gets paid to the employees in the other sectors. Further, other evidence differs as to which are the leading and lagging sectors. Sargan[5] found that the transport and scientific sectors appeared to lead the inflationary process, neither of these being production industries. Dicks-Mireaux[6] believes that the export and import competing industries

1 N. Kaldor, 'Economic Growth and the Problem of Inflation', *EC*, 1959.
2 A. Jones, *The New Inflation: The Politics and Prices and Incomes*, Penguin, 1972.
3 H. A. Turner and D. Jackson, 'On the Determination of the General Wage Level – A World Analysis,' or 'Unlimited Labour Forever', *EJ*, vol. 80, 1970, pp. 827-49.
4 J. Eatwell, J. Llewellyn and R. Tarling, 'Money Wage Inflation in Industrial Countries', *RES*, 1975.
5 J. D. Sargan, 'A Study in Wages and Prices in the UK 1949-69', in H. G. Johnson and A. Nobay (eds), *The Current Inflation*, Macmillan, 1971.
6 L. Dicks-Mireaux, 'International Factors', in H. G. Johnson and A. Nobay (eds), *The Current Inflation*, Macmillan, 1971.

have been the wage leaders in the recent inflation as a result of their profitability caused by the 1967 devaluation of sterling. Again, neither of these latter writers discusses the process by which the wage settlements in the leading industries are transmitted nationally.

IV.3 Incomes Policy

History: Since the mid-1960s different governments in the UK have used incomes and prices policies for a number of purposes.[1] The principal aim of these policies has been to reduce the rate of inflation, but important subsidiary aims have, from time to time, been to reduce the extent of restrictive labour market practices, to increase labour productivity generally, to encourage a shift in the structure of earnings and to improve the competitive environment in industry. Here we shall concentrate on the anti-inflationary aim.

There has been a wide variety of forms in the policies. For example, they have differed as to whether they were voluntary or compulsory, as to whether they had a flat rate norm (i.e. so many pounds per week) or a percentage norm, and as to whether they permitted exceptions or not. Thus from April 1965 to June 1966 the incomes policy was voluntary, i.e. there were no sanctions on those who chose to disregard its guidelines. From mid-1966 to mid-1967 the policy became both compulsory and more severely anti-inflationary in intent. After July 1967 there was a more ambiguous period where compliance with a somewhat more relaxed policy was 'essentially voluntary'.[2] Shortly after coming into power in June 1970, the Conservative government discontinued the incomes policy, but by mid-1971 they felt obliged to resume some direct action, with particular emphasis on achieving a gradual decline in the level of settlements in the public sector. By the autumn of 1972 they were trying to get TUC and CBI agreement on a more comprehensive but still voluntary policy; when this was not forthcoming, they announced a compulsory and initially severe incomes and prices policy in November of that year. This had three phases and lasted until a Labour government was elected in March 1974. After that time the statutory disciplines were ignored and a number of 'special cases' were recognized.

While in opposition between 1970 and 1974, the Labour Party had become officially hostile to incomes policies, particularly to those having statutory provisions. This was partly because there was scepticism of the economic advantages of such policies but much more because of political imperatives. In 1969, relations between the trade union movement and the Labour government had become extremely strained following the publication of a White Paper on industrial relations (*In Place of Strife*). During the subsequent period of opposition there were moves to restore friendly relations, and a particular expression of the rapprochement was the so-called Social Contract. Under this, a future Labour government would enjoy generalized and specific support from the trade union movement in return for legislation and policies designed to strengthen the position of the trade unions and their members. Among the matters on which the trade union leaders felt strongly

---

1 For a discussion of earlier policies see A. Fels, *The British Prices and Incomes Board,* Cambridge UP, 1972, particularly chapter 1.
2 The description is that of Fels, op. cit., chapter 1.

was the undesirability of statutory incomes policies. They felt that such policies, by undermining the role of free collective bargaining, struck at the very core of the justification for trade unions, at least as they are organized in the UK.

As a result, and in spite of quite exceptionally high wage inflation, the Labour government did virtually nothing directly to affect wage inflation between spring 1974 and summer 1975. However, a continuation of such a posture was widely thought to be impossible. It was not widely believed that in the absence of direct action wage inflation would quickly fall below 25–30% p.a. and it was recognized that such inflation as had already been experienced was going to be difficult to digest. On the other hand, there was great scepticism that a purely voluntary incomes policy, even if negotiated, would work.

In the event a very simple voluntary policy, albeit one with explicit sanctions held in reserve, was agreed between the government and the TUC and was adhered to very widely. This was followed, in the summer of 1976 and the summer of 1977, by two more stages, both fairly simple and neither backed with explicit sanctions, although during the third stage the government did take various disciplinary actions against firms that paid more than the suggested guidelines.

As with the choice between voluntary and statutory (a distinction that has by now become very difficult to make in practice) there have been changes in the type of norm used. Most of the early policies had percentage norms, but the Conservative government's Phase II, from April 1973 to September 1973, had a flat rate component (the exact formula was a permitted £1 + 4%). In July 1975 the Labour government announced a norm of £6 per week for everyone except those earning more than £8,500 per year, who were not allowed any increase at all. This was followed in the next year by a more complex formula of a minimum of £2.50 per week, a maximum of £4.00 per week, or, within those limits, 5%.

The effect of these flat rate guidelines, of course, is to reduce the relative earnings differentials between pay groups. This erosion of differentials certainly created political and industrial relations problems and probably began to affect adversely the allocation of labour. As a result, in Stage 3 of the Labour government's policy there was a reversion to a percentage norm (10% of earnings) plus some allowance for genuine productivity deals. Three other aspects of the norms are worth mentioning.

First, in November 1973 the Conservative government permitted a form of indexation, whereby workers could make agreements under which they would receive wage increases if the price level rose above a certain threshold. The intention here was that prices would not so rise and that the indexation clause would not in fact be triggered. This was an interesting idea and reflected the belief that wage settlements incorporate an allowance for expected future inflation. If most settlements include such a hedge against the future they will, in aggregate, raise costs and produce the very price rise they are seeking to protect against. If, therefore, the inflation hedge can everywhere be eliminated the rise in costs, and hence in prices, might be avoided. The indexation scheme was an attempt to eliminate the inflation hedge by making the compensation for price increases conditional upon their arrival rather than their prospect. Unfortunately the policy was a failure. The price index chosen was one that reflected the prices of imported goods, and many of these rose dramatically in 1973 as the major economies of the world boomed together. Once the threshold clauses were triggered a wage/price/wage spiral was set off because the wage compensation for price inflation was virtually 100%. Had a different index been used, or had commodity prices not exploded, or had the compensation not been roughly one for one, the policy might, in retrospect, have been judged more favourably.

The second point about norms is that there is no longer an attempt to relate them seriously to productivity increases. In the 1960s the ostensible purpose of the policy was to limit average wage increases to average productivity increases, thus securing constant unit labour costs for any given level of output. More recently, with inflation generally so much higher, the goal of constant unit labour costs is seen to be far too ambitious and has been substituted by the more modest aim of reducing the increase in unit labour costs over what it would otherwise have been.

The third point about norms is that recent incomes policies have been combined with tax policies, in that the Chancellor of the Exchequer has announced income tax reductions that are conditional on incomes policy success. For example, in March 1977 Mr Healey announced a 2p cut in the standard rate of income tax contingent upon the successful negotiation with the trade union movement of Stage 3 of the incomes policy. The theory behind this is that disposable incomes can rise (via the tax cuts) even if wage rates, and hence unit labour costs, do not. It also means that the wage rate or earnings norm is somewhat misleading because to it must be added the tax cuts, and these differ in value to different taxpayers.

The 1965-70 incomes policies permitted wage increases greater than the norm on four grounds: where there was a serious labour shortage in a particular industry, occupation or region; where the wages of a particular group of workers were 'seriously out of line' with their traditional place in the wage structure; for low-paid workers; and for productivity deals. More recent policies have also allowed exceptions for 'unsocial hours', and to allow the phased equalization of wage rates between the sexes to take place. The problem for the policy with most of the permitted exceptions is that they can often be used by powerful groups to circumvent its spirit. This is felt to be particularly true for productivity deals, which are often seen to be phoney.

Effectiveness of Incomes Policy: An incomes policy is likely to lead to some loss of allocative efficiency in the economy, by inhibiting changes in relative wages. Does it provide some compensating benefits by slowing down the rate of wage and price inflation below what it would otherwise have been?

The accumulated evidence on the effect on wage inflation of incomes policies as they have been applied in the UK suggests very strongly that they have generally been ineffective. Earnings increases are usually reduced below what they would otherwise have been in the early stages of the policy, but increasingly, and most notably when a government is compelled to dismantle the policy, earnings increase to reach the level where they would have been had no such policy ever existed.

For example a Department of Employment Working Party[1] estimated that over the years 1965, 1966 and 1967 earnings rose about 4% less than they otherwise would have done without a policy whilst in 1968 and 1969 earnings rose 4% more than they would have done had there never been a policy. The total impact of the policy was nil. This raises the question, why are incomes policies taken off? Presumably the answer is that, at least as they have been applied in the UK they become politically or economically unsustainable after a while.

This is precisely the conclusion reached in an extremely thorough study of the effect of incomes policies over the whole postwar period. The authors summarize all the recent literature and conclude 'incomes policy apparently has little effect

1 DE, *Prices and Earnings in 1951-69*, HMSO, 1971, para. 57.

either on the wage determination process or on the average rate of wage inflation.[1]

One reason for these findings is that incomes policies have often been introduced while the economy is being expanded. This was notably the case with the policies of the Conservative government in 1972 and 1973. It is precisely in such circumstances that one might expect least success because tight labour markets lead both workers and employers to try to circumvent the policy, the former because they want higher wages and the latter because they want more labour. Arguably one of the few incomes policy successes was with Stage 1 of the Labour government's policy in 1975. At the time, unemployment was rising rapidly and output was stagnant or falling, so that macroeconomic policy and the incomes policy were working in harmony against inflation. It could be argued that in these circumstances the incomes policy contributed nothing, that the success in reducing inflation should be ascribed to macroeconomic or monetary policy alone. However, most observers agree that the incomes policy at least caused the reduction in wage inflation to come earlier than it would otherwise have done.

REFERENCES AND FURTHER READING

A. B. Atkinson, *Economics of Inequality,* Clarendon Press, 1975.

British Journal of Industrial Relations, July 1977. Symposium on Labour Economics and Industrial Relations.

Department of Employment, *British Labour Statistics: Historical Abstract 1886–1968,* HMSO, 1971.

Department of Employment, *New Earnings Survey, 1977,* HMSO, 1977.

E. Hobsbawn, *Labouring Men,* Weidenfeld and Nicolson, 1968.

W. J. McCarthy (ed.), *Trade Unions,* Penguin, 1972.

E. H. Phelps Brown, *The Inequality of Pay,* Oxford UP, 1977.

---

1 M. Parkin *et al.,* 'The Impact of Incomes Policy on the Rate of Wage Change', in M. Parkin and M. Sumner (eds), *Incomes Policy and Inflation,* Manchester UP, 1972.

Statistical Appendix

TABLE A – 1

UK Gross Domestic Product, Expenditure (at 1970 prices), 1962-77, (£m)

Year	Consumers' Expenditure		General Government Final Consumption	Gross Domestic Capital Formation		Value of Physical Increase in Stocks and Work in Progress	Exports of Goods and Services	Total Final Expenditure at Market Prices	Imports of Goods and Services	Adjustment to Factor Cost[1]	Gross Domestic Product at Factor Cost[2]
	Durable Goods	Non-Durable Goods and Services		Excluding Dwellings	Dwellings						
1962[2]	1,693	24,587	7,804	5,197	1,177	12	7,358	47,788	− 7,494	−6,209	34,081
1963	1,958	25,466	7,929	5,254	1,204	201	7,663	49,675	− 7,769	−6,465	35,441
1964	2,134	26,150	8,057	6,038	1,503	936	7,996	52,814	− 8,541	−6,771	37,502
1965	2,128	26,626	8,268	6,342	1,558	616	8,395	53,933	− 8,644	−6,798	38,491
1966	2,085	27,231	8,489	6,494	1,603	420	8,725	55,047	− 8,873	−6,918	39,256
1967	2,218	27,724	8,973	6,996	1,784	390	8,864	56,949	− 9,502	−7,115	40,332
1968	2,371	28,303	9,004	7,314	1,868	482	9,898	59,240	−10,216	−7,278	41,746
1969	2,217	28,061	8,836	7,431	1,785	480	10,862	60,282	−10,559	−7,252	42,471
1970	2,408	29,260	8,964	7,810	1,643	416	11,466	61,967	−11,101	−7,539	43,327
1971	2,866	29,811	9,228	7,876	1,749	112	12,324	63,966	−11,659	−7,817	44,490
1972	3,442	31,077	9,626	7,798	1,838	35	12,501	66,317	−12,839	−8,416	45,062
1973	3,589	32,543	10,020	8,461	1,772	1,365	13,968	71,718	−14,393	−8,971	48,354
1974	3,026	32,656	10,233	8,362	1,639	561	14,817	71,294	−14,681	−8,881	47,732
1975	2,967	32,302	10,794	7,927	1,713	−842	14,361	69,222	−13,689	−8,806	46,727
1976	3,156	32,250	11,050	7,732	1,712	97	15,418	71,415	−14,207	−9,012	48,196
1977	3,105	32,028	11,027	7,554	1,518	423	16,342	71,997	−14,748	−9,055	48,194

Sources: NIBB, 1966-1976; ET (AS) 1977; ET April 1978.

Notes: 1. Adjustment to Factor Cost represents taxes on expenditure less subsidies valued at constant rates.
2. For the year 1962 the value of GDP as shown in the last column differs from the sum of its components by −£44m. This is because the various items have been separately linked to the later series based on 1970 prices. See NIBB, 1966-1976, p. 110.

TABLE A – 2

UK Prices, 1962-77: Index Numbers (1970 = 100)

Year	RETAIL PRICES (All Items)	CONSUMER GOODS AND SERVICES								
		Total	Food	Drink and Tobacco	Housing (incl. rent and rates)	Fuel and Light	Durable Goods	Clothing	All other Goods[1]	Services
1962	72.5	72.0	76.9	70.5	59.9	–	83.8	82.3	70.4	67.3
1963	73.9	73.4	78.2	71.4	64.1	–	80.9	83.5	72.2	69.2
1964	76.3	75.9	80.4	75.5	68.0	–	82.0	84.4	74.3	71.6
1965	80.0	79.5	83.2	82.8	72.5	–	83.3	86.5	78.1	74.8
1966	83.1	82.8	85.8	85.4	78.7	83.7	84.3	88.8	80.1	78.9
1967	85.2	85.2	87.8	86.6	83.3	86.7	85.4	90.1	81.8	82.8
1968	89.2	89.4	90.4	89.8	86.9	93.6	89.8	91.5	88.4	88.6
1969	94.0	94.4	95.4	96.1	91.8	96.2	93.5	95.0	94.0	93.8
1970	100.0	100.0	100.0	100.0	100.0	100.0	100.0	100.0	100.0	100.0
1971	109.4	108.3	109.4	104.2	110.7	109.4	107.8	106.8	107.8	109.6
1972	117.2	115.6	117.1	107.5	124.9	117.2	111.6	114.1	112.8	118.6
1973	128.0	125.1	131.4	110.6	138.9	120.5	116.1	125.0	119.5	131.9
1974	148.5	145.6	152.9	125.3	164.9	140.3	131.9	147.5	143.7	149.2
1975	184.4	179.5	187.7	158.1	203.9	182.7	163.4	168.5	178.6	182.8
1976	215.0	207.4	217.0	184.6	235.1	226.1	183.6	186.5	201.7	217.9
1977	249.0	236.9	254.2	215.5	265.1	260.5	212.1	209.8	231.9	238.8

Sources: *ET*, March 1978 and *ET (AS)*, 1977 (for retail prices): *NIER*, May 1978; February 1977, 1976; May 1975, 1974; November 1973.

Note: 1 For years 1962-5 series includes fuel and light.

Statistical Appendix

TABLE A – 3

UK Personal Income, Expenditure and Saving 1962-77 (£m)

PERSONAL INCOME BEFORE TAX

Year	Wages and Salaries	Forces Pay	Employers Contributions	Current Grants from Public Authorities[1]	Other Personal Income	Total[2]	Transfers Abroad (net)	UK Taxes on Income (Payments)
	1	2	3	4	5	6	7	8
1962	15,640	401	1,265	1,881	4,874	24,061	−10	2,430
1963	16,395	419	1,381	2,128	5,208	25,531	5	2,480
1964	17,765	450	1,504	2,250	5,572	27,541	10	2,751
1965	19,111	467	1,714	2,596	6,206	30,094	7	3,297
1966	20,389	523	1,902	2,825	6,570	32,209	22	3,689
1967	21,173	524	2,054	3,189	6,923	33,863	44	4,069
1968	22,566	542	2,300	3,679	7,408	36,495	55	4,524
1969	24,188	539	2,433	3,937	8,010	39,107	49	5,139
1970	26,984	658	2,773	4,334	8,564	43,313	34	5,850
1971	29,673	758	3,228	4,783	9,511	47,953	13	6,424
1972	33,141	862	3,913	5,844	10,772	54,532	57	6,592
1973	38,024	925	4,622	6,420	13,101	63,092	91	7,781
1974	45,856	1,071	5,811	7,869	15,513	76,120	86	10,430
1975	59,300	1,283	8,091	10,194	18,016	96,884	96	15,097
1976	67,185	1,473	9,966	12,824	20,938	112,386	69	17,610
1977	73,765	1,499	11,050	15,237	23,654	125,205	107	18,299

Sources: *NIBB, 1966-76* and previous issues; *ET (AS) 1977*; *ET*, April 1978.

Notes: 1 The figures exclude the net cost to public authorities of school meals and welfare foods provided free or at subsidized prices, also expenditure on legal aid. These are now included in public authorities' current expenditure on goods and services.

2 Before providing for depreciation and stock appreciation.

3 Before providing for additions to tax reserves.

Column 6 = 1 + 2 + 3 + 4 + 5

Column 10 = 6 − 7 − 8 − 9

Column 13 = 14 − 11

Column 15 = 10 − 14

National Insurance and Health Contributions	Total Personal Disposable Income[3]	CONSUMERS' EXPENDITURE					PERSONAL SAVINGS		Year
		Durable	Goods	Other					
		Amount £m	As % of P.D.I.	Amount £m		Total	Amount £m	As % of P.D.I.	
9	10	11	12	13		14	15	16	
1,197	20,444	1,419	6.9	17,511		18,930	1,514	7.4	1962
1,303	21,743	1,585	7.3	18,520		20,105	1,638	7.5	1963
1,444	23,336	1,749	7.5	19,711		21,460	1,876	8.0	1964
1,685	25,105	1,773	7.1	21,127		22,900	2,205	8.8	1965
1,804	26,694	1,757	6.6	22,503		24,260	2,434	9.1	1966
1,909	27,841	1,894	6.8	23,572		25,466	2,375	8.5	1967
2,165	29,751	2,128	7.2	25,262		27,390	2,361	7.9	1968
2,244	31,675	2,073	6.5	27,031		29,104	2,571	8.1	1969
2,654	34,775	2,408	6.9	29,288		31,668	3,107	8.9	1970
2,835	38,681	3,089	8.0	32,310		35,411	3,270	8.4	1971
3,333	44,550	3,840	8.6	36,104		39,929	4,621	10.4	1972
3,937	51,283	4,167	8.1	41,034		45,204	6,079	11.9	1973
5,000	60,604	3,990	6.6	47,992		51,962	8,642	14.3	1974
6,839	74,852	4,848	6.5	58,710		63,303	11,549	15.4	1975
8,419	86,288	5,795	6.7	67,892		73,424	12,864	14.9	1976
9,451	97,348	6,585	6.8	76,654		83,239	14,109	14.5	1977

TABLE A – 4
UK Population, Working Population, Unemployment, etc., 1962-77 (thousands)[1]

Year	Total Population (mid-year estimate)	Working Population	Employees in[2] Employment Males	Employees in[2] Employment Females	Employers and Self-Employed	H.M. Forces and Women's Services	Unemployed	Registered Unemployment (GB) Monthly Average	Unem-[3]ployment Rate %	Unfilled[4] Vacancies (GB) 'A' Monthly Average	Unfilled[4] Vacancies (GB) 'B' Monthly Average
1962	53,274	25,621	14,762	8,264	1,748	442	406	431.9	1.9	213.7	–
1963	53,552	25,719	14,772	8,289	1,735	427	496	520.6	2.3	196.3	–
1964	53,885	25,850	14,899	8,458	1,720	424	349	372.2	1.6	317.2	–
1965	54,218	26,045	15,015	8,606	1,702	423	299	317.0	1.4	384.4	–
1966	54,500	26,168	14,999	8,784	1,687	417	281	330.9	1.4	370.9	–
1966	54,500	25,632	14,843	8,410	1,681	417	281	330.9	1.4	370.9	–
1967	54,800	25,490	14,504	8,303	1,762	417	503	521.0	2.2	249.7	–
1968	55,049	25,378	14,306	8,344	1,786	400	542	549.4	2.4	271.3	–
1969	55,263	25,370	14,184	8,436	1,853	380	518	543.8	2.4	284.8	–
1970	55,421	25,300	14,002	8,470	1,902	372	555	582.2	2.5	259.6	–
1971	55,610	25,123	13,714	8,408	1,909	368	724	751.7	3.3	176.1	–
1972	55,781	25,194	13,608	8,512	1,899	371	804	835.0	3.7	189.3	–
1973	55,913	25,545	13,771	8,891	1,947	361	575	587.7	2.6	397.7	–
1974	55,922	25,602	13,659	9,131	1,925	345	542	585.2	2.6	298.8	94.6
1975	55,900	25,795	13,532	9,174	1,886	336	866	935.6	4.1	147.1	32.5
1976	55,886	26,093	13,388	9,151	1,886	336	1,332	1,304.0	5.6	118.7	23.6
1977	55,852	26,327	13,383	9,281	1,886	327	1,450	1,422.7	6.1	155.6	21.9

Sources: *AAS*, 1977; *MDS*, January 1978, and previous issues; *DEG*, May 1978, and previous issues.

Notes: 1 Estimates are for June each year unless otherwise stated; figures above the line refer to estimates on a National Insurance Card basis and below the line to a Census of Employment basis.

2 Estimates after June 1975 are provisional.

3 The unemployment rate is obtained by dividing the relevant monthly average unemployment figure by the relevant total employees (including unemployed) for the June of that year.

4 For 1962 to 1973 column 'A' refers to total vacancies. After 1973 column 'A' relates to vacancies notified to employment offices and column 'B' to vacancies notified to careers offices. These columns should not be added because of duplication in the series. Because of industrial action figures for 1974, 1975, 1976 and 1977 are averages of 11, 11, 10 and 11 months respectively.

UK Money Supply, Domestic Credit Expansion and Public Sector Borrowing Requirement, 1963-77 (£m)

Year	Money Supply[1] (M_1)	Money Supply[2] (Sterling M_3)	Change in Money Supply[3] (Sterling M_3)	Domestic Credit Expansion[4]	Bank Lending (Sterling) to Private Sector	Bank Lending (Sterling) to Public Sector	Purchases of Public Sector Debt by Private Sector	External Financing of Public Sector	Public Sector Borrowing Requirement[5]
	1	2	3	4	5	6	7	8	9
1963	7,322	11,411	not avail.	not avail.	not avail.	not avail.	594	103	842
1964	7,557	12,050	639	1,508	957	−380	504	656	989
1965	7,848	12,967	917	1,114	432	428	486	96	1,205
1966	7,844	13,406	439	711	34	220	262	413	961
1967	8,442	14,748	1,247	1,734	511	570	665	503	1,863
1968	8,784	15,757	1,009	1,969	538	112	−11	1,128	1,281
1969	8,812	16,132	375	−243	429	−362	354	−604	−466
1970	9,635	17,666	1,547	735	829	893	101	−1,333	−18
1971	11,088	20,111	2,455	1,190	1,627	1,648	2,104	−2,652	1,371
1972	12,657	25,443	4,927	6,674	5,510	−1,030	1,006	1,562	2,034
1973	13,303	32,046	6,702	8,066	5,972	1,134	2,290	767	4,195
1974	14,739	35,300	3,255	6,934	3,435	−370	3,165	2,572	6,375
1975	17,481	37,595	2,330	4,468	−384	3,081	5,603	1,024	10,520
1976	19,467	41,160	3,565	7,438	3,463	−163	6,085	3,003	9,410
1977	23,660	45,259	4,099	1,184	3,209	1,792	8,106	−5,480	5,707

Sources: All figures for this table were kindly supplied by the Bank of England. Recent revisions make it impossible to get consistent series for long runs of years from published sources. More recent figures for the various series may be found in *BEQB, ET* and *FS*. The Table is based on seasonally unadjusted data.

Notes: 1 M_1 consists of notes and coin in circulation plus sterling sight (or demand) deposits held by the private sector. Totals in column 1 are the amounts outstanding at the year end, not seasonally adjusted.

2 M_3 is a wide definition of the sterling money supply. It includes notes and coin in circulation together with all sterling deposits (including certificates of deposit) held by residents in the private and public sectors. Totals in column 2 are amounts outstanding at the year end, not seasonally adjusted.

3 Figures relate to the sum of the quarterly changes in M_3 (unadjusted). Because of slight differences in coverage the annual change in column 3 may not be identical with the first difference in M_3 as derived from column 2.

4 DCE is the increase in the domestic money stock after adjustment for any change in money balances caused directly by an external surplus or deficit. See chapter 2, section V. 1, and *BEQB*, March 1977.

5 The public sector includes the central government, the local authorities and public corporations. The borrowing requirement is discussed in chapter 2, section IV. 3.

TABLE A – 6

UK General Government: Current Account, 1961-76 (£m)

	1961	1962	1963	1964	1965
RECEIPTS					
Taxes on income:					
Central government	3,078	3,455	3,385	3,590	4,080
Taxes on expenditure:					
Central government	2,796	2,963	3,013	3,341	3,731
Local authorities[1]	831	916	1,014	1,096	1,228
National Insurance, etc., contributions:					
Central government	1,072	1,197	1,303	1,444	1,685
Gross Trading Surplus:					
Central government	46	17	17	24	24
Local authorities	62	67	75	80	88
Rent:					
Central government	29	27	18	19	22
Local authorities	252	270	287	317	363
Interest and Dividends, etc.:					
Central government[2]	280	373	338	391	428
Local authorities	40	48	52	59	70
Imputed Charge for Consumption of non-trading capital:					
Central government	38	41	44	48	51
Local authorities	94	101	111	120	128
TOTAL	8,618	9,475	9,657	10,529	11,898
EXPENDITURE					
Current Expenditure on Goods and Services:					
Central government	3,008	3,174	3,277	3,472	3,780
Local authorities	1,399	1,547	1,689	1,810	2,018
Non-Trading Capital Consumption:					
Central government	38	41	44	48	51
Local authorities	94	101	111	120	128
Subsidies:					
Central government	544	561	522	465	495
Local authorities	49	47	47	51	76
Current Grants to Personal Sector:					
Central government	1,665	1,829	2,065	2,176	2,507
Local authorities	43	52	63	74	89
Current Grants Abroad:					
Central government	118	121	132	163	177
Total expenditure excluding debt interest	6,958	7,473	7,950	8,379	9,321
Debt Interest:					
Central government	893	874	930	937	968
Local authorities[3]	211	240	269	320	380
Total Current Expenditure:	8,062	8,587	9,149	9,636	10,669
Balance: current surplus before providing for depreciation:					
Central government	369	671	240	562	936
Local authorities	187	217	268	331	293
TOTAL	8,618	9,475	9,657	10,529	11,898

Sources: NIBB 1966-76; figures for Central Government Rent and Interest, etc. (Receipts) 1961-5, kindly supplied by CSO.

Notes: 1 Rates.

2 Excluding interest on loans to local authorities.

3 Excluding interest on loans from central government.

1966	1967	1968	1969	1970	1971	1972	1973	1974	1975	1976
4,566	5,262	5,755	6,436	7,453	7,884	8,083	9,295	12,548	16,537	18,724
4,047	4,530	5,261	6,104	6,588	6,701	6,885	7,475	8,378	10,163	12,120
1,374	1,467	1,548	1,678	1,827	2,086	2,379	2,647	3,057	3,983	4,540
1,804	1,909	2,165	2,244	2,654	2,835	3,333	3,937	5,000	6,835	8,426
15	16	30	40	35	42	9	6	32	55	39
91	94	102	113	116	135	131	129	100	88	81
22	22	26	28	33	33	32	36	38	47	51
404	453	520	595	670	704	726	935	1,209	1,499	1,879
502	533	615	706	790	913	1,041	1,167	1,383	1,554	1,845
84	92	96	103	109	118	126	182	365	497	599
56	59	65	70	78	88	97	121	164	212	265
138	146	159	174	194	221	257	324	358	440	555
13,103	14,583	16,342	18,291	20,547	21,760	23,099	26,254	32,632	41,910	49,124
4,044	4,438	4,672	4,780	5,332	6,056	6,818	7,594	9,808	13,024	15,490
2,264	2,551	2,744	2,949	3,360	3,847	4,458	5,159	6,173	9,070	10,252
56	59	65	70	78	88	97	121	164	212	265
138	146	159	174	194	221	257	324	358	440	555
480	720	801	726	763	835	1,069	1,359	2,719	3,391	2,980
79	81	94	113	113	96	75	112	268	436	483
2,719	3,069	3,546	3,789	4,172	4,611	5,624	6,148	7,556	9,784	12,262
106	120	133	148	162	172	220	273	313	417	560
180	188	179	177	177	205	210	359	320	379	792
10,066	11,372	12,393	12,926	14,351	16,131	18,828	21,449	27,679	37,153	43,639
1,036	1,105	1,240	1,280	1,298	1,384	1,591	1,812	2,183	2,692	3,638
429	468	554	649	728	705	716	948	1,387	1,539	1,808
11,531	12,945	14,187	14,855	16,377	18,220	21,135	24,209	31,249	41,384	49,085
1,187	1,249	1,753	2,988	3,701	2,858	1,292	1,220	736	–915	–2,250
385	389	402	448	469	682	672	825	647	1,441	2,289
13,103	14,583	16,342	18,291	20,547	21,760	23,099	26,254	32,632	41,910	49,124

TABLE A – 7

UK Balance of Payments, 1962-77 (£m)

	Visible Trade			Invisibles			
				CURRENT ACCOUNT			
Year	Exports (f.o.b.)	Imports[2] (f.o.b.)	Visible Balance	Government Services and Transfers (net)	Private Services and Transfers (net)	Interest Profits and Dividends (net)	Invisible Balance
	1	2	3	4	5	6	7
1962	4,003	4,103	−100	−360	254	334	228
1963	4,295	4,375	−80	−382	195	398	211
1964	4,568	5,068	−500	−432	183	393	144
1965	4,913	5,136	−223	−446	208	435	197
1966	5,276	5,342	−66	−470	253	387	170
1967	5,241	5,796	−555	−462	339	378	255
1968	6,433	7,100	−667	−466	513	333	380
1969	7,269	7,425	−156	−467	565	498	596
1970	8,121	8,146	−25	−486	665	556	735
1971	9,060	8,781	279	−520	810	505	795
1972	9,450	10,151	−701	−561	854	534	827
1973	12,115	14,469	−2,354	−768	916	1,323	1,471
1974	16,539	21,734	−5,195	−858	1,232	1,306	1,680
1975	19,462	22,667	−3,205	−999	1,687	900	1,588
1976	25,422	28,932	−3,510	−1,549	2,684	1,516	2,651
1977	32,176	33,788	−1,612	−1,878	3,250	405	1,777

Sources: *UK Balance of Payments 1966-76* and previous issues; *ET (AS),* **1977,** *ET,* March 1978, *BEQB,* June 1978.

Notes: 1 For items relating to capital flows a + sign means an increase in liabilities or a decrease in assets, whilst a − sign means an increase in assets or a decrease in liabilities.

2 Including payments for US Military Aircraft and Missiles.

3 Figures for 1967 and 1968 include EEA losses on forward transactions. Figures for 1973 and 1974 include capital transfers.

4 Items for gold subscriptions to the IMF (1966 and 1970) and allocation of SDR's (1970, 1971, 1972) have been included in Official Financing for those years.

INVESTMENT AND OTHER CAPITAL TRANSACTIONS[1]

Current Balance	Official Long-term Capital	Overseas Long-term Investment in UK Private and Public Sectors	UK Private Long-term Investment Overseas	Other Capital Flows Mainly Short-Term	Total Investment and Other Capital Transactions	Balancing Item	Balance for Official Financing[3]	Total Official Financing[4]
8	9	10	11	12	13	14	15	16
128	−107	243	−242	103	−3	67	192	−192
131	−105	270	−320	56	−99	−90	−58	58
−356	−116	158	−399	56	−301	−38	−695	695
−26	−85	226	−368	−99	−326	−1	−353	353
104	−81	299	−303	−493	−578	−73	−547	591
−300	−59	414	−456	−396	−497	231	−671	671
−287	16	583	−727	−628	−756	−116	−1,410	1,410
440	−99	617	−679	−4	−165	412	687	−687
710	−205	828	−789	738	572	5	1,287	−1,420
1,074	−274	1,159	−836	1,767	1,816	256	3,146	−3,271
126	−255	893	−1,383	57	−688	−703	−1,265	1,141
−883	−254	1,827	−1,848	324	49	122	−771	771
−3,515	−276	2,530	−1,149	579	1,684	260	−1,646	1,646
−1,614	−288	1,762	−1,383	112	203	−51	−1,465	1,465
−859	−158	2,223	−2,331	−2,863	−3,129	360	−3,628	3,628
165	−283	5,195	−2,151	1,596	4,357	2,839	7,361	−7,361

TABLE A – 8
UK Reserves, External Liabilities in Sterling and Related Figures, 1962-77 (end period) (£m)

| Year | Gold Convertible Currency and SDRs[1] | External Sterling Liabilities[2] | | | | | | British Government Stocks Held by CMI[3],[4] | | Exchange Reserves in Sterling[5] |
| | | All Countries | | Sterling Area Countries[6] | | Oil Exporting Countries | | | | |
		CMI[3]	Other	CMI[3]	Other	CMI[3]	Other	(a)	(b)	
1962	1,002	1,268	1,551	766	823	–	–	1,044	–	2,312
1963	949	1,422	1,662	911	874	–	–	1,018	–	2,440
1964	827	1,349	1,704	894	931	–	–	1,087	–	2,436
1965	1,073	1,245	1,756	868	985	–	–	1,073	–	2,318
1966	1,107	1,267	1,684	849	1,030	–	–	1,037	1,135	2,304
1967	1,123	1,117	1,588	783	1,002	–	–	985	915	2,102
1968	1,009	959	1,460	712	984	–	–	961	880	1,920
1969	1,053	1,036	1,407	842	936	–	–	1,283	1,105	2,319
1970	1,178	1,166	1,673	968	1,111	–	–	1,381	1,180	2,547
1971	2,526	1,824	2,382	1,442	1,480	–	–	1,416	1,355	3,240
1972	2,404	2,046	2,291	1,718	1,319	–	–	1,572	1,280	3,618
1973	2,787	2,133	2,284	1,492	971	856	314	1,556	1,230	3,689
1974	2,890	3,581	2,500	–	–	2,678	344	1,421	1,053	4,634
1975	2,683	2,957	3,229	–	–	2,214	466	–	1,143	4,100
1976	2,426	1,536	3,484	–	–	685	497	–	1,103	2,639
1977	10,715	1,512	4,955	–	–	492	747	–	1,323	2,835

Sources: *UK Balance of Payments 1966-76* and previous issues. *ET*, March 1978.

Notes: 1 Total reserves expressed in dollars are converted to sterling at middle or central rates to end 1971 and at end-year middle market closing rates thereafter.

2 The series for 'Sterling Balances' has undergone several changes during the post-war period. The present series was introduced in 1971 and is described in the *Pink Book* for that year. There is a minor series break after 1973 in columns marked with a bar. Data for 1974 on the old basis is given in the *Pink Book*. Figures refer to banking and money market liabilities.

3 CMI = Central Monetary Institutions. This term includes International Organizations (except the IMF) but these holdings are relatively small. See *Pink Book* for details.

4 Column (a) reports holdings at nominal values whilst column (b) relates to approximate market values.

5 'Exchange Reserves in Sterling' is the sum of 'British Government Stocks' and External Liabilities to CMIs. Prior to 1974 it includes British Government Stocks at nominal values and thereafter at market values.

6 After 1973 the 'Sterling Area' classification was dropped from the series from which this Table is derived. The new area analysis is too detailed for inclusion here and reference should be made to *Pink Books* and *ET* for information.

TABLE A – 9

UK External Trade, 1962-77

| | Value of the External Trade of UK (£m) | | | | Volume Index Numbers 1975 = 100[3] | | | | Unit Value Index Numbers 1975 = 100[3] | | | | |
| | Imports (c.i.f.)[1] | | Exports (f.o.b.)[2] | | Imports | | Exports | | Imports | | Exports | | Terms of Trade[4] |
Year	Total	Manufactures	Total	Manufactures	Total (weight = 1000)	Manufactures (weight = 532)	Total (weight = 1000)	Manufactures (weight = 828)	Total (weight = 1000)	Manufactures (weight = 532)	Total (weight = 1000)	Manufactures (weight = 828)	
1962	4,628	1,556	4,062	3,336	54	32	51	51	32	37	37	37	115
1963	4,983	1,702	4,365	3,568	56	34	54	53	33	38	39	39	116
1964	5,696	2,161	4,565	3,773	62	41	56	55	34	39	39	40	115
1965	5,751	2,253	4,901	4,095	63	42	59	59	34	41	40	41	118
1966	5,949	2,471	5,255	4,390	64	44	60	60	35	42	42	43	121
1967	6,440	2,844	5,244	4,386	69	50	60	59	35	42	42	43	122
1968	7,900	3,772	6,442	5,413	76	58	68	68	39	48	46	47	117
1969	8,317	4,137	7,352	6,256	77	61	76	76	41	50	47	48	117
1970	9,163	4,672	8,170	6,913	81	65	77	77	42	53	51	52	120
1971	9,980	5,120	9,289	7,936	85	72	84	85	44	54	53	55	120
1972	11,301	6,223	9,906	8,418	93	85	86	86	46	56	56	58	122
1973	16,067	9,056	12,657	10,638	106	102	98	98	59	67	63	64	108
1974	23,492	12,075	16,820	13,907	107	107	102	103	89	87	82	81	92
1975	24,423	13,004	20,111	16,655	100	100	100	100	100	100	100	100	100
1976	31,569	17,222	26,024	21,616	106	109	109	109	123	123	121	121	99
1977	36,996	21,681	33,308	27,172	109	120	119	118	142	143	143	143	100

Sources: AAS, 1977, and previous issues; TI, 10 March 1978, 10 February 1978, 11 October 1973, 19 May 1978.

Notes: 1 Import figures differ from those given in Table A – 7 because of the inclusion of charges for insurance and freight. Apart from this, both series will differ because of certain adjustments made for valuation and coverage. Further explanation is given in the UK Balance of Payments 1966-76. Figures for 1970-7 are based on a revised classification. See TI, 10 March 1978.

2 Export figures do not contain any allowance for the under-recording of exports, and differ from figures in Table A – 7 on account of this and other coverage adjustments. Figures for 1970-7 are based on a revised classification. See TI, 10 March 1978.

3 Overseas Trade Statistics basis. Basic figures for 1962 kindly supplied by DI. Weights shown for 'manufactures' in the various columns apply to the series for 1970-7. Earlier figures are based on the previously used weighting system. See TI, 11 October 1973.

4 Export unit value index expressed as a percentage of the import unit value index. (This column is derived from unit value indices taken to one decimal point.)

TABLE A – 10

Productivity in UK, 1962-77: Index Numbers (1970 = 100)

Year	Output per Person Employed			Output per Man-Hour Worked
	Gross Domestic Product	Total Industrial Production	Manufacturing Industries	Manufacturing
1962	79.7	74.2	74.3	72.1
1963	82.2	77.6	78.2	75.9
1964	85.8	82.5	83.8	80.7
1965	87.5	84.1	85.4	83.3
1966	88.8	85.8	86.9	86.2
1967	91.6	90.0	90.2	90.1
1968	95.9	95.7	97.0	96.1
1969	97.9	98.5	99.3	98.3
1970	100.0	100.0	100.0	100.0
1971	103.3	103.3	102.8	104.9
1972	105.5	108.0	109.0	111.7
1973	109.5	114.9	117.4	118.0
1974	108.2	111.3	115.5	119.4
1975	106.7	109.9	113.4	118.5
1976	108.5	113.5	118.1	123.0
1977	109.9	114.4	117.6	121.4

Sources: NIER, May 1978; February 1977, 1976; May 1975, 1974; November 1973.

TABLE A – 11

Wages, Earnings (UK) and Salaries (GB), 1962-77: Index Numbers (1970 = 100)

Year	Weekly Rates of Wages	Hourly Rates of Wages	Average Weekly Earnings	Average Real Weekly Earnings[1]	Average Salary Earnings[2]	Average Real Salary Earnings[1]
	ALL INDUSTRIES					
1962	66.2	62.7	58.5	80.7	61.8	85.2
1963	68.6	65.0	60.8	82.3	65.1	88.1
1964	71.5	68.4	65.1	85.3	68.7	90.0
1965	74.6	72.6	70.0	87.5	74.6	93.2
1966	78.0	77.4	74.5	89.7	77.9	93.7
1967	81.0	80.5	77.0	90.4	81.4	95.5
1968	86.4	86.1	83.2	93.3	86.6	97.1
1969	91.0	90.8	89.7	95.4	93.4	99.4
1970	100.0	100.0	100.0	100.0	100.0	100.0
1971	112.9	113.2	111.3	101.7	111.7	102.1
1972	127.9	128.4	125.1	106.7	124.5	106.2
1973	145.4	146.5	142.5	111.3	138.0	107.8
1974	173.1	174.7	167.5	112.8	157.0	105.7
1975	224.5	226.8	212.3	115.1	202.9	110.0
1976	269.2	271.9	245.4	114.1	244.5	113.7
1977	287.5	290.5	270.4	108.6	167.3	107.3

Sources: (Wages and Earnings) *NIER*, May 1978; February 1977, 1976; May 1975, 1974; November 1973.
(Salaries) *DEG*, May 1978; December 1975.

Notes: 1 These are derived by deflating the indices for money earnings and salaries by the Retail Price Index from Table A – 2.

2 This index is compiled annually, in October before 1970 and in April since 1970. All index numbers in columns are related to April 1970 = 100. The index for October 1970 on the same basis is 105.9.
The figures before 1970 include some part-time workers.
The series covers all non-manual workers in 'All Industries'.

Index

'bears', 85
Beckerman, W., 35n, 52n
behavioural models, industrial, 170–2
Belgium
  growth rate, 50, 51
  as an open economy, 113
  output growth, 174, 175
  seller concentration, 197
Berle, A. A., 170n
Berrill, Sir Kenneth, 275
Beveridge, 261, 264
bills, 65, 67, 72, 76, 77
  definition, 65n; *see also* local authority
    bills; Treasury bills
Blackett, Lord, 213n
Blake, C., 210n
Blaug, M., 231 and n
block discounts, 80
BMC, 216
Boddy, D., 257n
Bonini, C. P., 215n
borrowings, local government, 88, 90
  nationalized industries, 76, 88
  overseas, 104–8, 119, 123, 141–2, 153,
    166
Bowe, C., 130n
Bowers, J., 13n, 226n, 228n
Brack, J., 257n
Bretton Woods Agreement, 159–61, 164
brick production industry, 215, 230
British American Tobacco, 203
British Gas Corporation, 189
British Insurance Association, 83
British Leyland, 218
British National Oil Corporation, 184
British Petroleum, 64
British Rail, 188, 189
British Road Services, 258
British Tourist Authority, 184
broadcasting, nationalization, 184
brokers, 67n
  discounts, 69
Bronfenbrenner, M., 14n
Brookings Report, 121
Brown, A. J., 40n, 203n, 207n
Browne, M., 250n, 251
Brumberg, R., 15n
Buck, T. W., 210n
Budgets, 25, 31, 32, 33, 35, 36, 87–92, 108,
  109
  1968, 12
  1970, 108
  1971, 108
  1972, 104, 108
  1973, 108
  1974, 29, 102, 108, 154–5
  1975, 108
  1976, 108–9
  1977, 109
  1978, 48, 52, 53, 218
building industry, 21

building societies, 21, 81–2
Building Societies Association, 81
buildings, investment in, 17, 21; *see also*
  housing
bullion brokers, 76
Bullock Committee, 272
'bulls', 85
Burkitt, B., 277
bus transport, 182, 183
business cycles, 8–9, 233

Cable, J., 257n, 279 and n
Cagan, P., 40n
Cairncross, Sir Alec, 31n, 35n, 51n, 130n,
  143n, 155n
Cairnes, 248
Cambridge Economic Policy Group, 146n
Campbell-Boross, L. F., 129n
Canada
  and General Agreement to Borrow, 161
  growth rate, 50
  strikes, 270
capital account, balance of payments, 152
  UK's external accounts, 114, 116
capital flow, 140, 147–55
  long-term, 152–5
  short-term, 123, 140, 141–2, 145, 147–
    52, 163, 164–5
capital formation, 217–18
capital gains tax, 94–5
capital stock
  adjustment principle, 6, 18, 20, 21
  depreciation, 97–8
  growth rate, 48, 49–50
  quality, 50
capital transfer tax, 101–2, 237, 239
car ownership, 181, 182, 183
Carter, C. F., 194n
cash, 64, 67, 69, 72, 75, 79, 90
'catching-up hypothesis', 50
Caves, R., 121n, 195n
Census of Population, 233
Census of Production, 195, 214
central government borrowing requirement,
  89–90
Central Statistical Office (CSO), 5, 27
certificate of deposit, 70
CET, *see* common external tariff
chemical industry
  capital/labour ratio, 173
  exports, 127, 128
  growth rate, 176
  relative importance, 173
  size structure, 172
Cheshire, P. C., 13
child benefits, 92, 261, 263, 264
Chiplin, B., 252n
Christopher, A., 264n
clearing banks, *see* London clearing banks;
  Scottish clearing banks
closed shops, 272, 277

Index

Index